Facing the Pacific

Facing the Pacific

Polynesia and the U.S. Imperial Imagination

Jeffrey Geiger

University of Hawai'i Press

Honolulu

Library of Congress Cataloging-in-Publication Data
Geiger, Jeffrey.
   Facing the Pacific : Polynesia and the U.S. imperial
imagination / Jeffrey Geiger.
        p. cm.
   Includes bibliographical references and index.
   ISBN-13: 978-0-8248-3066-3 (hardcover : alk. paper)
   1. Oceania—Relations—United States. 2. United States—
Relations—Oceania. 3. Imperialism—History—20th century.
4. Oceania—Foreign public opinion, American. 5. Public opinion—
United States—History—20th century. 6. Popular culture—
United States—History—20th century. 7. Oceania—In literature.
8. Imperialism in literature. 9. Oceania—In motion pictures.
10. Imperialism in motion pictures. I. Title.
   DU30.G45 2007
   303.48'296073—dc22

                                        2007000696

Designed by University of Hawai'i Press production staff
Printed by The Maple-Vail Book Manufacturing Group

Contents

Acknowledgments   vii

Introduction   1

1 The Garden and the Wilderness:
       Tropes of Order and Disorder   18

2 Idylls and Ruins:
       Frederick O'Brien in the Marquesas   74

3 Searching for Moana:
       Frances Hubbard and Robert J. Flaherty in Samoa   118

4 The Front and Back of Paradise:
       W. S. Van Dyke and MGM in Tahiti   160

5 The Homoerotic Exotic:
       From C. W. Stoddard to *Tabu*   192

Afterword   227

Notes   233

Bibliography   273

Index   297

Acknowledgments

This book could never have been completed without the support and guidance I've had over the (too many) years spent on the project. This includes sabbatical leaves provided by the University of Essex and support from the university's Research Promotion Fund, as well as the assistance of an Arts and Humanities Research Council Leave Fellowship.

I also owe a great debt to the following individuals and organizations for generously providing time, resources, and practical advice: Phil Frank of the Sausalito Historical Society; Patricia Keats of the California Historical Society of San Francisco; Sue Hodson of the Huntington Museum and Library, Pasadena; Scott Curtis, Barbara Hall, and especially Faye Thompson of the Margaret Herrick Library, Academy of Motion Picture Arts and Sciences; Jack Coogan of the Robert and Frances Flaherty Study Center at Claremont College; the Marin County Historical Society in California; the Butler Library at Columbia University; the Rush Rhees Library and Special Collections at the University of Rochester; Helen Pecheniuk at the National Library of Australia; the UCLA Film and Television archives; the Bancroft Library collections, University of California, Berkeley; the British Film Institute and library; and the National Maritime Museum, Greenwich. Thanks also to Elizabeth Deloughrey and the Pasifika list and to Jane Moulin for help with Marquesan language questions. Bette London and Frank Shuffelton hosted me as a visiting scholar on two occasions at the University of Rochester, giving me access to library facilities and Eastman House screenings that exposed me to resources I certainly would have missed otherwise. Many thanks to Masako Ikeda at the University of Hawai'i Press, for her enthusiasm and insights through each stage of the publication process; thanks also to Joanne Sandstrom and Ann Ludeman for their work on the manuscript.

I've been lucky enough to be part of a warm and congenial department at Essex, so I want to extend thanks to them for keeping it sane. I'm especially indebted to Peter Hulme, Fiona Venn, Rod Edmond, and the anonymous readers at the University of Hawai'i Press for their generous and detailed feedback, but would note that any errors or omissions that still remain are wholly the result of my own oversights.

The following people, too, provided intellectual and professional support, inspiration, or just good conversation along the way: Valerie Smith, Sam Weber, Teshome Gabriel, Martha Banta, Elizabeth Cowie, Sharon Willis, John Michael, Tom DiPiero, Morris and Georgia Eaves, Rachel Lee, Jonathan White, Francis Barker, Karin Littau, Iain Hamilton Grant, Shohini Chaudhuri, Colin Samson, Nicola Gray, Ken Plummer, Everard Longland, Jane Hindley, Cristina Fumagalli, John Gillies, Patricia Gillies, Graham Huggan, Sue Dobinson, Elena Coda, Randy Rutsky, Marilyn Manners, Kriss Ravetto-Biagioli, Sarika Chandra, and Shelley Salamensky. But my greatest debt is to Hal Gladfelder, for sticking with me through the ups and downs of completing this book. My far-flung family—my sister Nanci, my mother, my brother David and family, and Sue Banchero and family—all deserve thanks for their patience. I want to dedicate this book to my dear, and dearly missed, friend, Arthur Howes.

⤸

CHAPTERS 3 and 4 contain revised sections from articles that appeared elsewhere. Part of chapter 3 was published by the University of Texas Press as "Imagined Islands: *White Shadows in the South Seas* and Cultural Ambivalence," *Cinema Journal* 41.3 (Spring 2002), 98–121. Part of chapter 4 appeared as "Subaltern Looks and the Imperial Gaze: Charles Warren Stoddard's *South Sea Idyls*" in *Indiscretions: At the Intersection of Queer and Postcolonial Theory,* ed. Murat Aydemir (Amsterdam: Rodopi, 2007).

Introduction

Thus the old America passes away; behold a new America appears,
and her face is toward the Pacific.
— Hubert Howe Bancroft, *The New Pacific*

In the late 1990s, an advertisement for Fortunoff jewelers ran in upscale publications such as the *New Yorker* and the *New York Times Magazine:* it depicted a windswept beach and the blue waters of the Pacific; a miniature rowboat and a string of black pearls rested on the sand. An eighteenth-century map of the Society Islands was featured in an upper corner of the page, where "Otaheite" could just be made out—a detail that immediately worked to blur one's sense of present realities with past Pacific histories. At the bottom of the ad, two sentences similarly collapsed present and past, myth and history: "Our representative had to choose between a young Tahitian Princess and the cultured South Sea pearls. Fortunately, he was trained that duty comes first, giving you a much more agonizing choice: cash or charge."

On one level, the Fortunoff advertisement testifies to the persistent psychic hold that images of the South Pacific have on US audiences, a hold that still engenders popular fantasy from the film *Castaway* (1999) to the runaway TV hit *Lost* (2005), as well as reality programming such as *Survivor 4: Pearl Islands* (2003, shot on Nukuhiva) and *Survivor 5: Vanuatu* (2004). But the Fortunoff ad also suggests the more insidious and embedded stereotypes behind the Pacific island myth: the well-trained representative is obviously tempted, but too rational and civilized to accept the "savage" gift of the princess; he chooses money over sex, business over pleasure, sensible western enterprise over nonwestern self-indulgence. Behind the ad's innocuous appearance lies the myth of a primitive people frozen in time, occupying a site still ripe for commercial exploitation and sexual fantasy. Simply put, the advertisement attests to the linked pleasures that South Pacific islands have, over centuries, afforded the consuming gaze of the west—connoting solitude, release from cares, and, more recently, renewal from urbanized modern life—while promising economic rewards for those industrious enough to resist falling too deeply into reveries of Polynesian indulgence.

The persistence of this static image of Polynesia is remarkable, especially when one considers that it was already a long-standing cliché seventy-five years earlier, when Frederick O'Brien released his travel account *White Shadows in the South Seas* and helped to ignite a US obsession for all things Polynesian. As early as 1921—only a little over a year after O'Brien's debut—*Publisher's Weekly* was complaining that "the offices of the editors . . . are threatened with an early avalanche of South Sea material which menaces the pre-eminence of copra as the principal article of export from the Port of Papeete."[1] This book outlines the contours of this Polynesian vogue, looking at the ways the South Pacific was envisioned by an interrelated group of travelers seeking inspiration, regeneration, or simply a means to escape on distant Pacific islands. These visitors to the Pacific together enacted a kind of collective cathexis on a dispersed geographical and cultural area and at the same time carried along a substantial proportion of the US population in their wake.

Yet at the very moment that so many Americans were dreaming of isolated, unspoiled islands, Pacific nations were undergoing political and cultural upheavals: the culmination of well over 150 years of significant western political and commercial intervention in the region. The period during which these travels took place closely followed on the heels of the US appropriation of substantial portions of the Pacific—including the Philippines, the eastern islands of Samoa, Guam, and Hawai'i—as the US strove to secure its regional, and ultimately global, economic and political influence. Hence the idyllic fantasies that these visitors carried with them into Polynesia came up against some unexpectedly harsh realities: the legacies of colonialism, the inequities of economic imperialism, and the instability of any preconceived notion of American exceptionalism itself.

A Note on Terms

I should start by underlining some of the issues and contingencies relating to the use of terms in this book—beginning with the title. As the epigraph above suggests, the phrase "facing the Pacific" partly mimics the westward-gazing imperialism of expansionist scholars such as Bancroft, who, shortly after the US annexations, envisioned the Pacific as the natural extension of the ideology of manifest destiny. But my intention is not to perpetuate the view that US expansion into the

Pacific should fundamentally or unproblematically be viewed as continuous with manifest destiny. To do this, as Amy Kaplan has argued, might be to risk effectively repeating the teleological narrative that US imperialism has told about itself—that of the "inexorable westward march of empire."[2] This neat and unified narrative presents an overly coherent image of imperial expansion rather than reflecting the often incoherent "anarchy" and particularity of empire building that actually took place. Therefore, while the very fact of US territorial expansion is not under question, it is also important to keep in mind the ways that the ideology of manifest destiny served as a kind of self-spun myth that helped to project and displace homegrown desires, fears, and emerging cultural contradictions within the US: the whole field of "domestic" cultural politics—including North/South issues of slavery, Reconstruction, and Jim Crow segregation—sublimated in western expansionist fantasy. Though *Facing the Pacific* focuses narrowly on Polynesian fantasy after the First World War when commentators such as Bancroft were attempting to extend the life of manifest destiny, I suggest that these westward visions both reflected and helped to distract attention away from ongoing conflicts at home relating to the unity of US identity and nationhood, as the country experienced the upheavals of immigration, racial tension, and (perhaps more palpably than ever before) gender revolution.

There is an additional, and closely related, dimension to the title *Facing the Pacific*. As the writers and filmmakers examined here both engaged with and contested westward-facing expansionist fantasies, they also participated in a long history of *facing*—creating a kind of face for, putting a face on—Pacific islands and peoples, a face that conjured up dominant images of Polynesia and "types" of Pacific Islanders that would persist for many decades to come. This was a face that, on its surface, might have appeared to "show us them," but it was a typology that more often reflected, and was the by-product of, an ambivalent and contested US self-image at the same time.

The book's subtitle, *Polynesia and the US Imperial Imagination,* also could benefit from some further explanation, in that the west's terminology for Pacific places and peoples continues to be burdened by the debris of history, ideology, and cultural solipsism. Seemingly value-free terms such as "Polynesia," "Oceania," and "South Seas" have the ability to mask their roots in western histories and typologies, sublimating the roles they've played in producing universal fictions out of diverse localities. "Oceania" comprises the geographical categories of "Polynesia," "Melanesia," and "Micronesia"—islands that are "many," "black," or "small," respectively—a tripartite division usually traced back to the French explorer J. S. C.

Dumont D'Urville, who embarked on extended Pacific voyages in 1826–1829 and 1836–1839.[3] While recently reappropriated and reimagined (as in the strategic employment of the term Oceania by writers such as Epeli Hauʻofa and Albert Wendt), these categories have helped to configure zones of geographical, political, economic, social, historical, and linguistic commonality—but have also worked to homogenize the Pacific's diversity in all of these areas. Hauʻofa reminds us that Oceania should not typically be seen as a space of bounded territories, nations, and productive trade zones, but as a fluid network of peoples and cultures that once "moved and mingled unhindered by boundaries of the kind erected much later by imperial powers."[4] Jocelyn Linnekin suggests that "received categories such as Melanesia, Micronesia, and Polynesia have become increasingly vulnerable. They were in their inception artificial creations by Europeans—labels to make sense of the cultural, linguistic, and phenotypic contrasts and commonalities that they encountered."[5] But the absolute dismissal of terms such as "Polynesia" also might have its limits: Alfred Gell complicates Edmund Leach's claim that Polynesia might be "very nearly . . . [a] figment of the ethnographic imagination" by reaffirming the logic of conceiving certain Polynesian unities based on archaeological, linguistic, and historical evidence.[6] The problem for Gell is in not in recognizing the resemblances and common origin of Polynesian societies, but in overemphasizing the idea of a pan-Polynesian culture at the expense of marking cultural differences, heterogeneities, and uneven transformations over time. Gell's hesitancy in dismissing Polynesia as an organizing principle for ethnographic research makes sense within the remit of his comparative anthropological study, and he ultimately chooses to stress issues of cultural diversity while not fully dispensing with an overarching concept of Polynesia (though linked unified categories such as Melanesia, it needs to be said, lie on even shakier ground). My own project, concerned as it is with western constructs and fantasies, in a sense relies less on definitively answering the question of Polynesian unity than it responds to and interrogates a Polynesia imagined in western texts. The texts discussed in the following pages engage with islands encountered as part of the region known as Polynesia, and as such I make recourse to the term while attempting to keep its ideological and historical contexts—as well its strategic value—in constant view.

Another term that crops up in this book is "South Seas," two words that evoke both actual and fictional journeys across the limitless "Great South Sea" sighted by Vasco Nuñez de Balboa from the Panamanian isthmus in 1513. "South Seas" thus might correspond to a real sense of place, but it is also a mythical and textually constructed space, in a sense, outside place and history. I employ the term essentially to suggest a varied discourse of written and visual evocations of beaches, coral reefs, lagoons, coconut palms, and alluring native bodies, all holding the promise of sensual indulgence for western audiences. Herman Melville similarly identified "South Seas" as a tissue of overlapping texts and images: "South Seas is simply an equivalent term for Pacific Ocean. Then why not say Pacific Ocean at once?— Because one may have a lingering regard for certain old associations, linking the South Seas as a name with many pleasant and venerable books and voyages, full of well-remembered engravings."[7]

More recently, terms such as "Pacific Rim" and "Asia-Pacific region" have attempted to take in the wider postwar global exchanges, transformations, and perceptions that have marked the region. Yet these labels can also be seen as serving commercially driven, globalizing agendas of superpowers such as the US. For John Eperjesi, they are economic slogans that signify "smooth flows and big profits," compressing time and space, defying geographical and cultural realities.[8] Rob Wilson suggests they might further reflect attempts to forget colonial pasts: glossing Christopher Connery, he notes that "Pacific Rim" is an invention, an "American construct,"[9] while "Asia-Pacific"—though seen as an advance beyond "Pacific Rim"—still bespeaks a transnational community "where market-driven coprosperity and democratic nation-states will have come home to coexist; where North/South colonialism, orientalizing binaries, and world war are said to get washed away forever in the magical waters of the Pacific." Wilson further sees it as important to strike a balance between a positive global cultural imaginary and banner terms such as Pacific Rim that threaten to reinscribe the hierarchies and homogenizing tendencies of colonizing powers, absorbing Pacific localities into the East meets West free-market idealism of "Pacific Rimspeak" and the like.[10]

While a cautious approach to language is something of a commonplace to New Americanist scholarship, it is nonetheless worth recalling that even the term "America" is far from transparent. "America," as it commonly refers to the United States of America, of course elides and appropriates the rest of the Americas in one fell swoop; hence critics such as Malini Johar Schueller and Mary Renda have employed the neologisms "USAmerican" and "U.S. American," respectively, in their efforts to draw attention to the implicit imperialist gestures of the terms "America" and "American."[11] In this book, whenever possible and for the sake of both specificity and simplicity, I use "US" as both a noun and an adjective, though "American" as a noun for "resident/citizen of the United States" has generally been retained, because unfortunately we do not yet have a routine English equivalent of something like *estadounidense* in Spanish (though this term too can lead to confusion over another American "United States": Los Estados Unidos Mexicanos). Also, as an "American" myself, I hesitate to suggest a potentially privileged status as a critical outsider through the use of neologisms that could appear to distance my position from others who recognize themselves as "American." Thus "American" in this book refers to a construct of national identity and belonging, as well as being a label accepted by those who have constituted and recognized themselves within this group.

One final term, "imperialist," also warrants comment, though I could not hope to equal here something like Eperjesi's detailed anatomization of "imperialism" in *The Imperialist Imaginary.*[12] Still, I would like to draw on at least one point from Eperjesi's discussion: his highlighting of the increasingly economic sense of the word during the 1890s, and the ways that the US began to understand imperialism as a function of economic protectionism with the Spanish-American War that began in 1898 and the subsequent Filipino-American war that started in February 1899. These events form an important backdrop to the current study. Though the occupation of the Philippines carried with it all the ideological trappings of spreading freedom and civilizing the "savages," it was a policy explicitly linked to the economic interests of the US and the protection of the China trade in the midst of increasingly fierce international competition. This close cooperation between national military policy and private enterprise might suggest the ways that "imperialism" in the new sense of the word was in fact closely associated with "colonialism" in the old sense. Patrick Williams and Laura Chrisman offer useful definitions that link the practices of colonialism and imperialism, suggesting that the former can be primarily identified with the nineteenth-century European acquisition and expansion of overseas territories, while the latter encompasses the "more far-reaching" implications of economic and ideological domination that have come as a result of the colonial situation.[13] In other words, though we have "postcolonial" studies and do not yet have "postimperial" studies, it is important to keep in mind the very real political and structural continuities between colonialism and imperialism, both historically and as we currently understand the terms. It is in this broader sense that I employ the term "imperialism" in this book, though even as I write this, events such as the US military actions in Iraq are continually impelling us to reexamine the shifting assumptions behind these and other related terms. Eperjesi's assertion that "these days, imperialism is universally held to be a bad thing" begins to sound vulnerable, as we witness the return of so-called liberal imperialist scholarship, which emphasizes the limits of sovereignty and "extols the virtues of imperial power acting to promote human rights and democracy, intervening in order to 'civilize the uncivilized.'"[14]

The Production of "Whole Mythologies"

The cautious approach taken here to terminology is influenced by the work of contemporary writers and scholars such as Hau'ofa and Wendt, who have made a point of interrogating and resisting homogenizing labels for the Pacific's complex cultural dynamics. As Wendt puts it, the west created not just terminologies and typologies, but a "whole mythology" to refer to Pacific islands, a mythology that is "more revealing of *papalagi* fantasies and hang-ups, dreams and nightmares, prejudices and ways of viewing our crippled cosmos, than of our actual islands";[15] and these myths persist in western cultural fantasy. Explorers' accounts provided Enlightenment Europe with a concrete site on which to investigate, and reinvigorate, western mythologies. Empirical facts encountered on voyages of discovery promised to underwrite geographical myths of a lost continent, utopian myths of an ideal society, and origin myths of paradise and the tragic Fall. By the twentieth century, an extensive corpus of literary and visual representation had created a whole network of mythological "facts" about the Pacific, where truth and fiction were inextricably intertwined. Neil Rennie historicizes this process in *Far-fetched Facts,* describing the ways in which the discovery of the "South Seas" provided facts for philosophers that other authors embellished in turn with their own fabulations that were often popularly consumed as facts.[16] Friedrich Nietzsche neatly summed up the process of searching for mythic realities in other cultures, suggesting that the post-Enlightenment west found itself "stripped of myth . . . without any fixed and consecrated place of origin" and was thus "condemned to exhaust all possibilities and feed miserably and parasitically on every culture under the sun."[17]

A key theme underlying this book, then, is the notion that these "whole mythologies" about the South Pacific constitute a kind of euhemeristic phenomenon: that is, a collective attempt to explain, rationalize, and validate certain widely held myths as being grounded in historical truth, thus reviving the social role of mythical peoples, places, and events under the guise of presenting factual accounts. The term comes from the utopian writings of Euhemerus of Messene (4th century BC), whose *Sacred Scripture* was a novelized account of an imaginary voyage to a group of islands in the uncharted waters of the Indian Ocean, describing the way of life on its chief island, Panchaea. Euhemerus wasn't the first to conjure up a utopian marriage of myth and history, but his work, in particular—somewhat like the colonial myths about distant peoples and places that were to come later—was soon subject to the ideological manipulations of parties eager to deify their politicians as heroes in order to advance their political aims. We might see manifest destiny as one form of euhemeristic manipulation, of myth taken for history and used to political ends; the Enlightenment trope of Tahiti might be seen as another; and perhaps the prevailing image of Polynesia produced for US audiences in the 1920s could be seen as one more, closely related, phenomenon.

Gayatri Spivak explains western mythmaking about others as a self-centered ideological process and, couching her argument in psychoanalytic terms, sees the production of colonial images as linked to the construction of stable western subjectivities. Colonial images thus tend to represent the colonized essentially according to the terms of the colonizer's own self-image, as the "self-consolidating other" (as opposed to the "absolute other") so that the west "consolidated itself as sovereign subject by defining its colonies as 'Others,' even as it constituted them, for purposes of administration and the expansion of markets, into programmed near-images of that very sovereign self." [18] Building on this, Robert Young refers to the "narcissism" of the west—a narcissism that, in Pacific representations, might be seen to underpin and exploit perceptions of the "otherness" of island cultures. [19] As variously defined through fictional and nonfictional texts, photographs, films, and other media, Pacific "others" were framed by a largely self-reflecting colonial lens. Thus it could be said that while helping to feed productive global networks of knowledge and commerce, the colonial gaze onto the Pacific reinforced the concrete and conceptual gaps of geographical distance and cultural difference, producing myths of otherness that helped to shape and consolidate western identities.

It is undeniable that western narcissism inheres in constructions of Polynesia, yet this book also suggests that whatever "universal" tendencies towards greed, lust, spatial mastery, cultural chauvinism, ethnocentrism, racism, and religious solipsism underwrote the process of colonial and imperial expansion, there are certain distinctive features to western images of Polynesia that, like the islands themselves, cannot be reduced to a unitary or overarching theory of colonial-era representation. Rod Edmond suggests that colonialism (and, by extension, imperialism) was itself never a "unitary formation," while in the Pacific in particular,

the history of European presence . . . is not necessarily coterminous with the history of colonialism in the region. In particular, we need to distinguish between the early and later phases of contact. The inequality and subordination typical of contact in the late nineteenth century were not inevitably present in earlier exchanges between Europeans and Pacific islanders. . . . Just as it is mistaken to assume some identity of interest, even ultimately, in the category of Europe, the self, or, indeed, any single imperial power, it is also misleading to homogenize different Pacific societies, or assume consensus within any one of them. [20]

Edmond's observations help to tease out the contingencies and irregularities encountered when reading colonial texts marked by differing geographies, histories, and cultural influences. And while this notion hardly negates the value of theories such as Spivak's and Young's in helping to construct an overview of the functions of power as they relate to (western) identity formation in colonial discourse, still, as Edmond suggests, any attempt to conceive a "single global answer" to larger questions of the changing nature of colonialism through time tends to become problematic, given colonialism's "dispersed and differential impact" around the world. Indeed, specifically countering Young, Edmond argues that there can be no "general theoretical matrix" that might provide an "all encompassing framework for the analysis of each singular colonial instance" and that critics would be better off instead addressing these questions in specific historical and colonial situations.[21]

In reading island representations, it is important too to avoid characterizing island sites from continental perspectives, where islands tend to be seen "merely as metonyms of imperialism, rather than as specific locations generating their own potentially self-reflective colonial metaphors."[22] Nicholas Thomas has argued that European contact and established colonial relations in the Pacific can be seen as culturally "entangled": islands held under the sway of colonial and imperial forces were not *"tabula rasa"* for the wholesale projection of western power and representation; rather, each encounter generated local and distinctive knowledge and information.[23] Moreover, the authority of "western knowers," Thomas argues, hardly possessed the kind of epistemic mastery that has often been attributed to it.[24] Given that my own study strives to keep an eye on the peculiar relations between Polynesian islands and the US within a certain historical frame, I have had to recognize my indebtedness to the universalizing models of postcolonial theory while remaining cautious about theorizing away the particularities of time and place. On the one hand, this book investigates the overarching nature of the Polynesian fantasy in helping to consolidate dominant notions of modern American selfhood, but I also want to look at those modern Americans themselves and at their entanglements in Polynesian lives and cultures and their efforts to come to terms with the imperial power networks in which their works and lives were embedded.

Western fictions, travel accounts, ethnographies, films, and other kinds of representations created euhemeristic half-truths out of diverse Pacific islands and cultures. Indeed, as J. G. A. Pocock suggests in his analysis of Diderot, figures such as the South Seas "natural man" were inventions sited outside of (European) history: tropes that functioned to critique western Selves in the process of writing and revising western histories and identities.[25] Wendt's work suggests that responding to these myths and histories might not simply be a question of setting the record straight—of telling the absolute truth in the face of *pakeha* or *papalagi* lies. While not diminishing specific Oceanian identities, Oceanian writers and artists have been engaging with, reinscribing, and reshaping the received mythologies of the west. Scholars such as Futa Helu, Malama Meleisea, and ʻOkusitino Māhina have further attempted to rethink reductive notions of "legitimate" versus "illegitimate" facts themselves by redressing positivist dismissals of Oceanian-based histories and myths. "Myth may function in the interests of the dominant order," notes Māhina, "but equally may encourage usurpation." [26] This process in part involves reasserting the centrality of Pacific mythologies in the retracing of Pacific histories. Rather than privileging any single historical narrative, Helu, for example, outlines the interrelated nature of "three types of history"—island histories by foreigners, histories from indigenous perspectives, and histories hypothesized from the study of myths and oral traditions—arguing that there is "no logical difference between the three types of history (though procedural details can be very different)." [27] Without collapsing the distinctions between "western" and "Oceanian" positionalities, this kind of analysis performs a useful function for western texts as well: it neither valorizes nor rejects western histories out of hand, but helps to relativize the constructs of the west, placing them in relation to other narratives and other forms of historical understanding. It also helps us to consider the ways that the west's writing of island histories was another means for the west to write and revise mythical histories, and historical myths, about itself.

Imperialist Discourse

The readings in this book highlight the incessant duality of imperial representations. The creation of a whole mythology about Polynesia might on the one hand be summarized in a series of simple, truthful phrases: they came, they exploited resources and labor, they imposed their desires and superstitions, they invented stories and histories about us; yet the process was always more complicated and unstable than a Manichean framework positing "us" versus "them" might easily explain. European and US travelers mythologized Polynesia on their own terms, yet at the same time they overlapped and collided with local beliefs, behaviors, and practices, producing texts that can vividly reflect the irreducible nature of cultural encounters themselves. The textualization of Captain James Cook's legendary murder and apotheosis (in the European press as well as, it has been argued, in Hawaiʻi) after taking on the role of Lono—the god of fertility, fated to die—during the Makahiki festival has been a prominent example of this collision, both then and now. Here the apparent misreadings and misapprehensions that constituted the event meet subsequent revisions, clarifications, and scholarly interventions: history replaces myth replaces history, and so on.[28] Like the cultural encounter itself, the texts produced and reproduced in the wake of the encounter tend to be highly unpredictable and multifaceted, fraught with ironic reversals, ambiguities, ambivalences, and even resistance to dominant modes of representation.

We might begin to ask, as have critics such as Lisa Lowe, James Clifford, and Ali Behdad, to name just a few, whether the monolithic, oppositional categories of classic postcolonial criticism (which owes a great debt to Edward Said's work—in particular *Orientalism*) are not in many ways convenient and even reductive markers of the complex and, at times, contradictory dynamics of imperial domination and anti-imperial resistance. As Behdad suggests of certain orientalist texts, perhaps as we leaf through these works searching for counterhegemonic resistances to colonial power, we will frequently find ourselves disappointed: we might find, rather, "counterdiscursive practices" working *within* the system "as effects of its power relations."[29] In the case of this study, which looks at popular travel writing, documentaries, and Hollywood films produced shortly after the US had colonized many parts of Oceania and was exerting its influence on others, this differential approach to the interconnected operations of power, which questions the logic of ever being absolutely "inside" or "outside" imperial ideology, is especially relevant. These ideological and discursive slippages within what could be called "imperial discourse" might be even more palpable in certain US texts as opposed to those produced under the sway of "high" European colonialism: while the US engaged in some versions of direct colonial administration, it also tended to slide towards the less rigidly centralized and more ad hoc, free market–based economic imperialism that still characterizes its foreign policy.

The critical dismantling of the Manichean framework for viewing colonial and imperial power relations has been both enabling and problematic; power might be figured not as an automatically oppressive entity to be opposed en masse, but as a function of multiple relations between and among varying social, political, and discursive forces. To paraphrase Michel Foucault, the discourses of power can be seen as heterogeneous processes, rather than as hegemonic totalities, and may be said to enable, even as they repress, oppositional discourses.[30] To rupture a vertical model of power is to suggest that power is something that circulates, a "productive network" that runs through the whole of the "social body."[31] Colonial texts might create the effect of order and control, but as Lowe argues, the colonial text is neither monolithic nor internally consistent; representations are not characterized by "discursive consistency" but are, rather, heterogeneous and contradictory, both internally and when compared to each other. Difference, ambivalence, and heterogeneity are fundamental attributes of colonial representations; they allow, as Behdad has argued of orientalist texts, "the possibility of multiplication and dispersion" of ideas, experiences, perceptions.[32] But it is also worth recalling Schueller's caution that, particularly in US literary studies, seeing the circulation of power in Foucauldian terms has at times too easily allowed moments of resistance and challenges to the mechanisms of power to be collapsed back into a larger social network, leading to little beyond noting that "any significant cultural practice is complicit in the power it might think to be opposing."[33] Schueller recognizes that challenges to imperial structures, even if written from "within" those structures, are not always merely complicit with furthering an imperial will, but might ultimately serve as the groundwork of its undoing.

Dennis Porter also avoids an overly tidy theoretical framework for explaining textual power dynamics, but importantly stresses that the texts themselves (and not just a theoretical framework or method for approaching the text) frequently point to these ambivalences and heterogeneities, doing so "because the human subject's relation to language [and I would include here visual language, such as film] is such that he or she is never merely a passive reflector of collective speech. We leave our individual mark in our written and spoken utterances in ways of which we are aware, if at all, only after the fact."[34] Though the works examined here were produced when the US empire was extending its reach, their connotations and effects can be seen as more differential and problematic than summary notions of western cultural solipsism tend to allow: the texts are imbued with the give-and-take relations of travel, of distance from the familiar, of immersion in different ways of life. They also have a tendency to embody the paradoxes of island representations: marked by continental perceptions of islands as bounded, isolated sites remote from mainland centers of power, yet at other times incorporating a sense of the limitlessness, mobility, and interconnectedness of islands and island dwellers dispersed across vast expanses of ocean.

Overview

This book is not an exhaustive catalogue of the Polynesian-themed texts of the era.[35] Rather, I wanted to present a cohesive and interlinked narrative by limiting the investigation to a group of individuals who traveled and worked in Polynesia during what could be called the "long 1920s": the transitional period of economic recovery, boom, and downfall that followed the First World War and lasted into the early years of the Great Depression. This was also a last gasp, at least until World War II, for the westward-gazing imperialist strategies of the US.[36] These writers and filmmakers were all acquainted with each other and, in some cases, were long-time friends, and together they significantly contributed to introducing the US public to a new wave of postwar South Pacific representations. Those focused on here—the journalist Frederick O'Brien, husband and wife team Robert Flaherty and Frances Hubbard Flaherty, Hollywood director W. S. Van Dyke, and expatriate German director F. W. Murnau—participated at times openly and at other times covertly or subconsciously in the production of what Wendt calls whole mythologies about the region. Yet as I also hope to show, the work they produced is multifaceted and far from clear-cut or simplistic: most of these texts, even if at times complicit with the representational strategies of imperial power, cannot easily be dismissed as the end results of subjects wholly interpellated by an imperialist framework. If they sometimes unself-consciously adopt, at other levels they also confront, conventional social demands and prejudices.

The complex and at times disturbing quality of these texts arises from their tendency to enact a double gesture: they frequently repress or erase the "native" subjects *in* the text while empowering the authorial position *of* the text. Yet often those who strove to consolidate power in the colonial context were themselves marginal figures at home, disenfranchised in terms of gender, class, sexuality, or political affiliations. And while many of these works offer a well-worn nostalgic or solipsistic view of a precolonial paradise, in other, sometimes subtle, ways they reveal the rapid cultural and perceptual shifts that were taking place amidst a new social modernity and through the stylistic and political innovations of modernism. Polynesia often served as a screen—indeed, it often appeared as a vision on a film screen—onto which the cultural and ideological conflicts of the US could be displaced and projected, yet it also acted as a site where hidden, often forbidden, racial and sexual confusion and desire could be explored in sublimated form. As Antonio Gramsci suggested, to understand both the role of culture in "national-popular" hegemonic discourses and to comprehend the subaltern resistances existing within these formations, we have to consider the "real nexus" of the work—its fuller contexts as a socially produced text. We need to look carefully at where these texts come from, what modes of power or commerce facilitated them, how they were received and consumed by audiences. We also need to consider their absorption into the broader frameworks of culture and history.[37]

Thus this book starts by looking backwards, at a history of Polynesian representations. The first chapter aims to provide some useful historical, textual, and thematic contexts for looking at modern(ist) US representations of Polynesia, beginning with the Enlightenment and working forward to US expansion and up to the First World War. The heart of the story then begins in chapter 2, just as the war ended, when O'Brien released his best seller *White Shadows in the South Seas*, unleashing a wave of Polynesiana on the US public. This chapter positions the role of Polynesia in the US imagination just after the war and marks the ways that O'Brien's manifestly anticolonial text both accorded with and resisted dominant modes of received Pacific representations. The story continues by looking at O'Brien's friend and confidante Robert Flaherty and his wife, Frances Hubbard Flaherty, and examines the couple's collaborative work on *Moana* (1925). *Moana*'s well-intentioned nostalgia for a seemingly passing way of life is reexamined from the standpoint of salvage ethnography and as part of the larger ethnographic sensibility of the 1920s. Chapter 3 follows Flaherty's career in the Pacific by discussing his and Van Dyke's directorial pairing on the Hollywood version of *White Shadows in the South Seas* (1928) and Van Dyke's sequel, *The Pagan* (1929), focusing on the ways that fundamentally racist discourses can be embedded within manifestly anticolonial texts. The final chapter takes us up to 1931, with Flaherty and Murnau's "pure native"—and strongly homoerotic—romance, *Tabu*, the release of which was shortly followed by Murnau's death in a car accident in Santa Barbara. Encountered in these texts are various Polynesian islands and island groups: the Marquesas (O'Brien), Western Samoa (Flaherty), Tahiti (Flaherty and Van Dyke), and Tahiti, Bora Bora, and Morea (Flaherty and Murnau). At their most revealing, these texts offer insights into shifting notions of Polynesian otherness in the US imagination and their impact on US subjectivity: into the ways that US peoples as "mainlanders" sought solace and identification in images of distant islands.

Since this book deals with the links between the US and Polynesia, the omission of a lengthy discussion of the US relationship with Hawai'i should be briefly addressed here. The central importance of Hawai'i to the US, initiated in earnest with the American Board of Commissioners of Foreign Missions' indigenous conversion project in 1820 and culminating in the island group's annexation in 1898, cannot be underestimated: Hawai'i's annexation, like that of the Philippines, was critical to shoring up US military and commercial investment in the strategic Pacific arena, especially as it related to the China trade, while its appropriation as a territory played a substantial role in helping to push frontier ideology further westward into the Pacific. Yet by the time of O'Brien's, Flaherty's, Van Dyke's, and Murnau's Pacific travels, Hawai'i had been incorporated into an imagined US frontier, having long lost its mystique for the traveler in search of an "unmapped" paradise. The mythical Pacific remained an ideal to be met beyond the frontier's known horizon, while

Hawai'i was a safe travel option occupying the realms of tourism and international trade. A 1925 ad for the Hawai'i Tourist Bureau stresses the islands' selling point as familiarity, a kind of suburban garden of delights: "Here within easy reach lies Eden—for all folk who want rest, warmth, and new diversions.... Surrounded by modern conveniences and comforts, and with moderate living costs, you'll want to enjoy several weeks or months in this smiling territory of the U.S.A."[38]

Still, Hawaiian cultural fantasy that translated into the marketable culture kitsch of hula and ukuleles continued to inhere in the US popular imagination, and still does. In the 1910s, the play *Bird of Paradise* was touring the country, its advertising copy claiming that it was "beautiful, intensely atmospheric... Hawaii with its laughing, dancing maidens crowned and garlanded with brilliant flowers, maidens casting eyes of witchery on white strangers."[39] *Bird of Paradise* implied that Hawai'i could still conjure up enigmas of savagery no longer found on the "mainland," but certainly to the more diehard Pacific adventurer, Hawai'i's exotic potential had been tamed, domesticated, and, perhaps most telling of the limits of US fantasy—hybridized. Writing just before annexation, Mark Twain noted that "wealth has introduced changes; some of the old simplicities have disappeared."[40] As early as 1849, William Maxwell Wood could write of Honolulu's international flavor and diversity, which he considered one of the positive achievements of western civilization:

> When [Americans] hear of a wanderer amid the isles of the Pacific, [they] associate with him imaginings of barbarism, and sympathize with his severance from the artificial refinements of life; but here we are in those far away isles, and in a delicious climate, amid beautiful scenery; we are also in a handsome town, of five or six thousand inhabitants, with its strong and comfortable stone and white frame Venetian-shuttered houses, elegantly and luxuriously furnished...its churches, hotels, shipping, and wharves; palace, king, court, cabinet, and regular laws. We are surrounded by, not only natives, but Yankees of every grade, degree, and profession; Englishmen, Frenchmen, Germans, Italians, and Chinamen. In large and well-fitted stores we can procure whatever we want, from any part of the world.[41]

Hawai'i would serve as a physical and conceptual base upon which to push US ambitions farther west and south: Honolulu and the islands were transitional cultural spaces of transnational flow, perched between the comfort and safety of home and the purer, more intense exoticism promised by the imagined, as yet untamed, southern skies of Polynesia.[42]

TO PARAPHRASE Albert Wendt once more, the west created a mythology of Pacific peoples and places that in many ways had more to say about western fantasies and hang-ups than it did about Oceania's actual islands. It is, in a sense, precisely these *papalagi* fantasies and hang-ups that I am examining here, and as a result I remain keenly aware of this book's limitations. Perhaps most strongly, this book reflects my position as a so-called transatlantic scholar—marked by elements of both professional emplacement and displacement—working both in and between the US and Europe. It also reflects my background as a student and teacher of literature and film. No doubt if this book had been written from a different cultural, geographical, or disciplinary standpoint, these US-centered texts might have held less of a fascination for me, and the influences and expectations that frame the analyses would have led to very different conclusions.

Edmond has pointed out the problems of focusing solely on western representations, noting that "to concentrate on the conventions through which a culture was textualized while ignoring the actuality of what was represented is to risk a second-order repetition of the images, typologies, and projections under scrutiny."[43] This study works to recognize the cultural contexts in which these writers and filmmakers produced their texts, but it is also guided by a sense that the critique of western representations can be an important step towards comprehending the complicated and extensive process of empire building, and empire dissolution. The analyses here are about discovering inner conflicts and lacks of resolution—what Jean Narboni and Jean-Louis Comolli called the "cracks"—in apparently unified texts created under the weight of an increasingly sophisticated rhetoric of US imperialism by those who sought out encounters with cultural difference, where selves formed by the bonds and blinders of cultural and national affinities meet alternate ways of life formed by different affinities and horizons of experience.[44]

This book, then, is limited to reading modernist-era texts that reveal a distinctive, heightened relationship between US self-fashioning and received versions of Polynesia. Yet the texts discussed in the following chapters are in many respects neither peculiarly "modern" nor even very "American," just as US imperialism itself was never far removed from the structures of European colonial power it both contested and inherited. Texts are always haunted by their ancestors: as much as they are of their time, postwar US fantasies of Polynesia can be seen to have adapted and renewed much older—and primarily European—connotations, myths, and legends about the South Seas. Most forms of western travel have marked a return to an imagined past; as Rennie suggests, "Travel from civilization tended to be regressive, the traveller discovering not a new land so much as a new location for old, nostalgic fictions about places lost in the distant past, now found in the distant present."[45] The idea of traversing distance not only across space but also across time acquired a unique status in journeys to the South Pacific, where acts of travel were grounded in myths of discovering some version of a lost Eden, based partly on empirical "evidence" and partly on textual voyages of the imagination.

In looking at the following Polynesian-themed texts, we might be reminded that as we view the dreamlike landscapes of the "South Seas" and the bodies inscribed within them, the text's geographical and chronological displacement from its subject matter is nonetheless somehow marked, at every turn, with a belated sense of self-recognition. Dennis Porter notes that travel texts that have attempted to capture and "bring home" images of other places always show the mark of a certain déjà vu and that these visible and invisible ghosts can be understood in part through recourse to what Freud called the uncanny.[46] Porter thus describes a sense of the belatedness in the travel text that sets it apart from something like the explorer's account, for these visited places are always already haunted by the ghosts of previous texts and travelers who have gone before. In many of the works discussed in the following chapters, this sense of belatedness nearly overpowers the text's manifest content: the hegemony of the past threatens to turn present Pacific travels into simulacra of earlier observations. Yet the gap between textuality and reality tends to reassert itself: if travelers rarely find themselves amidst the rarified places and peoples they once read about and longed to encounter, the disordered and unpredictable experience of their own encounters inevitably gives rise to something new—if unexpected. The disaffected writers and artists examined here, who went to the Pacific in search of paradise, tended to return with a problematized sense not only of cultural otherness, but of home and selfhood. They returned telling tales that helped to feed, but also to unsettle, the ideological boundaries between here and there, home and away.

1 The Garden and the Wilderness
Tropes of Order and Disorder

Over the landscape there reigned the most hushed repose, which I almost feared to break, lest, like the enchanted gardens in the fairy tale, a single syllable might dissolve the spell. For a long time . . . I remained gazing around me, hardly able to comprehend by what means I had thus suddenly been made a spectator of such a scene.
—Herman Melville, *Typee*

We dropped down a thousand feet, and Typee lay beneath us. "Had a glimpse of the gardens of paradise been revealed to me I could scarcely have been more ravished with the sight"—so said Melville on the moment of his first view of the valley. He saw a garden. We saw a wilderness.
—Jack London, *The Cruise of the Snark*

It has often been observed that a key moment in history haunts almost all subsequent representations of Polynesia: the Enlightenment evocation of Polynesian islands—in particular Tahiti—as the embodiment of both Christian and neoclassical pastoral myths. Louis-Antoine de Bougainville named Tahiti "la Nouvelle Cythère," comparing its lush interior to the Elysian fields and to being "transported into the garden of Eden."[1] For Philibert Commerson, surgeon on Bougainville's voyage, this was the island of More's *Utopia* (1516) come to life: "This island made such an impression on me that I had already applied to it the name of Utopia, or the Fortunate Isle, which Thomas More has given to his ideal republic."[2] Joseph Banks would compare Tahiti to the pastoral, mythic, and imperial foundations of Britain itself: "The scene we saw was the truest picture of an arcadia of which we were going to be kings that the imagination can form."[3] These moments, which themselves entered into western legend, are what Jonathan Lamb has called "the sublime of the South Seas": highlighted encounters that served as synecdoches for what were in fact long, arduous, and frequently dull oceanic journeys.[4] These were also reassuring images, images of a secure and self-reflecting order from a dimly remembered past. This past, though obscure and accessed only through the grand narratives of the west, was invoked to help organize the strange sights and sensations of the South Seas. Such tropes of harmony and order tended to be short-lived, however, for if Polynesian encounters could hold up a mirror to the civilized self they could also, as Enlightenment critiques aimed at European morals and manners began to show in earnest, highlight the foreignness and failures of the west, seriously undermining any presumptions of omniscience.

I want to begin not so much with a framing argument as with some frames of reference for thinking about the cultural and discursive dynamics of the twentieth-century texts at the heart of this study. This chapter therefore highlights continuities in accounts of Pacific encounters, focusing on several recurrent features of South Seas discourse grounded in the period that Pamela Cheek refers to as the dawn of Enlightenment "globalization."[5] In particular, I want to elaborate on three areas: the twinned themes of violence and sexual spectacle, emerging taxonomies of difference, and the growing importance of visual documentation on voyages of discovery. My intention is not so much to intervene in the extensive scholarship on Enlightenment voyages as to track back from later US representations, using them as a kind of lens for rereading these highly influential narratives. I then outline some frameworks more specific to the US context: the still resonant accounts of Captain David Porter and Herman Melville, questions of imperialism and anti-imperialism, conceptions of Polynesian "whiteness," and the relativistic approaches to cultural difference that were having a strong impact on popular attitudes in the 1920s. What cuts across almost all of these accounts is a dialectical tension between the seemingly opposed tropes of disorder and order: between irrational, unpredictable "others" and rational, civilized "selves." These accounts begin to reveal this tension in their very attempts to discipline, via rhetorical and narrative means, the textualization of an unpredictable and disordered experience. Thus these explorers and travelers—often unwittingly, or at odds with their own complicity—were very much a part of the process of inscribing, controlling, knowing, and definitively mapping the "blank" spaces of the South Seas. Yet it also needs to be said that the encounter can also engender a meeting point, an ambivalent and often threatening space between the opposed poles of other and self, a space that the writers, artists, and filmmakers discussed in the following chapters attempted to negotiate in their island representations.

Violent Encounters / Sexual Scenes

In the epigraph above, Melville portrays the observer/outsider as stunned by the spectacle of the enchanted garden, fearing that the interruption of a single syllable could destroy the fragile perfection of the scene. The outsider's entrance ushers in the specter of violence, of violent penetration, replete with its gendered and hierarchical oppositions of active and passive, corruption and purity. The negotiation of violence, as Greg Dening's work suggests, is endemic to engaging with Pacific-related texts and to constructing and reconstructing Pacific ethnographies and histories.[6] Physical violence, senseless killings and mutilation, has been a central theme of texts that document Pacific encounters with the west, yet other forms of violence—economic, ideological, taxonomical, discursive, interpretive—have in many ways been no less potent, if perhaps more subtle. If the South Pacific—and in particular the Society Islands—was commonly figured as an idyll, written and oral histories also reveal the underside of this fantasy: voyagers were enraptured by islands that seemed briefly, miraculously, to embody their highest ideals, but were just as often horrified to find this mythic embodiment threatened by confused reactions to cultural difference and by the passions, hysterical reactions, fears, and bravado to which these encounters gave rise. The islands still bear these scars, from voyages of discovery to colonial expansion, commercial exploitation, military conflict, the annexation of territories, and finally to the deployment of nuclear weapons, as recently as 1996.[7]

As early as the sixteenth century, patterns of uncontrolled violence and subsequent hints of western self-loathing become visible in the accounts such as Antonio Pigafetta's of Magellan's major exploring voyage (1521) and Pedro Fernández de Quirós's journal of Mendaña's failed attempt to colonize the Solomons (1595). But what most strongly resonate in later US representations are mid-eighteenth-century accounts and the arrival of the so-called modern era of western contact with Polynesia. Captain Samuel Wallis, sailing in John Byron's former ship the *Dolphin,* anchored in Tahiti's Matavai Bay in June of 1767, and was the first European to lay claim to Tahiti, calling it "King George the Third's Island." Multiple versions of the event reflect the disruptive and unpredictable nature of the arrival.[8] Almost immediately an initial, tentatively friendly meeting between the English and Tahitians turned confrontational. Fearing petty theft and convinced that several canoes filled with men were intent on attack, Wallis became determined "to intimidate the Indians," and ordered a nine-pound canon to be fired over the islanders' heads (Hawkesworth, 1:435). Tahitians tossed stones from canoes and managed to "wound some of the [English] people." The native who threw the first stone was shot with a musket. Though Wallis was convinced that his firm hand had proven the English were a force to be reckoned with, the conflicts continued over the next four days. The problem with the Tahitians was not so much that they posed a direct threat to the well-armed ship, but that they threatened disorder, with their petty thefts and large numbers of canoes advancing on the *Dolphin*'s boats. Military force becomes the immediate response to a strange people who violate propriety and convention: Wallis fired cannons directly at "not less than three hundred canoes" (Hawkesworth, 1:444) that surrounded the ship, with at least one (Wallis's journal states "a few") "cut asunder" (Wallis, 59).

Closely bound to the violence of the Pacific encounter is the sexualization of the scene: indeed, the two can be seen as opposites side of the same coin. Lee Wallace contends that "from the first, imperial expansion in the Pacific has been imagined as a sexual event."[9] Wallis's Tahitian episode opens with a rather troubled sexual image, as native women who appear to play psychosexual games with sailors who have been many months at sea threaten to undermine the captain's authority. Women viewed from the ship's boats go about "stripping themselves naked"; they "endeavoured to allure" the sailors "by many wanton gestures, the meaning of which could not possibly be mistaken" (Hawkesworth, 1:438). Adopting the semifictionalized point of view of Wallis himself, John Hawkesworth (who in 1773 published the first "official" version of the British voyages) betrays little or no pleasure in relating the spectacle: the titillations of the voyeuristic scene might be obvious, but the narrative stays its detached, businesslike course. The narrator's stance, his guise of restraint, implies moral superiority and scientific objectivity while at the same time, in its conjuring of the erotics of sheer visibility, feeds the reader's desiring, imaginary gaze. This attempt at regulating the subjective pleasures of a disturbing and alluring spectacle might reflect the official strictures governing Hawkesworth's account, but it is interesting too because it reflects the inner tensions of similar, if sometimes less strict, disciplining regimes of subsequent accounts. Here "native" sexuality is observed from a safe distance, controlled through a self-consciously rational rhetoric of representation yet never quite escaping western erotic projections, perhaps typifying an Enlightenment-era tension between sexual regulation on the one hand and the proliferation of pornographic fantasy on the other.[10]

On 26 June, Wallis and his men ventured ashore to take possession of the island, but the scene again erupted, with "several thousands" of Tahitians coming towards the English through the woods. Retreating to the *Dolphin*, Wallis ordered cannons fired "into the wood in different parts." Nearby on a hill, women and children "had seated themselves to see the battle"; there were "several thousands who thought themselves in perfect security," out of range of the guns (Hawkesworth, 1:450). But—to convince them that they were not, in fact, secure—Wallis ordered the guns fired towards them. Hawkesworth's reinscription presents the scene as almost comical, but, two years later, the shock still resonated with the Tahitians. In 1769, Joseph Banks notes, "We have found by constant experience that these people may be frightned into any thing. They have often describd to us the terrour which the Dolphins guns put them into and when we ask how many people were killd they number names upon their fingers, some ten some twenty some thirty, and then say *worrow worow* the same word as is usd for a flock of birds or a shoal of fish: the Journals also serve to confirm this opinion" (3 July 1769). Given the antagonism of these early scenes it seems remarkable that, so the accounts state, later the same day the English established trading relations.

The following year, in April, Bougainville's *Boudeuse* and *Étoile* anchored in Tahiti's rocky Hitiaa lagoon for twelve days. As in Wallis's encounter, Bougainville's ships were met by the spectacle of women "stripped of the garments they generally dress in" (*Voyage*, 218). But in Bougainville's published narrative (which appeared in 1771, two years before Hawkesworth's *Account*), the spectacle becomes less an image of potentially disruptive sexuality than an invitation to indulge in a mythical reverie, less an effort at objective witnessing and businesslike self-denial than an opportunity for aesthetic and even comic textual pleasure. In a famous passage, Bougainville states,

> In spite of all our precautions, a young girl came on board, and placed herself upon the quarter-deck, near one of the hatchways, which was open, in order to give air to those who were heaving at the capstern below it. The girl carelessly dropt a cloth, which covered her, and appeared to the eyes of all beholders, such as Venus shewed herself to the Phrygian shepherd, having, indeed, the celestial form of that goddess. Both sailors and soldiers endeavoured to come to the hatchway; and the capstern was never hove with such alacrity than on this occasion. (*Voyage*, 218–219)

Bougainville's unpublished account summarizes the event simply as "a young and fine-looking girl came in one of the canoes, almost naked, who showed her vulva in exchange for small nails" (*Journal*, 60). The florid published version with its "Boticellian" scene establishes the mythic splendor of New Cythera: rising from the waters is a vision of perfection engineered to captivate the western gaze.[11] Bougainville's *Voyage* adds wry humor and tension, conjuring up the barely controlled desires of sex-starved sailors and a capstern (capstan) "hove with such alacrity."

Though hardly a convert to Rousseau's "savage man" thesis, Bougainville was within days describing an idealized picture of paradise: "These people breathe only rest and sensual pleasures.... And so I have named it New Cythera, and the protection of Minerva is necessary here as in the ancient Cythera to defend against the influence both of the climate and of the people's morals" (*Journal*, 63).[12] With this classical invocation, Bougainville raises the specter of a Tahiti that might meet its tragic fall as a result of its own indolence and sexual freedom, a theme that returns in explicitly Calvinistic terms in nineteenth- and twentieth-century meditations on the "fatal impact." Bougainville, however, soon learned of a more immediate threat. On the fifth day, an "Indian" was killed by a musket shot, and by the next day French soldiers had wounded several others. The garden of delight was threatening to turn into a battlefield. Partly because of his regard for the people—who, "apart from thefts . . . [were] the best people in the world"—Bougainville punished four soldiers, possibly quelling a rebellion (*Journal*, 68–70). He decided to leave after only ten days, taking with him Aotourou, an authentic natural man destined to be displayed to the Parisian elite—just as Furneux and Cook would take Mai (Omai) to London in 1776. Aotourou remained eleven months in Paris, where Bougainville was obliged to defend him against the critical barbs of skeptics who continued to cast aspersions on his idealized accounts. Even Johann Forster, translator of the first English edition of *A Voyage round the World* and scientist on Cook's second voyage, could not suppress adding to the critical violence, noting that Aotourou was less than an ideal type: "though our author has strongly pleaded . . . in behalf of Aotourou, it cannot, however, be denied that he was one of the most stupid fellows."[13] New Cythera, it would seem, needed a Minerva less to offer protection from itself than to protect it from the assaults of others.

James Cook's *Endeavour* approached Tahiti on 11 April 1769, arriving almost exactly a year after Bougainville.[14] Accompanying Cook was the natural historian and Fellow of the Royal Society Joseph Banks, whose Tahitian journal Cook would closely shadow in modeling his own account. Banks begins documenting the visit with the famous entry of 13 April, comparing Tahiti to Arcadia. Tahiti appears as an ordered, civil society, and within a day he is putting forward cultural comparisons reminiscent of Rousseau, concluding that Tahitians act in ways "at least equal to any we had seen in civilizd countries" (14 April). But on the third day, a sudden incident threatens to disrupt the delicate balance of the Tahitians' position among the ranks of the civilized—not because the Tahitians are seen as debased, but because the actions of Cook's men disturb the hierarchies embedded in the terms "civilized" and "savage" themselves.

Cook's voyage had been undertaken with the hindsight of past encounters and was under the unusually strict written instructions of Lord Morton, president of the Royal Society:

> Have it still in view that sheding the blood of those people is a crime of the highest nature:—They are human creatures, the work of the same omnipotent Author, equally under his care with the most polished European; perhaps being less offensive, more entitled to his favour.... No European Nation has a right to occupy any part of their country.... Therefore should they in a hostile manner oppose a landing, and kill some men in the attempt, even this would hardly justify firing among them, till every other gentle method had been tried. There are many ways to convince them of the Superiority of Europeans.[15]

Though the contradictions of an Enlightenment vision are visible in Morton's instructions, where European superiority sits uncomfortably alongside declarations of universal human equality, it is nonetheless an edict that reminded the voyagers not only of the moral and ethical stakes, but of the legal implications of conquest.[16] Morton's warnings were effectively annulled on the third day, when Banks notes that an "Indian" had snatched a musket and a midshipman "(maybe) imprudently" had ordered the marines to fire into a crowd of people, leaving "several shot" and finally killing the man who stole the musket. Banks states that the English are "guilty no doubt in some measure of the death of a man who the most severe laws of equity would not have condemned to so severe a punishment" (15 April), but he stops short of accusing the soldiers of lawlessness. Sydney Parkinson, one of the artists documenting the voyage, was far less compromising. Parkinson, a Quaker, calls the incident a "catastrophe," offering quite a different version of events:

> A boy, a midshipman, was the commanding officer, and, giving orders to fire, they obeyed with the greatest glee imaginable, as if they had been shooting at wild ducks, killed one stout man, and wounded many others. What a pity, that such brutality should be exercised by civilized people upon unarmed ignorant Indians![17] (15 April)

Parkinson's condemnation suggests a world upside-down, recalling the exasperated tone of de Quirós's journals two centuries earlier, documenting Mendaña's trigger-happy soldiers in the Marquesas: both authors are witnesses to spectacles of senseless violence but come across as isolated dissenters, powerless to seek justice or restore order amidst the anarchy of officialdom.

John Hawkesworth's rendering of the killing attempts to conform to the unornamented style of Cook's account, and both accounts are marked by the evasive tendencies of official reportage. Both Hawkesworth and Cook include details that ascribe blame for the violence to the Tahitian musket-stealer, and even suggest a planned conspiracy by the Tahitians against the English—details that do not appear in Banks or Parkinson. At the same time, Hawkesworth includes a detail that further absolves the English of wrongdoing, noting that after the marines fired into the crowd, "we afterwards learnt, that none of the others were either killed or wounded" (2:91). Though Banks himself never spells out the ways this event might have influenced his attitudes towards his fellow English, he increasingly, in the coming days and weeks, appears drawn towards engaging—culturally, physically, emotionally—in Tahitian life and customs.

Banks is the figure most commonly associated with sexual indulgence on Cook's first voyage; only twenty-five at the time, he is described by Roy Porter as "dashing, unmarried and free of formal responsibilities aboard ship [and] able to use this grandest of grand tours as young English gentlemen generally used Italy and France—for the pursuit of pleasure and adventure, and the sowing of wild oats."[18] On the day after the *Endeavour*'s arrival, Banks notes,

> we walkd freely about several large houses attended by the ladies who shewd us all kind of civilities our situation could admit of, but as there were no places of retirement, the houses being intirely without walls, we had not an opportunity of putting their politeness to every test that maybe some of us would not have faild to have done had circumstances been more favourable; indeed we had no reason to doubt any part of their politeness, as by their frequently pointing to the matts on the ground and sometimes by force seating themselves and us upon them they plainly shewd that they were much less jealous of observation than we were. (14 April)

Banks reads the lack of walls as signifying a lack of (sexual) shame but passes little judgment and seems pleased by the "politeness" he understands as sexual invitation. A month later he relates an incident that suggests not only his increasing physical and emotional investment in Tahitian life, but also his projections of sexual fantasy. A party arrives in a double canoe; cloths are laid on the ground, after which

> the foremost of the women, who seemd to be the principal, then stepd upon them and quickly unveiling all her charms gave me a most convenient opportunity of admiring them by turning herself gradualy round: 3 peices more [of cloth] were

laid and she repeated her part of the ceremony: the other three were then laid which made a treble covering of the ground between her and me, she then once more displayd her naked beauties and immediately marchd up to me. . . . In the evening Oborea and her favourite attendant *Othéothéa* pay us a visit, much to my satisfaction as the latter (my flame) has for some days been reported either ill or dead. (12 May)

The same incident is reported by Parkinson, who seems more focused on the cloths than on the display of nudity: "A woman passed along the next, having a great many clothes upon her, which she took off, and, spreading them upon the ground, turned round, and exposed herself quite naked: more garments being handed to her, by the company, she spread them also upon the ground . . . then the people gathered up all her clothes, took leave, and retired" (13 May). The perpetually chaste Captain Cook offers a more restrained version of Banks's "ceremony," adding the detail that the woman exposed herself "from the waist downwards" (93)—confirming an interest in displaying tattoos rather than sheer nudity.[19] Banks is nevertheless eager to discover sexual meaning in the acts, prevailing upon the women to stay behind, though they refuse. The juxtaposition of the morning's encounter with the appearance of his "flame" that evening—eliding a whole day's activities in the process—suggests the extent to which his desires are being projected onto his Tahitian hosts. Hawkesworth's presentation of the incident for the English public comes under the compelling heading "Some Ladies visit the Fort with very uncommon Ceremonies: The Indians attend Divine Service, and in the Evening exhibit a most extraordinary Spectacle." Yet Hawkesworth discreetly eliminates both Banks's entreaties towards the women in the morning and his romantic interest in Purea's (Oberea's) attendant in the evening, noting only that she was "an agreeable girl, whom they were the more pleased to see" (2:124).

One of the most notorious scenes of the "rites of Venus" related from the first voyage appears in Cook's account, and it would be highlighted four years later by Hawkesworth under the chapter heading "an Extraordinary Spectacle." Numerous critics have speculated about the "odd scene" witnessed by Cook on 14 May, described as an act of public sexual intercourse between a "young fellow above 6 feet high" and a girl of "10 or 12," who is encouraged by Purea and some other women (93–94). Except for certain comic embellishments, it is evident that Hawkesworth attempted to tone down the potentially volatile aspects of the story (by, for example, shortening the height of the man and making the girl slightly older) in anticipation of his English readership (2:128).[20] But there is a further alteration in Hawkesworth's account. Cook describes the girl being instructed by

Purea and the other women in the following manner: "far from shewing the least disapprobation . . . they instructed the girl how she should act her part, who young as she was, did not seem to want it" (94). Hawkesworth, perhaps attempting to clarify any faint ambiguity in the last phrase, changes the passage to "they gave instructions to the girl how to perform her part, which, young as she was, she did not seem much to stand in need of" (2:128). Cook's use of "want" instead of "need" leaves open the possibility of doubt: the girl likely does not need instruction, but also perhaps does not "want" her part in the act. Hawkesworth's "clarification" unambiguously imbues the young girl with experience and, it could be inferred, desire.[21] While the difference may seem superficial (and indeed Hawkesworth's accordance with Cook's version is basically clear), it is interesting that Hawkesworth's interpretation of Cook's eyewitness account erases even the slightest element of skepticism: if Cook's account has left the door ajar, Hawkesworth's shuts it. Similar to the elisions he made when reproducing Banks's "ceremony," above, Hawkesworth here others the act and its participants, deemphasizing wherever possible the give-and-take immediacy of the cultural encounter while emphasizing controlled acts of voyeurism and distancing. This suggests the subtle reappropriations that could take place when Tahitian-European encounters entered into the slippery realms of representation and eventually into popular fantasy.[22]

Subtle rhetorical gestures such as this one, along with others, no doubt helped the public to assess the Tahitian sex scenes in Hawkesworth's *Account* as pornographic. Indeed, the book caused a serious public scandal: such "impure" and "lascivious" descriptions could hardly belong to works of "fact." As Cheek suggests, "To describe sex without sensibility, without the characterization and heroic rhetoric of romances, without the veil of metaphor, and without the commonsense approach of sexual advice manuals, was to produce an image of foreign sexuality."[23] Hawkesworth himself died shortly after the book's release, suggesting that the vitriolic response dealt a fatal blow.[24] Though the strangeness of the Polynesian scene was likely heightened during Cook's and Banks's visit by the presence, unbeknownst to them, of *Arioi* performers known for their distinctive mixture of sexual display and entertainment, the excessive response to Hawkesworth's text nonetheless reflects the collision between erotic fantasies and social and rhetorical efforts to control them, and how homespun anxieties and desires towards transgression were projected onto Polynesian scenes. Clearly, an already existing popular fascination and discomfort with sexual representation coalesced around images of Polynesian sexuality and sexual display—images that, in spite of later, more measured revisions, would take on a legendary life of their own.[25] Yet a key problem also existed in the sense that, even within efforts to "other" or distance these anarchic Polynesian displays of sexuality, there always remained resemblance as well—and perhaps this was the greatest threat to civilized morals and manners. The Polynesian sex scene thus became a flashpoint around which a series of unresolved oppositions—distance and closeness, difference and sameness, fact and fantasy—continued to hover; indeed, the disbelief that greeted Hawkesworth's "factual" account would have merely exacerbated this more general lack of containment and consensus.

Towards a Taxonomy of Difference

The uncertain nature of the Polynesian encounter circulated not only around sex, but (and often at the same time) around physiological difference. George Robertson, master of Wallis's *Dolphin,* presents the ship's initial encounter of 23 June in the following manner: the Tahitians "brought a good many fine young Girls down [to the beach] of different colours, some was a light coper collour oy[rs] a mullato and some almost if not altogether White—this new sight Atract our mens fance a good dale, and the natives observed it, and made the Young Girls play a great many droll wanting [wanton] tricks, and the men made signs of friendship to entice our people ashoar" (148). Robertson's interest in skin color and its varieties—some young girls are almost, if not quite, white—is striking, particularly as it comes precisely at the moment the English are faced with what is being read as a sexual invitation.[26] These observations might imply curiosity more than prohibition: the fascination in the eighteenth century with natural history and the "varieties" of the human species, commonly seen as analogous to differences between animal species. Robertson continues the thread on 27 June when he notes that, in conjunction with the islanders' demand for the luxury of iron nails, "a new sort of trade" sprang up, "but it might be more properly called the old trade." The elderly men at this point brought out "several of the Young Girls . . . some a light coper colour oythers a mullato and some almost White. The old men made them stand in Rank, and made signs for our people to take which they lyked best, and as many as they lyked and for fear our men hade been Ignorant and not known how to use the poor young Girls, the old men made signs how we should behave to the Young women" (166). Robertson implicates the Tahitian patriarchy's use of "poor young Girls" perhaps in an attempt to shift responsibility for sexual contact away from the English, though he confesses there was ultimately little resistance: "the old trade went on merrily" until nails became scarce.

Questions of physiognomic difference were part and parcel of the Pacific sexual encounter, even if its meanings were far from transparent. Indeed, it is worth considering whether the scandal of Hawkesworth's *An Account of the Voyages* was on the whole a reflection of late-eighteenth-century English attitudes towards sex or whether it incorporated intertwined tensions relating to conceptions of racial and cultural difference. As Bridget Orr suggests, the taboo on miscegenation, at least in England, was not yet fully in place in the 1770s, but was "in the process of being constructed."[27] Cheek further highlights the differences between emerging sexual sensibilities in Britain and France: certainly Diderot's rendering of the polyamorous capabilities of Aotourou emphasizes light comedy rather than threat when he notes that "the holding of women in common was a custom so well established in his mind that he threw himself on the first European woman he met, and very seriously intended to show her the courtesy of Tahiti."[28] In England, the 1770s saw an increase in social anxieties over relations between African men and British women, as characterized in the widely rumored affair between Catherine Hyde, the Duchess of Queensbury, and her young Creole page and protégé, whom she named Soubise. Orr further cites the lampooning in verse of Banks's sexual liaisons in Tahiti as suggesting miscegenation fears.[29] Yet not all were "negative" images: the poem *Seventeen Hundred and Seventy Seven* (1777), a critique of British sexual disfunction, is dedicated to Omiah (Mai, Omai) and cites the allure and vigor of Tahitian sexuality. Cheek sees the question of race mixing with respect to Polynesians as following a somewhat different trajectory in France, where utopian narratives of regeneration through racial mixing, or hybridity, would engender notions of "perfectibility through sexual combination and reproduction."[30] She ultimately tracks twinned poles of racial thinking through the British and French traditions: race as essential character and race as degeneration.

As I suggest in the coming chapters, both of these racial tropes can be seen to inhabit modern US images of Polynesia. But the problem in both traditions of representing, and thus in some larger manner fixing, Polynesian race and sexuality remained the belated nature of the Pacific encounter. Enlightenment accounts of Tahiti came on the heels of existing beliefs about the peoples of the Americas, Africa, India, and the Orient, and conceptions of Polynesians were obviously influenced by these discourses. But Polynesian peoples for the most part remained—if we are to judge from the available voyaging accounts—under the sign of uncertainty, racially and culturally somewhat ambiguous. Society Islanders—and Tahitians, in particular—were widely theorized as ideal natural men, yet there was also much skepticism; after all, though often elevated, they were not likely to be claimed as *identical* to European peoples. Yet neither was there a consensus that they were wholly "other." Sustained approaches to Pacific ethnology were in their beginnings:

Polynesians had not yet been clearly categorized and racialized, while the racial theories that would come to dominate nineteenth-century social and cultural thinking were still in their infancy. Immanuel Kant's contested discussions of race began to appear in the 1770s, with "Bestimmung des Begriffs einer Menschenrace" published in 1785, though even here Kant admits that the discussion of Pacific "races" engenders uncertainty rather than fixed determination.[31] Arguably this ambiguity, rather than disappearing under the weight of nineteenth-century racial taxonomies, was to become a formative feature of Polynesian representations.

The emerging ethnological focus that would, in the coming century, strive to "correct" the problem of Polynesian ambiguity also began in earnest with the Enlightenment. Questions of human variety were already important, if not central, issues on Cook's first voyage. Banks's presence is evidence of an increasingly broad-based interest in the scientific value of voyages, which in this case included the natural sciences of botany and ethnography. Banks and his assistant Carl Solander were followers of Carl von Linné, who developed a formal system of biological classification based on hierarchies, a version of the seven-layered hierarchical system still in use today. Edmond concludes that during the eighteenth century there was a paradigm shift in the way in which Pacific peoples were being thought of and represented: "religiously framed colonialism was being replaced by natural history as the basis for constructing otherness."[32] Yet there was hardly universal acceptance of these methods: Linnaean systems of classification—and especially their application to human beings—became the object of public satire after Banks's Tahitian liaisons came to light.[33] Cook's second voyage (1772–1775) more firmly announced this shift towards a scientific, racialized, and comparative ethnology in categorizing human differences. This voyage included Johann Reinhold Forster and his son George, who acted as Cook's scientist and scientific draughtsman, respectively. The result of the elder Forster's presence was the monumental *Observations made during a Voyage round the World* (1778), a work that offers insights into the emergence of comparative racial typologies and the application of theories of "the varieties of species" to ethnographic speculation in the Pacific.

The list of Johann Forster's chapter and section headings is indicative of his systematic and hierarchical approach. *Observations* concludes with a lengthy chapter titled "Remarks on the Human Species in the South-Sea Isles," which includes eleven subsections with headings such as "On the Varieties of the Human Species, Relative to Colour, Size, Form, Habit, and Natural Turn of Mind in the Natives of the South-Sea Isles," "On the Causes of the Difference in the Races of Men in the South Seas, their Origin and Migration," and finally "Various Progress, which the Nations we saw, have made from the Savage State towards Civilization."

Forster's project reflects the desire to "make sense" of the diversity that he witnessed and read about, to create a comprehensible and overarching pattern, in many ways prefiguring nineteenth-century taxonomical practices. "Making the unfamiliar plausible in this way was consistent with the Linnaean ambitions of all the Forsters' work on the South Pacific," Lamb suggests; "their tables and classifications were designed to accommodate all facts, no matter how wonderful or outrageous, as information and knowledge."[34] In his Preface to the 1996 edition of *Observations,* Nicholas Thomas summarizes aspects of the work that relate to the later development of Pacific ethnography and physical anthropology, but he emphasizes that, while exhibiting a tendency to hierarchically pattern different species, Forster resisted the polygenist doctrine. As George Stocking suggests, it was the appearance of the Scottish philosopher Lord H. H. Kames's *Sketches of the History of Man* in 1774 that really marked the "reformulation of an old question" and started in earnest the controversy between monogenists and polygenists that would ultimately allow hierarchical concepts of human species to take root in the nineteenth century.[35] Though he openly engaged with Kames's ideas, Forster remained principally a monogenist, faithful to a vision of the unity of the human race, a concept that would become endangered in the coming century. The work of Johann Friedrich Blumenbach is a standard touchstone in this debate (*Beytraege zur Naturgeschichte* was published in 1795, while Blumenbach's University of Göttingen dissertation on human variety appeared in 1776), and though Blumenbach classified humanity into five familiar races, these racial divisions did not necessarily unseat perceptions of the essential unity of the human species, which was also "the premise for [Forster's own] exploration of its division into 'races' or 'varieties.'"[36]

In spite of this manifestly monogenist approach, when introducing the section of his study devoted to human varieties, Forster betrays the essentialism in which he grounds his theories, hinting at what Kay Flavell calls the rhetoric of "national physiognomies": "A Majestic size, red hair, a blue languishing eye, a remarkably fair complexion, and a warlike, intrepid, but open and generous temper distinguish the Teutonic tribes of the North of Europe, from the rest of mankind."[37] Though obviously far from a social constructivist, Forster's essentialism does not utterly fix human differences into static "types"; instead, Forster attributes human racial varieties to migration and variations in climatic conditions. These conditions, which shift from the ideal "temperate" zones to the "unhappy," "frozen" zones, engendered varying degrees of human degeneration, from the "courteous, elegant, and even refined" Society Islander to the "most debased of all human beings": the "wretched mortals toward the frozen zone" who have "degenerated and debased from that original happiness" (191–192).[38] Yet we also might find that, couched within a scientific framework of empirical and scholarly research, Forster's conclusions in many respects contain undertones of established western myths that help to order the present: these formulations are not very far from the narrative of Eden and the Fall from original grace conjured up by previous and future visitors.

Documenting Difference

The development of biological and ethnographic taxonomies to account for species variety required technologies of accurate representation. On the first voyage, Sydney Parkinson was meant to provide a visual account of Banks's specimens, while Alexander Buchan was hired to make drawings of human figures, dress, and ornaments. Buchan, probably an epileptic, died on 17 April 1769, only four days after his arrival in Tahiti. The value that Banks placed on ethnographic drawing becomes clear from his journal entry on the day of Buchan's death: "I sincerely regret him as an ingenious and good young man, but his Loss to me is irretrievable, my airy dreams of entertaining my freinds in England with the scenes that I am to see here are vanishd" (17 April). Banks here almost subsumes the human loss to the technical loss: his lament at the inability to entertain friends with the Pacific scenes he witnessed might be likened to the loss of a fine camera.

As Bernard Smith asserts, Cook's voyages affected an important shift in terms of the use of visual records on voyages of exploration. In particular, Smith isolates an emerging category of "documentary drawing" (as opposed to "inventive drawing" or "illustrative drawing") that might best describe the kinds of images that Cook's artists strove for. A documentary drawing works to replicate what the draughtsman sees, to "suppress the inventive and illustrative components" of perception;[39] moreover, documentary drawing tends to take place on the spot, or at least very close to the time that events are observed. A good example is Buchan's *A View of the* Endeavour's *Watering Place in the Bay of Good Success* (1769), possibly the first on-the-spot visual recording made by Europeans of an encounter with non-Europeans. The gouache painting would have been developed from pencil, pen, or wash studies done on site, anticipating the plein air painting of the nineteenth century.[40] The view affords a snapshot of interconnected activities and exchanges taking place between Cook's men and the Ona Indians of Patagonia, freezing for posterity various intertwined and representative moments of the encounter. The artist's high-angle position is authoritative: it spatially orientates the figures within the landscape, conveying a maximum amount of documentary information while minimizing the possibility of ambiguity or speculation.

While composing an on-site drawing or painting is obviously quite different from snapping a photograph, a number of key impulses are shared with photography, and even with early moving images, especially a belief in recording the actuality of real events—a belief invested in documentary drawing over other kinds of creative representations. Just as documentary drawing can be seen developing in the Pacific as part of an interest in accumulating scientific knowledge and ethnographic information, early cinema enjoyed an enhanced status in many camps and was employed as a key—and believed to be technically superior—visual artifact for scientific use. Like a number of the studies produced by Buchan (and later Parkinson and Herman Spöring) on Cook's voyage, nineteenth-century photography and later chronophotography was put to the service of physiological and ethnographic study in, notably, the work of Eadweard Muybridge in the US and physiol-

FIGURE 1. Alexander Buchan, *A View of the* Endeavour's *Watering Place in the Bay of Good Success,* 1769 (courtesy of the British Library).

ogists Etienne-Jules Marey and Félix-Louis Regnault in France. The ethnographic investigations of Cook's voyages foreshadow the practical and scientific ambitions underlying these later practices, and indeed anticipate the later elevation of visual ethnography to the level of science—or traditional visual anthropology—through its conscious combination of empirical study, collection of artifacts, and production of authoritative, on-the-spot documentary records.

Many elements of the ethnographic drawing done on Cook's voyages might be seen to anticipate nineteenth-century practices of using visual—and soon photographic—records to establish clearly defined ethnic "types" and conventions. Smith points out that Buchan and Parkinson both would likely have come under the sway of a number of books in the *Endeavour*'s library that established the illustrative ethnographic convention, among them George-Louis Leclerc de Buffon's *Histoire naturelle* (1749–1767). The pseudo-science of physiognomy was taking on some force in Cook's time, and discussion about the art of observing others and about the semiotics of bodies had been gaining ground from about 1750 (with Buffon) onward. Kay Flavell shows this in her discussion of the English physician James Parsons and Swiss physiognomist Johann Caspar Lavater, whose work suggests that the belief that physical characteristics could serve as a universal semiotics of the moral and intellectual attributes of persons was becoming well-established by the 1770s.[41] But it would be inaccurate to conclude that an artist such as Parkinson, who after Buchan's death took over much of the ethnographic drawing on the first voyage, was essentially detached from his subjects or fully invested in a physiognomic approach. Parkinson's work for Banks was performed long before the appearance of a systemized physical anthropology. As Stocking notes, there was almost "a complete lack of comparative human anatomical material" in the late eighteenth century, even of material related to the "great races." Buffon had known the Chinese, for example, only through other voyagers' accounts, not through direct physical evidence (*Race*, 29). The documentary illustrations of Cook's voyages were working in a scientific context still relatively unexplored and lacking in strong antecedents and conventions.[42]

Nonetheless, even the work of Parkinson—particularly in the ways it was interpreted and disseminated in engravings (such as *Heads of Divers Natives of the Islands of Otaheite, Huahine, and Oheiteroah* that appeared in Parkinson's *A Journal of a Voyage to the South Seas* [1773])—betrays tendencies towards producing physical typologies that hint at later projects in human taxonomy. These projects would become fully realized in the US during the mid-nineteenth century—when the racialized body would come to function as a universal sign—with the publication of texts such as Samuel George Morton's enormous volume *Crania Ameri-*

cana; or A Comparative View of the Skulls of Various Aboriginal Nations of North and South America (1839, influenced by Blumenbach's fivefold division of the human species), and George R. Gliddon's and Josiah C. Nott's *Types of Mankind* (1854), texts that strove to validate strict racial hierarchies through advancing a polygenist position.

It is debatable whether Forster's emerging taxonomies had a very strong influence on his shipmate William Hodges, who produced drawings and paintings on Cook's second voyage. The voyage's astronomer, William Wales, argued that the elder Foster in particular was disliked for his "arrogance" and "dogmatical" nature.[43] Hodges's presence on the voyage was nonetheless meant to have scientific value: his Admiralty brief specified that the artist was needed to "give a more perfect idea thereof than can be formed from written descriptions only."[44] Like Buchan and

FIGURE 2. Sydney Parkinson, *Heads of Divers Natives of the Islands of Otaheite, Huahine, and Oheiteroah*, 1773 (courtesy of the National Library of Australia).

Parkinson, however, Hodges, a landscape artist, was not academically trained as a figure draughtsman, a fact that suggests that ethnographic drawing would hardly have been his forte. Still, as John Bonehill argues of the sketches of *Otoo [Tu] King of Otaheite* (1773) and *Tynai-mai* of Raiatea (1773), Hodges's drawings evidence an emerging tension between offering direct likenesses of specific individuals and presenting representative "types" of the varieties of peoples encountered.[45] Thomas similarly looks at Hodges's representations of the peoples of Malakula, New Caledonia, and Tahiti in large-scale views (as opposed to detailed ethnographic portraiture) and concludes that these images can be seen to register responses to Forster's "varieties of the human species."[46]

Yet the views that Hodges produced for the Admiralty after returning to England, such as the epic *View Taken in the Bay of Otaheite Peha* (1776) and its nearly identical companion, *Tahiti Revisited* (1776), present a further dimension to Hodges's work, mixing images of exotic newness with the figures and gestures of classical antiquity, revealing the painter's investiture in the pastoral ideal and the cult of the picturesque. Hodge's epic paintings for the Admiralty, though of limited popularity at the time, presented an Arcadian paradise suffused with light, warmth, and ample, nude native bodies: white and pink-skinned, Grecian figures, with only slight marks of tattooing betraying geographical and cultural specificity. This was the "production of an alternative dream," a dream that was not a precise ethnographic project of carefully measured faces, bodies, and bodily gestures, but a model of paradise as a fantasy into which the expansive I/eye of the western (male) subject could project an idealized self.[47] On one level, then, Hodges's landscapes induce the sensations of warmth and luxurious sensuality while offering a voyeuristic "peep" at Polynesian life: they were invitations to the west, functioning effectively as a visual means to market a voluptuous South Pacific idyll. But the paintings also subtly stage a version of the sentiment suggested by Bougainville's invocation of Minerva that would come to dominate in the nineteenth century: that of *tristes tropiques* or the neoclassical notion of "Et in Arcadia ego," a phrase coined by Virgil that expresses, in an indirect way, "even in Arcadia, death is to be found." In both *View Taken in the Bay* and *Tahiti Revisited,* death stalks at the edges of the frame: a *ti'i* carving, signifying deified ancestors, overlooks the scene, while an elevated platform bearing a shrouded corpse appears in the background of the far right corner.[48]

On Cook's third and final voyage, the artist John Webber was engaged with Cook in a project of extensive ethnographic documentation and illustration. Through all three voyages we glimpse both the perpetuation of established themes and also the arrival of something new: ethnography as a key part of the systematic study of the Pacific along with the enhanced status of visual documentation on the scientific voyage, where emerging conceptions of human variety and "types" were being represented. Webber's illustrations for the third voyage thus also come under criticism: Smith argues not that they did not record truth, but that, like all documentary images, they recorded a highly selective truth. We can see the extremes of this in the engravings based on Webber's work, such as John Keyes Sherwin's *A Dance, in Otaheite,* with its highly stylized figures of classical European proportions and features. Webber's famous portrait of *Poedua* (1777) is another example of this kind of idealization: here the partially disrobed figure of Poedua is portrayed as "fused with a tropical nature," bound to an invitation of tropical delights.[49] Webber's images might thus be seen as individual portraits of a mythical, Arcadian Pacific: a site of desire and pleasure ripe for western cathexis and the capitalist venture that was already under way.

Cook's accounts tend to reflect his famed objectivity and stoicism, though by the second voyage an impression already begins to filter through of voyaging as repetition, of discovery as the despoliation of those encountered rather than an invitation to share in Enlightenment values. Amidst the accumulation and flow of knowledge, an appearance of degeneration seemed to be setting in—the garden was becoming a wilderness.[50] This sentiment was voiced in George Forster's controversial account of the second voyage, which aligned the physical violence wrought by Europeans with more widespread corruptions:

FIGURE 3. John Keyes Sherwin, *A Dance in Otaheite,* 1784 (courtesy of the National Library of Australia).

It is unhappy enough that the unavoidable consequence of all our voyages of discovery, has always been the loss of a number of innocent lives; but this heavy injury done to the little uncivilized communities which Europeans have visited, is trifling when compared to the irretrievable harm entailed upon them by corrupting their morals. . . . I fear that hitherto our intercourse has been wholly disadvantageous to the nations of the South Seas.[51]

By the third voyage, Smith notes, Cook was "still playing the role of an official philanthropist of the Enlightenment seeking to raise Pacific people from a savage state," but he must have been aware that he was in the midst of "a profound and unresolvable contradiction"—a contradiction no doubt that had already started to become visible with the brutality, as Parkinson called it, of the first voyage. Smith's conclusions are worth repeating here: Pacific peoples were not really facing the difference between civilization and savagery, as the Enlightenment might have seen it, but between "exploitation and extermination. . . . Those peoples who were sufficiently advanced to grasp the potential advantages of a market economy survived to become the colonial servants of their European masters; those who could not . . . were exterminated."[52]

The "American Pacific": From Porter to Melville

The Enlightenment established the South Seas utopia as both a "real" site, ripe for economic and territorial expansion, and an ideal space suited to the projection of less tangible desires for release, spatial mastery, and sensual indulgence. During the 1770s, the US was beginning to bring its own free-market values to the Pacific, when ships from the East Coast sailed around Cape Horn, heading for the transoceanic Chinese trade routes laid down by Spain, France, and Britain. "The American flag first reached China in 1784," notes David N. Leff in *Uncle Sam's Pacific Islets,* outlining in a single sentence the aims of US Pacific strategizing for the next two hundred years.[53] Spurred by the expansionist ideologies that were developed, if not born, in the eighteenth century (and soon harnessed to the ideology of manifest destiny), the growth of the "American Pacific" was grounded in the interconnected ideological forces of real politics and mythic invention.[54] As Mary Renda suggests, the republic of the United States was, from the outset, constructed out of and immersed in the ideology of empire insofar as colonial settlement and Indian wars established its very foundations.[55] One of the first colonizing gestures made by the recently decolonized nation took place in 1791, when Joseph Ingraham of the *Hope* claimed the northern islands of the Marquesas (Te Henua 'Enana)—called the Washington group—for the US, naming the islands after luminaries of the US Enlightenment such as Franklin, Adams, and Hancock. Three weeks later, Etienne Marchand reclaimed the whole of the Marquesas for France.[56]

The first large-scale US military conflict in the Pacific occurred when Captain David Porter—sometimes called "the first American imperialist"[57]—and the men of the USS *Essex* raided Taipivai on Nukuhiva, killing many of its "unhappy and heroic people."[58] Porter's actions would come to both fascinate and haunt US travelers in Polynesia—notably Herman Melville and Frederick O'Brien—who followed in his wake. The *Essex* stopped to refit at Taiohae harbor during the late stages of the War of 1812—a war, as T. Walter Herbert notes, that evinced a US desire to be recognized as a legitimate state, as one of the "community of nations."[59] In the Pacific, this will towards recognition met with a belief in the strategic importance of the Chinese trade routes, as reflected in Porter's early interest in the Marquesas and the increasing US involvement in Hawai'i. On arrival in Taiohae, Porter quickly established relations with the local inhabitants, the Tei'i, who claimed they were being menaced by a group from beyond the mountains, the Hapa'a. Acting in accordance with Porter's demands, the Tei'i disarmed and turned their weapons over to the Americans in exchange for an assurance of US military protection. Porter—who became known as Opoti—had close links to the Tei'i, including exchanging names with the patriarchal chief Keatonui ("Gattenewa") and having a romantic interest in Keatonui's daughter, Paetini ("Piteenee"), which Porter himself claimed was spurned. This intimate involvement with the Tei'i could in part explain why he found himself challenged by the Hapa'a. They called the Americans cowards, threatening to steal even the supreme signifiers of white arrival: the ship's sails. Like Wallis in Tahiti, Porter responded to threats of disorder with a conventional military show of force: he was determined to "let them see the effects of our cannon" (26) and the "folly of resisting our firearms with slings and spears" (28). Porter soon became convinced of an imminent Hapa'a threat and decided to launch a preemptive strike: "I thought that the sooner they were convinced of their folly, the better it would be for themselves and us" (29). The battle was not a success: many Tei'i were killed, and the triumphal Hapa'a "exposed their posteriors" and treated the US military with "the utmost contempt and derision." Pressing on, the Americans finally took casualties: five were shot dead, though one Hapa'a fought on until "the muzzle of the piece was presented to his forehead, where the top of his head was entirely blown off" (36–37).

Porter/Opoti formally took possession of the island on 19 November, demanding that the Tei'i swear allegiance to the US flag. The desire for international recognition is reflected in the fit of naming that followed: Nukuhiva was called "Madison's island," the newly constructed (with the Tei'i) fort called "Fort Madison," the Tei'i village "Madison's Ville," and the bay itself "Massachusetts Bay"—the latter name derived from another conquered people on another conquered land, affording an unintended irony to the proceedings. Porter's Declaration of Conquest embodied the paradoxes of the US Enlightenment vision: "Our rights to this island being founded on priority of discovery, conquest, and possession, cannot be disputed. But the natives, to secure themselves that friendly protection which their defenseless situation so much required, have requested to be admitted into the great American family, whose pure republican policy approaches so near their own" (79). The phrasing suggests an early whiff of what Renda calls "paternalist" discourse, a mode in which military occupation and diplomatic intervention is cleverly rendered as domestic protection, supporting a US imperial self-image as that of "benefactors helping out a needy, if recalcitrant, child."[60] The US, however, never ratified Porter's familial occupation of Nukuhiva, and thirty years later the French reclaimed the island group.

If the Hapa'a were difficult foes, the Taipi proved even worse. Excelling in insults, they called Porter and his men "white lizards, mere dirt," and shouted the "most contemptuous epithet which they could apply": they called Porter's men "the posteriors and the privates of the Taeehs" (69).[61] The famous "Typee war" that ensued was a temporary but significant blow: the skillful Taipi warriors severely tested the powers of the US forces, and the battle, which was meant to be swift and decisive, went on for days. Finally, Porter adopted a shock and awe strategy, burning a wide swath through the forests and villages of the valley, down to the sea. Porter recollected, "Wars are not always just, and are rarely free from excesses. However I may regret the harshness with which motives of self preservation, that operate every-where, compelled me . . ." (101). Yet he then notes with hindsight that "my conscience acquits me of any injustice." The Taipi, he states, brought the destruction upon themselves; it was a slaughter he was obliged to commit.

What makes Porter's account unsettling is not just its violence, but the Enlightenment contradictions at the text's heart. Porter praises Tei'i, Hapa'a, and then Taipi nobilities each in turn; even while battling them he professes love and admiration for his Marquesan enemies:

> I am inclined to believe that a more honest, or friendly and better disposed people does not exist under the sun. They have been stigmatized by the name savages; it is

a term wrongly applied; they rank high in the scale of human beings, whether we consider them morally, or physically. We find them brave, generous, honest, and benevolent, acute, ingenious, and intelligent, and the beauty, the regular proportions of their bodies, correspond with the perfections of their minds. (58)

This might merely be a form of military *sprezzatura:* to roundly defeat an enemy portrayed as ignorant and defenseless would hardly imply bravery or noble character. The comments could also have been a calculated strategy to encourage the US government to take a greater interest in possessing the islands. In either case, Porter conforms to the mission of the US Enlightenment: to bring the benefits of democracy, civilization, and perhaps above all market economics to a people who embody the physical grace and fighting grit needed to contribute to US growth and regeneration.

Thus Porter's *Journal* was not just a sensational report of adventure and heroism, but offered US readers enticing descriptions of South Sea islands, inserting lengthy passages devoted to flora, fauna, and geography, as well as numerous ethnographic details. In the process he helped to construct himself, as Nicholas Thomas points out, as engaged in the cultural life of the island, if also elevated: the *hakaʻiki,* the "warrior chief Opoti" that many Marquesans came to view him as.[62] Except for moments of irony or wry criticism of indigenous practices, Porter's tone strives for objectivity and a degree of parity with those he describes. His description of preparing kava, for instance, is relatively unadorned and respectful: kava is "a root possessing an intoxicating quality, with which the chiefs are very fond of indulging themselves. They employ persons of a lower class to chew it for them, and spit it into a wooden bowl; after which a small quantity of water is mixed with it" (53). Such details come alongside images of childlike simplicity: "in religion," Porter notes, "these people are mere children, their morais are their baby-houses, and their gods are their dolls" (119). Porter's text, perhaps appearing to modern readers as somewhat schizophrenic in its shifting registers of paternalist praise and blame, nonetheless also clearly aims to preserve an overarching sense of Marquesan peoples as rational and morally capable humans beings.

Like other accounts of the same period (the German-Russian circumnavigator Adam J. von Krusenstern's *Voyage round the World in the Years 1803–1806* appeared in English in 1813, and his chief scientist, Georg H. von Langsdorff, published *Voyages and Travels in Various Parts of the World* in English in 1813–1814, with a US edition in 1817), Porter's *Journal* helped to project a more accessible image of life on lush Pacific islands. At the same time, this relatively sympathetic view was coming up against more derisive accounts, especially with missionary reports written under the influence of Calvinistic doctrine, which commonly figured Polynesians as cruel, violent, and desperately in need of conversion. Publications that backed US missionary societies, such as the *Massachusetts Baptist Missionary Magazine* and *Niles Weekly Register,* dedicated to "evangelizing the heathen," portrayed groups like the Maoris and Society Islanders as indulging in frequent warfare, orgies, cannibalism, and infanticide.[63] "Hard primitivist" images of barbaric savagery thus accompanied, and in many ways played off of, "soft primitivist" images of noble savagery inherited from the Rousseauian tradition.[64]

The tone of texts such as those that chronicled Charles Wilkes's US naval scientific exploring expedition of 1838–1842 reveal how easily and concisely the rejection of the South Seas ideal could be performed. A Samoan *'ava* ceremony, for example, is described like this: "['*ava*] is prepared in the most disgusting way. The *ava* plant, *(piper mythisticum)* is chewed by the women, and then thrown into a large bowl—the saliva of the females, as in the manufacture of the *chica* among the Indians of Chili, being supposed to produce the necessary fermentation; water is then added.... Being now fit for use, it is guzzled down by the Samoan toper, in copious draughts."[65] The global cultural comparisons mark out the narrator's overseeing observational position, yet no effort is made to disguise the condescension, even derision, felt towards Samoans. Interestingly, much like Porter's before him, Wilkes's expedition would become perhaps best known for the controversial, strong-arm military tactics of its captain. Particularly problematic was the aggressive campaign Wilkes led in Fiji on Malolo, where the villages of Arro (Yaro) and Sualib were burned to the ground as revenge for the killing of two US officers in the midst of a trading dispute. At Wilkes's command, survivors crawled on their hands and knees towards him, begging for his pardon. One of Wilkes's crew, Charles Erskine, was so stunned by the events that he wrote, "Perhaps I may be pardoned for thinking it would have been better if the islands had never been discovered by Europeans; not that Christianity is a failure, but that our civilization is."[66]

As these accounts suggest, perpetually changing outlooks on strategic Pacific locales were expanding and testing Enlightenment idealizations and serving as focal points for the contradictions of the US imagination of otherness. As the century progressed, the more explicit political and commercial contours of the "American Pacific" were emerging with the help of events such as the British-Chinese Opium War and the Treaty of Nanking in 1842—when the United States found itself in a disadvantaged position regarding Pacific trade routes as a result of concessions granted to Britain, but managed to lobby for extended rights and thus achieved a stake in the Pacific on par with European powers.[67] The further signing of the Oregon Treaty in 1846 powerfully signaled the arrival, according to Arthur P. Dudden, of the "American Pacific empire," where US free-market liberalism would supplant established global powers: "no longer would Europe, with its African and Atlantic satrapies, define American lives and outlooks."[68] In 1850, California was declared the thirty-first state in the Union, and the vaunted ideology of manifest destiny effectively became a geopolitical reality. As the balance of power shifted west, California would become central to Pacific trade, furthering the West Coast's "tilt to the global space economy of capitalism that would continue for the next century and a half."[69] Closely linked to this capitalist tilt was the growth of US whaling routes in the Pacific, of which Porter had been a staunch defender. By mid-century, the importance of whaling was manifested in the US presence and investment in Hawai'i, the commercial plantation periphery to the emerging global centrality of the US.[70]

The early work of the literary figure most closely associated with the whaling industry, Herman Melville, offers insights into some of the more submerged doubts and cultural anxieties raised by this US expansion. On 23 June 1842, the twenty-two-year-old Melville deserted the *Acushnet* and alighted on Nukuhiva with his shipmate Richard Tobias Greene, known as Toby. There, Melville was "kidnapped" by the Taipis, an incident upon which he would shortly afterwards base the autobiographical novel *Typee: A Peep at Polynesian Life. Typee* and its rapidly produced sequel, *Omoo* (1847, based on a two-week stay on Eimeo), were unexpected successes, spurred by the popularity of seafaring adventures such as Richard Henry Dana's *Two Years before the Mast* (1840). Melville gained an international reputation—fame he would never again match during his lifetime.[71] Yet Melville's impact on the political and cultural sensibilities of 1920s travelers in the Pacific such as O'Brien and Flaherty cannot be overstated. As Herbert asserts, Melville (like these later travelers) did not come to the Pacific as a representative of the US government; he was not a "self-conscious emissary of civilization,"[72] but an ordinary commercial voyager. This may in part suggest why, from its outset, *Typee* seems less constrained by official rhetoric than accounts such as Porter's. It gestures instead towards a more radical agenda, even threatening to rupture the complacent assumptions of western cultural hierarchies:

> The enormities perpetrated in the South Seas upon some of the inoffensive islanders well nigh pass belief. These things are seldom proclaimed at home; they happen at the very ends of the earth; they are done in a corner, and there is none to reveal them. . . . With what horror do we regard the diabolical heathens, who, after all, have but avenged the unprovoked injuries which they have received. We breathe nothing but vengeance, and equip armed vessels to traverse thousands of miles of

ocean in order to execute summary punishment on the offenders. On arriving at their destination, they burn, slaughter, and destroy, according to the tenor of written instructions, and sailing away from the scene of devastation, call upon all Christendom to applaud their courage and their justice. How often is the term "savages" incorrectly applied![73]

Melville's ironic reversals threaten to turn the logic of imperial discourse on its head. Here he reframes Porter's contradictory messages by reinscribing them with at least one key difference: Porter's aversion to assigning absolute blame for his acts or admitting his own guilt is replaced by a more clear-cut schema of western aggressors and Polynesian victims. By the time of Melville's writing, the Marquesas was commonly being portrayed as a site of fearsome savagery—"cannibal isles." Porter's raid, however, is rewritten as a rape of paradise, as a scene of conquerors and conquered, with concomitant implications of the gendering of race and space. There is no suggestion of cause, no strategic or military justification, for such acts of conquest. *Typee* further addresses textual inscriptions of Polynesian travels, and attacks figures like Wilkes:

> Now, when the scientific voyager arrives at home with his collection of wonders, he attempts, perhaps, to give a description of some of the strange people he has been visiting. . . . Having had little time, and scarcely any opportunity to become acquainted with the customs he pretends to describe, he writes them down one after another in an off-hand haphazard style; and were the book thus produced to be translated into the tongue of the people of whom it purports to give the history, it would appear quite as wonderful to them as it does to the American public, and much more improbable. (Chap. 24, 170–171)

Though such passages appear at first unassailably critical of the hypocrisies of imperial knowledge-gathering, the embedded ironies of Melville's own position are less visible: his uncle had sailed with Langsdorff, while his cousin Thomas Melvill (possibly the basis for "Tommo") had visited Taipivai on the *Vincennes*.[74]

Malini Johar Schueller has argued that Melville's text appears on its surface to be anticolonial but is in fact "fraught with moments of colonial inscription."[75] It might be worth looking briefly at some of these critical approaches, since they shed light on ambivalences and contradictions not only within *Typee* itself, but also in the manifestly anti-imperialist sentiments that followed it. For Schueller, Melville articulates colonial tendencies through what Homi Bhabha calls a "strategy of disavowal," leaving Melville's narrative "replete with overt disavowals of Euro-American colonial prerogative at the same time as they repeat cultural colonialism through strategies of difference: creating racial boundary situations and describing natives through the scientific schemata of classification" (50). John Carlos Rowe suggests effectively the opposite position, arguing that "Melville's anthropological gesture in *Typee* destabilizes our very processes of understanding 'other' peoples. In that regard, *Typee* rejects the prevailing ethnographic models of its time and anticipates the more literary anthropologies of our own age."[76] While Rowe finds *Typee*'s westward-looking account to be in fact "articulating the horror at home" in echoing essential elements of the slave narrative (278), Schueller discovers embedded rearticulations of colonial discourses of gender, racial classification, and binaristic representations. Yet it is possible that Melville's text leaves room for both interpretations. As Schueller herself suggests, it is not so much a question of Melville's resistance to mid-nineteenth-century ideologies of racial and colonial thinking—the text clearly argues against presumptions of western superiority—as it is a question of whether *Typee* can constitute a "complete and absolute rupture" from colonial ideology (64). This question becomes central to engaging with manifestly anticolonial texts, such as those in the following chapters, that followed in Melville's footsteps. Indeed, *Typee* might be seen as an example of what Michel Foucault described as "mobile and transitory points of resistance" since there can ultimately be "no absolute resistance to absolute power" (qtd. in Schueller, "Indians," 64). But this abstract image of circulating power should not lead to conceptions of resistance as merely localized, ineffectual, or idly complicit. In her later work, Schueller cites the possibilities that anti-imperial enunciations can have a "deformative power" in relation to dominant discourses.[77]

But purely at the level of critique (which itself suggests forms of resistance), Melville's attention to a figure like Porter opens up explicit questions of US complicity in imperial projects both abroad and at home. By the time of *Moby-Dick*, Melville seems keenly aware that the growth of the American Pacific comes on the back of ongoing commercialism, culminating in an Asia-Pacific fantasy of Oceanic domination where "new built California towns, but yesterday planted by the recentest race of men" are directly linked to "low-lying, endless, unknown Archipelagoes, and impenetrable Japans" via islands overrun by the demands of US markets.[78] This attention to US market-driven expansionism can be contrasted to accounts of travelers such as William Maxwell Wood, who in *Wandering Sketches* (1849) includes a few pages about his visit to Nukuhiva and makes direct connections to American Indian genocide, repeating the widespread notion that the

Marquesan "race" was dying. At the same time, Wood represses the question of US complicity in Pacific commerce and colonization by focusing blame almost solely on the French. His praise for Hawai'i earlier in the narrative is thus juxtaposed with an attack on French control of the Marquesas: "The Marquesans are the finest race of savages I have ever seen, and it is much to be deplored that they are soon to disappear. . . . The French seem to have no wish to preserve them; on the contrary, I regret to say they are freely diffusing the means of destruction. The currency, or payment for their commodities was spirits and tobacco. . . . During our visit to the shore, we met several reeling from the [French] storehouses with bottles of fire-water in their hands."[79] In *Typee*'s third chapter (expurgated from the revised US edition), Melville similarly directs criticism at French colonizers, but his willingness to focus equally on Porter's destructive acts could be seen to draw attention to ongoing debates about US external and internal colonizing activities alike—the latter incorporating issues both of American Indian decimation and slavery.

Greg Dening admits that Melville's encounter with Polynesia "engendered in him a pessimism"[80] and that Melville's work thus suggests the rupture of easy binaristic associations such as good and evil, west and nonwest, civilization and savagery. As *Typee*'s protagonist plots his escape from Nukuhiva, he is forced to face his own inherent savagery and compulsion towards violence: "Even at the moment I felt horror at the act I was about to commit, but it was no time for pity or compunction, and with a true aim, and exerting all my strength, I dashed the boat-hook at him. It struck him just below the throat" (chap. 34, 252). For Dening, Mow-mow's murder sees the metaphysical poles of good and evil suspended, leaving only endless ambiguity and implying a loss of political clarity. This growing ambiguity, however, might be read as productive rather than as a shift towards apolitical ineffectiveness. *Typee* opens with a portrait of western aggressors and morally superior Polynesian natural men, but ends with something far more unsettling for western readers: fear, chase, physical violence, and escape from paradise. Even if *Typee*'s anxious retreat from the beach—from crossing over into cultural difference—implies a triumph of moral ambiguity, it does not necessarily undo the book's colonial critique. It does, however, complicate it. Indeed, rather than solely dismissing Porter's self-serving account of conquest, Melville's tale—while flirting with the boundaries between the real and the fanciful—ultimately draws out and even mimics Porter's self-contradictory textual flourishes. In so doing, Melville shows up the disordered ambivalences lurking beneath Porter's veneer of rhetorical and authorial control. "I felt horror at the act I was about to commit," states Tommo, revealing in all its frightening truth the western visitor's seemingly endless, and often interchangeable, capacity for both sympathy and violence.

Imperialism and Anti-imperialism

Perhaps the most appropriate starting point for a discussion of US expansion in the second half of the nineteenth century would be guano, a highly profitable commodity used as fertilizer. With the "guano wars" and Guano Act of 1856, Washington's leaders reinforced the legality of claiming territory in the name of commercial gains:

> Whenever any citizen of the United States discovers a deposit of guano on any island, rock, or key, not within the lawful jurisdiction of any other Government, and not occupied by the citizens of any other Government, and takes peaceable possession thereof, and occupies the same, such island, rock, or key may, at the discretion of the President, be considered as appertaining to the United States.[81]

Unincorporated territories such as Baker, Jarvis, Phoenix, Christmas, and Howland islands—along with Kingman Reef and the Johnston Atoll—were taken under this provision. At the same time copra was emerging as the primary industry in the region, with Germany holding the greatest stake in the business, increasing commercial competition over the coming decades, with substantial effects on its laborers.[82] As the commercial stakes got higher, a more ambitious and clearly defined agenda emerged under Abraham Lincoln's secretary of state, William Henry Seward, who envisioned the Pacific as a major component of the quest to develop a US "empire" that could gain control of world markets. In pre–Civil War speeches, Seward argued that the US could achieve global power through commercial competition, "depending not on armies nor even on wealth, but directly on invention and industry."[83] Though Seward's wider ambitions were never realized during his lifetime, shortly after the end of the Civil War, in 1867, he became directly responsible for bringing both Alaska and the Midway Islands under US control.

In spite of this widespread economic and ideological investment in the region, it has been argued that as late as the 1880s the US was exhibiting an ambivalent attitude towards undertaking heavy expansion in the Pacific. The US stake could be seen as meager compared to better-organized European colonial networks, and US interests were largely limited to those of private shippers and traders. Donald Johnson and Gary Dean Best note that in the 1860s, Apia, Lauthala, Suva, and Papeete had US consular representatives, but even these numbers began to diminish as France, Britain, and later Germany assumed control of various island groups. Though this diminished presence might be attributed more directly to the recovery period after the Civil War and to the economic crash of 1873 rather than to any lack of official interest, Johnson and Best argue that "there simply was no American colonial policy in the 1870s and 1880s, either in Congress or in the executive branch, although occasionally voices might be raised in favor of one or another expansive move."[84] A closer look suggests, however, that the US had hardly turned away from Pacific speculation and was in fact shifting focus on to a small number of highly strategic island sites.

For Walter LaFeber, the years 1850–1889 should be viewed as the "roots of empire," a period of preparation for the openly imperial land grabs of the 1890s.[85] US interests successfully negotiated in 1872 for the use of the harbor at Pago Pago, and the intimate involvement of Albert B. Steinberger—a self-styled "special agent" of the US State Department in Samoa who came to see himself as the future "arch-manipulator" of Samoan affairs—in the formation of a Samoan government in 1875 assured ongoing if "unofficial" US influence in the midst of subsequent governmental power shifts. As J. W. Davidson notes, "The Powers were not uninterested in Samoa, but their interest was centered upon their own advantage and that of their nationals"—these nationals being both increasing numbers of commercial settlers abroad and industrial-age consumers at home.[86] By 1878, US interests were officially entangled in Samoa, and by the late 1880s the secretary of state, Thomas Bayard, was explicitly linking US interest in Samoa to strategies of building an isthmian canal across Central America. It is not really possible, therefore, to separate out the interconnected US designs on the Pacific, Latin America, and the Caribbean. During this period, advocates of "preventive imperialism" urged for the acquisition of territories that were in danger of being taken by other nations, even while participation in illicit activities such as blackbirding continued unabated. It is estimated that, in 1844 alone, there had been between five hundred and six hundred indentured laborers aboard US vessels, with kidnappers such as William H. "Bully" Hayes achieving particular notoriety.[87] In a telling move, in 1872, nearly a decade after the end of the Civil War, the US Congress failed to pass a bill designed to suppress the ongoing trade of slave labor in the South Pacific.

The appearance of revisionist studies by William Appleman Williams, R. W. Van Alstyne, and LaFeber in the late 1950s and early 1960s helped to contest the once commonly held notion that the imperial expansion of the 1890s was effectively an aberration amidst predominantly isolationist US policies. Indeed, the sheer scale of the events that took place over an eighteen-month period between 1898 and 1899—when the US government took possession of Hawai'i, the eastern islands of Samoa, Wake Island, Guam, the Philippines, Puerto Rico, and Cuba (as an occupied country and protectorate)—suggests that these actions were hardly isolated or anomalous.[88] John R. Procter, serving on the US Civil Service Commission, summed up the events with a rhetorical panache that echoed Seward: "The year 1898 will be one of the epoch-marking years in the history of the United States. In this year is to be decided the great question of whether this country is to continue in its policy of political isolation, or is to take its rightful place among the great World-Powers, and assume the unselfish obligations and responsibilities demanded by the enlightened civilizations of the age."[89] Procter prophesied a "New Imperialism" rising from the ashes of old European imperialism, a system he described as a series of oppressive, centrally governed regimes that dated back to the Roman Empire. The Pacific could be seen as a natural extension of an ongoing policy of manifest destiny, as Dudden notes: "The United States of America spread itself across the North American mainland rapidly to the Pacific Ocean's shores and territories in Alaska, Hawaii, Samoa, and the Philippines, establishing an imperial sway before the end of the nineteenth century over extensive areas of the Pacific ocean."[90] But for dogmatists like Procter, the issue was not merely political, but also moral and explicitly racial, ideologically linking Pacific expansionism to the underlying Christian solipsism of manifest destiny (assisted by conversion narratives and a long tradition linking Native American and Polynesian "races")[91] and also to the white/black, North/South racial struggles of home. Procter's invocation of battles in the Philippines simultaneously praises the systems developed by "Teutonic ancestors" as models of social organization and finds them regenerated in US beliefs and practices: "From the blood of our heroes, shed at Santiago and Manila, there shall arise a New Imperialism, replacing the waning Imperialism of Old Rome; an Imperialism destined to carry world-wide the principles of Anglo-Saxon peace and justice, liberty and law."[92]

The underlying motivations behind expansionism were perhaps best expressed by President William McKinley, who offered the following personal and diplomatic reasons for intervention in the Philippines:

And one night it came to me in this way—I don't know how it was, but it came: 1) that we could not give them [the Philippines] back to Spain—that would be cowardly and dishonorable; 2) that we could not turn them over to France or Germany—our commercial rivals in the Orient—that would be bad business and discreditable; 3) that we could not leave them to themselves—they were unfit for self-government—and they would soon have anarchy and misrule over there worse than Spain's was; and 4) that there was nothing left for us to do but to take them all and to educate the Filipinos and uplift and civilize and Christianize them, and by God's grace do the very best we could by them as fellowmen for whom Christ also died.[93]

McKinley's missionary fervor is here conjoined with an ideology of racial uplift and a firm desire to see military order replace the "anarchy of misrule." With these objectives, the president placed the white man's burden firmly into US hands, perpetuating and extending colonial ambitions. Vincent Rafael reminds us that the Philippine mission was characterized by McKinley's policy of "benevolent assimilation," which incorporated a nostalgic vision of manifest destiny while at the same time patronizing and infantilizing Filipinos as the colonial children of the US, separating out the good ones from the "insurgents."[94] More than two hundred thousand of these Filipino insurgents would be killed during the three-year war that followed. Represented as benevolence, political and economic motives explicitly overlapped in the "American Pacific": 1898 would also see the founding of the American Asiatic Society, with its stated mission of working to "foster and safeguard American trade and commercial interests"—that is, to lobby to protect US trade routes across the Pacific—and to "co-operate with religious, educational, and philanthropic agencies designed to remove existing obstacles to the peaceful progress and well being of Asiatic peoples."[95] In 1899, the American Asiatic Society's secretary bluntly underlined its purposes when he offered an analysis of the annexation of the Philippines: "Had we no interests in China," he noted, "the possession of the Philippines would be meaningless."[96]

The negative impact of the 1898–1899 occupations and annexations hardly went unnoticed. The colonization of the Philippines, for example, led vocal anti-imperialists such as William James to argue that any possibility that the US could retain a moral advantage in international politics was now "lost forever":

> I confess that I wonder that you can still speak in as friendly way as you do of the President [McKinley]. Hasn't his policy in this matter (in addition to certainly losing us all our influence in those [Philippine] Islands in the end) lost us our unique past position among nations, of the only great one that could be a trusted mediator and arbiter, because the only one that was not a professional pirate? Now, (having puked up our ancient national soul after 5 minutes reflection, and turned pirate like the rest) we are in the chain of international hatreds, and every atom of our moral prestige lost forever.[97]

For James, the debate over expansion in the Pacific was "surely our second slavery question," pointedly collapsing the presumed gap between far-flung imperialist aggressions and domestic racial policies by highlighting the continuities of "external" and "internal" subjugations.

Advocates for expansion were nonetheless gaining the upper hand in the war of rhetoric, arguing that what once appeared to be limitless "free" space for advancement within US borders was now filling up. The Herculean feat of the transcontinental railroad, completed in 1869, had shrunk perceptions of space dramatically, reducing the traveling time from the East Coast to California from an arduous journey of months to one that could be done in under a week.[98] Ulysses S. Grant, recalling riding on an early railroad in Pennsylvania, noted the experience was like "annihilating space."[99] Perceptions of shrinking space were bolstered by statistical evidence: by 1890, the US Census Bureau had announced that the western frontier had officially closed. After the 1890 announcement, a range of scholarly and literary works lamented the loss of free and open land, indicating that a pervasive "frontier crisis" had entered US consciousness.[100] At the same time, rapid industrial expansion had added to the tendencies of "boom and bust" economies: depression had struck in 1873–1878 and 1882–1886 and would return with force in 1893 and last through 1897. Rekindling the visionary thinking of empire builders such as Seward, historian Hubert Howe Bancroft laid out plans for escaping what appeared an increasingly urbanized and unstable continental nation by reinvigorating manifest destiny across "the new Pacific." Bancroft wrote,

> The year 1898 was one of bewildering changes for the United States. In that year the last of mediaeval tyranny was driven from America. Our domain was extended east into the Atlantic and west into the Pacific, and across to Asia. The Pacific ocean, its waters, its islands, and its shores, as the world's theatre of commerce and industrial progression, attracted the attention of every nation, and a readjustment of affairs was demanded to meet new emergencies. Almost since yesterday, from the modest attitude of quiet industry the United States assumes the position of a world power, and enters, armed and alert, the arena of international rivalry as a colonizing force, with a willingness to accept the labor and responsibilities thence arising.

Bancroft then genders the new America: "Thus the old America passes away; behold a new America appears, and her face is toward the Pacific!"[101] The American Adam is wedded to an allegorical Eve, facing a space of forgetting and newness, untroubled by questions of genocide, broken treaty agreements, or trespassing on established land rights. Lush islands become the natural extensions of the bourgeois dream of private ownership, of home and hearth. Polynesia as a "virgin" territory could thus invigorate the American Dream—with its roots in More's *Utopia* and the mythic discovery of the "New World"—of the coming "American Century."

Yet the shift of US military and commercial power into the Pacific was not merely the logical extension of the westward march of empire; it might also be seen as part of the socio-spatial dynamics that Edward Soja has called "peripheralization," where the spatial mastery and centralization of one area (in this case the US West) becomes yoked to the commodification and distribution of power over peripheral areas—hence Pacific islands such as Hawai'i could become linked as plantation and tourist resources to the growth of California as part of the "same global dynamic."[102] At the same time, powerful ideological factors were at work. This period encompassed the rise of what Emily Rosenberg calls the ideology of liberal-developmentalism in US diplomatic policy: the belief in the adaptation of free-market enterprise as a fundamental principle for all nations, coupled with the growing acceptance of government intervention to protect private enterprise and speculation abroad. This ideology was quickly aligning itself with both religious and secular senses of the US "mission" overseas: the Christianization of non-Christian belief systems through radical conversion and the bringing of technological and professional know-how, or "progress," to "underdeveloped" peoples around the globe.[103]

Perhaps no single event better summed up the fine-tuning of the US imperial imaginary than at the World's Columbian Exposition in Chicago, which ran from May until October 1893. Staged to celebrate the 400th anniversary of America's "discovery" (though in fact delayed by a year), it attracted twenty-eight million people, a third of the US population at the time. Frederick Jackson Turner debuted his frontier thesis there, arguing that a vigorous America rose from westward expansion and its contact with, and mastery of, wildness. A new and grandiose model for the US sprang up in Chicago, signified in the monumental edifices of the main fairgrounds—the White City. Meanwhile, at the Midway Plaisance, a mile-long finger of land pointing west from the White City, live anthropological displays were juxtaposed with Egyptian belly dancers, international foods, and novel attractions including an ice railway and George Ferris's enormous revolving wheel.[104] As elsewhere saw the rise of imperial-era tourism, here the gaze over the Pacific could be experienced up close, even miniaturized, as in the panorama of the Kilauea volcano. For twenty-five cents, the amateur anthropologist could view (and, for two dollars, photograph) the live exhibits of peoples in the Javanese village or the live South Seas Islander exhibit.

What these voyeuristic displays hid from view were the larger implications and volatility of Pacific expansion, as New World powers such as Australia, New Zealand, and Japan, like the US, jockeyed for position amidst the more established colonial powers of Europe. It was thus hardly surprising when a rumor circulated, in 1907, that the US wanted to buy Tahiti from France for five million dollars, presaging the policies of "dollar diplomacy" that would shortly hold sway under William Howard Taft's administration.[105] The rampant commercial expansion envisioned as a dream during the notorious South Sea Bubble of 1720 was finally being realized: the Pacific was up for sale. Ultimately, the US would gain the upper hand in this commercial arena with the help of one of the great engineering feats of the twentieth century—the Panama Canal—a project that had for some time been seen by powers such as France as the linchpin to achieving Pacific dominance. At the 1893 exposition in Chicago, a one-hundred-square-foot model of the canal across Nicaragua had already brought this concept home to millions of Americans: the canal could do for US global expansion what the transcontinental railroad had done for the mastery of North America, yet on an even grander scale.[106]

The Pacific was becoming known as the great crossing ground, poised between Occident and Orient, between the colonial regimes of Europe and the emerging imperial and commercial superpowers of the New World. As Eugène Pelleray (of the French organization Comité de l'Océanie française, created to enhance the French presence in the Pacific) stated in 1911, the islands were seen by the west as "veritable oases in this immense aquatic desert" and valuable as "stopping points" and "refueling stations on the great maritime routes."[107] As predicted, the imminent opening of the Panama Canal further shifted the balance of power. The journal *Océanie française*—produced by the comité—stated,

> The Panama Canal is not only an instrument of economic conquest. The Panama Canal will also create incalculable consequences. It will permit an active reaffirmation of the Monroe Doctrine, altered from its original intent now for the sole profit of the Americans of the United States, to allow them to spread their star-spangled banner over all the coasts to the two oceans and in the ports of the two Americas. . . . Is not their ambition henceforth to see all the American states accept their mastery?[108]

The French clearly still felt the sting of the Monroe Doctrine's invocation, which, beginning in 1842, had prevented French intervention in "protectorates" such as Hawai'i.

US foreign investment, both economic and psychic, proceeded apace: between 1897 and 1914, before the First World War forced a temporary slowdown, US direct investments in overseas companies increased fourfold, while the immense popularity of missionary societies such as the YMCA, "rushing to convert the world to American-style Christianity within their lifetimes," continued to gain ground.[109]

When the war arrived, it did not spare the South Pacific: in 1914, Australian troops fought German and Melanesian soldiers in New Guinea, while soon after, a German ship bombarded Tahiti (rather than Samoa, because of the "high esteem" German naval commanders held for its population).[110] The Pacific, the strategic crossroads of competing powers, would end up as a stage upon which the great imperial conflicts of World War II would be acted out.

By the early twentieth century, what for Joseph Banks had actualized a true picture of pastoral origins now presented quite a different image: to many western travelers, this was a hybrid wilderness created by wave upon wave of traders, whaling ships, missionaries, settlers, blackbirders, beachcombers, and finally widespread annexation and direct colonial rule. Aldrich refers to this period as the apogee of colonial power in the Pacific, noting that it was also during this time that the *idea* of colonialism reached its zenith: when lobbyists for expansion and sophisticated modes of technical reproduction were helping assure that images supporting colonial ideology and identity were more widely disseminated than ever before.[111] The classic South Sea travel tale of escapist adventure and romance popularized during the late nineteenth and early twentieth centuries, closely identified with writers such as Charles Warren Stoddard, Louis Becke, Pierre Loti, Robert Louis Stevenson, and Henry Brook Adams, also was undergoing significant shifts in emphasis. Perhaps more than ever before, Pacific travelers were to be found lingering on a sense of disappointment, often stressing the gap between popular textual fantasy and the witnessing of colonial realities. "There is not much real native life now to be seen," wrote a disappointed Beatrice Grimshaw while visiting Apia in 1908, before continuing her quest for paradise.[112] That same year, the author J. H. M. Abbott noted, "The influence of the white man, both for good and for evil, is beginning to make its result noticeable. . . . Many of the ancient and barbarous customs of the natives are dying out. It is a pity that some of their more harmless usages should disappear . . . but a matter of congratulation that such horrible and ghastly practices as the burying alive of their old people are beginning to fall into abeyance."[113] Writing of his first encounter with Marquesas Islanders in 1924, Major A. J. A. Johnson observed people dressed in neatly pressed white shirts and khakis, and mused, "It was true, then, and the old picturesque costumes had vanished. We had been prepared, but all the same could not repress a feeling of disappointment."[114] But beyond merely disappointing travelers, Polynesian travels could conjure up worse: images of contamination, disease, and the tragic Fall would become recurring themes in US modernism's ambivalent conception of Polynesia, viewed both as a world of possibility and as a disappearing field of ruins.

Polynesian "Whiteness"

So far this chapter has outlined some of the ways that western representations effectively euhemerized an enduring and easily identified image of Polynesia, an image wherein elements of the real and imaginary were intermixed by western travelers and bound to prevailing beliefs and fantasies. With the nineteenth century rise of "exact" sciences such as anthropometry, linking physiology, ethnology, and emerging racial models, this euhemeristic process took on renewed force. The tripartite categories of "Polynesia," "Melanesia," and "Micronesia" became not just terms of geographical convenience, but strategically bolstered beliefs based on racial stereotyping that prevailed in both popular and scientific discourses. Melanesia means, literally, "black islands," and innumerable accounts draw unfavorable comparisons between different parts of the Pacific based upon racial hierarchies. As Jocelyn Linnekin notes, Polynesians since the time of Cook were generally portrayed as "sensual and hospitable," while Melanesians were "typically described as savage."[115] These commonplaces closely followed prevailing assumptions that linked character, race, and skin color to overarching, tripartite geographical and cultural categories.

Yet these representations never really offered consistent or predictable accounts of difference even within the "unified" category of Polynesia itself. "Hard primitivist" and "soft primitivist" representations often inhabited the same landscape, and tended to mirror rather than diametrically oppose each other. This overlapping dualism of the barbaric and pastoral savage persists and intensifies in early-twentieth-century accounts, and where apparently conflicting attitudes appear within a relatively unified western subject position or gaze. Polynesia remained a dream of paradise that beckoned travelers, but the very titles of books such as Grimshaw's *In the Strange South Seas* (1908) and Douglas Rannie's *My Adventures among South Sea Cannibals* (1912)[116]—or films such as the Bison Company's *The Headhunters* (1913) and William F. Adler's *Shipwrecked among the Cannibals* (1920)—suggest that this image contained other, competing conceptions and barely disguised derision. Yet these dualities nonetheless remain closely aligned. In Grimshaw's travel record and Adler's film, for example, we find reasonably sympathetic accounts of culture contact packaged under sensational hard primitive titles that appeal to popular paranoia about cultural and racial difference.

Hard primitivism was fostered and extended by late-eighteenth- and early-nineteenth-century scientific racism—the misused legacy of prominent physiologists such as Blumenbach—with its emphasis on determining essential human differences based on anthropometric (and in particular, craniological) studies, practices that formed the foundations of physical anthropology. The comparative anatomical studies of Blumenbach, along with figures such as Petrus Camper (1722–1789) and Georges Cuvier (1769–1832), had in effect broken with Enlightenment ethnological concepts and established the coming of biological determinism and empirical constructions of racial difference that would dominate mid-nineteenth-century thought. These theories not only posited profound constitutional, temperamental, and developmental differences between clearly defined racial "types," but offered a model of the evolutionary pyramid that placed Aryan and Anglo-Saxon civilization at the top of other, lesser, cultural and racial formations. As strictly descriptive typologies, these divisions were variously structured around the following categories: "Caucasoid," characterized by narrow faces and noses and fair skin; "Mongoloid" or "Oriental," with flat faces and noses and "yellowish" skin; "Australoid" (considered to be related to Caucasoids), with large noses, sloping foreheads, and light brown skin; "Congoid" or "Negroid," with large noses and black skin; and "Capoid," or Bushmen, relics of an earlier racial type, with short, flat faces and dark yellow skin. As argued in the US by texts such as Samuel George Morton's *Crania Americana*, physical attributes could serve as powerful universal human signifiers, and the racial wave theories that followed further refined the foundations of scientific racial divisions put into place by anthropometric studies. These conceptions were assisted by new technologies of visual reproduction that captured and displayed an index of material reality: an image of the bodies of others seemingly irrefutably superior to the deceptions of the naked eye. As Anne Maxwell suggests, to many of its strongest supporters photographic technology appeared to bury the errors of subjective vision "beneath the seamless surface of purely mechanistic technique."[117]

Yet paralleling the entrenchment of hard primitivism through race theories—certainly in the case of Polynesia—soft primitivism persisted, encompassing a diverse network of ambivalent yet nonetheless persistent notions that emphasized cultural, ethnic, and even racial sameness, rather than difference. Certainly the trope of Polynesian nobility was so embedded that Henry Adams could ironically refer to "civilization without trousers";[118] but what I would like to question is whether this encoding of the sameness of Polynesian bodies could be seen as pushing beyond these conventions to posit something closer to Polynesian "whiteness." Observing this tendency towards images of Polynesian-European sameness in English exploration narratives, Roy Porter suggests that "recent work on stereotypes has emphasised how cultures typically respond to the unfamiliar by emphasizing 'difference' and labelling it monstrous, bizarre, crazy, or other. Yet that is not always so; assimilation can be no less effective than anathematisation as a way of coping with the alien."[119] Throughout the nineteenth century, the image of Polynesian sameness as a means of appropriation occurred in different forms: it came amidst the identity crises of travelers who desperately wanted to escape the west and go native; it was scientifically validated in anthropology within diffusionist models of racial dispersion and development; it also appeared as a way to circumvent increasingly fixed and enforced taboos against miscegenation. Thus, rather than taking travelers somewhere else, into the realms of the foreign, the bizarre, or the unknown, the Pacific idyll was often constructed as a place of spiritual, psychic, and even racial return. The traveler left an increasingly mechanized and alienating civilized world to enter into a realm of an imagined, idealized familiar. This realm, many would claim, was the cradle of the white race.[120]

Primarily based on physical observations, the question of a Polynesian connection to Europeans was implicitly raised long before "race" was defined as an object of scientific enquiry. Even when Enlightenment beliefs in the unity of the human species are taken into account, it is clear that some people are immediately perceived as more "white" than others. On his first encounter with people in the Marquesas, de Quirós was met by four hundred islanders, whom he described as "almost white, and of very graceful shape . . . their skin was clear, showing them to be a strong and healthy race, and indeed robust."[121] Bougainville engages with the long tradition of classicizing Polynesian bodies, a practice typified by Hodges's work, and specifically conjoins visible whiteness and the cleanliness of Tahitians with European appearance, stating that "nothing distinguishes their features from those of Europeans: if they were cloathed; if they lived less in the open air, and were less to the sun at noon, they would be as white as ourselves: their hair in general is black" (*Voyage*, 249). The naturalist Commerson, on Bougainville's voyage, saw Tahitian women as the "rivals of Georgian women in beauty," connecting the whiteness of Georgian women of the Caucasus mountains (later engendering the racial classification, via Blumenbach, of "Caucasian") to Polynesian appearance.[122] George Robertson of Wallis's *Dolphin,* preoccupied with skin color in the context of cross-cultural sexual relations, hazarded a guess that Polynesians were in fact directly related to human "races" encountered in Europe, arguing that "this Race of White people in my opinion has a great resemblance to the Jews, which are Scaterd through all the knowen parts of the Earth" (228). In passages cited earlier, Robertson twice indicates the presence of "mullato" women, a term from Spanish implying not only the surface appearance of the skin but also a "mixed breed." Robertson seems to be considering—or wants his readers to consider—whether "white" essence might lie just below the skin's surface appearance. J. R. Forster similarly proposed continuity rather than absolute difference, noting that the "varieties of the human species" in the South Pacific could be placed more along the lines of a continuum caused chiefly by the climatic degeneration of temperate versus tropical zones; he thus arranged Pacific peoples starting with the "most beautiful variety," the Tahitians, moving down to the Malekulans, who were "black."[123]

As noted earlier, the idealization of Polynesian bodies would also be linked in certain cases to tropes of racial regeneration, notions of species rebirth in the discovery of peoples seemingly free from the inbred degeneration and decadence of western bodies. Cheek finds this thread particularly in the French tradition, where exoticist narratives such as Restif de la Bretonne's *Découverte australe par un homme volant* (*Austral Discovery by a Flying Man*, 1781) gave rise to arguments for the utopian "perfected body": the fantastic union of *métropole* and *antipodes,* where hybridity becomes "a tool for French regeneration, rather than as a vehicle for degeneration."[124] Shades of this image are present too in the later US tradition, where for reasons ranging from aesthetic appreciation to the desire to lift sanctions imposed on interracial sexual relations, and at times even to allow strategic political expediency, US voyagers such as David Porter explored the possibility that Polynesians might—even if marked by savagery—be almost white. As if anticipating the question of where the Marquesans might fit into the American mold, Porter's observations linger on physical characteristics, with a particular interest in the skin color of "the youths and girls," which "is of a light brown," while the men are "a dark copper-colour" (59). In applying coconut oil and turmeric, Porter explains, the women remove "the yellowness of the skin" and thus display "a fair and clear complexion, which might vie in beauty with our handsomest dames." He goes on to state that "the roses are then blooming on their cheeks, and the transparency of their skin enables you to trace their fine blue veins." The turmeric application engenders a metaphor suggesting that unsightly—and perhaps hybrid—yellowness can be removed, revealing the essence of "blue blood" beneath the skin's surface.

Typee's Fayaway, while never described as precisely white, also comes thrillingly close for Melville's narrator: "Her complexion was a rich and mantling olive, and when watching the glow upon her cheeks I could almost swear that beneath the transparent medium there lurked the blushes of a faint vermilion." Fayaway has "hair of deepest brown" that flows in "natural ringlets over her shoulders," teeth of "dazzling whiteness," and "strange blue eyes" (chap. 11, 85–86). Melville's "I could almost swear" that she bore the faint marks of whiteness is a key descriptive element, revealing not so much a secure knowledge based on scientific evidence as the longing of an amorous American struggling with the meeting of desire and visibility: he thinks he sees a self-reflecting whiteness in the skin and blue eyes of his beloved. Later in the novel, he expands on this idea to suggest that there might be "distinct races of men" even on Nukuhiva itself, and that in Taipivai he noticed "several young females whose skins were almost as white as any Saxon damsel's" (chap. 25, 182). Like Porter, Melville notes that the impression is in part artificially produced through the use of "papa" root and avoidance of the sun. But the impression is no less genuine, or significant, for being artificially achieved. Melville then itemizes a list of explorers who have extolled the beauty and lightness of the islanders, from Figueroa's account of Mendaña's voyages to the accounts of Cook, Charles Stewart, and Porter; he finally concludes that "the distinguishing characteristic of the Marquesas Islanders, and that which at once strikes you, is the European cast of their features—a peculiarity seldom observable among other uncivilized people" (chap. 25, 184). The "dark-hued Hawaiians" and "wooly-headed Feegees" do not, for Melville, rank as highly.[125]

But at least as significant as this desire to project whiteness onto a Polynesian canvas is the fact that Polynesians are, ultimately, never quite white enough. Polynesians may appear to be a white "race," but they never enter into what theories of whiteness have called the "unmarked" or normalizing realms of whiteness itself. The Polynesian becomes a reflection of the white voyager, visitor, or colonizer that is uncannily the same and at the same time irreducibly other, a fact that engenders both positive pleasures and paranoid fears. The colonial gesture of presenting the other as the "near image" (or in Homi Bhabha's terms, the "not quite") of the west's sovereign self is thus enacted at multiple levels, in widely varying contexts, but retains a certain consistency.[126] The appropriation of otherness thus extends not only to the realm of culture, per se, but also to emerging beliefs in more fixed and essential characteristics, such as race.

Melville's thematization of the complexities and ambivalences of whiteness in *Typee* expand into an overarching metaphor that came to mark much of his later work. As critics have noted, the theme of whiteness in Melville's oeuvre is ambivalent—the whiteness of the whale, the albatross, pearls—an ambivalence that begins to suggest ways that whiteness might be figured differentially, rather than monolithically, in the colonial context. Whiteness is desired in the other; at the same time it is never a fixed, secure trope for self-identity but rather a burden that the self wishes to cast off. In *White Jacket,* the figure of White Jacket must literally cast off whiteness—his "white jacket"—to save himself from death by drowning: "Sink! sink! oh shroud! thought I; sink forever! accursed jacket that thou art!"[127] What Melville calls in *Moby-Dick* "bodily whiteness" becomes a confused mirroring of self-in-other, where an idealized return to prelapsarian unity in the tropics effectively results in the problematic bleaching of native bodies. Yet whiteness is also marked by a kind of uncanny return of the repressed, recalling the shadow of death: "therefore, in his other moods, symbolize whatever grand or gracious thing he will by whiteness, no man can deny that in its profoundest idealized significance it calls up a peculiar apparition of the soul."[128] This apparition of whiteness reappears as a powerful trope in the work of later Pacific travelers such as O'Brien and Flaherty, where the whimsical desire for prelapsarian return is bolstered by a selective interpretation of theories of race and Polynesian origins, yet undercut by the impossibility of escaping selves grounded in the habits, desires, and racism of the west.

By the twentieth century, racial discourses in the US were mixing received scientific presumptions with the rise of a more systematized discipline of anthropology, and by the late 1910s and early 1920s, increasingly formalized notions of cultural relativism were entering into popular discussion and debate. While there is little space here to summarize the extensive range of the related theories circulating in the first third of the century, it is worth noting that in spite of the increasing influence of cultural and relativisitic thinking in ethnographic study, prominent purveyors of anthropometry continued to influence the understanding of Polynesians as a race well into the 1920s and 1930s. Peter Bellwood suggests that up until about 1895, Polynesians tended to be considered as a single racial group, but that afterwards "and for fifty years, the game of Polynesian origin-tracing reached a rather low level," citing John Fraser, J. Macmillan Brown, Louis R. Sullivan, Ralph Linton, and E. S. C. Handy in this group.[129] It is also important to note the persistence of craniology in the work of anthropologists such as Roland Burrage Dixon, who worked to multiply and hybridize types rather than consolidate a single Polynesian type. Dixon, a professor at Harvard and a student of Franz Boas who accompanied Boas on the famous Jesup North Pacific Expedition in the late 1890s, posited in "A New Theory of Polynesian Origins" (1920) that Polynesians could be assigned to four distinct racial categories: "Negrito," the oldest Polynesians, of the northern Hawaiian chain, characterized by a "short head" and a "broad, flat-bridged nose"; "Negroid," of the marginal islands of eastern Polynesia (the Marquesas), characterized by a "long head" and broad, flat nose; "Malay," of western Polynesia and southern Hawai'i, characterized by a short head and a long, narrow nose; and "Caucasoid," peoples of New Zealand and Hawai'i, with long heads and long, narrow noses.[130] Louis R. Sullivan, curator of physical anthropology at the American Museum of Natural History and author of works such as *The Essentials of Anthropometry: A Handbook for Explorers and Museum Collectors* (1923), posited similar categories a few years later in his armchair study of Polynesia based on E. S. Craighill and Willowdean C. Handy's Marquesan fieldwork, but noted that the Tongans, Samoans, and Tahitians constituted the "typical Polynesian" of the "Caucasoid" type, while Hawaiians and Marquesans were a "Mongoloid / Negroid mix."[131] As James Belich shows, there was widespread acceptance amongst *pakeha* scholars in New Zealand of a "whitened" or Aryanized Maori in the late nineteenth and early twentieth centuries, marked by the publication of a "remarkable little book" by Edward Tregear in 1892, *The Aryan Maori*. The Polynesian Society emerged around the same time, founded by Tregear and the genealogist Stephenson Percy Smith, whose *Hawaiki: The Whence of the Maori* (1896), based primarily on collected folklore, argued that Polynesians were descended of an Aryan population originally located in India.[132]

It is difficult to posit the precise extent to which these ongoing speculations influenced popular discourses and the amateur ethnography of US travelers in the early part of the twentieth century. References are scattered and often contradictory. Henry Adams's narrator Ariitaimai in *Tahiti* believes herself to belong to "the great Aryan race" (Arii); O'Brien's writings clearly show the influence of figures such as S. P. Smith.[133] O'Brien would parody figures such as E. S. C. Handy in his late 1920s theatrical adaptation of *White Shadows in the South Seas,* where an island-hopping American anthropologist arrives in the Marquesas to investigate "the origins of the Polynesians," engaging in the following exchange with a French missionary:

> FATHER SIMEON: The same race as ourselves? How is it possible, monsieur? They are dark and we are white!
>
> PROF. Archibald Trevelyan: They were as white as we were once. The sun of these latitudes has burned them.
>
> FATHER S.: One of our fathers had the same idea.
>
> PROF.: It is a mystery how and when they came, but I hope to identify the race by comparing their skulls with those of other living peoples.
>
> FATHER S.: And to prove this you are staying one day?[134]

Without this ironic touch, O'Brien proposes similar "Smithed" concepts of Polynesian origins near the beginning of the original *White Shadows in the South Seas,* where American readers were faced with the proposition that they shared an "ancient kinship" with Polynesians, who were of Caucasian blood. These and related theories might appear to offer superficial and nostalgic fantasies of Polynesian origins, but they also might be seen as flawed attempts to intervene into popular racist discourses.

The image of Polynesians and other "races" that Americans were encountering in the early decades of the twentieth century was highly variable and contested, shot through with competing representations of sameness and absolute otherness. As the US expanded abroad, internal definitions of American-ness were increasingly constricted. In the background to this discussion, of course, are events such as *Plessy v. Ferguson* (1896), which sanctioned social divisions based on race and racial appearance, and the rise of Oriental exclusion, which culminated with the passage of the Chinese Exclusion Act in 1882. Stereotypical "Oriental" representations that included Pacific Islanders regularly appeared during this era of Yellow Peril scares.[135] As Bernard Smith has suggested, this was nothing new: shades of orientalism long underpinned representations of Polynesia, predating the construction of racial categories in the Pacific, as suggested in the orientalist etchings accompanying Hawkesworth's *An Account of the Voyages Undertaken by the Order of his Present Majesty for Making Discoveries in the Southern Hemisphere* or in Joshua Reynolds's celebrated full-length portrait of Omai, completed in 1776.

But even as racial affiliations and divisions became of central importance in the US, official discourse moved back and forth on the degree to which certain groups should be included under the category of Oriental. Definitions of race were of utmost importance to gaining access to US citizenship, but the goalposts were constantly changing and the legal precedents were hopelessly unclear, as evidenced by Supreme Court cases such as *Ajkoy Kumar Mazumdar,* which in 1913 confirmed that Asian Indians could be classed as Caucasian. This decision was followed by the Immigration Act of 1917, which created an "Asiatic Barred Zone" blocking immigration from India, Burma, Siam, Afghanistan, Arabia, the Malay Islands, and Polynesia.

Even more important, the early years of the 1920s saw legal precedents regarding racial affiliation and citizenship shifting their emphases away from ethnological categories towards the sanctioning of popular conceptions of race. In 1922, in the case of *Ozawa v. The United States,* the Supreme Court attempted to define the term "white persons," here denying naturalization to a Japanese man because he didn't belong to the "Caucasian race." Briefly, it appeared the court was giving precedence to standard ethnological categories. But the Supreme Court then rejected scientific ethnological classification the following year in the *United States v. Thind* decision, in which a "high caste Hindu of full Indian blood," ethnologically classed as Caucasian, was denied the right to naturalization. "White person" was henceforth to be defined as it was popularly understood by the "common man." As the court stated,

What we now hold is that the words "free white persons" are words of common speech, to be interpreted in accordance with the understanding of the common man, synonymous with the word "Caucasian" only as that word is popularly understood. As so understood and used, whatever may be the speculations of the ethnologist, it does not include the body of people to whom the appellee belongs. It is a matter of familiar observation and knowledge that the physical group characteristics of the Hindus render them readily distinguishable from the various groups of persons in this country commonly recognized as white.[136]

The power to bestow whiteness therefore officially shifted to common knowledge and popular conceptions, a significant move that undermined ethnological definitions. The *Thind* case, in tandem with the Asiatic Barred Zone of 1917, was not surprisingly a "source of gratification to administrative officers," according to the commissioner of naturalization in 1923, Raymond F. Crist, since it provided simple geographical answers to previously confused conceptions of who was white and who would therefore be eligible for naturalization.[137]

The American travelers discussed in the following chapters thus mark a possible alternative to this trend in that they strive, with the assistance of ethnological theory, to forge a popular discourse of Polynesians as something closer to idealized—white—perceptions of American selfhood than to nonwhite "others." Many of these Pacific travelers closely studied early-twentieth-century theories of Polynesian Caucasoid or Aryan origins, which had gained momentum by assembling a varied speculative and scientific apparatus, from Charles Darwin's evolutionary theory and concepts of species dispersion to linguistic theories and theories of biological essentialism. Both O'Brien and Flaherty were influenced by figures such as Smith and the linguistic historian Abraham Fornander, who conjectured that Polynesians were living descendants of white "Caucasoids," presenting the following elaboration on the linguistic theories of the philologist Franz Bopp:

It may be proper here at the outset to say that I believe that I can show that the Polynesian family can be traced directly as having occupied the Asiatic Archipelago, from Sumatra to Timor, Gilolo, and the Philippines, previous to the occupation of that archipel by the present Malay family; that traces, though faint and few, lead up through Deccan to the north-west part of India and the shores of the Persian Gulf; that, when other traces here fail, yet the language points farther north, to the Aryan stock in its earlier days, long before the Vedic irruption in India, and that for long ages the Polynesian family was the recipient of a Cushite civilisation, and to such an extent as almost entirely to obscure its own consciousness of parentage and kindred to the Aryan stock.[138]

Fornander argues that Polynesians are Aryan, though they would have long ago forgotten any traces of their ancestry. A longtime resident of Hawaiʻi and a professor in Honolulu, Fornander was married to a Hawaiian—thus the scientific question of Polynesian origins engaged with his own role in what might potentially be classified as miscegenation, with its concomitant prohibitions and "scientific" arguments that mixed race relations led to the degeneration of the species.[139] Dispersion theories like those of Smith and Fornander defended the Polynesian "race" in the face of racist doctrines, but also perhaps unwittingly underpinned those very doctrines in their appeals to Caucasian legitimacy. Alongside these notions, migration theories such as J. Macmillan Brown's (which Peter Bellwood calls "one of the strangest theories of all time") posited that Polynesia was first settled by Caucasians using primitive Aryan languages, who had moved across land bridges from Japan and Easter Island.[140]

I am not suggesting that theories of Polynesian sameness dominated ethnological models at this time; indeed, they appeared as only one strand in a highly contested range of theories and beliefs. In addition to the anthropometric divisions of figures such as Dixon and Sullivan, the early-twentieth-century US saw the resurgence of what George Stocking calls "organismic" racial thinking modeled on the work of US social scientist William Z. Ripley. Stocking argues that it was through Ripley that what was left of polygenism in European physical anthropology had its impact in the US (though by 1921, Albert Churchward would argue that in Europe, at least, "if polygenism is not yet dead, few, I believe, there are to keep the dying embers alive, and these few can have no knowledge of the comparative anatomy and physiology of the lower human races").[141] In the late-nineteenth century, Ripley, while not strictly a physical anthropologist, suggested theories of dominant racial typologies that were relatively static, distilling from the strict racial categories of physical anthropology three more or less uniform racial types that carried the "essences of racial purity."[142] Stocking has located a current in early-twentieth-century US anthropology and social science that loosely adopted such typologies into patterns of thought that presented races as supraindividual entities that had a common "genius" or "soul" (the "genius" of the yellow race, the "soul" of the black, to which might be added, the "naturalness and ease" of the Polynesian) and whose earthly existence followed "the individual human life cycle of birth, growth, maturity, and perhaps even death."[143] The strains of this holistic, organismic approach found perhaps their most notorious formulation in 1916, in the influential racism of the zoologist Madison Grant's homage to Count de Gobineau's polygenism, *The Passing of the Great Race,* which posited races as separate biological species, positioning the Aryan and the idea of the noble Teuton against the essential inferiority of nonwhite races.[144] A similar approach can be found underlying Bancroft's expansionist image of the "New Pacific," where the Pacific basin is rightfully dominated by Anglo-Saxon Americans, their "gregarious" nature having been increasingly confined in a postfrontier, urbanized US:

> Here [in the Pacific] is room for a new regenerated humanity. . . . Here is room to spread out, with ocean air and frontage for all, and with endless facilities for many small cities instead of a few large ones. It is fitting that the Anglo-Saxon race should dominate these waters, and that English should be the language of the new civilization.[145]

Moreover, Bancroft continues, the islands are currently populated by a race of "red men," which again suggests the connections, going to back to before Ellis, between American Indian groups and Pacific Islanders. This time, however, the groups are not associated as common, tragic victims of the fatal impact but as conveniently weak objects primed for conquest.

What remains interesting in these overlapping and often conflicting racial discourses is that Polynesians are not merely absolute "others" that serve to stabilize notions of American subjectivity. As I began to suggest earlier, Polynesians, while sometimes viewed as embodying "white" features, are nonetheless never fully privileged to the unmarked status of whiteness. As Ross Chambers notes, whiteness is not itself usually compared with anything, but "other things are compared unfavorably with it." Whiteness is a "blank" racial category; it has "a touchstone quality of the normal, against which the members of marked categories are measured and, of course, found deviant, that is, wanting." [146] Polynesians in the accounts studied here are often compared to white, yet also always remain "marked" in some fashion. Rather than remaining unquestioned, a blank field of racial categorization, Polynesians appear to embody a more unsettling, in-between status, suggesting ambivalent and contested racial possibilities that threaten to denaturalize the ways that whiteness is constructed against a nonwhite field. Indeed, in most cases the problematic gestures of affinity between "white" and "almost white" in Polynesian representations tend ultimately to fragment into declarations of absolute difference, as will be seen in subsequent chapters. But where they do persist, as they do subtextually in Melville's persistent ambiguities, they begin to suggest at the very least that Polynesia, as seen through the lens of an emerging US modernity, offered peculiar representational possibilities quite distinct from colonial constructions of orientalism, African primitivism, and so on. This is perhaps what is most uncanny in US representations of Polynesia: the unstable and liminal appearance in Melville's "peculiar apparition of the soul," where a self-destroying "other" threatens to converge with the otherness of the self.[147]

Cultural Relativism

It is important to view the cultural relativism that emerged as a dominant mode of anthropological inquiry in the first third of the twentieth century as part of a developing tradition rather than as an absolute break with the past. Cultural relativism and anthropology never were the same thing, the latter always remaining tied on some level to the disciplinary histories, regimes, and practices that constituted it. Cultural relativism, on the other hand, might be glimpsed through a history of the cross-cultural encounter, which held the potential for travelers to reflect, often negatively, on the west as merely one form of social organization among others. Stocking argues that the historical development of anthropological relativism, though today mainly implying a general sense of critical detachment, involved "if not disillusion, at least a rejection of contemporary values and an alienation from contemporary society."[148] In these terms, one might include Bougainville's rapturous encounter in Tahiti that inspired Diderot's philosophical relativism or Cook's moments of cultural comparativism that at rare moments recalled elements of Montaigne's and Rousseau's theses. If not precisely suggesting utter alienation, these texts do envision forms of cultural detachment and critique.

Banks's journal, for example, reveals a dominant Eurocentric classicism when Banks names several Tahitians after Greek figures: one he calls Lycurgus for his ability to mete out justice, another is Hercules, "from the large size of his body" (17 April), and so on. But Banks's account suggests the uneven dynamics of the cross-cultural encounter, charting barely perceptible shifts and concessions in the balance of power. By 10 May, Banks notes that the "Indian name of the island, *Otahite*" had been recognized, stating "so therefore for the future I shall call it," perhaps subconsciously undermining Wallis's claim in the name of the British sovereign, and perhaps also addressing Cook's authoritative place-naming strategies based on northern maps, outlined by Obeyesekere. Banks also discovers the given names for his "Greeks": Lycurgus's "real name" is approximated as *Tubourai tamaide*, while Hercules is set down as *Tootahah* (Banks, 27–28 April).[149] Yet the Tahitians were also "not a little pleased to discover that we had [names] likewise."

Just as the English renamed the Tahitians, so the English find themselves with new or adapted Tahitian names. Banks writes, "I give here the List: Captn Cooke *Toote,* Dr Solander *Torano,* Mr Hicks *Hete,* Mr Gore *Toaro,* Mr Moloineux *Boba* from his Christian name Robert, Mr Monkhouse *Mato,* and myself *Tapáne*" (10 May). Banks's validation of these new names opens up the possibility of suspending cultural hierarchies, a cultural practice that involves, Talal Asad has suggested, "*learning to live another form of life* and to speak in another kind of language." [150]

Certainly, early beachcomber accounts suggest complex understandings of difference emerging before cultural anthropology's systematization of fieldwork and "participant observation." Vanessa Smith, glossing Dening, notes that crossing the beach, moving from shipboard towards island life, can signify a "liminal space in which social orders intersect in a context that is necessarily provisional and relativising." [151] Thirty years after Cook first encountered Polynesian islands and cultures, the Englishman Edward Robarts, a beachcomber in the Marquesas, embarked on an extensive experiment in comparative cultural living. Robarts deserted his ship the *New Euphrates* just before Christmas 1798 to live in the Marquesas, where he remained seven years, marrying a woman on Ua Pou and fathering a daughter. His experience of two cultures led to some striking moments of self-reflexive and comparative ethnographic reflections, worth quoting here at length:

> These [Marquesan] people have no correspondence with any other race of men but of their own class. They are separated from the rest of mankind at least 2000 Miles distance.... Here is man in his native state. But let me ask my Impartial reader a fair question. Which of the two is the greatest Savage, the man who has Every Education given him, or the poor untaught Indian who has none? Here is no Police Office, no Court of Requests. But turn ourselves and take a view of Hicks Hall, which stands at the Bottom of Clerkenwell Green, London & of the Publick Office in the Borough Southwark. Next is the office in Worship Street, Finsbury Square, and the one in Hatton Garden. Peep into Bow Street and stop at Tothill Fields. The above mentioned offices you will see daily crouded with the wretches of both sex, whose countenances and crimes are of the darkest hue. Here is a large field to reflect in and view the out casts of Europe, acting some of their tragic and their Comic Parts. Here you see the Queen, the Jilt, the Nun of easy virtue, the Beau, the Lounger and sometimes the simple Farmer in search of their watches or cash that the fair nuns of the Strand, Parliament Street, or the Hundreds of Drury have depriv'd them of the night before. Haveing thus painted with a favourable brush a few characters on the stage of Europe, [I] must now leave my courteous reader to his own private thoughts, and I trust that he will Join with me

in Lamenting the situation of those Benighted, but Hospitable race of mankind which Inhabit the several groupes of Isles in the South Seas.[152]

Robarts offers a quite sophisticated relativism that also functions as a mode of rhetorical irony not unlike Diderot's. Yet this is an irony resulting from experience and not armchair philosophical speculation about human nature, morality, or sexuality as in the European cultural debates animated by the Tahitian accounts. In Robarts's journals, his transcultural immersion begins to allow some of the complexities of Marquesan culture to emerge, and these articulations put into question, with great immediacy, the hierarchical cultural assumptions that deny complex subjectivity to those unwilling or unable to comply with western demands and expectations.

Another deserter in the Marquesas, Paul Gauguin, offered a number of relativistic observations in *Noa Noa* (1901), including this famous one: "'Savages!' This word came involuntarily to my lips when I looked at these black beings with their cannibal-like teeth. However, I already had a glimpse of their genuine, their strange grace." Gauguin continues,

> As they were to me, so was I to them, an object for observation, a cause of astonishment—one to whom everything was new, one who was ignorant of everything. For I knew neither their language, nor their customs, not even the simplest, most necessary manipulations. As each one of them was a savage to me, so was I a savage to each one of them. And which of us two was wrong? [153]

Though Gauguin's journals were prepared and augmented by his friend Charles Morice, and are not very reliable accounts of his final years, in many ways they thematize popular moves in modernist writing and representation towards relativist attitudes about culture and identity, with their meditations on human transience and fallibility, their questioning of absolute truths and their insistence on the arbitrariness of cultural affiliation. Ultimately, however, as Gauguin's paintings from Tahiti and the Marquesas suggest, this may not so much suggest crossing over into difference as a desire for youthful and racial regeneration, a coming into contact with an imagined primitive self. When it appeared in the US in late 1919, the first edition of O. F. Theis's translation of *Noa Noa* sold out within three weeks, suggesting that relativistic discourse was being popularly established just as more disciplined, postwar comparative anthropological approaches were arriving on the scene.[154]

In the various writings of missionaries, beachcombers, and other resident aliens in Polynesia, one can perceive the persistent echo of separation from and critical reflection on western cultures, often conjoined with idealistic desires to cross culture lines and escape, efface, or renew western selfhood. In 1889 the young Englishman Alfred St. Johnston released his Polynesian recollections in *Camping among Cannibals,* which appeared as part of the Macmillan Colonial Library series, circulated in the British colonies. On page after page St. Johnston extols the pleasures of the "splendid" and "radiant" Pacific locales (Tonga, Samoa, Fiji), full of "heat and brilliancy of light I cannot describe." [155] Soon, St. Johnston is questioning the "supercilious, patronising, and confoundedly impertinent manners that a white man generally assumes are not only horrible to me but incomprehensible. . . . I believe it has been chiefly my feeling of affection and fellowship with these Polynesians that has taken me so well all through the islands" (115). Meanwhile, questions of self-identity continue to arise: "I remember learning a hymn in my tender youth in which I thanked the Lord I was born an English child: I think I could have done it with greater truth had I been born a Pacific Island one" (31). After some weeks have elapsed, St. Johnston decides to remain with the natives as much as possible and to "shun all people of my own colour" (145). In Samoa, St. Johnston refers to himself and his companions as "us idle Samoans" (180), finally lamenting, "Oh why was I born a grovelling Englishman?" (205). Even more than the desire to go native—that is, to cross into the realms of racial or cultural difference, which would imply a loss of (western) self—these passages signal regeneration and a return to a lost or buried self, to a more noble form of life now lost to the west. Later institutionalized forms of cultural relativism often encoded these holistic, primitivist desires, as seen in Edward Sapir's or Margaret Mead's work, but at other levels relativist approaches were performing the important task of beginning to challenge the entrenched cultural hierarchies of the status quo.

In the years following the First World War, the opposing poles of elevation and derision that had long characterized primitivist fantasy were converging with the rise of the increasingly systematized and disciplined anthropological practice of cultural relativism. This was a time of profound, collective self-interrogation for Europe and the US. In the wake of a brutal war, civilization seemed to signify the opposite of progress: its new technologies engendered warfare, entropy, and destruction of the very values they were meant to guarantee. Around the same time, the public sphere was negotiating ongoing debates between the anthropological findings of Franz Boas at Columbia (and, soon after, Robert H. Lowie's psychoanalysis-inflected anthropology at Berkeley) and the resurgence of biological determinism, as exemplified in the holistic and organismic approach of Charles B. Davenport, leader of the American eugenics movement, and his collaborator, Madison Grant. In spite of the reactionary influence of the latter two, "culture" was rivaling "race" as the touchstone for discussions of social organization and identity, as famously defined by British ethnologist E. B. Tylor: "Culture or Civilization, taken in its wide ethnographic sense, is that complex whole which includes knowledge, belief, art, morals, law, custom, and any other capabilities and habits acquired by man as a member of society." [156]

As Stocking notes, however, in examining the pluralization of the culture concept, there were few usages of the plural of the term "culture" before 1900, and these only in the work of Franz Boas.[157] Boas, initially a physical anthropologist, had been influential in US academia since the 1890s for his work on American Indian groups; he released major works characterizing the relativist turn—*The Mind of Primitive Man* (1911) and *Kultur and Rasse* (1913)—just before the war, while Lowie's *Primitive Society*, a classic mixture of psychology and anthropology, was released shortly after the war, in 1919. Increasingly after the turn of the century, though never letting go of what Stocking calls the "residue of polygenist and evolutionary assumption which was the baggage of physical anthropology generally," [158] much of Boas's work was oriented towards transforming scientific debates on race by positing the primacy of culture over race as a means for understanding the diversity of human societies. His relationship to physical anthropology became further fragmented after the completion of his study of the descendants of immigrants, performed for the US Immigration Commission (1908–1920), which called into question the reliability of using human crania as primary tools for scientific ethnological study.[159]

Boas became leery of hard empiricism as it applied to the realm of culture, and his work, and followers, came to interrogate whether universal laws could govern how cultures worked. Boas's later views are summed up in his Foreword to Margaret Mead's *Coming of Age in Samoa* (1928):

We are accustomed to consider all those actions that are part and parcel of our own culture, standards which we follow automatically, as common to all mankind. They are deeply ingrained in our behaviour. We are moulded in their forms so that we cannot think but that they must be valid everywhere. . . . The anthropologist doubts the correctness of these views, but up to this time hardly anyone has taken the pains to identify himself sufficiently with a primitive population to obtain an insight into these problems.[160]

With this increasing emphasis on bias, horizons of understanding, and the limits of objectivity, Boas—and soon after, Boasians such as Alfred Kroeber, Edward Sapir, Ruth Benedict, Lowie, and Mead—helped to expand doubts about cultural (and to an extent, racial) fixity into the wider popular arena. Cultural anthropology explicitly questioned the presumption that there were ideal laws for governing cultures, including western cultures. Yet the discourses of race and cultural chauvinism in the US remained, as ever, complex, confused, and fraught with division. At the same time that Boas was developing some of his most challenging culture work, D. W. Griffith's epic ode to racism, *The Birth of a Nation* (1915), was breaking box office records across the US, shortly to be followed by the appearance of Madison Grant's reactionary study. Indeed, eugenicists had been visible at the 1915 San Francisco Panama-Pacific Exposition, and eugenicist sentiment would inhere in US popular culture well beyond World War II.[161]

On its surface, it seems that the idea of culture partly—perhaps largely—developed by Boas, and the relativistic streak in cultural anthropology, would have formed a powerful counternarrative to prevalent racist and ethnocentric tendencies that dominated nineteenth-century ethnological study and persisted unevenly into the twentieth century. Relativism promised to institutionalize tolerance towards cultural difference and suggested that the practices of other cultures could even poke holes in the ironclad façade of western civilization, increasingly considered—if one were to extrapolate from Boas's later writings—as itself multiple, situated amidst other global cultures. Moreover, that all cultures had their peculiar logic and inner workings and were not necessarily reducible to universal organizational structures was an idea further developed in Britain by the Functionalist approach of Bronislaw Malinowski. But relativism, which has often been seen as a clean break from the past, had a tendency to perpetuate the cultural hierarchies and atomizing theories of the previous century. Even when expressed by the most ardent Boasians, it is often a simultaneously progressive and regressive conception of the primitive that we encounter in these texts.

In the early 1920s, the Boasian view was expressed in the writing of Edward Sapir—associate, close friend, fellow poet, and colleague of Ruth Benedict and the intellectual guide and one-time lover of Margaret Mead.[162] In Sapir's influential article "Culture, Genuine and Spurious," which circulated in the early 1920s before appearing in the *American Journal of Sociology* in 1924, we find a vision of western cultural regeneration through an appeal to primitive types. Sapir sees the west as plagued by a form of "spiritual disharmony," and this phenomenon is particularly true "in the case of America, where a chronic state of cultural maladjustment has for so long a period reduced much of our higher life to sterile externality." [163] What Sapir seeks for US culture is the revitalization of what he labels a "genuine culture," a culture "deeper and more satisfying" (95), and he finds this ideal in the "frequent vitality of culture in less sophisticated levels":

> The Indian's salmon-spearing is a culturally higher type of activity than that of the telephone girl or mill hand simply because there is normally no sense of spiritual frustration during its prosecution, no feeling of subservience to tyrannous yet largely inchoate demands, because it works in naturally with all the rest of the Indian's activities instead of standing out as a desert patch of merely economic effort in the whole of life. (93)

Sapir's model is historical in many respects (evoking Elizabethan England and Periclean Athens as examples of genuine cultures) and suggests breaks from Boasian relativism, but it is also utopian, positing an ideal relationship of culture and environment against corrupt, self-conflicted cultural formations. This sense of US cultural sickness, as set against the spiritual health suggested metaphorically by the primitive, was echoed and expanded in Mead's work. In much of Mead's work, one encounters the term "primitive man" functioning as a metonym for a whole range of cultures and behaviors, suggesting that universal holisms could comfortably function within a manifestly pluralist approach. Mead often writes, for example, in the Manichean terms of them and us: "primitive man, secure in his closed and ordered universe, has a dignity that we have lost. He is all of a piece, he has few doubts and few confusions.... This homogeneity, this coherence, is something which may well fill us with envy." [164] The comparative anarchies and dangers posed by anthropological relativism are restored by tropes of order. Thus just as it would be wrong to reduce anthropology's history to a straightforward narrative that sees Boas as solely responsible for the study of cultures in the plural, it would be wrong to suggest that the Boasian worldview and its legacy led simply or unproblematically to pluralism. The ongoing dialectics of difference and sameness, the underlying discomfort with disordered cultural experience, and the irrepressible demand for identifiable holisms in describing the cultural encounter strongly mark the texts discussed in the following chapters.

↢

ALTHOUGH THE POSTWAR US came under the sway of popular and institutional forms of cultural relativism, this was not simply a freewheeling, liberal relativism embraced by modernism. In spite of the increasing openness within US culture itself, and especially in urban centers—where figures such as W. E. B. Du Bois were rewriting imperial narratives of the "white man's burden" and making intellectual inroads against Eurocentric concepts of culture—diversity and relativism were still sharing space, and sometimes butting heads, with received racial and cultural absolutes and reductivisms. Indeed, both the early accounts of Polynesia and those outlined in the following chapters share a deep fear of rupturing what are perceived as static cultural holisms. Bougainville, for example, saw that the French entrance into the scene engendered violence and disturbed his poetic ruminations: orderly paradise threatened to turn into an anarchic wilderness, and he abandoned it after only ten days. Since it always depended on a fragile, voyeuristic, and fundamentally backwards gaze at an exotic ideal, the Polynesian fantasy perhaps was to find its perfect partner in photography and cinema, media that promised to reverse civilization's spoliation by preserving a replica of the "real" prelapsarian ideal, even surpassing this as cinema captured the lost Pacific as a vibrant, bodily entity in motion. Perhaps technically reproduced images would even prove themselves superior to the real, allowing western viewers to endlessly reenter that ideal space without disturbing a thing.

2 Idylls and Ruins
Frederick O'Brien in the Marquesas

> We were going to the glamorous South Seas to film the life of the
> Polynesian as he had lived it in his islands before the white man came
> with his strange God, his strange manners, his strange and wonder-
> ful commodities. But Polynesia covers leagues and leagues of ocean,
> from Hawaii to New Zealand and Easter Island to Samoa. . . . Where
> in Polynesia could we find a people whose spirit was still strong? The
> answer we had from Frederick O'Brien.
> — Frances Flaherty, "Setting Up House and Shop"

Shortly after the unexpected success of *Nanook of the North*, Robert and Frances Flaherty met with Frederick O'Brien at the Coffee
House Club near Times Square with the painter George Biddle,
who had lived in Tahiti, and the singer Grace Moore. According to Flaherty, as
they were discussing ideas for his next film, O'Brien insisted he should go to the
"exact opposite" of *Nanook*'s frozen climate—the South Pacific. O'Brien suggested Safune, on Savai'i in Western Samoa, where Flaherty would ultimately end
up living with his family for nearly two years, filming *Moana*. Flaherty recalled
some time later O'Brien's saying, "I know what appeals to you more than anything else is the racial differences. . . . There [in Safune] the white man has had the
least influence."[1] O'Brien's advice echoed Flaherty's purist intentions. If Pacific
cultures were "dying" as a result of western interference, the Flahertys were seeking
a "strong" and unspoiled cultural mise-en-scène to match the heroics documented
in *Nanook*. Mixing the pleasures of exotic escape with the urgency of ethnological salvage, O'Brien told Flaherty he would be just in time to "catch" some of the
beautiful Samoan culture before it passed entirely away.[2]

O'Brien had spent several months in Samoa the previous year, traveling and
researching what would become his third, and ultimately last, published book,
Atolls of the Sun. In June 1921, towards the end of their brief but intense love affair,
he wrote to Jack London's widow, Charmian (Kittredge) London, "I am now living
at Safune, Savai'i, and your chart will show you where it is. It is the most beautiful

village I have seen in the South Seas, with a river so big that I row up it in a boat to the bathing place."[3] O'Brien goes on to say that he is living with a friend and intends to stay "a month or several months" while writing a book about Samoa—one that never materialized (*Atolls of the Sun* ended up focusing on the Tuamotu [Paumotu] Archipelago).[4] Two years later, the Flahertys arrived in Safune with a Paramount Studios expense account, taking a house "three-hundred and fifty yards from the sea"—the same house in which O'Brien had stayed. Frances's opinion of Safune was less enthusiastic than O'Brien's: "I cannot say that Safune turned out to be the most picturesque spot in the whole of the South Seas. Probably all of a hundred houses—thatched roofs, and curtains of woven coconut leaf to be let down in case of storms—stretched along the sandy beach."[5]

Before looking at the Flahertys' experiences in Samoa, however, it is worth considering why a filmmaker such as Flaherty, coming off a substantial box-office success, would so confidently trust the advice of a travel author that he would journey thousands of miles with his wife and three children, with thousands of dollars worth of film equipment and no planned scenario, to an unseen filming location in the middle of the Pacific. The answer lies partly in their recently established friendship and partly in the prominence that O'Brien enjoyed in the 1920s, a status that may be difficult to fathom given his obscurity now. But in the early 1920s, few would have disputed the claim made by the *San Francisco Call and Post* that O'Brien's books were "more successful than almost any other travel books of our time."[6] His first, *White Shadows in the South Seas,* had an enormous impact on the reading public, setting in motion a wave of popular interest in South Pacific–themed material that would last more than a decade. It also established him as a serious and sought-after writer: "Editors are clamoring on all sides for his work," noted a 1924 profile in *The Bookman,* "but it must be said of Freddie that he doesn't care very much about money."[7] In 1921, O'Brien estimated that a lecture tour of twenty appearances would net him $10,000: "I would hardly want to speak for less than $500," he wrote to Charmian London.[8] That same year, *Travel* magazine ran "Literary Couriers to Distant Places," an article depicting O'Brien next to other "victims of wanderlust" such as Joseph Conrad and Rudyard Kipling.[9]

O'Brien was, however, only briefly to remain in this company. Very little critical work about him has surfaced since his death in 1932, although the *Oxford Companion to American Literature* credits him with reviving popular interest in the works of Melville after the First World War and inspiring "a host of imitations exploiting the glamour of the Pacific islands."[10] Already fifty when *White Shadows in the South Seas* appeared, he considered literary success to be more of an accident than the culminating achievement of his career. Still, he enjoyed the advantages that came with fame: invitations to dine at the Algonquin Hotel and the P.E.N. club, a lucrative writing contract with William Randolph Hearst, friendships with Hugh Walpole, Margot Asquith, George Sterling, Sherwood Anderson, Charmian London, and Flaherty. Nevertheless, he insisted that he had "no optimism nor really much concern about achieving any reputation or return" from his work.[11] He referred to himself as a person without "a particle of initiative."[12] Indeed, the 1949 edition of Kunitz and Haycraft's *American Authors* begins his résumé with "hobo" before moving on to describe him as a journalist and author of several best-selling travel narratives. O'Brien was dropped from the 1955 edition, testifying to his increasing obscurity.

If O'Brien's work does deserve renewed attention it is not so much, perhaps, to resurrect him as a forgotten genius—though his humor, taut narrative style, and knack for richly evocative description still make for engrossing reading—as to explore his work's influence and the ways it might have been symptomatic of changes that were taking place in dominant US perceptions of the South Pacific. This, and the fact that O'Brien's work and its reception—particularly that of *White Shadows in the South Seas*—speak to widespread concerns at the time over the nature of the American character, over disputed definitions of what constituted a unified American culture, and over a rapidly intensifying political climate both at home and abroad. It is important to remember that for a few years after the First World War, O'Brien's books were among the most widely read material in the US that dealt with the South Pacific. This surge of interest in his island reminiscences caught both O'Brien and his publishers by surprise, but with hindsight it might be understood as linked to the paradoxical situation in which Americans found themselves in the wake of the 1898 territorial annexations and more recent European conflicts. The Monroe Doctrine of 1823 had confined US interests to the American continents, forbidding European interference in the western hemisphere; yet as a nation-state, after Teddy Roosevelt, it found itself in contradiction with its own continental self-perceptions, reinterpreting the Monroe Doctrine, enacting imperial strategies, and engaging in wars on foreign soil while, on the home front, remaining strongly invested in the liberating identity of a formerly colonized people.

O'Brien's writing reveals his efforts to come to terms with this paradox, suggesting a kind of split colonial subjectivity at work: he clearly longs for a prelapsarian paradise in the Pacific to match the myth of an American Eden, but he discovers only what he sees as the ruins of indigenous cultures and the remnants of past colonial conquests on the islands. What results is a sustained critique of imperial activity in the South Pacific, enlarging and politicizing an image of *tristes tropiques* found in writers such as Melville and Stevenson. Though largely stripped of its more expansive political critique, this image of Polynesia as a potentially ideal world exploited by the west would reappear in novels and films such as Nordhoff and Hall's fictional works and their screen adaptations. Formed amidst "other" peoples and places, O'Brien's accounts reflect the struggle to come to terms with global uncertainties and unstable concepts of American identity. *White Shadows in the South Seas,* then, might be seen less as a document of life among strange peoples and places than as a glimpse into an estrangement from the self—a self constructed out of the absolutes of cultural and national affiliation. As I hope to show, this estrangement, if painful, ultimately proved productive by leading to a more mobile image of US identity. This mobility clearly reflects contemporary modernist sensibilities of exile and displacement, yet at its most ambitious, it might suggest the emergence of transcultural and transnational identities.

Tramp, Beachcomber, and Tourist

Since the eighteenth century, wayward sailors, escapees from whaling ships, and travelers lured by inviting seas, beaches, palm trees, and sensual and sexual possibilities have entered into the world of island life as beachcombers. Unlike the explorers, traders, missionaries, and, later, anthropologists and reporters, whose official accounts tended to be driven by their professional affiliations, beachcombers chose to separate themselves from the binds of officialdom. Beachcombers were essentially cultural deserters: they behaved, dressed, and spoke in languages foreign to the west. Nonetheless, they were not natives, and their presence on the islands was often far from benign. Between 1774 and 1842 alone, more than 150 beachcombers came to live in the Marquesas. Yet while their presence inevitably affected cultural change, as Dening notes, beachcombers "enlarged the experience of the island by translating islanders' roles into their own more familiar ones. By their access to the worlds on the seaward side of the beaches they became mediators. They knew the moods and motivations of both sides and made intercourse possible."[13] A few, such as Edward Robarts, Jean Cabri, and William Torrey, left accounts of their experiences behind; Herman Melville, too, who expanded a three-week stay on Nukuhiva into *A Narrative of Four Months Residence,* is numbered among the beachcombers who left behind a record. Moreover, the digressive and episodic structure of most beachcomber accounts, like that of Melville's *Typee* and *Omoo* (which recall in turn the journal-entry style of explorers such as Cook and Bougainville) suggests a documentary immediacy that fractures many of the distancing mechanisms of fictional narratives, placing them perhaps closer to the realm of what Mikhail Bakhtin referred to as the dialogic.[14]

Though a self-declared beachcomber, O'Brien arrived in the Marquesas some time after beachcombing had become transplanted by more accessible forms of tourism. Writing in *The Bookman* in 1920, his self-description suggests a restless, romantic streak facilitated by the increasing ease of travel, rather than any fierce commitment to escape:

> I don't suppose that readers of *The Bookman* really care a continental that I am a Marylander, and was first a sailor and then a law student at a university; laborer, tramp, reporter, war correspondent, newspaper editor and publisher in the United States, Hawaii, and the Philippines, correspondent and traveler in Asia, Africa, and Europe...beachcomber in the South Seas, political writer, publicity and utility expert, acting state food administrator in California, and one of Herbert Hoover's assistants in Washington; and always a lover of sunsets on far shores...and also of being alone.[15]

This restless Irish American tramp and traveler fits the profile of the sometimes obscure first-person narrator of O'Brien's Pacific tales: one who tends to underline his status as a man of experience and adventure without revealing too much else. In *White Shadows in the South Seas,* the narrator/O'Brien notes that he "climbed on the foot of Vesuvius, Halaakela, Kilauea, Fuji, and Mayon, and the mountains of Asia and South America," though he offers few specifics as to when, how, or why—the lust for adventure perhaps being self-explanatory.[16] As a result, certain silences remain around the author of, and narrator in, O'Brien's text. This is partly because there is little biographical material to frame the narratives: no archives of papers or personal effects, just a smattering of personal correspondence, articles, book reviews, and three published travel books. But these silences also are the inevitable aftereffect of an author who inhabited so many professional skins and, by extension, social identities.

By cobbling together disparate accounts, one can reconstruct much of O'Brien's life. He was born into a comfortable Baltimore family of devout Irish Catholics in 1869; his father was a judge and former representative to Congress.[17] After attempting three years at Loyola Jesuit College in Baltimore, he dropped out and fled middle-class comforts. His travel narratives offer only glimpses of the range of experiences that followed. In 1887, he traveled by foot through Brazil and Venezuela, and then worked in asphalt pits in Trinidad. Returning to the US, he attempted to study law briefly, "plodding through irksome duties as a law clerk," but soon left to live as a hobo in the US West and South, slinging liquor at levee camps in Mississippi.[18] In 1894, he became a general in Coxey's Army, a vagabonding organization that marched from California to Washington, D.C., to draw attention to the legions of unemployed during the economic depression of the 1890s. "My first memory of Los Angeles is living in a warehouse on San Fernando street in '94, arming and outfitting for our migration (Coxey's army) to Washington," O'Brien later recalled; "I had walked from San Francisco to the [downtown] Plaza in 30 days."[19] The few that successfully made it to Washington were beaten up on arrival.

Tendencies towards leftist activism and moral indignation in the face of social injustice seemed to run in O'Brien's family. He describes his sister Mary as a similarly unorthodox figure: a Catholic Trotskyite who questioned received thinking while juggling conventionally opposed ideologies. "I may bring my sister to California," he wrote to the suffragist and poet Sara Bard Field. "If I do I fear we will both go to jail for she is an admirer of the foxtrotsky tho [*sic*] very Catholic. How she balances the Pope and Lenin I don't see, but she does."[20] Particularly in his letters, O'Brien reveals his radicalism and persistent refusal to accommodate the status quo. He rarely aligns himself with established doctrines, and he often gestures towards a more broad-based critique of accepted ideological binaries, perhaps because his politics were grounded in firsthand witnessing of the profoundly disorderly and illogical facts of everyday injustice. After a trip to Africa, he wrote to Field's husband, the philosophical anarchist Charles Erskine Wood:

> In Liberia . . . I saw the chief of police, in Sam Brown belt and with a gold star, torturing another Negro with whip and fire, within two blocks of a monument to the Liberian settlement, on which was: The Love of Liberty Brought Us Here. The secretary of state told me that "Booker Washington was a four flusher." The secretary of war said, "I have to put the fear of God into the hearts of those bush niggers."[21]

Drawn from direct observation and journalistic investigation, O'Brien's political statements had the potential to disturb convention, showing how political realities could grate against the most sacred social ideals. Yet his best-selling books were never really associated with a confrontational ideological stance, though they do contain pointed descriptions of social inequities. One of the issues I want to consider here is why O'Brien's politics tended to be overlooked by the broader public, even though his books are sympathetic to contemporary anti-imperialist movements, offering forthright criticisms of colonialism and of the emerging US global power relations. The answer might lie not only in the ways that O'Brien embedded his political position within an entertaining narrative like *White Shadows in the South Seas,* but also in the work's reception and the contexts of its release.

By the late 1890s, O'Brien had settled into journalistic work at the Columbus (Ohio) *Dispatch,* the *Honolulu Advertiser,* and the *San Francisco Chronicle;* from 1902 to 1909 he was editor of *Cablenews* in Manila. Experiences such as Coxey's Army and, later, of the aftermath of US aggression in the Philippines during the independence movement of 1899–1901, resulted in a lifelong concern with the rise of US imperial ambitions.[22] After the US invasion in 1915 of Port-au-Prince, Haiti—which was preemptively attacked before, it was claimed, Germany could seize financial and strategic control of the island—O'Brien noted with dismay the bipartisan aggression both in Hispaniola and in the Philippines: "I wish honestly I could go to Haiti and Santo Domingo, and print the truth about the US military murders there. . . . In the Philippines it is the same. We hell-roared through those islands, as Republicans, and now the Democrats have done as much in Haiti. The soldier, when not defending his country, is a merry butcher."[23] He long advocated independence for the Philippines (which finally became a reality in 1935, several years after his death), and had notes ready for a "Philippine novel" that was lost in transit with other manuscript materials after a Far East trip in early 1925.[24] In 1909, O'Brien returned to California, where he edited newspapers in Oxnard and Riverside, only to leave again in 1913, when he spent a year beachcombing in the Marquesas. By the time *White Shadows in the South Seas* appeared, bringing with it unexpected celebrity, he was then living "mostly in California, with a garden in the South, and a little blue house [called *Kaoha*] in Sausalito right over San Francisco Bay."[25] George Biddle, who first met O'Brien in Tahiti in 1920, had this to say: "The more I see of O'Brien the better I like him as a human being and the less I respect him as a writer. He is quite a character. A boon companion, warm, generous, merry, irrepressible. A wonderful storyteller in his cups—and almost illiterate."[26]

Postwar Horizons

For much of the early 1920s, US readers were under the spell of O'Brien's tales. According to *Publisher's Weekly, White Shadows in the South Seas* was the number 5 nonfiction best seller of 1920. The following year it increased its sales, appearing at number 2, while its sequel, *Mystic Isles of the South Seas,* was number 4. "The O'Brien cult spread like grass-fire," recalled one writer when O'Brien's death was announced in 1932.[27] The book's success is even more surprising when one considers that, at four dollars, *White Shadows* was twice the price of most trade books. O'Brien himself thought the price "prohibitive."[28] Library figures, then, might be a more reliable indicator. In 1920, *White Shadows* was the year's number 1 work of nonfiction, and in 1921 it was number 3, with *Mystic Isles* appearing at number 7.[29]

Yet *White Shadows* was not a book that many had thought publishable. Completed in 1914, it made a few publisher rounds before being shelved for nearly five years. In the end, though, this delay was probably the single most important factor in its success. Released by the Century Company during the week of 17 September 1919,[30] it appeared just as Americans were undergoing a tentative awakening after the First World War. The eleventh hour of 11 November 1918 had seen armistice in Europe, which officially ended most fighting, and seven months later (28 June 1919) the Versailles Treaty was signed. In the midst of celebrations, insecurities about the virtues of the civilized west were coming to the fore in the wake of the war's technological savagery. The social climate was one of postwar malaise: a few pages away from an article on O'Brien's travels in *Current Opinion* a satirical cartoon reads, "Getting the last boy out of the trenches," and is accompanied by a graphic image of a lifeless body dangling from a crane.[31] "The world is sick," O'Brien wrote to Charmian, "with more than fifty millions dead of the war, and grief and indecision as a cloud over the earth."[32] The horrors of war spurred desires for escape, not only because the west was haunted, but because people were anxious to rediscover the modern mobilities that had been obliterated by war. The outlook for tourism in *Publisher's Weekly* was positive, even if the attractions were grisly: "With routes from travelers and sightseers again open and personally conducted tours to the battlefields of Europe now advertised, it is safe to predict that travel books will again be in demand . . . after an absence of five years when they were found relegated to an obscure corner of the most remote shelf."[33]

Other large-scale social changes were taking place that were not directly linked to the war. In 1920, the Census Bureau classified the nation for the first time as a predominantly urban population, radically altering the image of the US as a rural, agrarian space with limitless potential for expansion. As David M. Wrobel notes, "The advent of the urban skyscraper served as a symbol of the transition, and the advent of new mass production techniques promoted spiraling growth in the automobile industry. The nation had become more 'citified' and more mobile."[34] Studies such as Louise Christine Odencrantz's *Italian Women in Industry* (1919) raised public awareness of this newly urbanized and ethnic population, with its waves of immigrants that now included Italians, Jews, Greeks, and Eastern Europeans. The postwar phase of the Americanization movement was asking fundamental questions about how to instill "American values" in these new arrivals and adding fuel to reactionary notions that traditional American life was being irrevocably lost. In the midst of these debates, the very concepts of "America" and "American" were being reevaluated.

With urbanization there were renewed anxieties about shrinking land opportunities—anxieties that mirrored and perpetuated the concerns that followed the Census Bureau's 1890 announcement that the continental frontier had officially closed. After 1890, a range of scholarly and literary works lamented the loss of free land, indicating that a pervasive frontier crisis had entered US consciousness.[35] At the same time, larger-than-life figures such as Frederick Jackson Turner ("The Significance of the Frontier in American History," 1893) and Teddy Roosevelt (*The Winning of the West*, 1889–1896) were helping to redefine and mythologize the open expanses of the West as the core of the American spirit and the source of the ideals of masculine self-reliance. Turner's thesis, which opens with the 1890 census report, argues, "Up to our own day American history has been in a large degree the history of colonization of the Great West"; but the census announcement marked "the closing of a great historic movement." The importance of the frontier included the fact that it kept America rugged, unlike the softening qualities of "old Europe": the frontier was "a military training school, keeping alive the power of resistance to aggression, and developing the stalwart and rugged qualities of the frontiersman."[36]

In October 1920, Turner's essay reappeared in *The Frontier in American History*, a well-received collection that reflected a revitalized idealization of the frontier. As Wrobel argues, the frontier image returned as an idyll that acted as a "kind of solace" during uncertain postwar years.[37] In the 1920s, postfrontier anxieties were enhanced by Malthusian debates that projected overpopulation and limited resources for a nation now pressed, so it would seem, against its continental boundaries. Best sellers such as Hal G. Evarts's *The Yellow Horde* (1921) and Edison Marshall's *The Voice of the Pack* (1920) and *The Strength of the Pines* (1921)—"a splendid novel of life in the open, of blood stirring adventure," as it was advertised—as well as numerous academic studies and popular films celebrated the joys and transformational powers of the unspoiled wilderness, enacting an imagined return to a pristine American Eden. During the war, the East Coast dentist Zane Grey became America's best-selling novelist, suggesting the widening gap between the image of the frontier and any sense of it as a real place. Nostalgia took hold as the frontier passed into memory, and reality, Wrobel notes, shifted into the realm of romance.[38] Early in 1920, Grey's *The Man of the Forest* revived the mythic

West in the postwar context, offering readers the chance to identify with protagonist Milt Dale, the rugged frontiersman, a "man's man, who lived in and for the wild"[39] (though even Milt Dale, having rescued his Eve from the wilderness, is ultimately subject to domestication). Grey's tale from "God's country" would go on to become the number 1 fiction seller of the year. Following an initial visit to Papeete in 1926, Grey too would shift the locus of the mythical frontier farther west with stories such as *Tales of Tahitian Waters* (1928) and *The Reef Girl* (published posthumously).

But it should not be thought that the perceived loss of the frontier solely initiated a full-scale retreat into nostalgic fictions; as suggested in the last chapter, manifest destiny had never really been abandoned. Desiring opportunities for free land, proponents of expansion were determined to see that the US continued to gain territories and hoped to persuade the public that dominance of the Pacific frontier could ensure America's future stability. Though policies such as John Hay's "Open Door Notes" of 1899, protecting US commerce in China, signaled the preeminence of commercial strategies over landed expansion, tracts such as Bancroft's *The New Pacific* offered jingoistic and racialized rhetoric that mythologized the land grabs of the American West and extended them to the next horizon. As Bancroft argued,

> The wealth of the Pacific, for the most part lightly held by inferior peoples, invites the presence of the strong and dominant. The great ocean has waited long for fit occupancy and ownership. . . . Many centuries must elapse before a crude culture planted in aboriginal regions can attain to a front rank; wherefore a transplanted civilization of a higher order were better here, and it should be drawn from the purest sources.[40]

No doubt *White Shadows in the South Seas,* through its sheer popularity, helped to shift the locus of the US imagination away from the western frontier and into the Pacific. Its islands, beaches, and open vistas formed a romanticized space upon which to focalize popular fantasies while providing an attainable, if distant, real place for material resources and capital. It is tempting, then, to see O'Brien as yet another beneficiary of a resilient US frontier ideology.

But if we look at *White Shadows* with even scant attention, it is difficult to attribute its success merely to a war-weary society's desires for release or to a new demand for stories of rugged individuals gazing over the Pacific frontier—assuming that all those who bought the book or borrowed it from the library actually read it. Because *White Shadows,* somewhat like US consciousness after the war, is simultaneously giddy and haunted. A narrative of release mixed with memory and loss, it presents a paradise scarred by violence taking place beyond the European conflicts of the war: long-standing and ongoing battles in the less visible war for imperial conquest. Although it would gain fame as a lighthearted adventure tale, *White Shadows* is exceedingly pessimistic: it fails to celebrate the discovery of a new frontier, nor does it echo the popular sentiments of something like Emerson Hough's popular *The Passing of the Frontier* (1918), which called for the perpetuation of the "frontier spirit" even in the midst of a vanishing geographical reality. Hough's book effectively internalized the frontier, arguing it was immanent to American character; O'Brien ignores or eludes explicit mention of the frontier.

At more subtle levels *White Shadows* might be suggesting that, if frontier spirit is indeed immanent to US character, there are nonetheless intractable consequences to expansionist ideologies. The book functions, therefore, as something akin to a return of the repressed. O'Brien's narrative questions the moral sanctity of frontier mentality by associating colonialism with genocide. On a metaphorical level, it reverses the common connotations of black and white in the colonial context, showing that the deathlike shadows that cut across the South Pacific emanate from a source in whiteness itself. There is no colonial light conjured up to brighten a savage and primeval darkness. Moreover, blackness and whiteness, with their prevailing connotations of evil and good, are not diametrically but dialectically opposed: each folds into and exerts an influence on the other. If *White Shadows* conjures up an imagined idyll, the idyll is set against this darkening backdrop. Descriptions of vibrant life and tropical lushness abound, but death lingers at the edges of almost every scene.

Reading *White Shadows*

White Shadows in the South Seas, Mystic Isles of the South Seas, and *Atolls of the Sun* essentially describe a single journey, but *Mystic Isles* and *Atolls* are actually "prequels" to *White Shadows,* which was published first. *White Shadows* opens with O'Brien sailing out of Papeete, while *Mystic Isles* marks the "true" start of the journey away from home, opening with O'Brien's departure from San Francisco Bay, bound for Tahiti. *Atolls of the Sun* continues the trip from Tahiti through the Tuamotu Archipelago, but, somewhat oddly, the final third of the book ends up overlapping with the Marquesas visit narrated in *White Shadows*. It could be that O'Brien, as his letters suggest, struggled to finish the third book and decided to introduce material that he and Rose Wilder Lane had cut from *White Shadows* (most notably, a chapter on tattooing that appears in *Atolls*).[41] But these efforts to fill the narrative gaps were not entirely successful, at least to many reviewers, who argued that in *Atolls* O'Brien was (like the South Seas craze more generally) running out of ideas.

White Shadows is made up of constantly shifting and digressive episodes, recalling at times Melville, Stoddard, Stevenson, London, and numerous less well-known beachcomber accounts. On its surface the plot seems complex, even messy, but an overview reveals a relatively straightforward structure: O'Brien leaves Papeete on the schooner *Morning Star*, arriving in Atuona on Hiva Oa, the largest of the southern group of islands, where Paul Gauguin spent his final years. He decides to abandon the schooner to settle in Atuona, enlists a "boy Friday," Nakohu (translated as Exploding Eggs), and moves into a blue, tin-roofed house, rumored to have been previously occupied by a leper. He journeys in a whaleboat to Vaitahu[42] on Tahuata, where he spends two weeks with Neo Afitu Atrien (translated as Seventh Man Who Wallows in the Mire) and his niece, Hinatini (translated as Vanquished Often). He explores Tahuata with Charles Alfred Le Moine, a painter who knew Gauguin in his last years. He returns to Hiva Oa, where he travels across the rugged interior of the island to visit a plantation site. He then journeys by whaleboat to Taiohae on Nukuhiva, where he meets the missionary Père Siméon Delmas. Shortly thereafter, he travels overland to Taipivai, leaving from Taiohae on the schooner *Roberta*, which he abandons because of a plague of cockroaches, ending up in Omo'a on Fatuiva, staying with the Swiss landowner and trader François Grelet. He then accompanies Grelet on a whaleboat along the coast of Fatuiva to Hanavave, where he stays with a missionary, Père Olivier. Returning to Omo'a, he is nearly abducted by a woman, and later crosses the mountains at dizzying heights. After sailing back to Atuona, he spends the remainder of the text focusing more specifically on ethnographic details: local medicine, fishing, surfing, listening to legends and tales. He finally departs on the steamship *Saint François* for Tahiti.

The plot suggests very little of revolutionary import, especially in the context of earlier South Seas travel and beachcomber accounts. Yet most episodes lead to textual excursions that contextualize, complicate, and broaden the scope of the basic journey. It is in these details that *White Shadows in the South Seas* appears to challenge some established clichés not just of the Marquesas, but of the roles of past Pacific colonialisms and current US interventions. The book was at least partially successful in this respect, and arguably helped to reestablish the ambivalent and darker postwar tone that had characterized Melville's work and that would reappear in subsequent South Pacific representations. More recently, a book such as Mel Kernahan's *White Savages in the South Seas* (1995), which deals with Tahitian travel, politics, and diaspora, even in its title elliptically engages with and updates some of O'Brien's more submerged ironies and critiques while avoiding his sometimes problematic rehashing of the enduring stereotypes and conventions of Pacific colonial discourse.

These problems include the ways in which characters are often sketched for comic effect and cultural difference is exploited for comedy. Like Jack London before him, O'Brien seems a bit too preoccupied with sensational stories of "long pig" feasts in the "cannibal isles." Several photographic plates feature reclining women, "South Seas maidens" with breasts displayed to the camera: the ethnographically sanctioned "goona goona" demanded by film producers and book publishers. Even counted as "documentary" evidence of Polynesians in a state of nature, the images, while no doubt racy, apparently were hardly shocking to mainstream audiences in 1919. Except for comments on the book's "delightful illustrations," few reviewers thought the photographs worth mentioning, testifying to the embeddedness and standardization of the "South Seas maiden" image.[43] Also problematic is the book's racial imagery, couched as it is in an apparently anticolonial stance (though racism and anticolonialism are not always mutually exclusive, as seen in the racial bias enforced by many Polynesia-philes against Melanesians). O'Brien's reveries on music, for example, evolve into egregious celebrations of human wildness and animal nature, recalling the cult of Josephine Baker and the *danse sauvage:* "there is release and exhilaration in the barbaric, syncopated songs and in the animal-like motions of the jazz dances with their wild and passionate attitudes. The rag-time melodies, coming straight from the jungles of Africa through the negro, call to impulses in man that are stifled in big cities, in factory and slum" (169). This may be O'Brien at his worst: suggesting that an emergent jazz culture might counter the ordering and controlling narratives of western musical traditions and therefore provide an escape from the status quo, yet also replicating fetishistic modernist images of a barbaric and liberating primitivism.

Though apparently unable or unwilling to draw attention to the limits and complicities of its racial images, at other times the text suggests a self-reflexive writing subject at work, pointing up the gaps in the univocal text and acknowledging that myriad voices are silenced in creating a "true" document of South Pacific life. O'Brien rarely makes claims to exhaustive or even accurate representations, implying that even a sympathetic traveler participating in local life might offer only the "feeble and misunderstanding" voice of a perpetually "alien" observer. Perhaps in an effort to avoid similar criticisms to those Melville aimed at the superficial scientific voyager, O'Brien notes,

Some day when deeper poverty falls on Asia or the fortunes of war give all the South Seas to the Samurai, these islands will again be peopled. But never again will they know such beautiful children of nature, passionate and brave, as have been destroyed here. They shall have passed as did the old Greeks, but they will have left no written record save the feeble and misunderstanding observations of a few alien visitors. (450)

Laced with references to children of nature and old Greeks, the passage recalls Rousseau, along with the neoclassicist aesthetic ideals of Bougainville, Banks, Parkinson, Hodges, and their legacy. In this sense O'Brien underscores his, and western history's, feeble and misunderstanding view of the Marquesas. At another level, though, the very stress on possibly speaking and writing in error encourages the possibility of dialogue. In this sense, *White Shadows* can be seen as attempting to work against the closed and authoritative conventions of much colonial discourse, allowing for falsehoods and fabrications to emerge. Rather than linger over its obvious problems, then, I would like to focus on the potential of *White Shadows* to act as what Roland Barthes called an open—or partially self-reflexive—text. At its best, *White Shadows* signals its intertextuality, revealing traces of the meanings and associations produced by the discourses about Polynesia that preceded and framed it.

Expectation

O'Brien's trip to the Marquesas has been said to have been inspired by Martin Johnson's lecture presentation film, *Jack London's Adventures in the South Seas Islands* (1913). This is probably not strictly true, given that O'Brien had a long-standing fascination with the idea of the South Seas, having voraciously read such writers as Stevenson, London, Becke, and Stoddard. The book's first few pages, perhaps self-referentially, thus contemplate a textualized Pacific before engaging in any authoritative reportage, conspiring with urbanized US readers who might be eager to indulge in imagined worlds away from "sky-touching buildings darkening the street" and "the artificially lighted cages of a thousand slaves to money-getting" (123). O'Brien seems closer to twenty than forty-five in these opening scenes, conjuring up images of adventure, youth, and romantic longing for exotic lands. This enthusiasm urges on the narrator's and the reader's desires for hedonistic travel: "something of the boyish thrill that filled me when I pored over the pages of Melville long ago returned while I stood on the deck of the *Morning Star,* plunging through the surging Pacific in the driving tropic rain" (7). This plunging, driving prose not only recalls the meter of Romantic verse, but mimics the forward movement that employs the tradition of travel writing, where the metaphor of traversing distance sustains both author and reader in their journeys from home to abroad, from familiar to foreign, from ignorance to new experiences and understandings. This opening strategy was something of a convention in Pacific travel literature: the early pages of *Typee* refer to the accounts of Cook, Stewart, and Porter, while the lesser known Alfred St. Johnston's *Camping among Cannibals* opens with a similar homage:

> Over the mere words "The South Pacific Islands" a strange glamour has for me always hung; a tissue of dreams, woven from the threads of narrative and description in old voyages and travels, has ever in my mind enwrapped them, and many a time, before there seemed to be a chance of my visiting them in reality, have I wandered in imagination along their golden sands and beneath their lofty groves of palms.[44]

O'Brien soon begins to recall openly fictional texts such as the Victorian "boy's own" adventure story, in which fearless endeavor in a world populated by savage races reinscribes a boy's masculine and imperial authority.[45] He asks, "Where is the boy who has not dreamed of the cannibal isles, those strange, fantastic places over the rim of the world, where naked brown men move like shadows through unimagined jungles, and horrid feasts are celebrated to the 'boom, boom, boom!' of the twelve foot drums?" (7). These shadows of naked brown men emerge from a confusion of savage fictions—recalling Ballantyne's *The Coral Island,* Conrad's simultaneously threatening and fascinating savagery, even *Tarzan*—though at this point O'Brien mentions only Melville. These ghostly shadows settle across the traveler's imaginary landscape and gesture beyond themselves into the realms of the unseen and unknown.

If the islands of the South Pacific supply a unique source for fantasy, O'Brien argues, this is partly because the world has been overrun by travel and tourism, its mysteries nearly conquered. Popular travel sights no longer excite the imagination: "years bring knowledge, paid for with the dreams of youth. The wide, vague world becomes familiar, becomes even common-place." Travels in London, Paris, Venice, "many-colored Cairo," the "desecrated crypts of the pyramids," and the "crumbling villages of Palestine" offer only recycled experiences (7). O'Brien's narrator seeks to invent and consume the new, and here in the middle of the Pacific is one of the last bastions where disaffected travelers might encounter the thrill of discovery, original rather than recycled experiences. This notion of western fantasy actualized in reality is returned to in both *Mystic Isles* and *Atolls*. In the former, O'Brien juxtaposes his own preconceptions against the public imagination in the wake of Cook's and Bougainville's accounts. As he sails south from San Francisco Bay, he recalls with intense anticipation that "what the great captains, and Loti, and Melville, Becke, and Stoddard, had written had been for years my intense delight. Now I was to realize the dream of my childhood. I could hardly live during the days of the voyage" (*Mystic*, 19). This leads to further meditations on textual constructions of the South Pacific and what they signified to the west:

> I remembered that Europe had been set afire emotionally by the first reports, the logs of the first captains of England and France who visited Tahiti. In that eighteenth century, for decades the return to nature had been the rallying cry of those who attacked the artificial and degraded state of society. The published and oral statements of the adventurers in Tahiti, their descriptions of the unrivaled beauty of the verdure, of reefs and palm, of the majestic stature of the men and the passionate charm of the women, the boundless health and simple happiness in which they dwelt, the climate, the limpid streams, the diving, swimming, games, and rarest food—all these had stirred the depressed Europe of the last days of the eighteenth and the first of the nineteenth centuries beyond the understanding by us cynical and more material people. The world still had its vision of perfection. (19–20)

O'Brien's narrative persona in *White Shadows* wants to recapture some of the newness and exhilaration of these early accounts, but already at the journey's start he senses the belatedness of his reveries.

We soon recognize that this adventurer is arriving at the tail end of a grandly artificial history. Even seventy years earlier, Melville amidst the Taipis felt he had "fallen in with a greatly traduced people." Melville was disappointed to find that his "hideous expectations" concerning Taipi warriors and the "diabolical malice with which they glutted their revenge upon the inanimate forms of the slain" were "nothing more than fables." He ends up feeling like "a 'prentice boy who, going to the play in the expectation of being delighted with a cut-and-thrust tragedy, is almost moved to tears of disappointment at the exhibition of a genteel comedy" (*Typee*, chap. 17, 128). Witnessing a violent skirmish a little later, Melville wonders if he should change his mind, but his point has been made: Pacific travels often leave one with the impression that experience is unlikely to live up to the sensations of the text. Charles Stewart, the missionary and chaplain aboard the USS *Vincennes* whom Melville cites as an influence, similarly pinpoints the falsehoods of previous accounts:

> Every new observation of the character of this wild race [the Taipis], persuades me more and more fully, that the fierce and vindictive deportment, reported of them in some instances towards foreigners, is attributable, in a great degree at least, and in a majority of cases, to the ill treatment and wrong suffered by them from previous visitors; and often, is the direct consequence of the imprudent measures and violent usage of the very persons who publish their ferocity to the world.[46]

White Shadows soon turns away from fictional and exploration accounts to meditate on theoretical and scientific discourses that might help to substantiate the explorers' utopian "vision of perfection." After introducing Darwinian theory, O'Brien proposes a return to a lost time: nothing less than a rediscovery of the origins of the white race. Leaving Papeete, he imagines a journey that releases him from time itself: "Before we saw the green banners of Tahiti's cocoanut palms again we would travel not only forward over leagues of tossing water but backwards across centuries of time. For in those islands isolated from the world for eons there remains a living fragment of the childhood of our Caucasian race.... And I was to see it, before it disappears forever" (7–8). The voyage becomes not only a journey backwards in time, echoing what Johannes Fabian has called an allochronic ethnographic discourse of the primitive, but also, in a very literal sense, a journey to Eden.[47] The "dominant blood" of Polynesian peoples is white; thus travelers to Polynesia might find Caucasian survivors of a lost continent, "isolated for untold centuries" (8).

O'Brien claims that his theories rely on passages from Darwin's *On the Origin of Species,* which conjecture geological phenomena on the basis of biological observations. In *Atolls of the Sun,* O'Brien embellishes his ideas with references to the lost continent of Pan, which afforded a "land bridge" for migrating Caucasian peoples. These peoples later intermixed with "new sailors of giant canoes" from Asia.[48] Related, often utopian, concepts of human dispersion can be seen elsewhere in modernist primitivism. In *Fantasia of the Unconscious,* D. H. Lawrence argues that once, before the flood, all civilizations were in dynamic contact: "In that world men lived, and taught, and knew, and were in one complete correspondence over all the earth. Men wandered back and forth from Atlantis to the Polynesian Continent as men now sail from Europe to America. The interchange was complete, and knowledge, science, was universal over the earth."[49] Theories of a sunken continent, though often absent of explicit racial speculations, had been voiced in a scientific context by Joseph Banks on Cook's first voyage, which was in part launched to research notions of a great South Sea continent. George Forster came closer to marrying race with sunken continent theories, suggesting that Oceanic peoples had first appeared on a continent called Mu, only a few mountains of which still emerged from the ocean. Related theories persisted and mutated throughout the nineteenth and twentieth centuries, as exemplified in influential works such as James Churchward's *The Lost Continent of Mu* (1926).

Shortly after O'Brien's travel books appeared, Churchward released his mystical archaeological tract, *The Lost Continent of Mu*, which contained similar lost continent theories reputedly garnered from an "old Hindu priest" in 1868. In 1924, Churchward made the national news with the announcement "Tablets Tell of Great Continent With 64,000,000 White Inhabitants That Was Swallowed Up by Pacific."[50] O'Brien's description in *Atolls* of the discovery of the ancient civilization's "cryptogram" and "the discovery of a new Rosetta stone" suggests Churchward's claim to have seen identical, inscribed "Naacal tablets" in Mexico and India, tablets that described the source of a great lost civilization in the Pacific. Churchward opens his book with the attention-catching claim that "the garden of Eden was not in Asia, but on a sunken continent in the Pacific Ocean."[51] As noted in the last chapter, more-authoritative scholars such as Abraham Fornander, Edward Tregear, and Stephenson Percy Smith, while largely steering clear of religious mysticism, had already offered a variety of interrelated dispersion theories of Polynesian and Maori origins based on theories of migrating Causasian peoples. R. M. Watson's *History of Samoa* (1918) advanced a similarly Smithist argument for Samoa, offering a wave theory that included racial hybridization: "From their appearance, from their undoubted relationship to other Polynesian peoples, it is probable that the Samoans are of an original Caucasian stock with which through the ages many strains, almost certainly including the malayoid and not entirely excluding the negrito, have combined to produce a distinctive people."[52] Racial wave theories such as these helped to prop up pseudo-religious associations between Polynesia and the true Eden, theories that hover around the edges of O'Brien's text. S. Percy Smith is mentioned in *White Shadows* (118), while the missionary Siméon Delmas of Taiohae (who shipped Marquesan spiders to Lucian Berland at the National Museum of Natural History as part of an investigation into the common origin of the archipelagos and assisted the publication of R. I. Dordillon's Marquesan dictionary in 1904) makes appearances in *White Shadows* and *Atolls in the Sun*.[53]

Robert Flaherty, too, was potentially envisioning a fantasy of white origins in *Moana,* which constructs its Samoan characters as a primeval family in a lost state of nature.

As noted in the last chapter, scattered images of Polynesian whiteness preceded scientific study of Pacific "races." Self-reflecting images that explained away cultural and physical differences helped to render the unfamiliar familiar, appropriating and consolidating otherness within the boundaries of the (white western) self. This was, however, a highly unsystematic appropriation, and arguably it existed at some distance from—and often in opposition to—mainstream racial ideologies. O'Brien's prelapsarian reveries suggest the ways that complex racial discourses have been negotiated through private reflection and public dissemination. In *White Shadows,* these discourses become a means through which the narrator can regulate both the closeness and distance he feels towards his Marquesan companions. He finally determines that (white) Americans and Marquesans are best seen as blood "cousins": "My savage friends, with their clear features, their large straight eyes and olive skins, showed still the traces of their Caucasian blood. . . . 'We are cousins,' I said to her, handing her a freshly-opened cocoanut which Exploding Eggs brought" (112). Seen positively, then, the belief that Polynesia held the cradle of Caucasian mankind might, at one level, have helped to unsettle, if not unseat, US expansionist arguments such as John R. Procter's and Hubert Howe Bancroft's, grounded as they were in positing essential racial differences. Seen less generously, the fantasy of white racial origins reinscribes evolutionary hierarchies: western civilization is the final flowering—or degenerated last gasp—of the Caucasian race, which is elsewhere dispersed in various stages of development around the globe.

Arrival

One of the earliest detailed accounts of western arrival in the Marquesas is that of Pedro Fernández de Quirós, the chief pilot on Alvaro de Mendaña's voyage to colonize the Solomon Islands. In 1595, heading across the South Sea with a motley group of colonizers, Mendaña sighted land, thinking he had, with little effort, arrived at the Solomons. On their approach, Mendaña's ships were met by at least seventy canoes. Many islanders climbed aboard, and soon became excited by the sailors' gifts of shirts and hats. They began "dancing and singing in their fashion," but also started to snatch various trinkets, foodstuffs, and other items. Agitated,

Mendaña ordered a gun to be fired, and a native was then stabbed with a sword, his wound "shown to the others." De Quirós documented the encounter: "one old man with a long and well-ordered beard, who cast fierce looks from his eyes . . . was shot in the forehead, and fell dead, with seven or eight others, while some were wounded."[54] The island turned out not to be one of the Solomons, but Fatuiva, over three thousand miles short of their destination. The colonizers soon sighted three other islands in the distance, and Mendaña acknowledged his mistake, naming these "new discoveries" La Magdalena (Fatuiva), San Pedro (Motane), Dominica (Hiva Oa), and Santa Cristina (Tahuata). The island group was called Las Marquesas de Mendoca in honor of his patron, the Marquis de Cañete, the viceroy of Peru.

Within days, islanders were being treated by Mendaña's soldiers as exotic fauna, or less. They were maimed and killed simply to set an example for others; soldiers pointed guns at natives because, they explained, their "diligence was to kill, because [they] liked to kill." Dead bodies were strung up on shore as evidence of the Spaniards' capabilities. All told, de Quirós estimated, two hundred islanders were killed in a two-week period, even if Mendaña's four armed ships "had little to fear from unarmed natives in canoes."[55] In the midst of this violence, de Quirós's observations of confusion and failed ideals can be seen to establish the contours of a sympathetic or "soft primitivist" discourse of Pacific peoples. The exasperated tone that marks the narrative would become a recognizable feature of Pacific travel accounts, where western travelers often represented themselves as frustrated yet passive witnesses to a spectacle of arresting beauty and widespread destruction.

As O'Brien sails towards the Marquesas on the *Morning Star,* even the ship's traderoom, which in O'Brien's boyhood fantasies opened the "door to romance," yields only depressing stories from the ship's resident trader, McHenry. Paradise has long been a fallen place, and seeds of doubt are planted suggesting that it might never really have been anything else. O'Brien hears that "now almost every island has its little store, and the trader has to pursue his buyers, who die so fast that he must move from island to island in search of population" (11). "Booze is boss" now, and hopeful visions of a return to an original racial harmony are extinguished. Fears of miscegenation are already made evident. McHenry and the ship's engineer, Ducat, nearly come to blows when McHenry makes a disparaging reference to Ducat's wife as his "kanaka woman" (14). *Kanaka,* a Hawaiian term for "human being" that refers to indigenous peoples, was widely associated with slave labor in the Pacific and used disparagingly. Writers such as London employ the term freely, though O'Brien deems it necessary to gloss its contexts: "no Tahitian says 'kanaka' of himself. It is a term of contempt. He might call his fellow so, but only as the American negro says 'nigger'" (241). Also aboard the ship is another unsettling omen in the figure of fellow passenger Lieutenant L'Hermier des Plants, a "very soft, sleek man . . . much before the mirror, combing and brushing and plucking," set to become the Marquesas' French governor (22).

O'Brien's first glimpse of the islands again recalls the rhetoric of Romanticism, but here he reverts to pathetic fallacy. Passing Fatuiva, he notes only the island's "stern, forbidding aspect," observing, "Rain fell drearily as we passed Fatuhiva, the first of the Marquesas Islands sighted from the south. . . . The Marquesas islands lay before us, dull spots of dark rock upon the gray water. . . . that gaunt, dark shore itself recalls that the history of the Marquesas is written in blood, a black spot upon the white race" (24–26). The imagined, utopian space is rapidly replaced with a tangible and visibly scarred place, and O'Brien's vision starts to disintegrate. Again he is indebted to writers such as Melville, who cites a similar if less explicit failure of expectation: "From the vague accounts we sometimes have of [the Marquesas'] beauty, many people are apt to picture to themselves enameled and softly swelling plains, shaded over with delicious groves. . . . The reality is very different; bold rock-bound coasts, with the surf beating high against the lofty cliffs" (*Typee*, chap. 2, 12). For Melville, first contact initiates meditations on *tapu* and death, and even "the brown shaven skull of one of the savages" floating in the water (13)—actually a swimmer hauling a string of coconuts—subtly suggests the bodily violence and physical dismemberment to come (an image that returns forcefully in Flaherty and Murnau's *Tabu*). Melville goes on to isolate the evils of Porter's raid and the French acquisition of the islands, while O'Brien's arrival suggests a more personalized and self-implicating guilt regarding the colonial atrocities that preceded him. The shadows of "naked brown men" imagined a few pages earlier are now transfigured into the white shadows that frame the narrative. Melville's ambiguous arrival nonetheless still gives an impression of life on the islands, echoing earlier exploration accounts, though he is surprised to see only male islanders in canoes, concluding that canoes are *tapu* to women. O'Brien is greeted by silence. The gray sea, the edifice of "frowning" cliffs, waterfalls like "gauzy wisps of chiffon" that "hardly veiled the black walls behind them" evoke a funeral shroud. Finally, a single outrigger canoe appears bearing Nakohu, a "slender Marquesan boy," whose "naked body was like a small and perfect statue" (31). In a gesture that oddly echoes the behavior of the colonists and labor kings he soon inveighs against, he engages Nakohu to be his "valet" for the equivalent of five cents per day.

By 1914, it would have been impossible to find the unspoiled island life con-jured up in books and rehearsed for the first few pages of *White Shadows;* still, this was a vision that would continue to play a major role in stories and films. The Marquesas was well-known as among the most heavily exploited island groups. The 1922 edition of *Stewart's Handbook*—the first year the handbook assembled "accurate accounts of . . . the whole of the groups and the detached islands" for "traders, tourists, and settlers"—starkly echoes fatal impact discourse and suggests that new batches of visitors seeking Pacific innocence will have to look elsewhere:

> The natives are said to surpass all other South Seas islanders in physical beauty. . . . But, although the French have long since put an end to civil warfare and canni-balism, the Marquesans are dying off with appalling rapidity, European vices and customs having done their work. In 1850 the islands were estimated to contain 50,000 inhabitants—now there are less than 3,000! The natives behold with dis-may the approaching extinction of their race, and have grown so despondent that they, never an industrious race, have now ceased altogether from production.[56]

As far as *Stewart's Handbook*—and O'Brien—could see, the fatal impact was lead-ing to extinction.

After encountering Nakohu, O'Brien's first experience of Hiva Oa is the cer-emonial greeting of the new French governor. He observes "men, tall and mas-sive . . . awkwardly constricted in ill-fitting, blue cotton overalls such as American laborers wear over their street clothes." He is not so far away, as it turns out, from the streets of an urbanized US and the bleakness of mechanized labor. His impres-sions are of automaton-like, passive subjugation: "Men and women were waiting with a kind of apathetic resignation; melancholy and unresisting despair seemed the only spirit left to them" (35). The governor's speech attempts to stir a sense of patriotic belonging, but the people listen "as if he spoke to someone in Tibet who wanted to sell a green elephant" (36). Only after wine is brought out do things become livelier; the drink "dissolve[s] melancholy" and a dance begins. O'Brien may appear to be embarking on yet another "verbose and patronizing account of cultural despair," as Nicholas Thomas describes many late-nineteenth- and early-twentieth-century travel accounts,[57] but he shortly after turns the lens around to reveal the governor, hidden away that night, with a pistol in hand and "pajamas of rose-colored silk," fearing for his life among his subjects. The line between us and them now clearly defined, O'Brien decides to find a middle ground—"to live among them" (40–41).

Fatal Impact

As O'Brien settles into daily life in Atuona he listens to the talk of traders and missionaries and concludes that the Marquesas is on an irreversible path of decline. The degenerating influence of the west has bred decay: people have been wasted by diseases, exploited by commercial interests. The tropics are paradoxically lush and barren; nature itself, a "melancholy wilderness," mourns the passing of the people: "a spirit of gloom seemed to rise from the shadowed declivity, from the silence of the mournful wood and the damp darkness of the leaf-hidden earth" (305). Though he finds time for adventures—a battle with a giant octopus, surfing an enormous wave for a half-mile into shore, diving thirty feet into tropical pools— these distractions seem never very far from a haunted, chiaroscuro backdrop. His observations seem to emphasize the aesthetic aspects of this lingering death, a fate both horrible and strangely poetic:

> The score of houses strung along the upper reaches of Atuona Valley were silent at this hour, and everywhere native houses were decaying, their falling walls and sunken roofs remembering the thousands who once had their homes here. . . . The rotting homes of the Marquesan people speak more eloquently of death than do sunken graves. (126)

The islands appear as fields of ruins for the contemplative gaze of the western traveler. Later, as he sails past the silent valleys of Fatuiva, the moribund scene suggests a kind of gothic beauty: "death hung like a cloud over the desolate wilderness of these valleys, over the stern and gloomy cliffs, black and forbidding, carved into monstrous shapes and rimmed with the fantastic patterns made by the unresting sea" (347).

Notions of the fatal impact, like the myth of the prelapsarian South Pacific, had a long discursive history. As Greg Dening notes, even by 1863, "No one talked profusely of the handsome men and beautiful women on the beach. They remarked instead on ophthalmia, skin eruptions, bloated limbs and wasted bodies coughing mercilessly in the corners of their huts."[58] Throughout *White Shadows,* O'Brien persistently evokes fatal impact discourse, that "insistent and ubiquitous" narrative of inevitable extinction, as Rod Edmond calls it, that, by the late-nineteenth century, had become a "colonialist mantra."[59] In *White Shadows,* a phrase that mutated throughout Pacific accounts of the nineteenth century—"The coral waxes, the palm grows, but man departs"[60]—reappears as *"E tupu te fau; e toro to farero, e mou te taata":* "The hibiscus shall grow, the coral shall spread, and man shall cease" (131). The phrase is elegiac, and, like all elegies, it implies the inevitable defeat of humanity that comes with the passage of time. The fatal impact appears in this sense as a metaphor: a metaphor for the experience of change, a trope that both dematerializes and removes agency from island peoples, translating depopulation into an aestheticized image that masks the dynamics of culture contact and the structures of power. As Dening notes, "As populations withered, reflections on their dying did not concern so much guilt about what was introduced across the beach as the inability of the primitive to adapt. Their dying was a weakness."[61] Edmond's work further suggests that the fatal impact embodies too the west's fear of its own extinction. Fatal impact discourse extended to many corners of the globe: to US travelers it was not just an "external" phenomenon, but had already been broadly thematized in accounts of American Indian genocide. Henry David Thoreau remarked on the decline and disappearance of Indian cultures as a tragedy, yet unavoidable since the Indian was closely linked to other "savages" and was therefore naturally "degraded by contact with the civilized man."[62]

No doubt *White Shadows* was influenced by Stevenson's *In the South Seas* (published posthumously in 1896, based on his voyaging journals), in which the visibility of the fatal impact in the Marquesas becomes a leitmotif that mirrors Stevenson's own fragile state of health:

> She began with a smiling sadness, and looking on me out of melancholy eyes, to lament the decease of her own people. "Ici pas de Kanaques," said she; and taking the baby from her breast, she held it out to me with both her hands. "Tenez—a little baby like this; then dead. All the Kanaques die. Then no more." The smile, and this instancing by the girl-mother of her own tiny flesh and blood, affected me strangely; they spoke of so tranquil a despair.[63]

Stevenson witnesses failing life and externalizes the imminence of his own death; encountering the fatal impact everywhere in his brief meetings with local people, he grafts his own vulnerability onto the bodies of Marquesan others. Dening has little patience for Stevenson's indulgence in death and his admiration for the fortitude of colonizers and missionaries: "Stevenson in his comfortable little yacht *Casco* could not forget the latent savage that lived inside every calico shirt and under every tattooed skin. He enjoyed the island's gloom and silence and admired the simple brothers and priests who lived on the edge of violence and built tiny chapels as if they were cathedrals."[64] Yet Stevenson's influence, for better and worse, on travelers such as O'Brien might lie beyond its apparent solipsism: *In the South Seas* also projects a vulnerable and ambivalent traveling subject that complicates the all-seeing eye/I of more official travel accounts. Stevenson's narrative "I" is a suffering rather than heroic voyager, constantly torn from the secure confines of the intact, healthy western body to examine the sufferings of others. The figure authoring and authorizing representation here is transient and struggling towards empathy: a fading presence destined to join other ghosts of the Pacific, ultimately raising questions that haunt the text's sometimes manifestly positive images of advancing civilization.

Nor is Stevenson's view entirely apolitical, as he observes exploitative labor practices in the Pacific aimed not only at islanders but at immigrant laborers such as the Chinese. In the Marquesas, he familiarizes colonial hegemony by recalling the British eradication of Scottish Highland groups, leading to what he refers to as the "Highland metaphor." On its surface, this would seem to form part of a tradition sporadically glimpsed in travel accounts by Sydney Parkinson, George Forster, or, more forcefully, Melville. But as much as Stevenson evokes a sense of oppression and injustice, what appears chiefly to interest him in the Marquesas is the uncanny aesthetic of native destruction, a phenomenon marked not by protest but by something far more demure: "so tranquil a despair." Depopulation is presented as the workings of fate, the inevitable corruption of the race: "the Marquesan, never industrious, begins now to cease altogether from production" (32); natives are "mild, uncomplaining creatures (like children in a prison)" who "yawn and await death" (42). Meanwhile, replacing this languid and appealing—but unproductive—race are the productive forces of industry. Passing Atuona, Stevenson notes, "It is but a few years since this valley was a place choked with jungle, the debatable land and battleground of cannibals." The valley, now a plantation, wears instead "so smiling an appearance: cleared, planted, built upon, supplied with railways, boat-houses, and bath-houses" (105). The plantation is owned by an industrious member of the emerging dominant race in the region—an Anglo-Saxon American named Captain John Hart—who has produced order and cleanliness out of space where, within recent memory, Stevenson is told, "young men picked up a human foot, and provocatively staring at the [white] stranger, grinned and nibbled at the heel" (106).

As Edmond notes, Stevenson's voyage would ultimately lead to an image of an oceanic world beyond death, capable of adapting and surviving,[65] but in the Marquesas he found a site that reflected his own mortality, a place of walking ghosts and spirits. If renewal is in store, it appears chiefly to arrive through natural selection and western progress. Stevenson weighs various arguments to explain depopulation, among them the coming of plantations, which led to displacement from traditional dwellings, but rejects them one by one: "I have heard the mortality of the Maoris attributed to [the] marshy vicinity of their plantations. How plausible! And yet the Marquesans are dying out in the same houses where their fathers multiplied" (39). He concludes that depopulation in the Marquesas and Hawai'i is attributable to promiscuity: the "debauched" Marquesans and the "notoriously lax" Hawaiians compare unfavorably to the "most chaste" and "most temperate" Samoans (40–41). In 1924, Major A. P. A. Johnson documented a discussion with a missionary on Hiva Oa that resonates with similar claims of wanton sexuality and self-inflicted degeneration: "It is such a great tragedy that such a splendid people should disappear . . . [but] like Adam and Eve in Eden, they had their Paradise, but they preferred the evil to the good, and by their own acts—cannibalism, immorality, and the rest—they signed their own death warrant."[66] The idea looks both backward—to Bougainville's invocation of Minerva to save Polynesia from its own amorality and the later apotheosis of the chaste Captain Cook—and forward, to global discourses of illnesses such as AIDS as self-inflicted and preventable through monogamy and chastity.[67]

Notions of the fatal impact moved not only Pacific travelers, but a whole generation of US anthropologists and the salvage projects of their followers. But just as the traditional anthropological project has been criticized for its rhetorical tendency to freeze Pacific cultures in the static pose of the rescued past, the notion of the fatal impact, as Wendt, Subramani, Dening, and others have noted, posits a nondynamic and isolationist model of Pacific cultures. Wendt sees it as an outmoded and racist idea, arguing, "According to these theories and views we, the indigenous, have been hapless victims and losers in the process of cultural contact and interaction; our cultures have been 'diluted' and 'corrupted'; we have even 'lost' them." Wendt prefers concepts that recognize that all cultures "are becoming, changing in order to survive, absorbing foreign influences, continuing, growing."[68] Cross-cultural contact has engendered radical change, and this contact was corrosive and violent for many populations of the Pacific, but to posit the disappearance of a culture is to assume that cultures are static and measurable quantities. It reinforces binaries, as Dening notes, allowing for the invention of "weak" as opposed to "strong" cultures. It positions anthropological reconstructions of the Marquesas as the "true" culture, inventing a "museum piece out of time."[69]

Fatal impact theory gave currency to salvage ethnography—or the "great rescue missions," in Mead's words[70]—of anthropologists such as Malinowski, Reo Fortune, Gregory Bateson, and Mead herself. In addition, it provided writers and artists with remnants of disappearing cultures, an ideal focus for emotional cathexis and aesthetic contemplation. On this level the fatal impact provided a convenient metaphor for expressing, if not redressing, colonial ills.[71] Glossing George Lukács, Edward Said has suggested that many modernist texts tend to be characterized by a "formal irony" that constitutes a response to the "disturbing appearance" of "various Others, whose provenance was the imperial domain." This "self-conscious passivity" in modernism arose from a culture uncertain about whether or how to give up imperial control, resulting in "paralyzed gestures of aestheticized powerlessness" rather than political engagement.[72] For Said, much modernist literature—such as the phrase he notes as "no, not yet . . . no, not here" that closes E. M. Forster's *A Passage to India* (1924)—becomes an inscription of personal stasis rather than potential social transformation.[73] In many ways Said's formulation helps to explain the persistence of the fatal impact as a dominant metaphor in modernist texts coming to terms with the fringes of the colonial metropole. As both a measurable entity and as a metaphor for the impact of commerce and colonization, it withholds agency from others while translating the west's inability or unwillingness to affect positive change into the inevitability of fate, of death. Flaherty's *Nanook of the North* (1922), for example, scrupulously avoids showing an Inuit culture coming to terms with the impact of technology and change, and closes with an image of a sleeping Allakariallak (Nanook) that invokes a death mask. The fatal impact is a sublimated yet terrible knowledge shared by the collective: it does not need to be explained. There are other, embedded cultural roots to the fatal impact as metaphor, as will be explored shortly: the fatal impact's aesthetic tensions of beauty and death tap into a modernist fascination with Romanticism and the cult of the ruin.

Yet the obsession with death and decay is not left as pure rhetorical artifice: O'Brien, like Stevenson, tries to go beyond the simplifications of the fatal impact and connect his book's darker undertones to local beliefs and practices. Observing customs relating to death and dying as he attends the funeral of a woman, Aumia, who died of consumption after spending weeks calmly gazing on her own coffin, O'Brien discusses concepts of *havai'i* (the afterlife) and *po* (the darkness). He suggests that "all Marquesans live in the shadow of that day [of death]" (161). Dening's "silent land" is also grounded in beliefs connected to dying: "The past lay heavily on Te Henua. The dead still occupied the land. They were everywhere to be seen and were at all times remembered. The dead stayed mostly where they had lived. Sometimes they still sat . . . in white *tapa,* their heads crowned with feathers, at their necks pearl and turtle-shell gorgets."[74] For Dening, western visitors of the eighteenth and nineteenth centuries had an almost necrophilic interest in the funerary customs of the Marquesan people, and O'Brien appears to be no different. But Aumia's funeral also incites more politically engaged—if essentially oppositional—meditations on the implications of these deaths, which O'Brien calls "a relief from the oppression of alien and unsympathetic white men" (156).

If O'Brien's text seems invested in a discourse that provides static models of victimhood and cultural decay, at certain moments we can glimpse a politicized and historicized position that challenges traditional renderings of the fatal impact as divine violence. One way he does this is to make explicit the links between native bodies and western capital, exposing a socioeconomic system based on the exploitation of labor and resources, rather than reinscribing oppositional models of strong and weak cultures. It would be easy for O'Brien to blame the French, as did many of his predecessors. But although he lampoons the false civilities of French colonists, the critique avoids the standard retreat into American exceptionalism. There is no "smiling plantation" here that promises a colonial order will emerge from a convulsive transition. Indeed, when staying on a plantation on Fatuiva with the Swiss settler Grelet, O'Brien surveys a depleted population and a failed business amidst lush flora. The landowner bewails his inability to expand his plantation because the natives "die too fast," after which O'Brien meditates on the physical and psychic impact of capitalism:

> [Grelet] voiced the wail of the successful man the world over. If he could get labor, he could turn it into building his dreams to reality, into filling his ships with his goods for his profit. But he had not the labor, for the fruits of a commercial civilization had killed the islanders who had had their own dreams, their own ships, and their own pleasures in life. (320–321)

Depopulation appears not as inevitability, but instead is attributed to western commercial gain based on the value of physical labor and goods. O'Brien further posits western subjectivity constructed under the sway of expansionist commercial ideologies against subjectivities that suggest alternative realities, desires, and ways of seeing the world. In *Atolls,* he expands his critique of the industrial mechanization of human lives in the scramble for colonial gain—the minting of "gold for the white labor kings" (276)—arguing that commercial prospecting has profoundly endangered existing social systems:

> With the entire Marquesan economic and social system disrupted, food was not so easily procurable, and they were driven to work by commands, taxes, fines, and

the novel and killing incentives of rum and opium. The whites taught men to sell their lives, and women to sell their charms. Happiness and health were destroyed because the white man came here only to gratify his cupidity. (165)

The question becomes not just one of widespread disease, waste, and loss, but of the physical and social dynamics of predatory commercial practices and cultural hegemonies.

O'Brien also makes efforts to analyze the implications of contact and the resulting shifts in cultural practice, rather than simply documenting its visible effects. In *Atolls*, he considers the role of *tapu* in Marquesan life and concludes that the "utter disregard" that white outsiders showed in trespassing the intricate and hierarchical bonds of the *tapu* system may have undermined Marquesan daily life. He argues, "The abandonment of *tapus* under the ridicule and profanation of the whites relaxed the whole intricate but sustaining Marquesan economy. Combined with the ending of the power of chiefs of hereditary caste [*haka'iki*], the doing away with *tapus* as laws set the natives hopelessly adrift on an uncharted sea" (284). Dening, while desiring to avoid western models and certitudes about Marquesan life "before contact," offers a not dissimilar reading of *tapu* and *haka'iki* as having served as organizing metaphors for Marquesan culture: "Enata [the people] used *tapu* as a metaphor to understand themselves. The coming of Aoe [western outsiders] made a bridgehead for agnosticism. The consequent personal and social trauma in the islands gave witness to how difficult it was to reconstruct another metaphor."[75] Though this is still a kind of model, a version of "speaking for" the other, it is one that uses ethnological knowledge as a bridge for coming to terms with the complex give-and-take of culture contact. And it suggests that O'Brien's text is not totally free of ethnographic analysis even while it professes its idleness.

The Marquesas did not have to wait long for more authoritative and comprehensive cultural documentation than O'Brien could offer. Almost exactly a year after *White Shadows* appeared, Edward Smith Craighill Handy and his wife, Willowdean, arrived in the Marquesas from the Bernice P. Bishop Museum in Honolulu to begin nine months' fieldwork, a project that would lead to the monumental *The Native Culture in the Marquesas* (1923), Willowdean's *Tattooing in the Marquesas* (1922), and other publications. E. S. C. Handy points out in his introduction that "as a matter of fact only the lingering shreds of the ancient culture remain" and then paints a brief portrait of Marquesan life in the early 1920s.[76] But ultimately, as Dening suggests, even if Handy caught aspects of "the essential flexibility of Marquesan culture," his work is presented as a timeless and universal accounting of cultural practice: "The culture he caught was static for all that. He portrayed it without time or change, without history or individuals."[77] To the outside world, the Marquesas remained caught in a "zero point" outside time. Paradoxically, perhaps, the flexibility and immediacy of O'Brien's first-person narrative provides a more immediate sense of Marquesan life in the midst of an emerging, uneven, global modernity.

Colonial Ruins

In *White Shadows*, the fatal impact is not simply a metaphor that pronounces the divine fate of the Marquesas; it becomes part of a cultural dynamic that engages both "them" and "us." Earlier I suggested that elements of *White Shadows* might function as a return of the repressed. O'Brien's text often reveals less about the Marquesas than it does about the process of defining the self in the midst of cultural difference—and clearly all is not right with the western self. Escape from mechanized civilization to renewal amidst the primitive will not be a simple, nor even perhaps attainable, goal.

O'Brien's splitting from the civilized self is neither clean nor complete. He is never at rest; he is hardly at one with fellow westerners on the islands but neither, as much as he would like, is he able to really identify with the Marquesans around him. His primary motivation is escape, but a history of western deceit refuses to be suppressed either by distance or desire. During his first night in Atuona, ghosts of silenced lives constitute this perpetual return, haunting him from the corners: "Soon from out of the brick oven . . . whispering forms that slid along the slippery floor and leaped about the seats where many long since dead had sat . . . the Celtic vision of my forefathers, that strange mixture of the terrors of the Druid and soggarth, danced on the creaking floor, and witch-lights gleamed on ceiling and timbers" (42–43). Throughout *White Shadows* these ghosts rise up, phantasmagoric figures projected and dispersed in the form of allegorical fragments and dream images, suggesting that primitivist desires for return to mythic origins may unleash unexpected and unwanted nightmares. Ali Behdad has noted that "the field of the Other is often thematized in colonial fiction as the site of the uncanny surrounded by images of foreignness,"[78] but O'Brien seems less haunted by foreign others than by the specters of home, the "Celtic vision of my forefathers." Even at this distance, he cannot disavow western subjectivity, nor (given his Catholicism) the collective sins of his ancestors.

In keeping with this reappearance of the horrors of home, O'Brien experiences his starkest moments of self-recognition not when viewing the apparent ruins of

Marquesan culture and the fatal impact, but when contemplating the remnants of fading and past colonialisms. Visiting Père Siméon Delmas, he notes the missionary's "soiled soutane" and the "half unhinged" door of the church, the priest's "pitifully shabby room" telling of the "passing of an institution once possessing grandeur and force" (280–281). The journey to Vaitahu on Tahuata leads him to a similar conclusion:

> It was Standard Oil, sending around the world its *tipoti,* or tin cans, filled with illuminating fluid cheaper than that of the whale, that ended the days of the ships in Vait-hua [*sic*], and they sailed away for the last time, leaving an island so depopulated that its few remaining people could slip back into the life of the days before the whites came. (66)

The days of Melville's whalers are gone. The passing of French colonists and US commercial interests give the islands an appearance, in part, of recovery and retreat to the past. Ironically, Tahuata perhaps more closely approximates an imagined Adamic wilderness—a lush island with no other people. "The day of whites had passed," O'Brien contends (momentarily forgetting the significance of his own presence). In this vision of faded colonialism, it is not only the lingering fragments of indigenous cultures wasted by the west that serve as ruins for contemplation, but the failed period of high colonial administration. Broken roads, reduced to overgrown trails and rivulets, empty buildings and "tumble-down shanties," and handfuls of "motley half-castes lounging under trees" are colonialism's remnants.

Colonial ruins are strewn alongside evidence of the fatal impact, and O'Brien retraces these paths of conquerors, colonizers, beachcombers, and traders. A history of mistreatment and miscomprehension is framed as the failure of the west, which marks the corruption of Enlightenment ideals. In Vaitahu, he visits the graves of "the sailors who first raised the standard for France in these islands," Edouard Halley and Laffon de Ladebat—who were killed in a skirmish with the local population. Halley, left in command of Vaitahu in 1842, found himself in a confusing power struggle: the population was declining, and the *haka'iki,* Iotete, would not cooperate with him. Like Porter, he seemed to understand only shows of force; thus he intervened in the election of a new king, Maheono. Iotete refused to leave the island, so, imagining that only force could achieve his bidding, Halley attempted to push Iotete into exile. The resulting skirmish left Halley, Ladebat, and forty Marquesans dead. All that remains of the French, O'Brien notes, are stones and overgrown monuments, a "mausoleum" housed in "the eternal jungle"

(84). The ruins of colonists and voluntary exiles abound: in Atuona, remnants of Paul Gauguin's house are merely lines "sketched upon the fertile soil" (147). The search for Gauguin's grave on a hill above the valley yields only the memento mori of other graves, "mounds marked by small stones along the sides, with crosses of rusted iron filigree showing skulls and other symbols of death," where hibiscus sprouts "blood-red on the sunken graves" (151–153).

During a journey to Taipivai, O'Brien locates the scene of Porter's 1813 raid. The tale of Porter's aggressions further suggests a need for reexamination of those fictional and historical narratives that spurred his earlier longings for adventure. Common beliefs in a paternal US rescuing the Pacific from the hands of European colonizers are put into question as he searches for the Taipi. Porter himself painted his attack in almost surreal terms, conjoining aesthetic contemplation with acts of destruction: "We continued our march up the valley, and met along the way several beautiful villages, which were set on fire, and at length arrived at their capital, for it deserves the name of one.... I very reluctantly set fire to it. The beauty and regularity of this place was such, as to strike every spectator with astonishment" (Porter, 102). Critical accounts chiefly cite Porter's brutality, but it is perhaps not so much the violent acts themselves as the vertiginous contradictions at the heart of the text that haunted later US travelers. Prefiguring a now-classic utterance such as Bill Kilgore's "I love the smell of napalm in the morning" in *Apocalypse Now* (1979), Porter gazes at the lushness of Taipivai in the morning light "in all its beauty" and then destroys it: "a long line of smoking ruins now marked our traces from one end to the other." He then addresses a strange, backhanded apology to the Taipi: "Unhappy and heroic people, the victims of your own courage and mistaken pride ... the instruments of your own punishment shed tears of pity over your misfortunes" (Porter, 105). Returning to the site, O'Brien finds himself surrounded by stark reminders of Porter's ruthlessness: "a loneliness indescribable and terrible ... a feeling of doom and death was in the motionless air" (306–307).

There is no symbolic reconstruction here of a high colonial order, just as there is no real impression of a unified colonial body at the text's center; there are simply stark remnants for contemplation, marking distance from any pregiven unity of the colonial scene. This is the underside of imperial order: imperialism not only destroys its others but also shatters the west's idealism, killing the imagination itself. The west comes to see itself as nothing more than a degenerate force. *White Shadows* thus confronts Turner's thesis that American character was forged in contact with the wilderness and therefore is a regenerative force created in opposition to "old Europe." O'Brien refutes American exceptionalism and suggests instead that US imperial aims are merely the opposite side of the same coin, aligned with European practices and interests. Furthermore, he suggests, "old Europe's" problems, and failures, on the colonial front are now US problems.

Raymond Williams notes that the term "civilization" implied the simultaneity of process, progress, and order: "[The term] has behind it the general spirit of the Enlightenment, with its emphasis on secular and progressive human self-development. Civilization expressed this sense of historical process, but also celebrated the associated sense of modernity: an achieved condition of refinement and order."[79] Undermining the concept of civilization as progress is the spectacle of the ruin. Walter Benjamin suggests the connotations associated with ruins, where the mortified landscape of western history is revealed through enigmatic emblems that hold the promise of a knowledge that is never fully possessed: "In the ruin history has physically merged into the setting. And in this guise history does not assume the form of the process of an eternal life so much as that of irresistible decay."[80] It is this sense of irresistible decay and not Enlightenment progress that O'Brien evokes via the compelling yet stark western ruins on the islands. Here *White Shadows* not only begins to suggest the failures of a colonial past, but also implies a critique of the interlinked ideals of post-Enlightenment modernity and the emerging "American Century."

On several occasions, O'Brien's observations shift from colonial ruins to the living remnants of the colonists themselves. Here the colonial body appears as a fragmented and discarded shell. When he arrives on Hiva Oa, one of the first things he witnesses is a "squalid dwelling" with battered windows that disclose "a wretched mingling of native bareness with poverty-stricken European fittings" (34). The site of wretched mingling is populated by a "ragged Frenchman" and three girls, "as blonde as German *Mädchens*," whose "white delicate faces and blue eyes, in such surroundings, struck one like a blow" (34). After being assured that "there is no native blood in those girls," O'Brien discovers the man is called Baufré, once married to the daughter of a former officer in the British Indian Light Cavalry, himself a *sous officier* in the French colonial forces, now reduced to "native" squalor. Though colonial hierarchies are revisited here, in that the ultimate tragedy of the white is to fall to the level of the native, there is a second dimension to the figure of Baufré, who crosses the increasingly blurred boundaries between colonizer and colonized, where degeneracy might now be defined by what Ann Laura Stoler calls mobile discourses of empire.[81] In the figure of Baufré, degeneracy is characterized by veering off the colonial course domestically and culturally, registering uncertainty and indeterminacy concerning the categorical definitions of civilized, white European versus degenerate native.[82]

O'Brien seems fascinated by these living, bodily ruins, which inhabit the interstitial regions between neatly defined colonialist categories. These figures not only underscore the distance from—and thus disruption of—"noble" imperial origins, but offer physical examples of an increasingly self-divided colonialism. They also perhaps elliptically recall Marquesan mythology and the figure of Pohu, whose exploits suggested the body divided into parts and parts recombined into wholes.[83] The hermit Hemeury François, a more extreme and terrifying version of Baufré, appears near the end of the narrative and bookends Baufré's appearance near the beginning. Hemeury François represents a figure disavowed by O'Brien: one of the culturally indeterminate and unnatural "freaks" of paradise he might become if he stays too long. Originally a "Breton of Brest," Hemeury is now a hermit living in the shadows of a banana grove, a "remnant of a man, a crooked skeleton in dirty rags, his face a parchment of wrinkles." His white flesh is "the deadly white of the morgue" (429). Here whiteness metonymically recalls the specters of the uncanny, and death itself. His whiteness, too, is a ghastly visible signifier of a western and masculine desire that, unchecked, becomes a curse in the tropics: he lives in perpetual, unrequited love for a Marquesan femme fatale, a woman who continues to live below him on the mountain, still alone and threatening to lure the unsuspecting traveler into the savage "poison" of her embrace (434). It is likely that self-divided characters such as Hemeury, and not O'Brien himself, served as models for Matthew Lloyd, the "derelict of the Seven Seas" who would later appear as the protagonist seeking renewal in Van Dyke's film version of the book. Yet if the Hollywood version, as I will suggest, strives to reappropriate the protagonist's fall and to redeem the shattered colonial body, O'Brien himself never hints at such redemption. Fantasies such as these belong to an earlier and simpler time.

An Impassable Abyss

White Shadows in the South Seas vacillates between self-critique and sensual, textual indulgence, between ironic self-reflexivity and absorption into the mythical paradise it at times believes it recognizes as fact. Behdad has referred to the split in the writing subject of the colonial travel text, which reflects the split in the discourse of mid-nineteenth-century orientalism. Behdad proposes a reading of the colonialist text that "takes into account the possibility of a split between the manifest text, which is the scene of 'white' authorial writing (the agency of knowing in the work), and the 'unconscious' discourse as the site where the unspoken and the unspeakable surface in the manifest text through the speaking subject's lapses and uncertainties."[84] These lapses are what postcolonial readers focus on to produce critical complexity out of what was once read as the seamlessly monolithic language of colonial order. In *White Shadows in the South Seas*, much of the text actually foregrounds these lapses and uncertainties concerning colonial domination. But, Behdad suggests, the text cannot precisely be labeled counterhegemonic simply because the unspoken and unspeakable fact of colonial doubt appears to usurp the manifest text, thus producing an anticolonial stance.

For if at times O'Brien's book seems to have more in common with the hidden histories of Howard Zinn's *People's History of the United States* than it does with the travel tales of his contemporaries, at other times it carefully avoids subverting convention. In particular, the narrative is hesitant when it comes to images of eroticized bodies, especially when these bodies threaten contact with the narrator himself. Moments of visual pleasure occur, to be sure, and O'Brien often praises the native body, both male and female. But generally these images are safely masked as aesthetic appraisals. On one key occasion, when O'Brien describes visiting Charles Alfred Le Moine's cabin in Vaitahu, an encounter with the erotics of native visibility is elaborately staged in terms of art versus life. One of the artist's canvases strikes O'Brien: there an image of "laughing, clear-eyed" native beauty seems to seductively "speak from the canvas." The gap between art and life is soon bridged, and the "model in life" appears:

> Turning from the dingy interior of his cabin, I saw in the sunlight beyond the door his model in life. Le Moine had not the brush to do her justice. Vanquished Often, as Hinatini means, was perhaps thirteen years old, with a grace of carriage, a beauty and perfection of features, a rich coloring no canvas could depict. Her skin was a warm olive hue, with tinges of red in the cheeks and the lips cherryripe. Her eyes were dark brown, large, melting, childishly introspective. Her hands were shapely, and her little bare feet, arched, rosy-nailed, were like flowers in the sand. (64)

The image plays on the contrasts of darkness and light, where the darkened, museum-like interior of the cabin imprisons the lifeless mimesis of the artist's canvas, while in sunlight Hinatini reveals what Benjamin has called the transfiguring flash of synthetic meaning.[85] O'Brien's Hinatini is suddenly, vividly *there*, embodied and proffered directly to the reader: a kind of living Poedua or Fayaway. By foregrounding his written description against the inadequate mimesis of Le Moine's painting, O'Brien works to remove the mimetic distance of the text and imbues it with the immediacy of eyewitness testimony. His observing eye then moves on to a more anthropological and physiological comparison of native bodies and gestures against prudish, degenerated western bodies: "Their chests are broad and deep, their bosoms, even girls of Vanquished Often's age, rounded, superb, and their limbs have an ease of motion, an animal-like litheness unknown to our clothed and dress-bound women" (65). The visit to Tahuata—which, O'Brien has argued, more closely resembles an originary paradise than other islands—offers the US traveler opportunities to release sexual desires normally kept in check by guilty associations with colonial exploitation. These problematic, voyeuristic erotics circle the periphery of *White Shadows* and in turn facilitate the scopic desires of western readers.

Yet these sudden flashes of desire also inevitably usher in the specters of "wretched mingling"—figures such as Baufré and the hermit Hemeury François—and in these ambivalent moments the narrator suddenly needs to redefine his stable subjectivity against what is, resolutely, *not* of the self. Though offered the opportunity to "marry" Hinatini, he refuses, suddenly invoking an oddly Linnaean differentiation between animal "mating" behaviors: "She was but a child, I said; Americans did not mate with children" (71). Perhaps O'Brien was keeping one eye on his US audiences: though the coming Jazz Age might demand titillation, there were still strict prohibitions against transgression, immorality, vice—in a word, deviance. The seduction scene then takes a more curious turn. In an approximation of Wallis's *lome lome* experience at the house of Purea—and characterized by a similar passive acquiescence—O'Brien is seduced by Hinatini, who massages his back, and then by her uncle, who massages his chest, so that "I was beset before and aft by the most tender and friendly advances of the Marquesan race" (71). The foreignness of the native body promises to liberate repressed longings, enabling the simultaneous exploration not only of cross-racial heterosexual but also homoerotic desires. The scene ignites a brief flirtation with the sexualities explored in the tropics by O'Brien's literary ancestors: Loti, chronicling the seductions of his young Tahitian mistress, Rarahu; Gauguin, who took an adolescent mistress on Hiva Oa but also sang the praises of the "androgyne" Jotefa in Tahiti; even Stoddard's transsexual and homosexual paradise in Molokai. The Marquesans joke with O'Brien, noting that the "white man does not follow the white man's *tapus*," but the author's strict New England roots finally hold sway and he stops the seduction—the white *tapu* seems inescapable even at this great distance.

That night O'Brien awakes from "fitful dreams" to feel a "serpent" upon his inner thigh: a poisonous centipede. Had he greater physical restraint, he imagines, he could allow the serpent to "crawl its slow way over his perfectly controlled body" (72). But he has none: he wrenches the centipede off with a corkscrew. He then states, "I was ever aware that [paradise's] beauty concealed a deadly menace to the white man who listened too long to the rustle of its palms and the murmur of its stream" (73). The islands continue to beckon, but they begin to threaten a destruction of a white self constructed of western mores, cultural conventions, taboos.

For Greg Dening, the beach in the Marquesas is both a real place and a metaphor for cultural crossings. Crossing the beach implies entering into new worlds, while abandoning the accompanying baggage of institutions and cultural practices. For Dening, of the hundreds of authors that have mentioned the Marquesas—including Loti, Stevenson, London, and Heyerdahl—none of them ever really crossed the beach. He suggests that few Aoe (outsiders, westerners) were able to fully explore a world beyond their habits, texts, and preconceptions. It is worth asking, then, whether O'Brien crossed the beach during his year in the Marquesas. The answer seems to be no, even though he tries to relativize the west, to point up the ills of colonialism, and to qualify his own position as author and controlling force behind the text. He even raises the possibility of crossing over, states that the sound of drums "made one want to be a savage" (167), that he "felt [himself] Marquesan" after a nude swim, or that he "might have been a Marquesan" had the sands of genetic history shifted differently; he comes even closer when drunk on kava. Yet compared to a beachcomber such as Robarts, who stayed for seven years, became an adopted son, a husband, and father, and who fought alongside those he called "my own tribe,"[86] O'Brien gives the impression of being a long-stay tourist.

And unlike Robarts, O'Brien's fleeting impressions of cultural unity are the result of an admixture of racial theories of Caucasian sameness and physical observation rather than an embracing of difference. Regardless of what might have been O'Brien's "actual" sexual activities on the islands, the mores and strictures of home cannot be ignored—the text itself may be grounded in the "over there" but is patrolled by the strictures of "here"—and the moments of greatest stress appear when the narrator is on the brink of a loss of (masculine, western, heterosexual) self. He is twice exposed to the (here seemingly emasculating) custom of *pekio* (or "second husband") and on both occasions ironically invokes discourses about his trained impulses towards "chivalry": "Chivalry is not a primitive emotion," he notes, "but it dies hard in the civilized brain" (414). He retreats more adamantly after his rapturous encounter with Hinatini near Le Moine's cabin, concluding that "the [cultural] abyss is impassable": "Savage peoples can never understand our philosophy, our complex springs of action. They may ape our manners, wear our ornaments, and seek our company, but their souls remain indifferent" (68).

O'Brien's staunch refusal to engage in the social custom of exchanging names during his stay further suggests his frequently self-conscious need to cling to a differentiated western identity. Yet even the imperious Porter had (probably strategically) engaged in name exchange during his period in Nukuhiva. Alfred Gell notes that Marquesan name-exchange "annulled differences": if the *tapu* system strongly marked the boundaries of personal identities, name-exchange suggested the possibility of labile, multiple identities.[87] Though professedly comfortable with the boundary marking of *tapu,* O'Brien carefully avoids becoming entangled in name-exchange and the shape-shifting of cultural identity it threatens to initiate.

Thus at the heart of O'Brien's text is a contradiction. On the one hand he clings to fantasies of common racial origins and the fragmented image of a ruined Eden in the Pacific; on the other he backs away from a loss of self—physically, psychically, culturally—not from a lack of desire, but because he believes in the unbridgeable separation of civilized and savage. As Paul Lyons concludes,

> In O'Brien's emphasis on an ineffaceable difference between Islanders and whites —an emphasis most visible in his articles and reviews, in which the critique of Western destructiveness drops out—O'Brien reveals his connection to the worldview, fundamental to twentieth-century tourism, which feeds on difference, and is underwritten by the current science of the period which argued that the savage mind was prelogical or analogical.[88]

But in *White Shadows,* at least, there seems to remain a deeper contradiction. Even while basing many of his suppositions and hesitations on the "abyss" of absolute difference, O'Brien has, wittingly or unwittingly, constructed a world where there is little possibility of crossing over, because there is no palpable "other" or "savage" to cross over to, though there are past cultural and ideological constructions of savagery. Crossings and efforts to escape the west ultimately produce nothing more than a return to the uncanny soul of whiteness and the repressed realms of the self.

Though Polynesian cultures have managed to survive the near-genocidal colonial encounter, images of fragmentation, not regeneration, tend to dominate in O'Brien's textualized Marquesas. Yet it is clear too that the emerging world that *White Shadows* depicts has already outpaced the racial constructs and white man's *tapu*s of its author-narrator. New ethnic and cultural formations are taking place, and a highly mobile figure like O'Brien is intractably taking part in these changes. In spite of his expectations, there are few, if any, examples of racial or cultural purity on the islands. French, Chinese, and US settlers are everywhere in evidence; most of his neighbors are racially mixed or have themselves intermarried; it even could be said that O'Brien's borrowed theories of Polynesian origins in epic sea migrations and eventual racial mixing describe a distinctly Americanized narrative arc. All of this suggests the ongoing mobility of colonial modernity, but it also might offer a glimpse of the emerging mobilization and creolization of ethnicities, cultures, and identities that will follow in the wake of colonialism. It may even gesture towards the optimistic image of the American Pacific "altering and dissolving" into Asian / Pacific or globalist identities that, as Rob Wilson suggests, could at their best deform or critique the trajectory of US frontier expansion and the statist legacies of manifest destiny.[89]

O'Brien might refuse to exchange names, but he actively encourages the exchange of cultural trivia, songs, histories, tale telling. Just prior to the closing passages of *White Shadows*, O'Brien offers an indeterminate and open-ended episode that imagines the Marquesas as an interdependent global entity rather than an isolated and dying land. As he prepares to leave Hiva Oa for California, his neighbor Mauitetai receives a letter from her son, Pahorai Calizte. The letter is a snapshot of a distant place, America, and describes new experiences and emerging identities abroad. The son seeks permission to marry:

> She is *moi kanahau;* as beautiful as the flowers of the *hutu* in my beloved valley of Atuona. She is not of America. She is of Chile. She has paid many piasters for the coming here. She has paid forty piasters. She has been at home in Las Palmas, in the islands of small golden birds. (439)

Via Philadelphia, the Marquesas meets Chile and the Islas Canarias, as translated with an effort to "preserve the flavor of the original" by an expatriate Californian. Perhaps this meeting of Mauitetai's "wandering boy" and his intended might be seen to go beyond the conventional sense of modernist exile and displacement to suggest diasporic and emerging "hybrid" or creolized cultures. The letter closes with a coda, "Coot pae, mama," which dumbfounds its readers, for it recalls neither Marquesan nor French. Finally O'Brien recognizes the mobility and adaptability of language itself: "*Coot pae* is pronounced Coot Pye, and Coot Pye was Pahorai Calizte's way of imitating the American for *Apae Kaoha.* 'Good-bye, mama,' was his quite Philadelphia closing of his letter to his mother" (442). This introduction to the Marquesan *apae kaoha* also sets up the *"apae! kaoha e!"* that ends the book, reminding readers that even as the narrative travels "out there," distances and differences are rapidly closing, and simultaneously transforming fixed concepts of home and away. One begins to perceive a tear in the fabric of Manichean colonial discourse, a rupture perhaps always present, if not always visible.

⌒

IN EARLY 1920, the Century Company decided to publish Charmian London's introductory letter to O'Brien as a means to jumpstart the sales of *White Shadows.* The advertisement read, in its entirety:

My Dear Mr. O'Brien:

You lucky, lucky man . . . to have been what you've been, seen what you've seen, and, best of all, to have been a MAN and with the capacity so to appreciate your opportunity. George Sterling wrote to me, "Don't fail to read 'WHITE SHADOWS IN THE SOUTH SEA.'" I did not hurry to possess myself of your book. Really, to be frank, I am jealous of my South Seas. . . . I almost shrink from opening a new book about them, for fear of disappointment. I have so many disappointments of the kind. So I did not buy your book before I came away to spend this winter in Hawaii. But, around the holidays, on Maui, on the vast slopes of Haleakala, I found your book on every hand . . . and every one begging me to read it. And then I fell. . . . And now it is a pleasure to have confessed.

I do not often envy any one; but I do envy your man-experience. I have been about a bit myself in the strange places . . . but with a man. To go, as a man may, alone, now, would be my dream; but I may not, because I am a woman. I think the favorite book in my library is that great romance the "South Sea Directory."

How fortunate you were, to be on Hiva-Oa (which I only saw from Nuku-Hiva), and to find so many remnants of the real Marquesans, to see, even a few perfect types. I have just simply reveled in your descriptions. . . .

I like the way you have called a spade a spade. It is such splendid, straightforward stuff, all your book. . . .

Many words I have written in this letter; but they do not convey, I am sure, half of what your book means to me. Have you read my LOG? Rough and young as it is, I think you might like it.

Many will write you about yours . . . but few, at least women, can be more intelligently appreciative than I, who have mourned in Taipi Vai, and looked aside into deserted Haapa. . . .

And now, please let me thank you for your book. It has enriched my life.
Very sincerely yours,

(signed) CHARMAIN [*sic*] LONDON (Mrs. Jack.) [90]

Century's idea paid off, and the advertisement helped the book to become an established best seller. Cleverly, the ad offers a carefully edited version of Charmian—rather than standard sensationalistic advertising copy—to create the impression that O'Brien is a "real man" with "man-experience" straight out of popular adventure books. Charmian Kittredge also, curiously, is positioned as a voyeur on Pacific travels, closer to the armchair reader of *White Shadows* than the extensive voyager and author she actually was. As novelist Harold Bell Wright wrote in 1916, "The wilderness is a land where a man, to live, must be a man."[91] Highlighting the masculine virtues of O'Brien's rugged individualism helped to sell *White Shadows,* though in the book O'Brien actually expresses a dislike of hunting (123)—which is the polar opposite of London, who whiled away the hours shooting goats on Nukuhiva—and devotes a lengthy section to a discussion of matriarchal cultures and polyandry on the islands (109–112). The latter discussion once again recalls Edward Robarts, who exhibits tolerance and respect for Marquesan custom but is concerned that the practice of *pekio* would be the most difficult for western readers to come to terms with: "One man may have several women," he wrote, "but for one woman to have several men I think is a pill hard to digest."[92]

Much of the subtlety of *White Shadows* seems to have been lost in the translation from idiosyncratic travel narrative to popular phenomenon. Though far from being a political manifesto, O'Brien's book would have been a suitably entertaining vehicle for delivering a cautionary ideological message to US audiences regarding the implications of imperial expansion. But even its more explicit messages were largely ignored, as a curious sketch of O'Brien in *The Bookman* makes clear:

> He claims that it is all true—those white shadows in the South Seas really fell upon him and enveloped him; yet some of us, hoping we are still blessed with brains, have wondered late and long just what "white shadows" may be. We never found out in that fascinating volume. We are still in the dark, so to speak. The style is charming—just as the man is; but where does fact end, and fiction begin?[93]

O'Brien's image of the white shadow is, in fact, explained in the book, though not in the context of Polynesian cultures. Rather, O'Brien makes a much more pointed association between US politics in the Pacific and the violence towards indigenous peoples at home. The white shadow thus appears as the Americans' need to "take into account the shadow of the white on the red" (164). This links manifest destiny to US expansion in the Pacific, applying theories of migration, race, and the fatal impact to the treatment of American Indians, albeit through stereotypical color coding (164).

Few readers, it seems, picked up on the book's more serious implications or noted the ways that *White Shadows* specifically implicated US imperialism. If they did, reviews scrupulously overlooked it: the book received excellent notices, most praising its breezy escapism. The American Library Association Booklist called it "delightful," the *New York Call* praised its "subtle sense of humor" and "delicate sensitiveness," while the *Review* saw it as "clever and picturesque."[94] O'Brien received similar notices for *Mystic Isles of the South Seas* (a title that suggests a more self-conscious pandering to popular taste), the *New York Times* praising its "charm and insouciance of description."[95] By this time O'Brien was aware that reviewers were not coming to terms with the unsettling undertones of his books, and he wrote to Charmian London that reviews, in any case, meant "very little": "The reviewers compare it favorably, even asparagusly, with *White Shadows*. No reviewer but *one* senses my meaning outside of romance. He vaguely put it in the *NY Post*. The others quote and chatter."[96] Critics continue to overlook O'Brien; Dening's overview of late-nineteenth- and twentieth-century writers who came to the Marquesas, for example, skips from Jack London, who visited for ten days in December 1907, to Thor and Liv Heyerdahl, who stayed a year on Fatuiva in 1937.

But if my sense is correct in suggesting that the cultural role of *White Shadows* was more akin to a return of the repressed, then the book acted on the US public more as an allegory or dreamscape than as a didactic tract. Readers could follow a journey not only across physical space but across psychological terrain, to a beautiful and disruptive world where the tensions and failures of civilization's ideals were displaced on to a fading population and where the potentially threatening cultural practices of others were mediated by a narrator who might flirt with difference but would ultimately hold the line on the taboos and restrictions of home. Still it could be said that in many respects *White Shadows* furthered the popular rise of cultural relativism, which would find one of its most salient expressions in the novelistic, easily consumed relativism of Margaret Mead.

The South Pacific fad would perfectly exemplify the Jazz Age, an era known for relaxed morals, social innovations, and cultural fetishisms. But *White Shadows'* success, and the scores of imitations it produced—including writers that would come to prominence in the 1920s such as Nordhoff and Hall and Robert Dean Frisbie—would paradoxically prove instrumental to O'Brien's decline. His literary career ended up having at least one thing in common with that of his hero Herman Melville: sudden fame followed by increasing obscurity. By autumn 1921, O'Brien found himself plagued by rumors of declining sales, which his publisher attributed to "the general opinion . . . that the South Seas had been killed by the burlesque book, *The Cruise of the Kawa*."[97] By the end of the year, there had been "a tremendous slump" in sales. O'Brien expressed his fears to Charmian: "The bottom is out of the book market for me. Yet I cannot believe that reputation is not cumulative or that burlesque can effectually kill realer work."[98] Published under the pseudonym Walter E. Taprock, *The Cruise of the Kawa* opens with a "Publisher's Note" that makes clear just how quickly the South Seas literary market had become saturated:

> Of late the lure of the South Seas has laid its gentle spell rather overwhelmingly upon American readers. To be unread in Polynesiana is to be intellectually *declasse*. ...In the face of this avid appetite for tropic-scented literature, one may well imagine the satisfaction of a publisher when offered opportunity of association with such an expedition as that of the *Kawa*.[99]

O'Brien was beginning to wonder whether the phenomenon that his work had initiated was becoming a monster of his own making. Reviews remained positive, but at the same time they acknowledged that the South Seas literary moment was passing. On the appearance of *Atolls of the Sun* in 1922, one reviewer suggested, "Of course, the flood of South Seas books which the success of 'White Shadows' brought upon us has probably taken the edge off the public appetite. But if the order of publication had been reversed, and the 'Atolls' had come first, I see no reason why it would not have made equally as great a stir as its illustrious predecessor."[100]

With declining book sales and increasing financial difficulties, O'Brien's history of heavy drinking began to catch up with him. His partner for the last twelve years of his life, the journalist Margaret Wickham Watson (O'Brien remained married throughout his life to Gertrude O'Brien, who lived in Glendale, California) wrote of their troubles in 1924, "I am a little alarmed and worried at Fred's continual inability to work. When I went to Kaoha [O'Brien's house in Sausalito] at 2 this afternoon he told me he had not been able to do anything. . . . It seems as though all his artistic creative force had left him."[101] A year later she writes: "A year has passed and Fred has done no work at all. . . . I wonder what our life is to be."[102] Bouts of drinking continued, with extended periods of ill health. With no other source of income beyond writing, financial troubles began to set in, and were exacerbated by a continuing peripatetic lifestyle, including extensive trips to Europe in 1923 and 1925 with Watson, both of them in search of creative inspiration. To make matters worse, by the mid-1920s Rose Wilder Lane had begun legal proceedings, claiming she was coauthor of *White Shadows in the South Seas* and demanding royalties for her substantial contributions to the book, though the suit was settled out of court.[103] Writing to Charmian London, O'Brien remained defiant: "Be assured that I do not mind if anyone says that I am a drunkard or that I do not write my books. Don't try to straighten me out in the minds of people. Let me be just as crooked as they think I am."[104] By the end of 1925, after a trip to Europe, O'Brien was writing again and hoping to sell various versions of his South Pacific stories, such as "The Calm One" (a theatrical version of *White Shadows*), "The Pearls of Puka Puka," and "Rena" to Hollywood. By September 1925, Watson was noting that three publishers had expressed interest in O'Brien's (as yet unwritten) autobiography. In 1928, the appearance of MGM's *White Shadows in the South Seas* briefly revived his fortunes, and new trade editions of his books appeared. Still, MGM had rejected his concept for the screenplay, and, with the help of Robert Flaherty, the film ended up much closer to a Hollywood version of *Typee*.

In January 1932, O'Brien died of congestive heart failure in Sausalito. In the previous years he had published very little new material outside of some short articles and reviews, though he had become a radio personality in San Francisco and was displaying his characteristic flair for humor, political commentary, and storytelling. His partner, Margaret Watson, continued to circulate the manuscripts of his collected letters and his autobiography, now called *Paper Wings*, for two years after his death. The Depression had now set in, and publishers were drastically cutting back their lists. Watson inserted a newspaper clipping into her diary in 1932: "Many a book that would have seen yesterday's light will never see today's."[105] She committed suicide in 1934, shooting herself in the chest while alone in her apartment in San Francisco. Shortly afterwards, O'Brien's unpublished manuscripts disappeared from view.

3 Searching for Moana
Frances Hubbard and Robert J. Flaherty in Samoa

> Perhaps the public imagines that the charms of the savages can be
> appropriated through the medium of these photographs. Not content
> with having eliminated savage life, and unaware of even having done
> so, it feels the need feverishly to appease the nostalgic cannibalism of
> history with the shadows of those that history has already destroyed.
>
> — Claude Lévi-Strauss, *Tristes Tropiques*

The day after *Nanook of the North*'s premiere (11 June 1922), the *New York Times* could barely contain its excitement about the film's previously unknown director. Through the dynamism and immediacy of his images, Flaherty had managed to bring "life itself" from far-off Hudson Bay in Canada directly into New York's Capitol Theatre: "Beside this film the usual photoplay, the so-called 'dramatic' work of the screen, becomes as thin and blank as the celluloid on which it is printed."[1] *Nanook* was more real, more vibrant than mere fictions. A month later, the *Times* singled out *Nanook* as "one of the screen's finest achievements," and the film, which had cost about $53,000 to make, would ultimately earn nearly $300,000 on its first US run.[2] As Paul Rotha has pointed out, it was "wholly in Hollywood's character" for the major film company that had actually rejected Flaherty's initial offer to distribute *Nanook*—Paramount Pictures Corporation—to offer Flaherty a lucrative opportunity to produce his next film. A major reason for this change of heart was due to Jesse L. Lasky, the production head of Famous Players Lasky, who was himself known to harbor a taste for adventure, sometimes taking camping trips with Zane Grey to remote locales.[3]

The Lasky deal—which would lead to a fateful conversation with Frederick O'Brien about Samoa a few days later—left Flaherty full of expectation at the prospect of a secure future in filmmaking. Writing to his brother David in the hopes of persuading him to come along to Samoa as a production assistant, Flaherty noted that, as Famous [Players Lasky] own or control over 9000 theatres you might imagine what they can do with a year's advance advertising. . . . My contract with Famous is a wonder—giving me complete control of production, which few directors get with M.P. [*sic*] companies—and besides series in these biographic forms in various places after Samoa. . . . I get 40% of the film profits and an allowance of $15,000 a year. All the comforts of this family are at the expense of the company! The bookings on this film by the time it is completed will be $500,000, probably very much more than that. So much for *Nanook* refutations.[4]

Clearly, Flaherty saw his next film as merely the first in a line of biographical adventures shot in remote or exotic locations, like *Nanook.* On 27 April 1923, after spending a day in Sausalito with O'Brien and Margaret Watson, Robert and Frances set out from San Francisco on the steamer *Sonoma,* accompanied by their three children. They would stay on Savai'i simply—the island then thought by some to be the originary site of the Polynesian "race," and associated with the warrior goddess and prophet Nafanua, now strongly linked to a pre-Christian Samoa[5]—for twenty months.

It could safely be said that the Flahertys arrived in Safune largely naïve about the culture and political context they were entering into. They had read Stevenson, Safroni-Middleton, Beatrice Grimshaw—whatever they could get their hands on about the South Seas—but they also harbored fantasies of a precolonial "pure" culture that might be captured on film. German control of Western Samoa had been ceded to New Zealand after World War I, but German influence and officials were still everywhere in evidence—notably in the person of the Flaherty's eccentric "host" in Safune, Felix David. Resentment also remained over the New Zealand administration's failures during the 1918 influenza epidemic, which had killed 22 percent of the population while leaving Eastern Samoa, which had been successfully quarantined by the US, largely untouched. As Malama Meleisea notes, the early to mid-1920s was a period of economic instability and incipient social unrest, when initial optimism over the appointment of General George Spafford Richardson as chief administrator was shifting towards tensions between local customs and hierarchies—*fa'a Samoa*—and the bureaucratic needs of western colonialism to restrict and codify traditional ways. New laws such as the Samoan Offenders Ordinance of 1922 gave the colonial administrator powers to banish the use of chiefly titles, placing colonial forces in direct conflict with Samoan tradition and perceptions of autonomy.[6] Into this postwar climate of uncertain relations between *fa'a Samoa,* middle-class white and mixed-race settlers, and paternalist

colonial imperatives towards improvement, modernization, and increased pro-
ductivity through centralized authority, the Flahertys arrived with their mobile
Paramount studio. They would return to California with an astounding 240,000
feet of unedited film in December of 1924. As it turned out, the finished version of
Moana ended up bearing little relation to *Nanook*'s biographical format and was a
financial disappointment for Lasky and Paramount Pictures; yet it would turn out
to be the only one of Flaherty's three projects in the South Pacific that he would
see through to completion.

Flaherty's Legacy

In "Cinema and Exploration" André Bazin writes of the "gradual formation of a
mythology" of the exotic in the early-twentieth-century films of Europe and the
US that evolved "from *Moana* . . . to *Tabu,* by way of *White Shadows.*"[7] It is no
coincidence that all three works are marked by Flaherty's participation. Orson
Welles placed the humble documentarist, who struggled creatively and financially
for most of his thirty-year career, amidst the pantheon of great US artists and think-
ers, such as Thoreau and Whitman, who helped to define the essence of American
values and established the nation's distinctive self-identity as a unified "people"
and culture marked by a preeminent faith in the individual. Welles further noted,
"I don't see where he fits into films at all, except as being one of the two or three
greatest people who ever worked in the medium."[8] Welles clearly recognized a soul
mate: Flaherty, particularly after his death in 1951, was never viewed amidst the
ranks of the money-obsessed forces of Hollywood. Fred Zinnemann, who began
his career as Flaherty's assistant in the 1930s recalled that "Flaherty, invited to Hollywood, entered this glittering, soft, insecure community like a being from outer
space."[9] Flaherty was seen as an outsider, and at the same time was lofted above
the status quo.

Yet increasingly, critics have mounted an attack on the construction of what
has come to be known as the "Flaherty Myth"[10] and have stressed the ways that
even his most celebrated documentaries—*Nanook, Moana, Man of Aran* (1934),
and the Standard Oil–financed *Louisiana Story* (1948)—are inauthentic, semifictionalized works at best. The problem lies not so much in the ways that Flaherty's
work tends to blur the line between fantasy and reality as in its deceptive narrative
strategies, which naturalize the staging and reinvention of native life that was performed for his camera. Certainly Flaherty's legacy, which helped him to become
known as the "father" of US documentary film, has undergone a great deal of revi-

sion since Richard Corliss's "Robert Flaherty: The Man and the Iron Myth" (1973) derided the "sanctimonious reverence" accorded to him after his death (230).[11]

While Flaherty was alive there was a widespread assumption—much of it encouraged by Flaherty and Frances in their publicity efforts—that films such as *Nanook, The Land* (1940), and *Man of Aran* should be seen as exemplary of the social and heuristic function of nonfiction motion pictures. *Moana*, for its part, reputedly inspired the first use of the word "documentary" to describe a film's content, in John Grierson's anonymous review of 1926 (though Grierson used "documentary" here as an adjective, saying the film had "documentary value"). But it should not be thought that all audiences initially believed in the truth-value of Flaherty's films; in fact Flaherty has long divided public opinion. Shortly after its release, *Nanook*'s authenticity was interrogated by the explorer Vilhjalmur Stefansson, who noted that the Inuit had for generations hunted with guns, though Flaherty portrayed them as only having primitive weapons (one intertitle insists that the Inuit still hunted with nothing more substantial than harpoons). Stefansson further pointed out that the seal hunt sequence was an obvious fake, since the animal that is finally pulled from beneath the ice is clearly "still and dead."[12] After the release of *Man of Aran* in 1934, Ivor Montagu complained that "no less than Hollywood, Flaherty is busy turning reality into romance. The tragedy is that, being a poet with a poet's eye, his lie is the greater, for he can make the romance seem real."[13] More recently and perhaps most incisively, Fatimah Rony has seen *Nanook of the North* as a prime example of ethnographic taxidermy; she glosses both Stephen Bann's *The Clothing of Clio* (1984), which considers the taxidermic impulse on nineteenth-century historical writing, and Donna Haraway's "Teddy Bear Patriarchy," which examines the cultural role of Carl Akeley's dioramas and taxidermic displays at New York's American Museum of Natural History. Taxidermy, Rony notes, is an effort "to protect against loss, in order that the body may be transcended"; it fulfills, in Haraway's words, "the fatal desire to represent, to be whole."[14] Such representations eschew obvious cultural contact, conflict, and emergence in favor of creating an idealized, frozen image of the (presumed dying or dead) culture in question. In the case of *Moana*, one of its release subtitles, *A Romance of the Golden Age*, suggests this perpetuation of the taxidermic impulse that lies behind many colonial-era ethnographic productions. As "romantic ethnography,"[15] *Moana* elides evidence of culture contact and constructs the same technology-free mise-en-scène that was envisioned in *Nanook*.

In the latter, the strategic absence of technology is perhaps best revealed in the scene in which Nanook (played by Allakariallak) is shown encountering a gramophone, an object that acts as an odd visual oxymoron against the backdrop of the remote frozen north. Allakariallak's feigned ignorance of technology (though he worked behind the scenes as one of Flaherty's technical assistants) is further underscored as he tries to bite the record. The scene removes Nanook from the present, distancing him as well from the technological world of both filmmaker and audience. In response, films such as George Stoney's *Robert Flaherty's Man of Aran: How the Myth Was Made* (1979) and Claude Massot's *Nanook Revisited* (1990) reveal the elisions in Flaherty's work, the latter demonstrating the tensions between the film's once-celebrated academic status and reactions by Inuits to the film, who found comedy rather than serious drama in scenes like the seal-hunting episode. *Moana* carries with it similar problems, reinforcing the opposition of civilized and primitive by eliding the presence of the filmmaker and the trappings of technology—the very technology that had made it possible to visualize this primitive world out of time.

In the last few decades, the very legitimacy of universal documentary truth—not to mention its value—has come under intense questioning, and Flaherty, having established many features of the form, has also become the focus of its problems. Even if most audiences, as Jay Ruby has argued, continue to believe documentary images to be "accurate representations of reality, unless they are overtly altered,"[16] there have always been enough skeptical and cine-literate viewers around to cast doubt on documentary's accuracy. It has become almost axiomatic—since the advent of poststructural criticism's thorough interrogation of representation and its modes of operation—that the authenticity of the documentary, like all forms of representation, is intimately bound to issues of power, subjective choice, and ideological influence. Bill Nichols has thus asked how it is possible "to *represent* another person when any representation threatens diminution, fabrication, and distortion," a question that seems to be still largely disputed in documentary and ethnographic practice.[17] The greater the interrogation of cinematic authenticity, the more these interrogations underscore the unavoidable fact that nonfictional representations can never recover the actual presence they strive to recreate, in spite of the photographic record's status as a technological "index" of the events and objects it inscribes. Michael Moore's *Fahrenheit 9/11* (2004) shows its awareness of these issues in one of the film's most affecting scenes when Lila Lipscomb, who has lost her son in the Iraq war, is accosted by a female bystander who shouts "This is all a stage," after which the bereaved mother launches into a powerful defense of the truth of her experience as it is captured by the film. By revealing the potential falsehoods of the medium, the bystander's interruption paradoxically allows Moore's film to more fully claim its authenticity, and the moment lends added weight to Lipscomb's highly emotional scene in front of the White House that follows.

Critics such as Linda Williams have convincingly argued for documentary's continued relevance, suggesting that even in a climate of postmodern skepticism and generic hybridity, nonfiction filmmaking can be valuable for its ability to reveal complex relative and contingent truths rather than unified or absolute truth.[18] Flaherty nonetheless continues to be criticized on numerous fronts: those who expect documentary representations to be accurate and unmediated reality continue to draw attention to the ways the films lie, while those who accept documentary's falsehoods and inconsistencies still fault him for lacking complexity and minimizing film's self-reflexive potential. For his own part Flaherty, in writings and interviews, openly admitted his films' manipulations, detailing his use of staging, reenactments, and castings of actors.

Controversies concerning the factual status of documentary images began long before Flaherty picked up a camera. As Bernard Smith has shown, the representation of documentary information based on firsthand witnessing during South Pacific travels had come under attack as early as 1773, with the appearance of Hawkesworth's *Account* of the major English voyages. A few years later, George Forster's *A Voyage round the World* was highly critical of an engraving of the people of Eua that was based on William Hodges's documentary drawings done on site. Having witnessed the encounter, Forster strongly objected to the representation provided by *The Landing at Middleburgh, one of the Friendly Isles,* which was published in *Cook's Voyage toward the South Pole and round the World* in 1777. Forster noted,

> Mr. Hodges designed this memorable interview in an elegant picture, which has been engraved for captain Cook's account of this voyage. The same candour with which I have made it a rule to commend the performances of this ingenious artist, whenever they are characteristic of the objects which he meant to represent, obliges me to mention, that this piece, in which the execution of Mr. Sherwin cannot be too much admired, does not convey any adequate idea of the natives of Ea-oowhe or of Tonga Tabbo. The plates which ornamented the history of captain Cook's former voyage, have been justly criticised, because they exhibited to our eyes the pleasing forms of antique figures and draperies, instead of those Indians of which we wished to form an idea. But it is greatly to be feared, that Mr. Hodges has lost the sketches and drawings which he made from *Nature* in the course of the voyage, and supplied the deficiency in this case, from his own elegant ideas.

The connoisseur will find Greek contours and features in this picture, which have never existed in the South Sea. He will admire an elegant flowing robe which involves the whole head and body, in an island where women very rarely cover the shoulders and breast; and he will be struck with awe and delight by the figure of a divine old man, with a long white beard, though all the people of Eaoowhe shave themselves with muscle shells.[19]

Hodges's original sketches had been reinterpreted not only in the engraving by John K. Sherwin (an intervention that Forster acknowledges), but perhaps also in a composite drawing done by Giovanni Battista Cipriani,[20] but he nonetheless lays the blame on Hodges for the embellishments imposed on his own remembered image. Forster seems to expect verifiable truth in technically reproduced drawings. He further objects to the "elevation" of the Tongans to the level of ancient Greeks, suggesting that such embellishments distort the truth. Indeed, it could be said that Forster objects to what is now labeled ethnocentrism (hence identifying an ethnocentrism that underpins Enlightenment notions of civilization and the primitive more generally). Forster's published comments ultimately set off counterarguments attesting to the veracity of Hodges's images, notably from William Wales, who argued, "I am authorized by Mr. Hodges to assure the Doctor, that he has not lost any of his original sketches, and that every figure, so far as it relates to their dress, manners, or customs, are to be found amongst them, actually drawn from the persons which he saw; even the 'divine old man with the long white beard,' is amongst them." Wales continues by suggesting that Hodges's elevation of the native figure to the level of classical Greeks was hardly foreign to Forster's own embellished prose, citing Forster's own accounts of native women as "handsome, with flowing curls which hung down on their bosoms," and with statures "graceful, and form exquisitely proportioned," "their features full of sweetness," "their large dark eyes sparkled with fire," and so on.[21] Smith suggests that engravers of Pacific peoples never again represented them for an official publication "as though they were actors in a Greek play in an English country garden" and that emphasis was thereafter placed on "faithful" depictions.[22] Though practical changes may have followed from this well-publicized controversy, it is clear that even the indexical veracity provided much later by photographic technology couldn't fully prevent the production of Pacific images every bit as embellished and controversial as *The Landing at Middleburgh*.

Flaherty's *Moana* continues this historical debate concerning documentary inscription and the reproduction of ethnographic observations in the Pacific. As in any documentary image, there are expectations of truthfulness and accuracy, though *Moana,* it should be noted, was made before the rise of the truth-telling claims of cinéma vérité (late 1950s–1970s), direct cinema, and Free Cinema, before Mass Observation, before Grierson's social documentary movement in Britain argued for film's social relevance. In short, Flaherty rarely made the sort of claims to truth and "fly on the wall" immediacy that later came to define the genre. *Nanook* appeared in the same year that saw the birth of Dziga Vertov's *Kino Pravda* in the USSR, but seminal films such as *Man with a Movie Camera* did not appear until 1929, and even the latter features manipulation and fictionalization.[23] It is interesting, then, that one of the first reviews of *Nanook* suggests that contemporary audiences were hardly deluded and were well aware of the film's factual limitations. The reviewer makes clear the difference between producing pure fictions and presenting an "illusion of reality":

> The average photoplay does not reproduce life. Through the obvious artificialities of its treatment, through the unconcealed mechanics of its operation, through its reflection of a distorted or incomplete conception of life, rather than of life itself, it usually fails to be true to any aspect of human existence. It is not realistic in any sense. It remains fiction, something fabricated. It never achieves the illusion of reality. But "Nanook of the North," also seeking to give an impression of reality is real on the screen.[24]

Nanook may be illusion, but it is not purely fictional. Similarly, in introducing Frances's 1925 series of publicity articles in *Asia* on the making of *Moana,* L. D. Froelick acknowledged that the film offered an illusion of reality, yet still operated on the level of the real. Froelick appears aware of the film's illusory and possibly euhemeristic qualities, but curiously this awareness does not conflict with his experience of the film as an encounter with a real place. Describing his first viewing of *Moana,* Froelick draws attention to the artifice of the medium, but he still revels in the ways the film imbues the spectator with an "I was there" authority: "I have seen these people of Samoa, not as a dream nor as the created image of a story, but as action, swift and vital—and I have never been to Samoa."[25] Representation here invites the viewer to experience a virtual (yet no less substantial for being so) reality. As for Flaherty's deceptive use of typecasting and acting, Froelick does not think that artificial techniques like acting devalue the authenticity of documentary information. Indeed, he notes that Flaherty's rapport with his Samoan players "released the full genius of these Samoans for naturalness. Of course, they acted, but they lived their lives while acting."[26] Here is perhaps one clue to Froelick's belief in the film: in subtly recalling notions of William Z. Ripley's racial "genius" (the "naturalness" and unselfconsciousness of Polynesians appears to make them natural actors), he manages to conjure up a "deeper truth," rendering questions of the film's authenticity irrelevant.

Frances Flaherty's *Asia* prepublicity articles are similarly uninhibited regarding *Moana*'s fictionalizations. The aim of Flaherty's film, with Paramount behind it, was the popular "theatrical screen," as Frances would insist many times over in the coming years, since there were few commercial alternatives for those interested in making films of an ethnographic or educational nature.[27] In her *Asia* articles she documents the "trials" of picking the perfect Samoan stars, emphasizing that making *Moana* encapsulated all of the trouble, and glamour, of most conventional Hollywood fictions. Their first choice for female star, Taioʻa, is described in the glowing terms of a Hollywood "It" girl: "She had the appeal. That was just what we were looking for. Every one fell at Taioʻa's feet. She was like all screen stars, petted and spoiled and flattered by an adoring multitude."[28] Frances describes the searches and screen tests undertaken to find "the incidental characters to make up the typical Samoan family," continuing, "It was no easy task to find them. Strange as it may seem, types that photograph well are few. In these equatorial latitudes of lotus ease, thought has molded the faces not deeply, if at all, and in repose they become curiously empty" ("Behind the Scenes," 747). The process of choosing Samoan "types" continued apace: describing their search for a child star for the film, she notes, "Many of the Samoan children are not well built. They develop into splendid men and women, but as children they are not at all promising, perhaps because, after they have been weaned, they have a hard time in getting adjusted to a suitable diet. Peʻa was a perfect specimen, however, and every bit as worthy a representative of Samoan boyhood as Tom Sawyer or Penrod of the youth of America" ("Behind the Scenes," 752). The Flahertys clearly were less interested in representative images of Samoan peoples than they were in finding stock figures that could appeal to US audience expectations. Carrying on in true studio fashion, they renamed their young star Peʻa (flying fox) and eliminated references to his real name, Finauga (disputation).[29]

In addition to questions of fabrication, the issue of colonial complicity has dogged Flaherty's work. Rony situates *Nanook* amidst the colonial-era ethnographic spectacle: aligned to the circuslike atmosphere of late-nineteenth- and early-twentieth-century world's fairs and traveling shows that presented living peoples as ethnographic exhibits. Compounding these postcolonial debates is Flaherty's background as an explorer, mapmaker, and prospector—activities that have explicitly linked him to an imperialist project.[30] In his early career, Flaherty followed in the footsteps of his father, who worked with US Steel and introduced his son to the Canadian railroad builder and financier Sir William Mackenzie (whom Flaherty called "the Cecil Rhodes of Canada"), an encounter that marked a turning point in his life.[31] In *My Eskimo Friends* (1924), Flaherty recounts several expeditions into the Canadian north for Mackenzie, noting how, for his third major expedition in 1913, he decided to include a camera. In this sense, his filmmaking career was a direct outgrowth of geographical and commercial prospecting. Furthermore, *Nanook of the North* was sponsored by the French fur company Revillon Frères, and, as many have observed, a number of scenes not only represent the colonial-era fur industry as benign and friendly, but also provide product placements for Revillon (which was in staunch competition with Hudson's Bay Company at the time), especially the scene at the trading post, which presents the fur trade as a harmless diversion.[32] As early as 1926, Terry Ramsay's *A Million and One Nights* called *Nanook* "propaganda for Revillon Frères."[33]

Flaherty stated, "First I was an explorer, then I was an artist," a phrase repeated by Frances in interviews after her husband's death.[34] Certainly the mark of the imperial explorer inheres in many of Flaherty's films. *Nanook* conjures up the discovery of unknown worlds beyond the frontiers of civilization, while *Moana* recalls nostalgia for untouched primitive life amidst natural surroundings. The dominant cultural myths of pastoral nature, incisively anatomized by Raymond Williams in *The Country and the City,* inhere in *Moana,* though these myths are here projected onto an idealized primitive island perhaps most tantalizing for remaining pure, integrated, and at a distance: "the sea," *Moana*'s intertitles exclaim, "warm as the air and generous as the soil." For Corliss, mythic nostalgia manifested itself in Flaherty's desire to discover elemental truths about humanity and to "project them onto the mind screens of the rest of us, who may have forgotten them in our century-long rush toward catatonic computerism."[35] This will towards authenticating and narrating elemental truths did not always translate into accurate representations, and Flaherty had a tendency to project his personal ideologies onto the subjects of his films. Like *Nanook,* for example, *Moana* offers an artificial family molded on a combination of cultural "types" and bourgeois US ideals.

It is hardly possible, then, to view *Moana* primarily from the standpoint of the filmic world created within the film's duration, since an accumulation of extrafilmic information and commentary has effectively reconstructed what we see on the screen and what it means. Perhaps if we can put aside debates that have raged around Flaherty's cinematic constructions and begin to think of them along the lines of documentary fictions, then Flaherty's work can be viewed as both flawed and innovative: deeply indebted to discourses of fantastic savagery while also grounded in modernist desires to rescue holistic cultures and values. Films such as *Nanook* and *Moana* thus continue to raise questions about the uncomfortable marriage of ideology and aesthetics, primitivist nostalgia and the making of modern selves.

Culture Gardens

Flaherty's work forms part of what George Stocking has called the "ethnographic sensibility" of the 1920s and early 1930s: a growing individual and collective interest in producing more systematized and informed views of cultural difference than the travelogues and voyaging accounts of previous generations, an interest that nonetheless still lacked the more precise rules and scientific trappings of an emerging modern discipline of anthropology. As discussed in chapter 1, the 1920s was the beginning of the "classical" period of modern anthropology, which took an emerging concept of "culture" (as opposed to hierarchical conceptions of "civilization") as its focal issue and subject matter.[36] As Susan Hegeman notes, "Where 'civilization' invites comparisons of advancement with the 'savage' others, 'culture' allows for the possibility of a comparative operation in which one's own group's particular 'genius' may be understood in the context of those other people, irrespective of levels of 'advancement.'"[37] The ethnographic sensibility was shared by individuals from professions ranging from the purely creative to the academically trained, most of them interested in foregrounding the idea of culture as the framework determining human identities and social networks. An early and prominent visual manifestation of this movement was the monumental undertaking of Edward S. Curtis, whose twenty-volume photographic study ennobling "vanishing" American Indians, *The North American Indian,* was partly financed by his fanciful ethnographic film, *In the Land of the Headhunters* (1914), made among the Kwakiutl Indians. Essential to this quest for knowledge were those cultures that Edward Sapir called the "genuine" cultures of "less civilized" regions, which Sapir thought signified the idea of civilization in its purest form. Genuine cultures appear as truer representatives of "internal" and "harmonious" human interrelations,[38] and relations with the environment, than what could be viewed amidst—to quote Lynd and Lynd's influential 1929 study of "Middletown"—"the dust and clatter of [Middletown's] new industrialism." Hence the genuine culture promised a glimpse into humanity's rhythms apart from the mundane world where "people intently engaged day after day in some largely routinized, specialized occupation."[39]

The surprise popular success of *Nanook* was an indication of audiences eager to imagine and experience genuine culture, audiences seeking something more resonant than lighthearted travelogues and adventures. It also showed that the amateur ethnographer was not yet too seriously excluded by the increasing pressures on anthropological research to perform in the context of scientific discourses and methods—as suggested, for example, by Malinowski's detailed outlines of anthropological methods in *Argonauts of the Western Pacific*. As Stocking notes, "In the 1920s the mapping of the 'geography of culture' of cultural criticism overlapped that of cultural anthropology to an extent that we may not appreciate today, when the boundaries between academic anthropology and the outside world are more sharply imagined."[40] Though Flaherty never trained as an anthropologist (even his attempts at studying mineralogy at college level ended in failure), he nevertheless believed that his work did have ethnographic value. As he recalled of making *Nanook*, "I had planned to depict an ethnoligical [*sic*] film of life covering the various phases of their hunting, travel, domestic life, and religion in as much of a narrative form as is possible."[41] On this level, Flaherty projects a certain seriousness that surpasses the self-confessed ethnological limitations of travel accounts such as Frederick O'Brien's. As Jay Ruby notes, when Frances was in New York City in 1915, drumming up support for another Arctic expedition, she approached several prominent anthropologists, including Boas, the "foremost ethnologist and authority on the Eskimo of America."[42] Frances's meeting with Boas yielded no forthcoming support, but some years afterwards Boas is reported to have viewed *Nanook*. Writing to Will Hays, head of the Motion Picture Producers and Distributors of America (MPPDA), in 1933, Boas "suggested that it might be possible for anthropologists and filmmakers to make films collaboratively that would be both 'scientifically' useful and popular at the box office."[43] Ruby argues that there is little evidence that anthropologists were very interested in the ethnographic usefulness of Flaherty's films—hardly surprising considering that the self-image of cultural anthropology after the mid-1920s was of a discipline increasingly aligned to the sciences. This emergence of the discipline can be seen quite clearly in the Introduction to *Coming of Age in Samoa* (a study that few would now consider "hard science"), where Mead argues that the validity and verifiability of an "anthropological method" is the only option for those who "wish to conduct a human experiment but . . . lack the power either to construct the experimental conditions or to find controlled examples of those conditions."[44] It is likely that many anthropologists would have distanced themselves from Flaherty, who was already, by the 1930s and 1940s, a focus of debates about falsification.

Still, in the 1920s it would have been more difficult to draw clear divisions between cultural anthropology's emerging methods and Flaherty's work. Writing from Samoa in 1925 during her first experience of fieldwork, Mead describes inventing research methods for what would become the "human experiment" outlined in *Coming of Age in Samoa*, by using images from "a magazine story on Robert Flaherty's *Moana*."[45] Indeed, years later Mead would confess that her Samoan diorama in the Peoples of the Pacific Hall in the American Museum of Natural History, completed in 1972, was based on a scene from *Moana*.[46] Clearly, western conceptions of the South Pacific remained one-sided well into the twentieth century. To paraphrase Trinh T. Minh-ha, this was a process that revolved around us talking to us about them.[47] In the 1920s, these traveling myths were at home within both distinct disciplines and discursive modes, and traversing the spaces between disciplines and genres, between elite epistemological frameworks and popular consumption.

As Johannes Fabian observes, in Ernst Bloch's critique of Oswald Spengler's historical relativism, *Decline of the West* (translated into English in 1926), Bloch speaks of Spengler's tendency to construct "gardens of culture" out of historical material.[48] The phrase aptly describes the ethnographic sensibility of the 1920s US: Spengler's evolutionary models of "culture" and "civilization" had a significant impact on some of cultural anthropology's key figures.[49] Bloch suggests that, in Spengler's culture gardens, "quite artfully, historical relativism is here turned into something static; it is being caught in cultural monads, that is culture souls without windows, with no links among each other, yet full of mirrors facing inside."[50] It is this double gesture, at once erecting walls that create cultural monads and then placing oneself at the center—with a panoptic view inside an endlessly signifying and self-contained cultural discourse—that could be said to define the mastery of the ethnographer. In creating this centered, often heroic, figure, the ethnographic eye constructs an image of a stable "internal" subject position and of order and control (a control no doubt rapidly disappearing amidst the externalized and spurious cultures of the west).[51] As Haraway suggests, "Relativism is a way of being nowhere while claiming to be everywhere equally.... Relativism is the perfect mirror twin of totalization in the ideologies of objectivity; both deny the stakes in location, embodiment, and partial perspective; both make it impossible to see well."[52]

This panoptic illusion was literally rendered in 1920s and early 1930s ethnographic work such as Mead's. Mead often not just conjured up an "I was there" authority, but employed a rhetorical style that could produce a precise illusion of an absent presence in order to adopt an omniscient perspective. In *Growing Up in New Guinea* (1930), Mead writes,

> From a thatched house on piles, built in the center of the Manus [Titan] village of Peri [Pere], I learned the native language, the children's games, the intricacies of social organization, economic custom and religious belief and practice which formed the social framework within which the child grows up. In my large living room, on the wide verandas, on the tiny islet adjoining the houses, in the surrounding lagoon, the children played all day and I watched them, now from the midst of a play group, now from behind the concealment of thatched walls. I rode in their canoes, attended their feasts, watched in the house of mourning and sat severely still while the mediums conversed with the spirits of the dead. I observed the children when no grown-up people were present, and I watched their behaviour towards their parents. Within a social setting which I learned to know intimately enough not to offend against the hundreds of name tabus, I watched the Manus baby, the Manus child, the Manus adolescent.[53]

This rhythmic, repetitive passage is typical of Mead's authoritative style, where the speaking "I" and the observing eye mimics an infinitely repeated yet firmly centered subject, whose sole activity is a nearly mechanical process of watching and documenting. The ethnographic eye is a "participant observer": a detached, panoptic deity, both absent and present, a figure that reveals and conceals itself at will, sometimes openly participating, sometimes cloaking its purposes. And as Mead's consistently comparative approach to anthropology testified, these gardens of culture were investigated and created to examine not so much the "alien" cultures themselves as to throw light on the west's own vanishing sense of cultural fixity and stability.

Flaherty's methods intersected with anthropological practice in other ways as well, as reflected in his developing techniques of "shared ethnography," beginning with *Nanook,* where he screened rushes to his Inuit subjects, whom he relied upon for feedback. Flaherty employed Inuit assistants to hold cameras, work on sets, and perform the painstaking task of washing film for a minimum of twenty minutes in ice-cold water.[54] In Safune, Flaherty screened a number of films, including *Nanook,* which Frances reported "made little impression on [the Samoans]" since "they had no intellectual life and no imagination for anything outside their own placid islands."⁵⁵ (She belies this conclusion elsewhere, however, when she notes the excitement caused among the Samoans by screenings of Henrik Galeen and Paul Wegener's Expressionist fantasy *The Golem* [1920]).⁵⁶ The Flahertys were heavily reliant on so-called native informants, particularly on their "pure Samoan" interpreter, Fialelei, and were otherwise dependent on their two Samoan "boys" who worked as their assistants washing film in the cool water provided by a nearby cave ("Setting Up," 645, 647).

Flaherty's enlistment of native participation (usually as assistants) in making his films has often been praised as a forerunner of shared anthropology; indeed, if one thinks of knowledge making as an epistemological circle, then Flaherty's method was unusual in that the circle was not limited to the producers and consumers of western knowledge; it enlisted and encouraged "other" perspectives. But as Trinh has argued, shared ethnography can also imply more complex power relations, in which "shared" itself becomes a relative term. The shared ethnographic project can develop into a system in which, "to authenticate the work, it becomes therefore most important to prove or make evident how this Other has participated in the making of his/her own image.... Power therefore has to be shared...so that its effect may continue to circulate; but it will be shared only partly, with much caution, and on the condition that the share is *given*, not taken."⁵⁷ Though skeptical, such a critique does not give up on the value of the ethnographic approach or even deny a need to provide information about alternate cultural formations. It is, however, concerned with highlighting both a tradition of one-sidedness in the system of ethnographic "exchange" and a tendency on the part of western institutions to elide the power inequalities and colonial dependencies that have been preconditions for gathering cultural information. This version of native participation, coupled with a desire to maintain full control over the project, is suggested in Frances's description of the couple's translator, Fialelei, "granddaughter of the famous chief Seumanutafu...friend and counselor of Stevenson" ("Setting Up," 645), who is thanked in the film's opening credits. Frances writes, "She was a godsend, because the Chinaboy could not speak a word of English, only Samoan. Through her I translated all my household orders. She soon learned to take charge of the women in the village who did our laundry and the others who came to clean the house and do the daily work, and she developed into a most responsible housekeeper" ("Setting Up," 645). At one level Frances's independence from housework—even from managing the housework—reinforces her position as a writer and filmmaker and as her husband's colleague rather than "Mrs. Flaherty." But her professional independence is purchased on the back of her "native informant" Fialelei, and the ideals of ethnographic exchange dissipate into standard cultural hierarchies and presumptions.

Salvage

One of the main motivations behind the ethnographic sensibility, and what James Clifford has called culture collecting, was the prevailing notion of the fatal impact inherited from the nineteenth century.[58] As I've already suggested, discourses of the fatal impact provided western artists with a means to contemplate Polynesia as a beautiful yet troubling spectacle, a romanticized scene of passive (and in many versions, self-inflicted) destruction—what Stevenson called in the Marquesas a "widespread depression and acceptance of the national end."[59] Taking up this theme in the 1920s, those with ethnographic interests were engaging with a discourse that had shifted from aesthetic contemplation towards action: there were widespread calls to salvage whatever could be saved before the tragic end. Salvage served as an overarching metaphor for an anthropological practice that was beginning to require fieldwork as a mode of intervention—though this remained a defensive action, clearly, and one that posed no direct challenges to global colonial and commercial networks and that never fully interrogated the concept of the fatal impact itself. Perhaps the most visible US purveyor of salvage anthropology in the Pacific was Mead, who claimed that her anthropological career was directly inspired by the ethical implications of rescuing cultures. In a conversation in 1929 with her father, in which he predicted that the US had "ten years before the next war," Mead responded, "Then let's get our field notes written up as quickly as possible, so we can get back to the field to rescue as many cultures as we can before the war comes that may wipe them out altogether."[60] Mead attributed her zeal for cultural rescue to Boas, whom she portrayed in military fashion as a strategist with only a few graduate students to "deploy" on rescuing missions around the world, "much as if he were a general with only a handful of troops available to save the whole country."[61] Salvage ethnography was not only geared towards rescue, but, as the progeny of fatal impact discourse, permitted a fatalistic view of western progress and indigenous death. This binaristic view was easily translated into hierarchical concepts of "real," immediate (western) cultures versus metonymically preserved "other" cultures, which were figured as specimens: barely living museum artifacts saved from the bulldozers of history.

Clifford shows salvage ethnography as stemming from an anthropological generation that just preceded Mead's early career. A. L. Kroeber in Berkeley recorded the languages and lore of California's "disappearing" indigenous populations, while Malinowski suggested that the only future for the authentic Trobriand Islands culture was in the taxidermy of his texts: "just now... when men fully trained for the work have begun to travel into savage countries and study their inhabitants—these die away under our very eyes."[62] George Marcus has remarked on the urgency felt among ethnographers concerned with salvage, portraying themselves as heroic archivists working "before the deluge." The west may be advancing, and "signs of fundamental change are apparent, but the ethnographer is able to salvage a cultural state on the verge of transformation."[63] Mead, perhaps unintentionally, highlights the paradoxes of the salvage project when she notes that the very nation responsible for one of the most aggressive policies of territorial expansion was now responsibly planning to rescue cultural remnants of its victims: "Americans had been held firmly to the basic tasks of collecting masses of vanishing materials from the members of dying American Indian cultures, and it was in terms of the urgency of this salvage task that I decided to become an anthropologist."[64]

Clifford further identifies a more liminal, nostalgic impulse: that of preserving the authenticity—or one might say a "real sense"—of a culture rather than merely collecting the objects and descriptions themselves. The ethics of salvage are thus predicated on imagining what constituted the essence of a culture before the corruption of western influence. Each generation, Clifford suggests, thus imagines the pastoral purity of an era just left behind: "a 'good country' is perpetually ruined and lamented by each successive period, producing an unbroken chain of losses leading back ultimately to... Eden."[65] The South Pacific, the quintessential version of vanishing paradise, easily entered into this frame. Mead conjures up the urgency of saving "priceless and so-soon-to-vanish" Pacific cultures in *Growing Up in New Guinea,* where myths of prelapsarian return intersect with the urgency of rescue.[66] As Clifford suggests, anthropologists were inspired to rescue not only artifacts, but essences; indeed, Mead's frequently stated goal, which echoes the larger aims of cultural anthropology, was to distill and reproduce the internal logic of "whole" cultures in her work.[67] Perhaps rescuing Eden was possible after all.

As Clifford has argued, the ideology of salvage contributed to reinforcing the terms of west and nonwest in essential oppositions, rather than seeing the two in a relationship of fluid and dynamic exchange.[68] Moreover, one of the essential contradictions of salvage, and one that makes it seem a quintessentially modernist project, lies in the relation of the particular to the universal: that is, one can never really salvage wholes, only fragments. The very essence of salvage connotes ruins, leavings, and leftovers put to other uses—not the sort of cultural wholes that anthropologists such as Malinowski and Mead wished to represent in their work. Still, as many would argue, it would be wrong to deny that forms of recording and archiving have their uses: languages and cultural memories are fragile things, and have had a very real tendency to disappear.

Flaherty, while hardly a systematic collector, was interested in reconstructing authentic pictures of cultural life; he was also suspicious of the west's colonial influence and convinced of the reality of the fatal impact. The extent of his commitment to containing and preserving what he viewed as the disappearing purity of Polynesian cultures became fully clear when he attempted, in 1929, to implement a radical change in US government policy in the Pacific by calling for indigenous "preserves." While doing preproduction for what was to become *Tabu*, Flaherty worked on the idea in conjunction with James Norman Hall, Flaherty's drinking buddy and a longtime resident of Tahiti. In a passionate letter to the representative of the US consulate, Flaherty suggested that the "unexploited" island of Manu'a was the ideal site for such a cultural preserve.[69] Hall wrote at the same time, requesting that American Samoa be made a cultural "sanctuary" under the protection of the US government:

> Not the slightest attempt is made to preserve for them their indigenous life and culture which every enlightened visitor to the South Seas from the time of Wallis and Captain Cook down to the present, has thought so well worth preservation. ... Could not these islands, so small and unimportant commercially, be set aside for the benefit of their native inhabitants, and incidentally, for our own? Could not the Samoans be ... actively helped to throw off all influence alien to them ... in short, to live as Samoans, in the tradition and after the manner of their ancestors? ... It is a matter of concern in the same way that the preservation of bird life, of wild game, of great natural parks for the enjoyment and refreshment of mankind, is a matter of public concern.[70]

Flaherty's letter noted that "Mr. Hall, Mr. Murnau, Mr. Nordhoff, and myself" all believed the proposal to be a sound one. While egregious both as a concept and in its expression (with comparisons of native cultures to animal life), the proposal obviously attempts to speak in a language that government officials might comprehend; it also differs from more conventional ethnographic salvage techniques in suggesting a solution that includes the possibility of a living Samoan culture, though very much at the cost of its being in the world. Hall and Flaherty's proposal is a dream of a "real" and accessible culture out of time, the preservation of a people outside history, removed from the degenerating forces of global change. Although the US government appears to have taken little interest in the proposal, the intensity of the salvage impulse behind *Moana* becomes clearer.

Scopophilia and the Native Body

I want to turn now to an issue that more directly engages with *Moana* as a visual text: namely, the inscription of the "primitive" body and the filmmakers' fascination with recording—and indulging in—the spectacle of the human form. There is little question that the broad appeal and infinite reproducibility offered by motion picture technology opened the mythical South Seas to its widest audiences.[71] Certainly this was true in the US, where the rise of the motion picture business at the beginning of the twentieth century closely coincided with the closure of the frontier and the extension of US power in the Pacific region. Film has an indexical link to material reality, and many still accept it as superior to, and more immediate than, artistic impressions or written descriptions. As Gilberto Perez argues, photographs suggest both evidence and presence: "An imprint gives evidence of what has been; an image gives presence to what it depicts. A photograph gives evidence of what it depicts and gives presence to what has been. It is a documentary image as a painting can never be, not because it is necessarily more realistic than a painting but because it has a necessary material connection with reality."[72] The moving image was able to take this insubstantial yet palpable material connection a step further: it captured time, recording the dynamic, mobile landscapes of distant islands, dissecting the gestural nuances of the native body. The visceral immediacy of seeing "life itself" on the screen—as the *New York Times* suggested of *Nanook*—was the miracle of nonfiction cinema.

Yet the "indexical" image of Samoa that the Flahertys chose to represent was essentially reactionary: Samoan culture was far from untouched, and photographic records by Apia-based photographers such as Thomas Andrew had already, some decades before, worked to intervene in the myth of Samoa as a tourist paradise by producing images that reflected the political tensions and cultural shifts underlying Samoan colonialism and commerce.[73] The Flahertys opted instead for the well-worn cliché of the South Seas body free from the fetters of clothing, illness, or worry over material gain, a body divorced from mental preoccupations and modern pessimism. Frederick O'Brien distilled this modernist reinscription of untroubled, childlike corporeality in *White Shadows:* "Their bodies had not become a burden on the soul, but, light and strong and unrestrained, were part of it. They did not know that they had bodies; they only leaped, danced, flung themselves in and out of the sea, part of a large, happy, and harmonious universe" (166). This is a desexed body to be admired and desired, both an object of the gaze and a figure onto which audiences project an imagined, simpler subjectivity, a fetishism of an uncorrupted physique that disavows the spurious fragmentation of life in the mechanized west in favor of a simpler and more integrated physical universe. The geopolitical reality of the Pacific becomes a psychic screen projecting a fantasy of liberation—subverting inherited moral strictures, inventing lost figures of sexual innocence.

Moana, with its lush settings, Samoan actors chosen as best of type, and rich panchromatic textures, is a true exercise in scopophilia. Its peculiar focus on the body even caused one *New York Times* article to floridly describe Polynesians as a cult of narcissists and body worshippers: "Not any people in the world, ancient or modern, ranked human beauty higher in the list of life's gifts than did the people of these islands. In the star-scattered archipelagos of the Pacific tropics a dozen tawny races or breeds of superb physical endowment made their bodies wondrous temples for their free souls."[74] Similarly enthusiastic after seeing Flaherty's film in Paris in 1926, André Gide noted in his diary, "I have never seen anything more voluptuous."[75] This focus on the body further connects Flaherty to the preoccupations of anthropology, which, Rony notes, always had "a voracious appetite for the Primitive body" in its "authentic" state, the careful study of which, it was hoped, could ameliorate the artificial conditions of the urbanized western body.[76]

Moana appeals to scopophilic desires, but ethnographic scopophilia in the postcolonial context has become, justifiably, deeply embedded in a sense of guilt. Dissonance sets in when western viewers enraptured by exotic images recognize that, beautiful or not, they have been created through fundamental power inequalities and, frequently, abuses of colonial privilege. Indeed, as Bill Nichols, Christian Hansen, and Catherine Needham have collectively argued, the pleasures of visual ethnography might be seen as analogical to the more explicitly voyeuristic pleasures of pornography. Both ethnography and pornography, Nichols et al. argue, rely on techniques of distanciation, containment of excess, the illusion of empirical realism, and narrative realism created through expository means.[77] Most conventional pornography invents a "pornotopia" of the body for the scopophilic pleasure of the male spectator, while ethnography entraps native bodies in an "ethnotopia" of limitless observation to satisfy a western epistephilic hunger for anthropological data. While a suggestive comparison, it has been argued that this kind of analogical approach is potentially restrictive in its reading of both ethnography and pornography, since the critique of scopophilia ("pleasure in viewing") strives to bracket pleasure by offering a more or less unified model of modes of representation that are in fact quite varied. Still, a film such as *Moana* seems to exemplify an extensive history of intersections between ethnographic and pornographic ways of seeing, between scholarly epistephilia and popular scopophilia.

Moana is a stunning visual ode to the Samoan landscape and the Samoan body that encodes the interwoven sexual and racial discourses constructing Polynesia for the west in the 1920s. At times it overwhelmingly suggests an ethnographic sensibility; at others it veers towards the voyeurisms encouraged by pornography. At times the film aims to reconstruct Samoa as a concrete, historical world, taking advantage of the presumptions of documentary fidelity and offering captivating location photography and close-up ethnographic details that underscore an impression of what Nichols has called (in the context of *Louisiana Story*) documentary's "indexical fidelity" and "historical facticity."[78] At other times the film clearly appeals to structures of fantasy more closely aligned to fiction. *Moana* is not a homogeneous art object but a text imbued with the mobile meanings of the historical reality it represents, and its effects on audiences need to be considered as heterogeneous, differential, and historically situated. From here to the end of this chapter I want to raise several questions with regard to *Moana*'s differential impact on audiences, asking along the way: Whose visual pleasure was (or is) actually being catered to? Did the film address a primarily unified audience, or was its appeal more unpredictable? Perhaps as *Moana* weaves its exotic and erotic fabric, the text itself can be seen to gesture towards some of the competing perspectives and give-and-take entanglements that its dominant framing strives to contain. It is important, then, to look at the ways that popular ethnography such as *Moana* might have interacted with and encouraged the voyeurism and active looking of marginalized audiences (such as women, homosexuals, immigrants) even as it misrepresented the films' indigenous subjects. Moreover, it is worth considering where a film's constricted meanings might begin to crack under certain pressures—conscious or unconscious—exerted by the film's subjects themselves. After all, these were not the naïve natives without history constructed by the film's narrative and mise-en-scène. The contextual and close readings of *Moana* that follow are thus based on the supposition that colonial texts might generate semantic ambiguities, even while appearing manifestly hermetic and unified.

The Female Gaze

Auteurist readings of Flaherty's films have focused on the theme of masculine adventure, which encapsulates "universal" themes such as man against nature, the survival of the fittest, and the role of the patriarch in familial relations. While much about this general impression is accurate, it might be argued that the films cannot necessarily be reduced to these themes alone. Even from an auteurist perspective, *Moana* is a peculiar case in Flaherty's oeuvre, since it seems to minimize many of these universalizing motifs. The Flahertys were among the first to admit that there were fundamental thematic differences between *Nanook* and *Moana*, particularly with regard to a masculinist interest in a hero struggling against natural elements. It is worth considering whether this shift was signaled by the full-time participation of Frances. While *Nanook* seems very much the work of a dedicated professional explorer, made while Frances was at home with her children in a "placid Connecticut suburb,"[79] *Moana* was a collaboration between husband and wife, with brother David acting as assistant. Likewise, the major films that followed *Moana* without Frances—*Man of Aran, The Land,* and *Louisiana Story*—continued the struggle with nature themes developed in *Nanook*.

Flaherty's biographer Richard Griffith offers a suggestive portrait of Frances:

> Somewhere off to one side there was usually a motionless figure with a light meter in one hand and a camera in the other, silently snapping her own record of the scene. Frances Flaherty says her role in their work was that of Cassandra, continually snuffing out ideas by explaining their pitfalls and impracticalities to her enthusiastic husband. Flaherty put it just the other way round. He used to say that after the exciting evening discussions of the next day's work, came the cold light of morning in which all his beautiful ideas seemed crippled and dead. It was then that Frances stepped forward.[80]

Frances inhabits the edges of Flaherty's frame as well as the margins of his fame. Surprisingly little has been written concerning Frances's collaborations with her husband, perhaps because such an approach might disturb the mystique of the documentary auteur. Patricia Zimmerman notes that many even believed that the yearly Flaherty film seminars, established by Frances in 1955 (four years after Flaherty died), had been started by Robert. These legends "betray a masculinist, homogenizing deification of Flaherty the man as spawning an institution in his own likeness."[81]

Yet Frances's figure constantly changes depending on the angle of view. When Margaret Watson and Frederick O'Brien met the Flahertys in Sausalito a few days before they left for Tahiti, Watson observed,

> Mrs. F[laherty] very dignified, a bit austere and New Englandy. F[rederick] didn't like her he feels she exerts a repressive influence over her husband and would like to extend it to his friends. F[rederick] hates this quality in women. He told me that B[ob] F[laherty] was much of a pagan; even had children by an Esquimo woman. "He would not have done that" said F., "if he really cherished his wife."[82]

Perhaps Watson's comments reveal as much about O'Brien's attitudes towards outspoken women as they do about Frances's public persona; nonetheless, this hardly portrays the silent female figure off to the side, and instead begins to suggest the extent to which Frances's "stepping forward" was integral to *Moana*'s realization. Several years later at work on *Tabu*, this time without Frances, Flaherty would hold up *Moana* as their ideal collaborative project. Moments before his ship was to sail from San Francisco, Flaherty wrote to Frances,

> I want to work only with you—Fred [Murnau] is wonderful and all that but how more and more I loathe the contriving—this story business—when all these things are over *Moana* will shine as it has always shone. Life is going to be a failure if we don't do these things together—just ourselves.... More and more I realize how great *Moana* is. I shall never be happy until we do it again.[83]

Moana is the only one of Flaherty's three Pacific films that he completed. Frances's name appears in the opening credits with Flaherty's: the only film that the two ever jointly signed (though *Acoma*, in production in the Southwest several years later but never finished, was also meant to be coproduced). The opening titles further cite Robert and Frances as the "authors" of the film, while in her letters, journals, and *Asia* articles, Frances consistently employs the collective "we" to describe the makers of *Moana*—revealing perhaps not only the extent of her own contribution but also the professional public persona she wanted to project. But my interest in Frances stems less from a desire to recover agency and authorship in a collaborative project than to suggest ways of refiguring the critique of *Moana* and possibly to shift emphasis away from an image of masculinist directorial control that overshadows Flaherty's films. At the same time, Frances's being female does not automatically guarantee that she introduced a counterhegemonic perspective, nor does her presence necessarily suggest that *Moana* eludes the fundamental problems of colonial-era representation found in *Nanook*. As the anecdotes below suggest, as a desiring subject Frances practiced her own exclusions, her own fetishisms, and indeed, she kept her own camera on hand to frame and record the scene.

In her *Asia* articles, Frances contends that two breakthroughs occurred that would ultimately set *Moana* apart from other ethnographic travelogues such as Merian C. Cooper and Ernest B. Shoedsack's *Grass* (1925), and even from *Nanook*. The first came when Flaherty began to experiment loading his camera with panchromatic film stock, normally reserved for color and special effects, and known to be more unwieldy and fragile than the traditional orthochromatic black-and-white film. The panchromatic results "gave an extraordinary stereoscopic effect. The figures jumped right out of the screen" ("Setting Up," 711). As the *New York Times* noted in 1928, "Under panchromatic, you can get, without make-up, the difference between the delicate pink blush of a maiden, the blue of a 'black eye,' and the resplendent 'rum blossom' of a drunkard's nose."[84] Yet the discovery was not purely aesthetic. As Frances writes, the more palpable textures of panchromatic film were especially useful for Samoan skin tones, which in earlier experiments rendered in orthochromatic "came out black like negroes. There was nothing pleasant about them at all" (711). The lightening of Samoan skin through the use of panchromatic film—while conveniently following Hollywood hierarchies of skin color—could also be said to have helped affirm, in one compact gesture, a mythical vision of the cradle of the Caucasian race.

Frances's eagerness to make the case for *Moana*'s importance took on even stronger racial contours in earlier drafts of her article. In a letter to *Asia*'s editor in February 1925, she draws on the traditional tripartite division of Pacific peoples to differentiate shades of blackness from whiteness, with associated degrees of savagery and civility:

> You know, a Polynesian film has not been made—the so called 'South Seas' films have all been Melanesian, made in the New Hebrides of the cannibal blacks as hideous as they come, and then some if possible. The Polynesians are the Tahitians, the Marquesans, the Samoans. . . . You know they are exactly like us, these people. Color notwithstanding, they are as familiar to me as you, or anyone we know.[85]

Frances here perpetuates a belief in racial hierarchies informed by earlier ethnographic categories going back, unevenly, to Johann Forster, where climatic elements were seen to have engendered varying physical and temperamental characteristics. Though perhaps less "other" than Melanesians, the Samoans in Frances's view still remain "simple" because "the environment is perfect as it is. It has never demanded of the people the development of any intellectual life, any ingenuity, any adaptation to change." Continuing this line of thought, Frances describes their two Samoan film assistants, Samuelu and Imo, who washed and looked after the developed film, noting that the former is "six feet of physical perfection, carrying himself as only a Polynesian can, plastic strength in every line of his body.... His crisp black hair was arranged immaculately clear of his quite Caucasian brow" ("Setting Up," 710). Samoans are assigned to the top of the racial hierarchy, "like us" except with skin of "golden bronze,"[86] yet are clearly more interesting for their bodies than their minds: climate and cultural "simplicity," Frances claims, have rendered the race lethargic.

A second breakthrough involved the film's theme. More than a year had gone by in Safune, and Flaherty was still making tests and randomly shooting local scenes. The two had not established any narrative: "we were shaken by doubts ... much of [what they were seeing and filming] seemed trivial, unrelated, lacking in pattern."[87] Arguably, these digressions and uncertainties remain evident even in the finished film. The Flahertys had gone to Samoa with their "big idea" of filming another *Nanook of the North,* hoping to find another patriarchal hero dressed in native garb, like Nanook—a "sturdy, dignified chief and head of a family" ("Setting Up," 648)—combined with that indefinable sense of Hollywood "It": "Our idea was to find a man like Nanook, whose character would shine out of his face in the same way," Frances wrote; "which was the face that was going to be *the* face for the screen?" ("Setting Up," 710). As Frances further recalled,

> We were making a film for Hollywood, and we were very conscious of that fact. Bob had no illusions whatever as to what Paramount expected of him in the way of thrills and sensations for the box-office. All the way down on the steamer we talked about it, about the sea-monsters there doubtless were around those islands; doubtless the Samoans had encounters, fights for their lives, with them.[88]

But sightings of the giant octopi and sharks that they had read about in *White Shadows in the South Seas* never materialized, though while they searched for action the Flahertys were treated to extravagant feasts and dances, were seated through long conversations, were watching food being prepared. Thinking they knew their target Hollywood audience, the Flahertys "tortured themselves" with the question of how to create audience interest out of the everyday rhythms of Samoan life:

"We knew that our white compatriots could not see any film material in these people and their simple lives. The Samoans were neither interesting nor attractive to them. What did we think we could find in them?" ("Setting Up," 710).

After months of searching for the "necessary element of struggle" to create narrative tension, Frances finally argues, it was decided that through the visual power of panchromatic film stock, the recording of everyday activities could itself sustain a narrative. She notes that after all, "old primitive Polynesian life was changing"; it was "a fleeting ghost" that needed to be "caught for the American screen" ("Fa'a Samoa," 1085). The film would capture the image of that ghost, frozen and anaesthetized and remarkably beautiful: "the drama of our picture should lie in its sheer beauty," Frances wrote, "the beauty of *fa'a Samoa,* rendered by panchromatic film" ("Setting Up," 711). Frances offers an almost Pateresque transposition of drama and beauty in describing the film: beauty does not substitute for drama, but drama itself arises from the epiphany of experiencing a sublime aesthetic. This aesthetic largely arises from a focus on the gestures and textures of the body. William Murphy appropriately describes Flaherty's camera movements in *Moana* as "caressing,"[89] imbuing the apparatus with a tactility that intersects with western desires to reach out and touch an enigmatic native other. To render these bodies with technical precision and sensual fullness—this was a modern fantasy of envisioning and embalming the golden age. Thus the Flahertys filmed everyday Samoan life with a view to producing visual pleasure over narrative tension, ending up with one of the first full-length documentaries to focus primarily on domestic themes (though documentary shorts had taken domestic life as their subjects as early as the Lumières). This emphasis on day-to-day rhythms amounts to the visual celebration of domesticity in an exotic setting, which has led critics such as Richard Barsam, in noticeably gendered language, to go so far as to compare *Nanook's* "universal" poetic appeal to *Moana's* domestic blandness. Nanook's figure is thus "an Eskimo father, as well as a father for all mankind, and his concerns and instincts are those of all people." There is, however, "nothing universal" in *Moana,* who is merely a "benign" adolescent with a "passive, older" father.[90]

Moana's prepublicity took full advantage of stereotypes of civilized sophistication and elemental, primitive corporeality: west is to nonwest as mind is to body. Eden is a state of innocence and blissful ignorance:

These people have no thought-life, no intellect. They are back in the days before the Fall; they have not tasted of the Tree of Knowledge. . . . For us are the rough, rugged heights, the struggle, the slipping, the falling, the heartache, the pain, the vision, the hope, the faith, the despair; for them, a beautiful plain, sun-blessed, fertile, flower-spread, balm-kissed, a plain where life runs in and out and in and out like an unending repetition of a song. ("Fa'a Samoa," 1085)

Such confident ethnographic and authorial gestures, which strive to reduce the people among whom the Flahertys been living for over a year—and who Frances notes elsewhere had in many cases traveled abroad, gone to missionary schools, spoke English and drove cars ("Setting Up," 649)—into accessible caricatures, are nonetheless at other times equally matched by expressions of the fragility of Frances's autonomous, civilized selfhood. At times she seems on the verge of a crisis in the presence of an unknowable other: "I cannot tell you the words that he spoke, but—phrase by phrase ... measured, like music—simply, oh, so very simply, with dignity and beauty he spoke, in a manner that filled me with deep wonder, the deepest and truest things we know of comfort and love. 'Who are these people?' I cried within myself. 'Who are you! Who are you!'"[91] The phrases mirror Frances's frustration at never fully understanding the other she seeks to represent. The text shifts from a self-directed question ("Who are these people?"), which tacitly anticipates a possible response from her "inward" self, to an exclamation directed outside the self, towards an-other or interlocutor. But "Who are you!" is an ejaculation that doesn't invite or expect an exchange of information. Her unspeakable question, then (Who are you? Or, who do I imagine you are, therefore, who am I?), can only be asked inwardly, reflecting the broader gaps and ruptures between western subjectivity and the unnamable alterity of its imagined others.

Yet the instability Frances feels in desiring but being unable to bridge the gap of difference is partially erased by the presence of the camera, which reasserts safe distances collapsed by immersion in another culture. In certain respects the camera "solves" the dilemma of otherness, replacing sentimental affinity with scientific voyeurism:

Through the blur of that afternoon, dancing arms and dancing feet faded in and out, in and out of my benumbed consciousness. I could see ... a dreadful woman with elephantiasis; and another one seemingly half-witted, with half-witted grin, who insisted upon keeping herself exactly in the eye of Bob's camera. "Get her, get her!" I almost screamed at him. "Get her just like that and we'll go back to New York!" ("A Search for Animal and Sea Sequences," 957)

Frances's ambivalent longing to lose herself in the Polynesian context she inhabits beckons, seduces, and threatens excess, yet is finally contained by the camera's eye.

Her "benumbed consciousness" shifts to frenzied attention when life is framed by an imagined lens, and visions of an escape from paradise beckon with the cry of "get her."

It is perhaps significant that this moment of ambivalence arrives while she is watching a dance. Indeed, Frances notes, it was only after observing the spectacle of dance, day after day, that it was decided to abandon plans for an adventure film. Dance, with its linked emphases on cultural display, physicality, and naturalized performance, ultimately would serve as an organizing theme of the film. But it was not the "dreadful" dancing women with elephantiasis that would find their way into the finished film; *Moana*'s vision of *fa'a Samoa* would, rather, depend on idealized and often eroticized images of beauty. This fascination with the body's texture, physicality, and movement—both individual bodies and bodies in close, sometimes erotic, interaction—remains one of the film's most striking elements. Much of *Moana,* with its focus on disembodied hands and limbs performing traditional tasks, belies a scopic fascination that has its roots in nineteenth-century anthropology's obsession with medical taxonomies of the body. This fascination is envisioned in technical and aesthetic decisions made by Flaherty, such as the frequent use of medium close-up and close-up framing (which helps to mythify *Moana*'s stars) mixed with the use of long lenses and repositioning the portable Akeley camera at a distance so that it could fluidly and unintrusively follow its subjects' motions.

Moana

From its opening frames, *Moana* conjures a world out of time, like an epic poem. After opening with a quote from Stevenson, the first shot features a treetop against open sky; then the camera tilts down into dense vegetation, from which the central characters emerge, dressed in traditional lavalavas, bundling leaves. The image suggests first contact, but this is not a traditional encounter scene of white explorers greeted by canoes and islanders waving from the beach; indeed, there really is no encounter, no contact envisioned here at all. The presence of the white traveler is absent, replaced by the all-seeing but unseen ethnographic eye. *Moana* is creating a dream of a lost paradise, and its participants—apart from the gesture of "shared ethnography" in the opening credits thanking Fialelei—become frozen in a lopsided allochronic framework, denied a shared conception of contemporaneity and thus of shared human experience.

One viewer, L. D. Froelick, tried to reconstruct his experience of watching the opening shots:

FIGURE 4. "The lovers" in a scene from *Moana* (courtesy of the Academy of Motion Picture Arts and Sciences).

I came there, oddly enough, not by airplane, but, in fancy, through the sky. There is no such sky in our country—probably nowhere else on earth, save here in the South Pacific. . . . Puffs of white—clouds that swell and belly before your eyes, that carry children into enchanted lands of far-off castles—have always been there. . . . I saw a silver tree-top against this sky. My eyes followed down its trunk, and there was land—Safune, a village on the island of Savai'i, in British Samoa. Real land, real people.[92]

The term *papalagi* literally means "sky bursters" because when white people first sailed close to the islands it was believed that they had burst through the domes of heaven, rupturing the known universe.[93] *Moana*'s *papalagi* vision similarly arrives from the sky, moving from the panchromatic treetops to view the land and people below. For Froelick, the conscious movement from sky to land helps to imbue the film with the immediacy of "being there," of moving from outside to inside, finally encountering the technical replica of Safune as real land and real people. As noted above, viewers such as Froelick were well aware of *Moana*'s "reality effect," though few found that the blurring of fantasy and fact hindered (and some found that it enhanced) the film's pleasures. Robert Littell, writing in the *New Republic,* focused on the role of fantasy in the film but saw *Moana*'s obvious fictions as basically irrelevant to its overall impact:

> The Heaven in the South Seas which the white man thought he had discovered was not for him at all. It might have lasted for the native. In a very few corners some traces of it may still be found. Whether Mr. Flaherty found these corners intact, or whether he welded traces of the real thing with his imagination of it does not matter. His recreation remains a living reconstruction, not a tourist's grouping of local colors in an album.[94]

At the same time Grierson's review, even while employing the technical term "documentary," situated the film a little closer to fantasy than reality, placing it "on the idyllic shelf that includes all those poems which sing of the loveliness of sea and land and air."[95]

If *Moana* is a visual poem, it is a poem created through the formal techniques of epic distanciation, and might be placed on a continuum with the historical epics anatomized by Mikhail Bakhtin, which Bakhtin saw as constructed—using an appropriately visual reference—"in the zone of an absolute distanced image."[96] The epic creates an absolute and monochronic, as opposed to a contingent and relative, past. Implicit here also is the parallel relationship between Bakhtin's concept of writing and time and Fabian's notion of the allochronic discourse of anthropology, which targets the rhetoric of time in ethnographic texts. For Bakhtin, the epic past

> is both monochronic and valorized (hierarchical); it lacks any relativity, that is, any gradual, purely temporal progression that might connect it with the present. It is walled off absolutely from all subsequent times, and above all those times in which the singer and his listeners are located. This boundary, consequently, is immanent in the form of the epic itself and is felt and heard in its every word.[97]

The epic past for Bakhtin is "walled off" from the present not only because of the epic's discursive strategies, but because it constructs an authorial position also cut off from this past: the narrator is "a man speaking about a past that is to him inaccessible."[98] Closed off are the possibilities of open-endedness, indecision, and indeterminacy that for Bakhtin define the world of the present and the possibility of dialogic interaction. Similarly, *Moana* is a visual text that engages with both the ethnographic present and the walled-off poetic world of the epic. The narrator here is the absent, omniscient cinematic apparatus, fabricating a past that is otherwise inaccessible to both technology and the modern viewer.

Perhaps this is why the characters, both as "others" and as idealized projections of the viewing self, are seen searching at the beginning of the film. They are literally searching for Pe'a (Finauga), the film's impish child star, but the scene metaphorically suggests they are looking for something else too: perhaps the film will seek out our own origins, lost to time. Wandering the garden, they brush aside luxuriant leaves and call to one another. In a gesture not dissimilar to *Nanook*, near the film's beginning we are introduced to a close-knit family: Fa'angase; her intended husband, Moana (Ta'avale); Moana's brother Pe'a; their mother, Tu'ungaita; and father, Tafunga. Intertitles informationally describe some of the objects being gathered, such as taro root, while also noting that "Mother Tu'ungaita carries mulberry sticks." Though we don't know it yet, most of these objects will take on significance—some in unexpected ways—as subsequent scenes unfold. Laden with bundles, the group trails back down to the village, while another camera tilt, this time from the forest floor back to the top of the tree used in the opening shot, bookends the scene as a balanced and harmonious idyll.

Though Frances claimed that *Moana* was thematically and rhythmically a departure from adventure films such as *Nanook,* the next scene does suggest their lingering desires to discover action and thrills. An intertitle announces that the family is "on the trail of the jungle's one dangerous animal," and the scene opens with distant human figures emerging from the primeval forest, carrying a long pole. One of the film's central dramatic techniques—the withholding of narrative information—is introduced here. As established by the first camera tilt down from the trees, which leaves viewers in anticipation of what will be glimpsed below, several scenes show actions without explaining agency or purpose, revealing them only near the scene's end. Here several shots show Moana, Pe'a, and their father manipulating the ground cover and setting the pole in place before the key intertitle, "The Snare," makes it clear that a trap is being set, though the prey is still unknown. Flaherty's technique encourages the viewer's absorption into a complete process that lacks explanation. Thus viewers are obligated to make an effort along with the actors on the screen: we "solve" the dilemma or task nearly in real time. A momentary interlude introduces us to the first eroticized encounter between the film's two young stars, as Moana "finds a vine" and pours water into the mouth of Faʻangase. Perhaps anticipating the camera's gaze, she continues to hold her arms tightly across—thus concealing—her chest; Flaherty cuts to a sensuous close-up of her face. In an effort to grab fickle US audiences early on in the narrative, sex is intercut with violence: after a few establishing shots, we return to the forest, where an epic struggle is taking place with a wild pig, which lunges as Moana baits it with a stick. "More than one Safune man has been killed by tusks such as those," states a title card, with a close-up of the pig's head as it gasps for air. A later scene continues the focus on hunting and killing, this time of a turtle, which is drowned as it struggles in the water. On shore, Moana and Faʻangase caress and splash the animal, Faʻangase even propping it up and kissing the back of its head, its dying face displayed to the camera in an anthropomorphic fashion. Holes are drilled in the shell, ropes attached, and Peʻa drags it away along the beach.

After the pig hunt, the first of the aquatic segments depicts Moana and his father fishing, the clear water offering a glimpse of what is taking place below the surface. Here the limitations of Flaherty's Akeley camera are visible; very shortly afterwards, underwater scenes would become an essential component of the South Seas film. Flaherty credited the success of the sequence to panchromatic film: "the transparency of the water . . . was due of course to the color correction in the green coupled with a staging that enabled me to use the camera high above the water, so that the water itself acted as a reading glass before the camera." [99] Towards the end of the scene, Faʻangase appears once again, now waist deep in the water—a classical nymph with her breasts exposed to the camera, perhaps the shot most telling of *Moana*'s need to pander to clichéd South Seas fantasy and now-entrenched Hollywood expectations. [100]

Immediately following this documentation of work, struggle, and play is perhaps the most conventional ethnographic scene in the film, titled "Mother Tuʻungaita has a dress to make." The scene recalls the ethnographic interludes of nineteenth-century voyaging and travel accounts and of novels such as *Typee*: here the camera, mainly through tight close-ups of hands, tools, and the gathered mulberry bark mentioned in the opening scene, explains with very few intertitles the process of preparing cloth. The emerging tapa is really the scene's star, a fact further reinforced when we glimpse Faʻangase assisting later in the scene—now fully clothed and providing few voyeuristic distractions from the artisan and task at hand. A similar scene that continues the domestic theme later shows "Mother Tuʻungaita's cookhouse," and again features close-ups of disembodied hands performing traditional tasks. A series of balanced elements thus underlie and structure the film: orderly pairings and echoes of scenes that encode the worlds of masculine and feminine, action and relaxation, danger and domesticity, all enacted against a sublime landscape of mountains, forest, and sea.

Continuing the narrative strategy of withholding information, and free of authoritative intertitles, we observe Peʻa (whom Froelick calls the film's "Peter Pan")[101] testing the strength of a loop made of vine, while Moana sharpens a piece of wood nearby. Both shots offer medium close-ups, suggesting harmony and balance between the two brothers, until Flaherty cuts suddenly to a long shot of a palm tree that stretches out of the frame. Peʻa slowly climbs until he moves out of the top of the frame, the camera tilts up, and again Peʻa traverses the frame, until with another tilt we reach the dizzying heights of the tree. The scene visualizes another stock observation from South Seas travel writing and literature, and almost perfectly matches a passage from *Typee*, a book to which Flaherty often referred:

> Many children of the valley... take a broad and stout piece of bark, and secure either end of it to their ankles; so that when the feet thus confined are extended apart, a space of little more than twelve inches is left between them. This contrivance greatly facilitates the act of climbing. The band pressed against the tree, and closely embracing it, yields a pretty firm support.... In this way I have seen little children, scarcely five years of age, fearlessly climbing the slender pole of a young cocoa-nut tree, and while hanging perhaps fifty feet from the ground, receive the plaudits of their parents beneath, who clapped their hands, and encouraged them to mount still higher. What, thought I... would the nervous mothers of America and England say to a similar display of hardihood in any of their children? (Chap. 29, 214–215)

Barsam has linked the shot to the scopic limits of Flaherty's camera and his experiments with new lenses that "did not always result in shots that record all of the action necessary to convey their full meaning."[102] But the effect does appear intentional, since it is echoed by strategies of withholding information elsewhere in film, and the scene even concludes with a slightly comical flourish. Moana's task is revealed at the same time: several shots have to this point shown him working with his hands just offscreen; now we see in his hands a pointed stick being used to open coconuts. He shouts to Peʻa above, encouraging him, Flaherty perhaps offering comfort to the "nervous mothers of America and England."

After several spectacular shots of the sea and an inconclusive scene in which the characters head into breakers and capsize their canoe, we encounter another classic scene that follows an unexplained, complete process to its end, in which Pe'a, finding a "telltale bit of evidence—an empty coconut shell," searches the rocks for an as-yet-unidentified culprit. Pe'a starts a fire by rubbing sticks and waves the smoking brush near a rock crevice from which, after an enigmatic pause, he manages to pull out a robber crab, which is displayed, by now dead and cooked, to the camera. This technique became a mainstay of the observational documentary, which attempts to minimize disruptions (such as intertitles) to the filmed process unfolding in close to real time; and as suggested above, some critics read the technique as a collaborative strategy that engages the audience as detectives piecing together clues.[103] On the other hand, it also might be seen to place the viewer in a contradictory position: the audience is privileged to the clinical intimacy offered by the close-up yet denied information about the processes being enacted. While appearing to invite participation, these scenes might also reinscribe the mastery of the filmmaker, leaving viewers as displaced voyeurs: only the filmmaker is both in the know and on the scene.

The seventy-seven-minute version of *Moana* that had its official premiere in February 1926 at New York's Rialto Theater was misleadingly subtitled *The Love Life of a South Seas Siren*. That theatergoers would soon discover that the siren was actually male must have seemed irrelevant to Paramount executives hoping to draw in winter-weary audiences eager to witness the exotic landscapes and sensuous bodies of the South Seas. And though Fa'angase is exposed from the waist up throughout much of the film, supposedly one Paramount publicity woman complained at a preview that there were not enough bare breasts.[104] *Daily Variety* was a little more impressed by the film's voyeuristic possibilities, and though it thought the "mildly entertaining" film would play to "many walkouts" around the country, there remained "a sidelight," in that "the majority of the young women screened are nude to the waist, while the men are simply covered by a waist cloth."[105] In fact, physical contact between Moana and Fa'angase is either absent or encoded for most of the film; only in the final twenty minutes does a picture of the "loves" of the male "South Seas siren" emerge. With the intertitle "The end of the day for Fa'angase and Moana," the mood shifts: Fa'angase decorates Moana's body with flowers and ankle bangles made of shells, then massages him with oil. Though the intertitles instruct us that the ritual is about "anointing with perfumed oil, and an age old rite of the siva," the actors appear far less serious: both are laughing, and Fa'angase administers a playful slap to Moana's back. Throughout the scene, Flaherty's "caressing" lens focuses mainly on Moana's body, not Fa'angase's, and as Moana and his betrothed rise and begin to perform the *siva*, Moana fills the frame, the intertitles celebrating his skill, his "pride in beauty," and his "pride of strength."

Wondrous depictions of dance performances, and of the Samoan *siva* in particular, were conventions in literature on Polynesia. Henry Adams's travel companion in Samoa, John La Farge, waxed poetic on seeing the *siva,* noting that "no motion of a western dancer but would seem stiff beside such an ownership of the body." Adams sent photographs back to his friend John Hay in the US, further embellishing the scene: "you must supply for yourself the color, the movement, the play of muscle and feature, and the whole tropical atmosphere."[106] But whereas written accounts tended to emphasize the *siva*'s sensuality, fluidity, and grace, Flaherty's film provides an oddly circumscribed gaze: the camera is low to the ground, the framing uncomfortably tight as Moana dances with bent knees, nearly touching the ground, while Fa'angase dances standing upright, an afterthought almost entirely out of the frame. Barsam again attributes the oddness of Flaherty's framing to an awkward use of lenses,[107] but the effect makes no less an impact: the camera becomes a fixed and limited observer, occupying a point of view that approximates the low-angle perspective of Moana's watching family members, their encouraging glances intercut into the dance. But what kinds of looks are facilitated by Flaherty's choices? *Moana* clearly exceeds the epistemological limits and expectations

FIGURE 5. The *siva* (courtesy of the British Film Institute).

of ethnographic documentation; indeed, as *Daily Variety*'s salacious review has already shown, the film was hardly received as serious ethnography. This scene also differs from the scientific voyeurism underlying the tapa- and food-preparation sequences, as Ta'avale's performance is revealed as self-aware and intricately stylized. It is perhaps this four-minute scene of Ta'avale's *siva*, and not the artificially reproduced moments of native life shown elsewhere, that thus remains the most striking and interactive in the film. Yet also striking is Fa'angase, if only for her disappearance from the scene. Rony's reading of "ethnographic spectacle" is suggestive of this dynamic: the native woman tends to be mute, unnamed, as typified by the silent, staring Bride of Kong in the Skull Island sequence of *King Kong* (1933). There is "no other for the other" if the white woman is other to the white man, and the native man other to the white woman; the native woman is thus "excluded from the space of production."[108]

In her comments on shooting the scene, Frances cathects on, classicizes, and feminizes her male star, imbuing him albeit with a "powerful" femininity: "His powerful shoulders and legs are as smooth and graceful as a girl's. He has the torso of a Greek."[109] Steve Neale's suggestion that, traditionally, males who are sexually displayed on the screen are feminized in ways similar to women because Hollywood anticipates the ideal spectator as male, and thus has to stifle the homoerotic possibility of men looking at men, is suggestive but unsatisfactory in this case.[110] The Flahertys' excitement as they watched their panchromatic reproduction of the *siva* was that their Samoan stars "stood out from the screen bodily... living and beautiful and dramatic" ("Fa'a Samoa," 1088). Their delight in the scene (and realization of its value), along with Frances's perception of an eroticized, feminine Ta'avale might be seen to move in a number of directions at once: on the one hand it engages with a history of native male feminization by (mostly male) western observers in Polynesia; on the other it suggests the projected desires of modern female cinemagoers.[111] The "native" point-of-view framing and careful cinematic aesthetics of Moana's dance might be seen to provide a kind of safe zone that represses the problems of western voyeurism: allowing for the indulgence of interconnected libidinal desires, encouraging marginal heterosexual and homoerotic viewing pleasures under the cover of darkness in the theater.

Indeed, David Flaherty's journal entries on Ta'avale outdo even Frances's musings; he begins by imagining Ta'avale glimpsed through Frances's eyes: "Ta'avale is 18 years old. To Mrs. Flaherty belongs the credit for discovering him; but I am sure that she saw him first for that fawn-like bronze body of heroic proportions yet with the elasticity and the suppleness of a perfect animal.... We gasp at the marvelous grace and rhythm of his rippling arms and his esthetic hands, at the suppleness and god-like beauty of his body."[112] In explaining the inclusion of the *siva* in the film, David makes it unerringly clear that its purpose was to epitomize (and possibly problematize) the intense sexuality associated with the South Seas—both as an actual place, as a fantasy, and as a cinematic phenomenon:

> It is a beauty of which the outside world knows nothing, of which it perhaps dreams but never realizes. It is at once a confirmation and contradiction of the world's dream of the South Seas—to wit, a paradise of sex, of lovely women, a playground of voluptuousness. For that there's abundant sex interest in the dance of Ta'avale and Fa'anase [*sic*] cannot be denied. Ta'avale is the epitome of masculine appeal, quite as much I am sure as Valentino.[113]

Anxious to avoid being seen (and seeing himself) as a shameless voyeur, David convinces himself that the appeal of the scene is "purely aesthetic—animated masterpieces of a great sculptor"—and softens his own self-proclaimed sexual desires with a final appeal to art over baser instincts. Of all *Moana*'s scenes, this one perhaps most clearly attests to Frances's role as creative force, while also confirming an insistent homoeroticism implied in Robert Flaherty's career-long preoccupation with masculine bodies and behaviors.

Though the film unfolds in an episodic and seemingly aimless manner that runs counter to Hollywood expectations, intertitles inform us that what we have been seeing is in fact leading to a climax: Moana's ritual *tatau*. The scene was carefully prearranged: *tatau*ing had been legally prohibited and long discouraged by missionaries, and it is unlikely that Ta'avale would have undergone the process were it not for the Flahertys' urging.[114] Though suggestive to some of sado-masochism on Flaherty's part (Barsam calls the *tatau*ing a "physical disfigurement" that must have made it more difficult for Ta'avale in his "inevitable absorption into the Westernized culture"[115]) Samoans did not, as Meleisea points out, always readily conform to Calvinist prohibitions and doctrines; it would be reasonable to accept Rotha's claim that Ta'avale was ultimately "proud" of the results.[116] Polynesian tattooing had long fascinated, mystified, and alarmed western travelers: for missionaries the tattoo was emblematic of savagery; for figures ranging from beachcombers to anthropologists, tattoos promised access to that other world across the beach. Alfred Gell's comparative work on Polynesian tattooing, while justifiably cautious of pan-Polynesian reductivism, aims to dispel tattooing's more general associations in the west with degeneracy, criminality, and barbarism (as argued famously by Lombroso) and rather to consider the tattoo in terms of what Marquesans call *pahu tiki:* "wrapping in images." Critics such as Albert Wendt have updated such assertions, noting continuities rather than disruptions to Samoan *tatau*ing—the "highest form of clothing"—highlighting its ongoing cultural and aesthetic currency in the context of the "postcolonial body."[117]

As much as Moana's *tatau* was orchestrated by and for *papalagi*, critics who have derided the scene for its sadism restrict the multiple meanings generated not only by the filming of the act but by Moana's *tatau* itself, and might even be problematically reinscribing past missionary cries of barbarism. Gell suggests that tattooing might be seen as a form of "character armor" that both defends the social person (an apotropaic "second skin") and reconstitutes that person; it is the construction not just of a design on the skin but of a kind of new-grown body as a whole.[118] In this light Moana's *tatau* is significant not just in the terms encouraged by the film—a sign of Moana's journey away from youth, the pain indicative of the painful transition into manhood—but as a movement towards a new kind of social self, differentiated from but also intimately linked to the social network. On this level the Flahertys' renaming of Finauga as Pe'a, whether intentional or fortuitous, is interesting: Moana's *pe'a* (the whole *tatau*, but especially the back part, which is the focus of the film's scene) forms a bodily and metaphorical link to his fictional "brother," mimicking and at the same time transforming the film's eurocentric familial inventions. The *pe'a* might also incorporate deeper connections to Samoan mythology located specifically in Savai'i. Gell speculates on the connections between the two meanings of *pe'a*—"flying fox" and "*tatau*"—and recalls the legend of the warrior goddess Nafanua, who is closely associated with Falealupo in the northwestern reaches of Savai'i (Safune is roughly forty-five kilometers east of Falealupo). Stranded on an inhospitable island, Nafanua was saved by flying foxes, and the flying fox has been figured as a protector, a savior; in short, it is a "very exalted animal indeed."[119] Pe'a's name, projected and made visible in the *tatau*, might thus complicate the visible, overlapping relations between older and younger kin, protector and protected.

Yet the scene also intersects with *papalagi* fantasy: viewing the tattooed body can suggest, in certain western terms, examining an unclothed body. Historically, as suggested earlier of Joseph Banks's witnessing of nudity during what he called a Tahitian "ceremony," possible confusion about the displays of tattooing versus displays of nudity accompanied the projection of fantasy and the sexualization of Polynesians. Along similar lines, Lee Wallace suggests that the tattoo's hypervisibility facilitated a homoerotic gaze at the native male body.[120] *Moana* further presents the *tatau* scene as a ritual seen through a constructed native (participant-informer) point of view, therefore conferring a self-ethnographic status that helps to disguise any erotic connotations. Gaylyn Studlar's analysis of the specular function of violence and the unveiled male body in mainstream cinema of the 1920s suggests yet another dimension to this: she suggests in the case of John Barrymore's romantic melodramas that the male body "serves as a visual vehicle through which the order of 'feminine' love is constructed from the moral disorder of 'masculine' sexual desire."[121] Ritual scenes of violence thus can serve a "higher" purpose than that of the spectator's sexual arousal: the spectacle of male suffering (usually for the woman he loves) offers a free view of the unclothed male body, yet also reaffirms the transcendent values of an enduring heterosexual love. In related instances, violence to the male body can serve as a "cover" for the desiring female gaze, allowing the woman to "quietly violate the taboo against women scrutinizing, objectifying, and therefore threatening to commodify men."[122] We might note this pattern as Moana undergoes his trial: Fa'angase devotedly stands over him, sometimes dabbing his wounds with a bloody cloth as his face registers pain. Ultimately, however, it would be reductive to read the scene as just another case of western sadism and voyeurism. The *pe'a* revealed at the end of Moana's ordeal may encompass the visual markers of community, the connection of the parts to the whole, the individual to the collective. While Flaherty's vision is essentially ahistorical and denies the viewer access to the complex political and hierarchical dynamics connected to the *tatau* in Samoa, it does encourage the partial understanding of curious *papalagi* onlookers and the desire to find out more.

Viewings of *Moana*—which captures and "imprisons," according to Grierson's review, the body of the native—continue to raise questions about the cultural, sexual, and racial fetishization of Polynesia. The meanings signified in the film fragment, open to multiple interpretations, continually shift as they reemerge from the past and are recontextualized and renewed by multiple subject positions. But one thing remains clear: *Moana* will probably never escape the critique of reproducing the native body for the pleasure of western viewers, though the film's palpable homoeroticism and its address to the female gaze suggest the potential range of its effects. In texts such as these, where modernity and coloniality converge, the disparities between the emerging gazes of postmodern heterogeneity and postcolonial liberation begin to reveal themselves: *Moana* seems to simultaneously engage, implicate, and liberate those others rendered invisible within once-monolithic conceptions of the "western observer."

⌐

PARAMOUNT DEMANDED extensive cuts to Flaherty's first version (Hugh Gray states the studio "hacked it to pieces" and destroyed the negatives), after which *Moana* faced an uphill battle towards general release.[123] Paramount decided the film was not marketable, but finally agreed to do screenings in six of the "hardest boiled" towns on its test list.[124] Its initial box-office performance offers a few clues to its actual appeal: after a savvy letter-writing campaign to magazines and lecture societies spearheaded by Flaherty and the National Board of Review, the film opened successfully in Jacksonville, Florida; Austin, Texas; Lincoln, Nebraska; and Poughkeepsie, New York; though it failed in Pueblo, Colorado. The general pattern, established at the Imperial Theater in Asheville, North Carolina, was of a strong opening (in the first three days at the Imperial it made $1,857.10, a house record), quickly followed by diminishing box-office returns. As the manager of a theater in Lincoln put it, "The picture did real well considering how much the biggest part of the audience disliked it. Receipts on the picture daily were bigger than anything that we had played outside the *Ten Commandments*. I feel like the attendance came more for curiosity than for the real educational value of the picture."[125] The film's apparently serious nature could not measure up to the curiosity value of the Polynesian spectacle: "Most come to the theater to be entertained and amused rather than educated and enlightened," complained the manager at the Imperial.[126] At a preview in Mamaroneck the film was shown, according to the manager, to "a large foreign element including many Italians. It is a highly demonstrative audience, and will follow the most simple western with breathless interest, and will horseplay any picture which is above its mentality." Because of the "exceedingly hot" evening and the "exceedingly trying" conditions inside the theater, the manager feared the audience would be restless, and that the "rougher element would audibly make remarks at the nudity of the girl." But the manager found the results were "quite the contrary. . . . The entire audience remained engrossed throughout the picture, and there was not one single instance evident of the picture being received objectionably."[127]

Many reviewers were also positive. Robert Sherwood in *McCall's* (a magazine aimed at women) called it "film of the month" in June 1926, and though it was banned by the censor in Toronto for indecency, it had a relatively successful critical reception. At the end of 1926 *Moana* appeared on the *New York Sun*'s "Ten Best Films" list at number 7.[128] But perhaps one of the most incisive reviews came not from US newspapers, but in a letter to David Flaherty from a missionary in Samoa, who was less than positive, arguing that the film had failed to capture the textures and rhythms of Samoan life. The film first screened in Apia on 17 May 1926, with the governor-general of New Zealand present and the house completely packed. Though it was obviously commercially successful in colonial Apia, David's missionary friend found the film disappointing; it was essentially artificial, and he found himself hurried along by abrupt editing and rapid scene transitions:

I did feel as though I was rushed along from scene to scene with a bewildering activity and knowing the Samoans so well and their eternal patience and calmness about things, [it] somewhat disturbed my composure. I could not get down to the film for it would not get down to me. As soon as I sat back and wanted to see a scene through, it was off to something else.[129]

There were other letters from Samoa: several members of *Moana*'s cast and supporting crew continued to write to the Flahertys. Ta'avale wrote in 1925, just a few months before audiences around the US would begin purchasing tickets to watch his *siva*. He makes a subtle but decisive point about his impoverished—both economically and emotionally—state after the filming was completed:

> My heart is broken when I think of you all, and when I look at the house you lived in I cry in my heart. I never get any rest because I am thinking of you and your love for me. May good luck follow your family. You were very kind to me on the day you went away. I am poor, I have nothing, but from my poverty I send you my love. Please send me a picture of myself. Are you coming back to Samoa or not? Is it well with our picture? I have no more works, only love, to send to you all. I send you my love for your kindness to me. I hope I get a picture of myself.[130]

Though Ta'avale hints that he might be expecting something more in return for his work, he asks only for a picture of himself (twice), a token of his flirtation with stardom. As Frances noted in *Asia*, Flaherty was nicknamed "The Millionaire" when he arrived in Safune with his Paramount expense account, and the Flahertys, she claims, were charged exorbitant prices for services while in Samoa: "When the villagers did bring food to sell, it was at prices that would be ridiculous in a New York market" ("Setting Up House," 644). It is probably just as well that the Samoans had some economic forethought on the production site since very little Paramount money seems to have found its way back to Samoa once the shooting ended. A little over a week after Ta'avale wrote his letter, Tu'ungaita offered a similar sentiment: "I write you in my poverty; I cannot express my feelings."[131]

As *Moana* slipped into legend and obscurity in the coming decades, a few people attempted to revive the film and even to retrace its forgotten cast members. In 1954, Nancy Phelan, a visual aid officer working for the South Pacific Commission, brought the film to (Eastern) Samoa, showing it on Tituila, where she noted that the audience "laughed at the Samoan words on the screen, and at the most ordinary scenes, such as pulling up taro." She, perhaps in error, concludes that the laughter is a form of self-consciousness, "mixed with surprise at seeing Samoans in a film." After the screening, an "older man" asked for the film to be shown again for the children, since it "showed so many things *fa'a Samoa* that are no longer seen; they wanted their children to see Samoan life as it was and as it should be." No doubt Flaherty would have delighted in this reaction: his highly wrought image of cultural order and nostalgia for the past offered both universal appeal and came full circle to Samoa, showing the Samoans how life should be lived.

When Phelan seeks out the film's two leads—both living and working in Apia—the nostalgic appeal of Flaherty's idealized images to a post–World War II Samoa becomes clearer. Phelan finds that while Fa'angase has become "very fat but very beautiful" and is working "making tea for the Gold Star taxi drivers," Ta'avale has been working years in the Apia shipyards:

> I had rather expected to find him fat and handsome like Fa'agase, but he is quite small, rather shrunken and lined. I had to look at him several times before I could recognize the features of the young Moana. I asked him if he still danced the *siva*, but he said he was now too old [he would have been in his late forties]. He told me that the older people in the film were dead but that the little boy Pe'a still lives in Safune.[132]

Finauga (Pe'a) continued to live in Safune in the coming decades and was encountered there by a German camera crew in 1996–1997, aged eighty-four. He briefly appears in "Samoa: All You Can Eat," an episode of Axel Engstfeld's *Second Glance* (1999), which retraces Flaherty's steps in Samoa, Ireland, and the US Midwest. Finauga is shown watching television, reminiscing about the day Frances Flaherty "discovered" him while he was collecting cigarette butts with his friends near her house. "We always had to smile, smile, smile," he recalls, looking at photographs from the *Moana* shoot, "even once as we almost drowned in the surf—I came up for air and smiled. They kept telling us that the movie wouldn't work if we didn't smile."

4 The Front and Back of Paradise
W. S. Van Dyke and MGM in Tahiti

> Life is not real. It is an illusion, a screen upon which each one writes
> the reactions upon himself of his sensory knowledge. The individual
> is the moving camera, and what he calls life is his projection of the
> panorama about him—not more actual than the figures and storms
> upon the cinema screen. In this book I have put the film that passed
> through my mind in wild places, and among natural people.
> —Frederick O'Brien, *Atolls of the Sun*

As suggested in chapter 2, Frederick O'Brien's *White Shadows in the South Seas* presented US audiences a largely critical account of imperialist hegemony in the South Pacific that consolidated and expanded on the skeptical perspectives of earlier works, notably *Typee*. When it finally debuted nearly ten years later, MGM's screen adaptation retained remnants of O'Brien's anticolonial sentiments—even if, at the same time, it clearly had transformed a work of "factual" reminiscence into pure Hollywood fantasy. The film quickly earned critical accolades, the surrealist Ado Kyrou calling it "one of the most beautiful poems about love we have been given to see . . . a miracle that plunges us into total wonder."[1] Taking up a more explicitly political position, French critic Hervé Dumont argued that the film reflected the "courage" of its director, W. S. Van Dyke, in the face of the "most reactionary figures in the film industry." Dumont recognized that the film might exploit an "old American myth of lost innocence," but at the same time, Van Dyke "denounces the white scourge with an unaccustomed force, dealing with colonial exploitation and racism."[2] But it should not be thought that everyone has been kind to *White Shadows*: André Bazin referred to the film as "instant exoticism," while recent critics have seen it as a primitivist display of taxidermy, fueled by colonial guilt.[3]

Indeed, this cinematic "miracle" and the man who became the primary directorial force behind it, Van Dyke, seen together produce a more complex psychological and social image of US attitudes towards its neighbors in the Pacific than a cursory viewing of the film might suggest. As this chapter will show, even an auteur-inflected perspective such as Dumont's can take on new shades of meaning when new contextual information comes to light. In this case I'm referring to the discovery, in an attic trunk of a Los Angeles home in the 1990s, of Van Dyke's personal journal, in which he obsessively wrote daily entries while shooting the film on location in Tahiti.[4] Van Dyke's journal touches on far more than the technical and practical aspects of mounting the complicated on-location shoot: it also brings to light a more complex and self-contradictory view of the director than has previously been seen. Indeed, Van Dyke's journal can be seen to unravel the presumption that MGM's *White Shadows* is fundamentally a diatribe against colonial exploitation—at least not in the straightforward sense that critics such as Dumont have tended to read it.

My intention is to place the film in its broader contexts, a process that, inevitably, can expose certain ideological contradictions and historical discontinuities. If this was true of *Moana*'s documentary fictionalizations it is also true of mainstream Hollywood films' more consistent (and well-funded) formal coherence, which, as Jean-Louis Comolli and Jean Narboni have suggested, can reveal under close critical interrogation an ideological text "riddled with cracks."[5] This chapter thus considers *White Shadows in the South Seas* partly as popular entertainment and partly as a nexus of intersecting cultural desires (escape from modern corruption and degeneration, the virgin paradise, the South Seas maiden) and fears (of cultural, racial, and sexual difference, of losing the self in the process of going native), and looks at its sequel, *The Pagan* (1929, also directed by Van Dyke) for the ways it both perpetuates and complicates these notions. Both films project the ambivalence at the heart of conceiving otherness and speak at least as much to US attitudes and beliefs regarding its own emerging cultural history and collective identity as they do to the question of representing the west's others.

Indelible Tattoos

As early as 1922, O'Brien began circulating a scenario for a film version of *White Shadows*. He wrote to Charmian London expressing his anticipation in 1922: "Hearst has the scenario of *White Shadows,* the play, to see whether he wants it for the movies, or something else."[6] A short time later he is already beginning to sound exasperated: "I spent two days at Hollywood last week; horrible days / They want the *Calm One* [the play of *White Shadows*] for William Russell, a fathead."[7] Five years later, in 1927, the idea for the film still was being shifted back and forth among various moneymen in Hollywood; that same year, O'Brien submitted a detailed screen concept to MGM. In this version, he decided to base his treatment not on *White Shadows* itself, but on a "folktale" recounted in his third book, *Atolls of the Sun,* which had been far less popular than its predecessors. The tale contains faint echoes of Edward Robarts's or James Wilson's experiences as beachcombers, particularly in relation to Marquesan warrior culture. But chiefly it reflects O'Brien's fascination with the still-suppressed art of tattooing, which he sees as a remarkable yet paradoxical art form: on the one hand part of a living, ongoing process passed down through generations, on the other, an ephemeral art object drawn on the body itself, which goes with its possessor into the grave.[8]

The metaphorical significance of tattooing is stressed in both versions of the tale, and with it ideas of time, change, and decay; of the layering and juxtaposition of stories and images; and of the transformation of the signifying power of skin itself. This is suggested when O'Brien grafts a Marquesan storyteller into the book's narrative: an acclaimed tattoo artist called Puhi Enata, who tells of a white man from a privileged background who finds himself in the Marquesas, suddenly without any social position or public respect. He falls passionately in love with Titihuti, the "maddening, matchless" daughter of a chief. With her wild dancing and fantastically tattooed legs, Titihuti embodies the allure of the tropics—femininized, intensely erotic, uncontrollable—that gives rise to masculine desires for possession and even violent conquest. To win her over, the white man (who is specified as "American" in O'Brien's screen version) demands to be tattooed, to become "a man among men in the Marquesas."[9] This desire to embody the perceived masculine attributes of a Marquesan might suggest the appeal of an idealized primitive sexuality just at a moment when the US was witnessing fixed assumptions of masculinity and femininity thrown into flux and uncertainty. In 1927, Will Durant wrote in "The Modern Woman" of the "turbulent transition which has come upon all our institutions." The social upheaval of emancipation had "made men effeminate and women masculine; like occupations, like surroundings, and like stimuli [have] fashioned the two sexes almost into one."[10] In O'Brien's / Puhi Enata's tale, the westerner's attempt to reattain a masculine essence is only partially successful: after undergoing the arduous and painful tattooing process, the candlenut marks across his face stand out black on his white skin, instead of "blue as the deep waters of the sea."[11] He is called Tohiki for his intimidating appearance, and becomes a fierce warrior. Still, Titihuti, in the tradition of one version of the Polynesian maiden as a flirtatious femme fatale, refuses to accept him.

The protagonist is tormented and alone, but fate intervenes with a letter announcing that his father has died, leaving him with a large sum of money and family responsibilities at home. O'Brien's screen version sets the scene:

Many, many hours he...looks at his face in the water, for he knows that he can never return to America and to his own folks with those stripes of terror on his face. You must remember that he is blond, with yellow or brown hair, and that he has white skin and that those marks of the candlenut ink, which are blue on the tawny skin of the Marquesan, are black as sepia on the fair-skinned man. He becomes horrible to himself—repellent, and he meditates suicide.[12]

The American undergoes a rare ritual to remove the tattoos, requiring the literal etching of unrealized gender and racial desires upon his skin: retracing "the milk of a woman" into the crevices of the black marks. The treatment is successful, and he prepares to return to America. Yet in moments of passion, the tattoos return, now burning bright red instead of black against the whiteness of his face. The indelible markings have been interiorized, and are now likened to disfigurement and disease: "a leper's sign upon his brow."[13] The tattoo becomes a liminal sign of abjection both suppressed and desired, threatening to unmask alterity. For Gell, the tattoo in Polynesian societies can be seen as a form of body armor or protective clothing, but he stresses too its liminal and double nature: constituted both as design on the surface of the body and ink fused with and beneath the skin, the tattoo suggest the external applied and absorbed into the interior. It is "an inside of an outside and an outside of an inside": an opening of the body on to multiple selves and social and spiritual meanings.[14] In effect, O'Brien's / Puhi Enata's tale suggests the hazards of inserting the body into this complex web of meanings as an outsider, while more generally allegorizing the dangers of crossing the imaginary frontier between the west and its others. At the same time the tale might offer a glimpse of O'Brien's own unstable sense of cultural identity as a longtime global wanderer.

O'Brien's film treatment of the tale foregrounds some of the hallmarks of earlier fictional South Sea island films such as *Aloha Oe* (1915), *Hidden Pearls* (1918), and *The Shark Master* (1921), which betray an intense desire to become immersed in a primitive world that promises to restore simpler, more stable categories for positive identification, perceived as under attack in the west.[15] Yet the narrative also suggests coexisting fears of being indelibly marked by falling too deeply into the primal, sensual power of the cultural other. It is easier, perhaps, simply to stay at home, resigned to the superficial and commodified boundaries of the civilized. Even paradise is "out there," and can destroy the wanderer's ability to return to the comforts and bourgeois values of home. Sigmund Freud's *Civilization and Its Discontents* (1930) suggests a similar relationship: the community—or in this case, "civilization"—"assumes no other form than that of the family." If the child (either of the family or the community) wishes the father killed (either the "actual" father or that of the patriarchal family of "civilization"), then the scars of ambivalence and alterity will remain throughout life because of the rebellious individual's sublimated and displaced guilt.[16] In the tattooing tale, the young man quite literally wears the physical marks of his rebelliousness and guilt. He has attempted to obliterate the governing power and law of civilization by severing all ties to the west. Similarly, his family affiliations have been abandoned: his father, already psychically dead, passes away during his absence. It is too late to restore the integrity of these lost affiliations: any hopes for return are shattered by the ingrained guilt of past transgressions.

In the screenplay version, a disturbing pattern arises from the American's relationship to sexuality and the feminine, even after he returns home: his repressed tattoos reappear in full force on the night of his wedding. *Atolls of the Sun*'s tale, on the other hand, offers an understated humor more typical of O'Brien's travel narratives: the white man returns to "his own island," and simply tries to prevent detection by always remaining calm (leading to one of the working titles, "The Calm One").[17] Both versions raise themes and tensions that would find their way into the film, and both resonate with the history of Polynesian textualization, particularly ideas of imagined cross-cultural contact, the desire to escape and "go native," masculine erotic projections, and the impossible longing for a return to precontact life.[18] O'Brien's ambitious scenario was, in the end, rejected by MGM.

Staging the Exotic

On 3 August 1928, W. S. "Woody" Van Dyke's film version (from Ray Doyle's and Jack Cunningham's scenarios) of what the credits call O'Brien's "world famous" travel account premiered amidst the orientalist splendor of Grauman's Chinese Theater in Hollywood. The evening offered a primitivist extravaganza. Patrons received an elaborate program, designed as "an exact reproduction of an original tapa cloth pattern as made by the South Sea Island natives from the bark fibre of cocoanut palms," which promised indulgence in an exotic spectacle. The film was preceded by Sid Grauman's live Prologue, "The Tropics," which began with "special atmospheric music," followed by Kenneth Olds, "most famous of all male Hawaiian dancers," Samoan chieftains, and native dancers and instrumentalists headed by the "celebrated" Prince Lei Lani.[19] A true inheritor of the late-nineteenth-century marriage of anthropology and photography, the film's premiere featured a strange mix of primitivism and technophilia: this "torrid romance of the tropics" was also MGM's first sound picture. The sound effects were largely limited to bird calls and native wailing incorporated into the musical score, along with a postsynchronized—and now famous—"hello" uttered by Monte Blue in the middle of the film. The premier also included a demonstration of synchronized sound in the form of a filmed introduction presented by Van Dyke, in which he recounted the trials of shooting the film. D. W. Griffith flew in from New York to address the audience after the screening. In subsequent months the film would become a critical and popular success, easily earning back its unusually high costs and entering the record books as the film that rescued MGM from the brink of financial collapse.[20]

The rich images of the South Seas clearly satisfied the scopic demands of the (chiefly) silent cinema: Clyde De Vinna's cinematography would win him an Academy Award, while Floyd Crosby, who served as assistant on the film, would go on to win two years later for *Tabu.* As Raymond F. Betts suggests, "Just as the Western film embraced space, the one set in the South Seas captured light."[21] Many reviews praised the film's superb camerawork. *Daily Variety* noted, "The panchromatic work in this feature is outstanding. It's so good it very likely makes these Marquesas Islands look better than they really are." Yet as much as it is tempting to suggest that exotic spectacle alone lured summer crowds into theaters to watch the overheated locales of *White Shadows in the South Seas,* the same review suggests that the lush scenery and native bodies might not be enough to justify its two-dollar price.[22] Much about the film was designed to appeal on more conventional levels: it featured technological wizardry, melodrama and, especially, fast-paced action. "The biggest kick," *Film Daily* proclaimed two days after the premiere, "is in viewing of native pearl divers at work under the seas, showing one caught in immense clam shell, with his rescue by another as shark and octopus hover around."[23]

This was precisely the kind of action sequence that MGM executives had hoped a director like Van Dyke could bring to the film. Well-known as "one-take Woody," Van Dyke had originally been hired to make the film under the title of associate director with Robert Flaherty, largely to play against Flaherty's care for detail and his signature visual style. In a 1936 *Photoplay* interview, critic Howard Sharpe noted, "[Van Dyke] has no thought of ever making a picture of which the critics might shout 'this is a painting given movement, this is life on celluloid, this is ART!'" When asked to what he attributed his string of successes after *White Shadows*—including *Trader Horn* (1931), *Tarzan, the Ape Man* (1932), *The Thin Man* (1934), and *San Francisco* (1936)—Van Dyke's answer was typically acerbic: "I did a job for which I was paid. I took excellent stories and great box office names and put them together. The result was inevitable. I would have had to have been a pretty punk director to make flops out of sure-fire material like that."[24] Before *White Shadows,* he had been known for directing "quickies" and serials, such as Ruth Roland's *The Avenging Arrow* (1921) and *White Eagle* (1922), which rivaled the success of Pearl White's *The Perils of Pauline.* One of Van Dyke's ruling virtues, as far as studios were concerned, was his speed; he was not known for his technical or formal precision. But precisely how Van Dyke came to be drafted into the *White Shadows* project remains contested. According to accounts by Paul Rotha and William Murphy, *White Shadows* was originally purchased by David O. Selznick for his protégé, Van Dyke; Selznick, it is said, was interested in the book's evocative title alone. The production supervisor Hunt Stromberg insisted on engaging documentary filmmaker Robert Flaherty as codirector, and this disagreement, among others, led to Selznick's first split with MGM.[25]

Van Dyke was insulted by the title "associate director" and by the implication that he was meant to handle the "general, run of the mill stuff," while Flaherty was assigned to handle all of the "delicate stuff" with native actors and ethnographic footage.[26] Van Dyke's anger and resentment were apparently immense, adding to the arduous pressures of the overseas shoot, which would be one of the first of its kind for a large-scale Hollywood film. After arriving on location, he wrote to his script clerk and girlfriend in Hollywood, Josephine Chippo, pointing out Flaherty's shortcomings:

> If we ever see *Moana* running again anywhere I want to take you, just to show you how much of it is real and unreal. Almost all of it is staged. Natives doing things that they never do or did. And he knew no more about the camera than he did natives. Think his wife and brother must be responsible for his other films. I know very damn little about natives, but I bet I know more than he does. I know too damn much about them anyway.[27]

Several scenes in *White Shadows* do in fact suggest evidence of Flaherty's influence, if not his "touch," particularly those of feasting and dancing half-way through the film, which at times appear nearly identical to those in *Moana.* Van Dyke states in his journals, however, that all the filming was his: "Have had to retake all of Flaherty's stuff. It was putrid. He not only knows nothing about pictures but also nothing of natives."[28] Van Dyke, the fictional storyteller, is intent on pointing up the constructed fictions of Flaherty's ethnography, though ultimately one of the publicity angles for selling his own *White Shadows* to the public would be to claim it as an authentic "camera record" of real events. Thus *White Shadows'* opening titles herald it as an accurate record of O'Brien's adventures, declaring, "produced

and photographed on the locations and with the ancient native tribes of the Marquesas Islands in the South Seas." The Internet Movie Database still makes this
claim. Van Dyke, in fact, made the film roughly nine hundred miles away in Tahiti,
with lead actors shipped over from Hollywood and an amateur Tahitian cast.[29] The
tension that grew up between Van Dyke and Flaherty—the former an investment
guarantee brought in to sell the film to audiences hungry for action and melodrama, the latter now famous for his intense concerns for preserving the "fleeting
ghost" of indigenous cultures—indicates the stakes behind separating fiction from
fact and myth from history in South Pacific inscriptions.

Not only Van Dyke expressed a dislike of Flaherty's methods, which were diametrically opposed to Hollywood's time-and-money-managed goals. Clyde De
Vinna, also writing to Chippo, wrote that Flaherty was too "visionary" and imprac-
tical: "This Flaherty is as big a false alarm as I ever saw—so utterly ignorant of
pictures and everything connected with them that it has exhausted the patience
of everyone in the troupe and most of the time we go around flaring at each other
like a pack of strange bulldogs."[30] Van Dyke was similarly disturbed by Flaherty's
"ignorance" and could not appreciate his seemingly bizarre desire to get closer to
local life: "Flaherty gave me a heart failure yesterday for a moment or two when he
said that he would like to live here for the rest of his life. But after I had had him
arrested and the alienists had examined him, they pronounced him more or less
sane and harmless."[31] As tensions between the two directors mounted, Flaherty
was to spend more time on his own; two months into the shoot Van Dyke writes,
"Flaherty has been on one location for a week that should have been finished in
three hours."[32] A popular story recounts that Flaherty finally told members of the
crew, after spotting them on their hands and knees listening to a radio broadcast
from Hollywood's Coconut Grove, "Why not go back to California and make the
picture in the Coconut Grove there?"[33]

Indeed, Flaherty was taking his time over shooting, working according to his
customary methods—or lack thereof. Since the moderate failure of *Moana,* money
had become tighter and work more sporadic: *Moana*'s "carte blanche" contract
had not been the guarantee of long-term filmmaking success he had expected.
Since leaving Samoa, Flaherty had completed only two minor films, *The Pottery-
maker* (1925), sponsored by the New York Metropolitan Museum of Art, and a
fifteen-minute film about Manhattan, *Twenty-four Dollar Island* (1927), a film that
slightly predated the best-known "city symphony" film, Walter Ruttmann's *Berlin: The Symphony of a City* (1927). Flaherty's letters to Frances (who was in Arizona with David Flaherty beginning work on their ill-fated American Indian film,
Acoma) in autumn 1927 state that he had originally been planning, with Laurence

Stallings, on doing a version of *Typee* for Irving Thalberg, but was satisfied with the Ray Doyle script that was now shaping up, which he claims in any case as "my own invention really."[34] He left San Francisco on 30 November 1927, full of enthusiasm, like the rest of the film's crew, and pleased with the opportunity for well-paid work and travel. "Tahiti is incredible," he wrote to Frances, arriving at dawn to witness "the most romantic and entrancing scene I've ever seen—just one of those moments that are really a whole lifetime."[35] He imagined returning to make a film with Frances and paints glowing scenes in letter after letter, perhaps in an effort to displace fears of an unfulfilling assignment with MGM. Soon enough he is writing of his frustrations with a crew and codirector constantly homesick for their "paradise Hollywood,"[36] but he continues to imagine an alternate film to be made with Frances: "The richness that is in this country . . . the film we'll do—we'll know our continuity beforehand, then build and build—can't you see it all . . . because we love each other—confident in our ability—without worry—it will be as much because we love each other that we'll do it all—it will be the greatest film."[37]

Flaherty, like O'Brien before him, immediately became acquainted with the hard-drinking group at the social club Cercle Bougainville, which at the time included Charles Nordhoff and James Norman Hall. With Hall and camera assistant Floyd Crosby, he left Tahiti on scouting trips to Raiahea, Huahine, Tahaa, and Bora Bora in search of locations and native cast members, all the while complaining of the artistic and cultural limitations of the Hollywood method. Hall wrote of the "sacrifices" his friend was forced to make: "It is really a downright shame that he has to tie himself up with the 'interests' [of Hollywood] and can't be free to make the kind of pictures that only he can make."[38] But even well into February, Flaherty was writing optimistically to Frances that he was gaining practical knowledge of fast shooting and "short cuts," this in spite of the assembly-line approach of the crew, the superficiality and vanity of stars such as Monte Blue, and the fact that he was "sweating blood."[39] Tempers were running high, and Flaherty would finally exit in March, *Variety* tactfully reporting "a difference of opinion" on the set.[40] David O. Selznick recalled years later, "Flaherty was a real poet, a marvelous man who clearly could never work within the commercial setup. He had to work on his own."[41]

"Troppophobia"

Even after being released from working with Flaherty, Van Dyke was highly distressed about what he was coming to see as his state of exile in Tahiti. He kept a detailed record of his stay in a journal intended for Josephine Chippo that betrays his increasing agitation. Yet this account is more than merely an anecdotal supplement to the film. Van Dyke's journal makes explicit certain underlying tensions that are elided or obscured on the screen, offering a glimpse into Van Dyke's attitudes towards cultural and racial difference that at first appear worlds away from the unstable image of *tristes tropiques* envisioned both at the core of the film and in O'Brien's travel narrative.

Van Dyke arrived in December 1927, having sailed ten days and several thousand miles in search of the authentically exotic. But he writes of being upset in discovering that, much like a flimsy Hollywood set, there is both a front and a back to paradise:

> When you get in and on the island, the vegetation is very beautiful at first sight . . . but when you have seen it for a few days you begin to notice the ugly features also; such as the dead and dried foliage that clings to the green; the worm holes and the damp rot on the barks. . . . The bay is beautiful and I would like to swim in it but I am reminded of the constant danger of sharks. The natives are plentiful and I would like to get out and play with them but I am told that the great majority of them are full of syphilis.[42]

The aesthetic purity of the scene is marked by threats of danger, even death. In O'Brien's travel narrative, the disease that threatens the islands is explicitly associated with the age-old problems of western paternalism, commercial exploitation, and violence. In Van Dyke's description, the worm holes and damp rot that mark the "ugly features" of paradise recall with striking clarity a very different convention: that of the dissimulating face of a diseased woman—an allegorical legacy concisely anatomized by Sander Gilman. Gilman has connected the categories of gender and disease by tracing a genealogy of the representation of syphilis and its equation to the figure of woman, offering images that palpably represent the "front" and "back" of the disease from the late-fifteenth century onward. In a mid-nineteenth-century French edition of the poem *Syphilis* by Fracastoro (which gave the disease its name in the sixteenth century), Gilman finds on the title page a nineteenth-century variation of a Baroque emblem, "representing the choice of Hercules, tempted by Voluptas, the vice of luxury, behind whose mask the temptress hides her ugliness."[43] For Gilman, at this point "vice" has become "disease," and seduction has become infection. In Van Dyke's comments, the seductive, alien landscape is gendered feminine, perpetually threatening to enfold the wary traveler in its unhealthy and degenerate embrace.[44]

Revealingly, Van Dyke's observations regarding the front and back of the Tahitian landscape are always juxtaposed with growing concerns about his relationship with Chippo and his anxieties over their separation. Van Dyke, who had sworn to celibacy while in Tahiti, expresses in his letters increasingly fantastic erotic fears and often launches into possessive rages over Chippo that at times seem to verge on the hysterical.[45] These fears about femininity, hygiene, and disease, particularly in the context of the colonial South Pacific, suggest a more widespread paranoia of the dissimulating faces of sexual and cultural difference. This is further implied as the director's stream-of-consciousness narrative rapidly moves from observations about the landscape to remarks about Tahitian women: "[I] have been sadly disillusioned in regard to the beauty of native women. I even heard someone say something once about native charm. It is all a delusion and a snare."[46] The diseased specters Van Dyke discovers abroad no doubt allegorize certain masculine anxieties lurking at home. The Tahitian landscape's beauty conceals degeneration, while native women mask their corruption: sirens of the South Seas. Even to "play" with natives—which ambiguously could imply either social or sexual contact—is forbidden because it threatens exposure to syphilitic decay. Later during the shoot, Van Dyke's paranoia about native contagion appears to escalate into neurotic phobias: "Just a nasty loathing for everything here including the picture. Even hate to touch things. One of the best things they do down here is to shake hands. You can do it a hundred times a day. . . . I want to run and wash every time I shake hands with anyone."[47] He seems to be worried that the islands will forever brand him. Van Dyke describes a state aligned to that of O'Brien's tattooed American, who is indelibly marked through contact with the primitive. Tahiti "has left its mark on me. I'm branded by the damned country and I think that for the rest of my life it will lurk in the back of my mind as some fearful nightmare or boogy that will get me if I don't watch out."[48] Yet unlike O'Brien's young American, Van Dyke's tattoo does not inscribe an ambivalent urge to acquire a new skin, perhaps to embody multiple selves—even explore or engage with one's own alterity—but rather suggests a dread of something he will be unable to wash away: a desire to unambiguously, and perhaps violently, exclude unclean contact with the primitive. This might even be seen as a kind of extreme phobia of any flirtation with going native—a kind of "troppophobia" ("going troppo" was a slang term for going native/going crazy, thought to derive from Darwin, Australia, where going troppo meant losing one's head in the extreme humidity).

The director's writing expresses a desire to sever any links to Tahitians, "half-castes," Chinese—that is, those who cannot be assimilated into a self-reflecting sense of unified American and masculine selfhood. He writes to Chippo, "This place is sure a degenerate's paradise. Some of our gang are wallowing in it.... These natives represent a very little different strata to me than the negro. And they smell about as bad except when they are all daubed with perfume."[49] These cross-currents (xenophobia, US racial stereotypes, discourses of degeneration) visible in Van Dyke's writing could be dismissed as inconsequential or momentary lapses of reason, yet they return explicitly and with mythic force in such Van Dyke films as the Academy Award–nominated adventure *Trader Horn,* set in Africa, with its odd, almost surreal intercutting of De Vinna's ethnographic footage with staged scenes of native orgies, human sacrifices, and tribal blood sports.

In spite of the obvious problems with Van Dyke's position, simply to chastise the director with the advantage of postcolonial and postmodern hindsight is not my intention. His letters and journals attest to the multiple, often deeply contradictory and confused interweaving of prominent racial discourses in the US that have been explored throughout this book, tendencies that still mark our own social and discursive practices. They also suggest the ways that linked imperialisms interacted and collapsed upon one another in transnational contexts—Van Dyke's exporting of close-minded US racial slurs to Tahiti is facilitated by MGM's global reach. Clearly, for Van Dyke, shooting his film far from home, the islands refused to provide any object that he could seize upon, identify with, or offer up as an example that embodied the preconceived illusion of tropical paradise that continued to dominate in the US at the time. In his journals, Tahiti appears as a depressed and fallen place that encompasses the extremes of Dante's vision: paradise is called a "hell hole." Soon the metaphorical relationship between sexual and cultural alienation becomes even more closely interwoven, and the blurring of vice and disease is made explicit, perhaps thinly veiling a reference to Van Dyke's own strict sexual abstinence and the disappointed myth of potent primitive sexuality: "The men have the right idea down here. Everything droops. Even the foliage.... Everything is tired. There doesn't seem to be a semblance of native life left on the island. Everything is of the bastardized variety. The natives are not altogether French and the French are only partly native."[50]

This bastardized offspring of colonial mixing seems somehow the fault of Tahiti itself. It is this impure, sexually fallen and literally infertile—"drooping"—reality that the director finds himself constantly in need of disguising, making up, smoothing over, and revitalizing in his film. *White Shadows in the South Seas* ultimately highlights the ways that film images can encode the relationship between desire and representation: appearing to penetrate the truth of the "passive" peoples and landscape of the South Pacific, it succeeds not so much in capturing others as in representing the idea of otherness in the US imagination.[51]

The lapse Van Dyke marks between the false front and corrupted back of the exotic ideal extends to his ethnic actors as well (in his journals he reserves praise for his male lead, Monte Blue, alone). For the role of the virgin princess Fayaway, MGM sent over Rena Bush and the Mexican American Raquel Torres, leaving it to Van Dyke to choose between them. Though MGM's publicity machine would later call Torres "M.G.M.'s sensational little 'find' from Mexico," Van Dyke claimed "neither one of the girls [could] do a damn thing," though he finally settled on the "little bit cockeyed" Torres.[52] Still, the director was distressed by the skin tone of his actress: "I wired the studio telling them to tell the girl to sunburn on the way down," Van Dyke writes, "but of course she didn't do it and she is way too light to work with the other natives and is going to have to make up."[53] Van Dyke's preoccupation with skin color is partly due to his perceptions of visual continuity and verisimilitude in the film, but also may underscore his fear of permitting any "native" actresses to look too white—a fear not so much in evidence in the 1930s, for example, in films such as Frank Lloyd's *Mutiny on the Bounty* (1935, featuring the Mexican actress Movita Castenada and the Hawaiian Mamo Clark) and John Ford's *The Hurricane* (1937, with "native" leads Dorothy Lamour and John Hall).[54] As Jane Gaines has noted in her discussion of *The Scar of Shame* (1928), a "race picture" released around the same time as *White Shadows,* white producers tended to want to represent racial difference graphically on the screen: in other words, it had to be distinctly, visibly clear who was white and who was not. This fact worked against lighter-skinned African American actors, for "black and white film stock registered too much truth—on the screen racially mixed actors looked white."[55] Van Dyke's concern with how skin color will register on screen further points up the ideological gap between Flaherty and Van Dyke (and perhaps between Flaherty and Hollywood expectations of Polynesian racial visibility more generally). The difference between Torres's "whiteness" and the Polynesian actors' "blackness" was probably more pronounced because of the tonal range of *White Shadows'* orthochromatic stock: Flaherty's panchromatic success with *Moana* had not yet fully converted Hollywood practice. In making his Mexican lead "blacker," Van Dyke lays bare not only the highly uneven conceptions of Polynesian racial visibility, but also the racial presumptions and visual manipulations that take place behind Hollywood's "seamless" simulacrum of the real. Two years later, while filming *Tabu*, Flaherty would continue to complain of *White Shadows'* "negroid flesh tones and all."[56]

Paradoxically for Van Dyke, the material reality of Tahiti only obstructs the production of a fantasy that MGM had hoped the film's indigenous people and real locations could authenticate. The director finally lays blame on Tahiti by employing some all-too-familiar racial slurs: "We went originally to pick out some good-looking natives. What chance. Such a thing is turning out to be a myth. Some of them would look good in a cage."[57] The comment is a more extreme version of a common trope that can be found, albeit with some kind of poetic intention (or irony?), in sympathetic accounts such as John Grierson's review of *Moana*, where "primitive beings" are described as "caught and imprisoned" by Flaherty's filmic gaze.[58] Such comments implicitly recall cinema's links to the nineteenth-century ethnographic spectacle, where native bodies could be encountered as displays in the circuslike atmosphere of live exhibits and world's fairs. Here, though, the effect is more complete: the cinematic native rarely looks back at the audience; there is little or no implied interaction between observer and observed; the native specimen never leaves the enclosure and walks amidst the crowds as they did in the fairgrounds. The finished version of *White Shadows* would exquisitely perform this final act of native imprisonment, even while offering shades of O'Brien's skepticism and a convincing veneer of anticolonialism.

MGM's *White Shadows*

In spite of the film's production difficulties and Van Dyke's adversarial relationship to the Tahitian locale, the core of the film returns viewers to the mythic ideal of the Polynesian island as a prelapsarian idyll. Opening shots of pristine postcard images fill the screen with open vistas and vast horizons, like the spacious establishing shots of a Western. The intertitles tell us that the islands have been "for happy centuries the last remnant of an earthly paradise." But this spatial openness is soon ruptured by images showing the islands as cramped, soulless factories, manned by peoples enslaved to the demands of ruthless white traders. With a title that announces, "Today—the results of 'civilization,'" a lengthy shot tracks left to right along a beach, then cuts to a traveling shot in the opposite direction. We briefly see a man with limbs bloated by elephantiasis leaning against a tree, then glimpse unkempt houses, chickens, goats, and pigs running loose, and amidst them a mix of "Marquesan" men and women, some wearing pareus and others in heavy, missionary-influenced dress. The shot unravels the customary left-to-right coherence of the written text, and finally the viewer's gaze is drawn into the entrance of an island trading post.

The trading post is a classic scene of US frontier decadence: the patrons drink, dance, and loll about, recalling the chaotic saloon scenes of the Western, a genre familiar to Van Dyke from his earlier directing career. Inside, the trader Sebastian

(Robert Anderson) cajoles a pearl from a diver, Makia, by placing a watch on his wrist with a gesture that is at once condescending and proprietary. Rather than performing what Rony has referred to as the racializing of gender in colonialist films such as *Trader Horn,* this scene suggests the gendering of race and the classic feminization of the Polynesian male, here suggesting too the disavowal of those masculine anxieties revealed in Van Dyke's journals.[59] Sebastian, replete with phallic cigar, lets his hand linger a bit too long on Makia's arm, while the watch calls to mind Hollywood clichés of sugar daddies proffering trinkets to eager flappers. The homoerotics of the scene serve a dual and perhaps contradictory function. Sebastian emerges as the stock figure of the homosexualized villain, but homoeroticism here also might be seen to unsettle some of the more rigid dichotomies of heterosexual and homosexual, masculine and feminine, the west and its others—dichotomies that are often hierarchical assumptions in the colonial and Hollywood contexts.[60] This scene is repeated in slightly different form near the film's end when Sebastian, as the first trader to reach a precolonial island paradise, holds a watch—a "nice tick-tock"—to the ear of an innocent native girl (Rena Bush) and exchanges it for what she, in her unsullied native state, sees as a common and worthless pearl. In both scenes the watch becomes a prominent trope, referring to time as the corrupting influence on primitive life, rupturing both the unity of what Fabian has called the ethnographic present and the native's harmonious synchrony—their connection with timeless nature. Both the technology and strict chronology of the west appear as signs of its sickness and contagion, which ravage the pure bodies of the islanders.

The opening scenes of corruption set the tone for the film. The film's white protagonist, Matthew Lloyd (Monte Blue), is introduced as a trained doctor who has been reduced to alcoholism and is a passive spectator to the tragedy of island exploitation. Sebastian, resplendent in white clothes and a colonial bush helmet, notices an inscription on Lloyd's stethoscope that points to past voyaging glories: "Presented to Dr. Lloyd, by the boys, S.S. *Empress of India,* 1917." He remarks on Lloyd's fall from grace, telling him, "You're a disgrace to the white race." Lloyd freely renounces his profession, and his very selfhood, responding drunkenly, "I'm ashamed to be white." A homeless "derelict of the Seven Seas," Monte Blue's character continues the tradition of alcoholic wanderers going back to Harry Carey in *McVeagh of the South Seas* (1914) and Willard Mack in *Aloha Oe.*[61] Lloyd is also a professional, once trained to cure the ravages of commercial accidents and western diseases and now faced with an epidemic—a fatal impact—that extends far beyond one individual's powers of healing and containment. Beneath the narrative, then, flows a persistent undercurrent of white guilt and the threat of impurity and contagion, here inverted so that the contagion is embodied not by the syphilitic and bastardized natives mentioned by Van Dyke, but by the degenerating and fatal influence of white "civilization"—a term now self-consciously bracketed by quotation marks in the film's intertitles.

The film cuts to the underwater sequences celebrated by critics, which document the dangers of bursting veins and collapsing lungs: a giant shark stalks the divers; a clam seizes a foot; an octopus extends its slithery tentacles. Like automatons in a factory, the commodified divers descend into the depths one by one, ascending with blood running or half dead. Faced with yet another critical case, Lloyd confronts Sebastian, who defends himself with the pious arrogance of a slave owner. Lloyd deals a blow that sends the trader reeling into the sea, then desperately attempts to revive the diver, while the wails of "Old Naku," the victim's father, fill the soundtrack. But in spite of his efforts, Lloyd loses yet another patient. He returns to drinking, and cries out into the existential void, "Civilization—God!" But his cry dwindles to absurd and hysterical laughter as he watches well-dressed western dandies and "happy natives" dance in an alcohol-induced stupor nearby.

In spite of these initial efforts to perform a critique of western hegemony, the spectacle of a degenerate and degenerating west becomes absorbed into a narrative that revitalizes the lost-island myth while blurring the boundaries between exotic fiction and ethnographic document. As Raymond F. Betts suggests, the purifying gaze of the Hollywood lens strove to construct the South Pacific as an illusionary island. *White Shadows* situates this illusion at its core, and in the process loses sight of some of the deeper ambivalences that marked O'Brien's travel account and his screen treatment.[62] Unable to linger for long among the ruins of the west's others, the film escapes with Lloyd to a fantasy of monologic unity and reassuring timelessness on a far-off, solitary atoll. In scenes suggesting a classic rite of passage, Lloyd arrives here only after undergoing physical pain and exposure to the elements. First Lloyd is tricked by Sebastian's henchman, who is shown receiving a glimmering white pearl—by now established as the film's key signifier of white greed. In an image that recalls crucifixion, the doctor is strapped to the wheel of a drifting ship whose crew has been killed by bubonic plague. The allusions to crucifixion may have been intentional, in light of passages in Van Dyke's journal: hearing the complaints of the film crew, Van Dyke believed he was the only one of them who had truly suffered. He wrote, "There were about 42 versions [in the Bible] of the crucifiction [*sic*]. Every one had something to say about it except the one who was crucified. Think that I am the only one who was really crucified on this picture."[63] The sequence gives way to a stock element of the South Seas film—a violent storm and shipwreck—whereupon Lloyd finds himself resurrected and discovers, like Crusoe, that he has been washed up on an apparently unpopulated island.

It is possible to read the escapist narrative at the heart of *White Shadows in the South Seas* as a dream or fantasy sequence, especially if one wants to consider that the film might be self-reflexively gesturing towards the historical textualization of the South Pacific as a site of western fantasy. Certainly, as I've suggested earlier, the unspoiled island at the heart of the film would have been known, at least to most audiences in 1927–1928, as an invention. So the film's central fantasy envisions an impossible dream of personal and cultural holism, reflected in a narrative that stages a return to the coherence and order of a precolonial world. This rediscovered unity is clearly marked out as preferable to the voidlike abyss ("Civilization—God!") experienced by Lloyd, the exhausted and fragmented figure of both colonialism and modernity. But the presence of this precolonial illusion also reminds us of the relationship of self to other in primitivist fantasy, which, as Henrietta Moore has observed, is marked not only by the desirability of going native, but also by anxiety.[64] Going native threatens to erase difference and therefore implies a loss of self—fears that disturb the conscious desires of O'Brien's tattooed American and that also signal the fall of the hero in *White Shadows in the South Seas.*

Recovered from his ordeal, Lloyd briefly uses his "native" knowledge to engage in some rudimentary survival tactics, and notices the presence of human habitation on another nearby island. Soon he is peeping through dense foliage at nude women bathing and tossing flowers, the camera mimicking the forward movement of Lloyd's voyeuristic gaze with a lingering zoom through the leaves, enacting an explicit convergence of Lloyd's, the viewer's, and the camera's eye in the scopophilic pleasure of viewing. Lloyd's famous (and somewhat comical) "Hello"—MGM's first synchronized word—echoes across the gap of difference. The power of cinema to construct masculine desire is communicated through the delicate gauze of De Vinna's lens filters, through which Lloyd and the viewer are afforded brief and tastefully framed glimpses of nude women tossing their hair and athletically diving from rocks. Here, through the visual codes of ethnographic spectacle, what Nichols et al. have collectively called the ethnopornographic gaze is realized.[65]

In the scene we are introduced to Fayaway, a character who first appeared in Ray Doyle's script treatment.[66] A carefully composed shot depicts Torres at the edge of a pool, catching and tossing flowers into water that reflects the figures of her companions. The close-up shot of Torres's Fayaway, at first unaware of Lloyd's and the camera's gaze, encodes the exotic as the object of western and masculine pleasure; indeed, Torres prefigures the success of Dorothy Lamour, whose embodiment of the exotic would appear ten years later in *The Hurricane. White Shadows'* Fayaway is on one level a standard version of the South Sea maiden handed down from Enlightenment representation, but more specifically she can be traced to her namesake in *Typee,* who is an erotic vision of "full lips" and "teeth of dazzling whiteness" that looked like "the milk-white seeds of 'arta,' a fruit of the valley, which, when cleft in twain, shows them reposing in rows on either side, imbedded in the rich and juicy pulp" (chap. 11, 85). She is Tommo's "peculiar favorite," the innocent yet ripely sensual opposite of the Marquesan women who dance with "abandoned voluptuousness" during the ship's first night in Nukuhiva, for Fayaway has the "easy unstudied graces of a child of nature." Unlike her embodiment in Torres, however, Melville's Fayaway is not free of the "hideous blemish of tattooing." In fact, three dots mark Fayaway's lips, dots that Melville's narrator somewhat defensively maintains were "minute . . . no bigger than pin-heads," and "at a little distance were not at all discernable" (86). Sex and gender are constitutive signifiers once again: Tommo's relief at Fayaway's lack of tattooing is contrasted with his wonderment of the "remarkable" male tattoo a few pages earlier (78). Melville

FIGURE 6. Lloyd (Monte Blue) glimpses bathing women in *White Shadows in the South Seas* (courtesy of the British Film Institute).

might have been grateful for the distancing and fetishistic power of the cinema: there are no blemishes in MGM's constellation of stars. In any case, it is unlikely that tattoos on either sex would have found a place in Hollywood's marketable vision of Polynesian beauty, as evident in the negative studio response to O'Brien's tattoo-dominated screenplay.

Lloyd is an outsider to this world, but he eagerly seeks entrance and, most important, redemption. But the voyeuristic unity of the audience's and Lloyd's gaze at the bathing women soon collapses: the women do not linger in view of Lloyd's gaze but flee from it in fear. This action not only reinforces the idea that voyeurism relies upon strictly maintained distance as a coefficient of pleasure, but also serves as a warning to Lloyd as an ethnographic observer, who should remain an *absent* presence in his cultural encounter—a voyager safely glimpsing the spectacle from offshore—lest he endanger the perfect harmony of the savage scene. The necessity of preserving distance at this point also seems to underscore the contention of Nichols et al. that both ethnography and pornography promise something they cannot deliver: "the ultimate pleasure of knowing the Other. On this promise of sexual or cultural knowledge they depend, but they are also condemned to do nothing more than make it available for representation."[67]

But the film does attempt to encode an intimate sense of knowing the other, and in the ensuing scene the island inhabitants, after hunting for Lloyd, contemplate the miracle of his white skin and ponder whether he is a "white god." Lloyd collapses and is taken to a palm-roofed house, where he is massaged back to life in a scene that graphically defines first contact: numerous disembodied feminine hands massage Lloyd's white flesh in a series of tight close-ups. The images revisit an archetypal scene in Pacific fantasy: Captain Samuel Wallis's experience of *lome lome* during his stay in Tahiti in 1767. Hawkesworth notes that on 11 July, Wallis encountered Purea, wife of the chief of the southern district of Papara, who would come to be known as Queen Oberea.[68] The next day Wallis is invited to shore, but is taken ill and finds himself too weak to walk on his own. In Hawkesworth's version, Wallis is carried by a sort of Amazonian Purea over puddles "with as little trouble as it would have cost me to have lifted over a child if I had been well" (1: 464). Wallis enters Purea's house, where four young girls give him and his ailing companions the *lome lome* treatment:

> As soon as we entered the house, [Purea] made us sit down, and then calling four young girls, she assisted them to take off my shoes, draw down my stockings, and pull off my coat, and then directed them to smooth down the skin, and gently chafe it with their hands. The same operation was also performed upon the first

lieutenant and purser. . . . I found great benefit . . . from the chafing, and so did the lieutenant and purser. (1: 463)

Wallis is dressed again, not in his own clothes, but in a tapa: "At first I declined the acceptance of this favour, but being unwilling not to feel pleased with what was intended to please me, I acquiesced." Though it has hardly met with universal approval,[69] the scene conjures up themes often repeated in later accounts and suggests how the narration of Polynesian encounters was immediately bound to sexual (if often deferred or cryptic) fantasy. Wallis's sensual "chafing" also establishes the theme of the western protagonist's renewal and transformation as a willing (though as this version emphasizes, passive) participant in a foreign cultural—and often sexualized—experience. Wallis's "acquiescence" at his moment of physical and spiritual weakness suggests the desire, implicit or repressed in most accounts, to cross over to—and at a certain level, to physically embody—the world of the primitive. Indeed, the *lome lome* incident bears a strong resemblance to the classic "morning after" scenario, as if Wallis were insisting that he was too drunk—or in this case too ill, or weak—to resist Purea's strong advances. In Hawkesworth's narrative, Wallis's change into the tapa initiates a shift in attitude, and not long afterwards Hawkesworth's Wallis is referring to the Tahitian people, whom he and his men had shortly before been shooting at and killing, as "our Indian friends" (1: 476). Nonetheless, there are strict limits to Wallis's crossing over: the narrator's assertions of passive acquiescence allow him to maintain psychic distance while participating in a scene of cultural difference. And rather than suggesting an easy transfer of cultural identities, the stress on changing clothes alone suggests that Wallis's version of going native exists chiefly at the level of masquerade and superficial appearance: a disembodied guise of otherness that displaces bodily transgression by highlighting the essence of the European self beneath the tapa.

The progression of events in *White Shadows* follows a similar trajectory, but here Van Dyke's and De Vinna's choice of shots makes explicit the encounter's erotic elements. When the camera moves from a removed distance to intimate closeness, ethnotopia becomes pornotopia, and any problems of cross-cultural interpretation or social difference are dissolved in the intensity of physical contact. The palpable presence of Lloyd's white body, as the nexus of native and feminine desire, replicates and recolonizes the language of the pornographic film where, as Nichols and others have suggested, the phallic "star" takes center stage, ordering and demystifying any potential threats embodied by feminine (and in this case native) desire. The intense focus on disembodied body parts again suggests a fragmentation and anatomization reminiscent both of conventional pornographies and the probing ethnographic lens. And though the moment can be read as a realization of interracial sexual contact, before the act can pose a threat it is relegitimized through the authority of an ethnographic pretext: intertitles interrupt the action to state that this is all a demonstration of "the secret and sacred massage of Polynesia." Though beautifully photographed—focusing only on hands, faces, and Monte Blue's head and torso—the bodies in evidence here create a sanitized spectacle of white and masculine potency. As the scene ends, a two-shot reveals the leads exchanging desiring and knowing glances. As in the Wallis story, the physical contact of *lome lome* seems to animate the possibility of "becoming" Polynesian and tests the fine line between "them" and "us."

As if to underline the film's ethnographic credentials at this key moment, the ensuing sequence of the "Great Feast" in which the tribe of Mehevi celebrates could, even with its sleek production values and oversized scale, have been cut directly from *Moana*—though where Flaherty had one boy climbing a coconut palm, *White Shadows* shows a dozen, descending the trunks together like Busby Berkeley dancers; instead of one turtle being captured in the sea, there are two; and so on. The cooking sequence replicates Flaherty's "Mother Tuʻungaita's Cook-house" sequence nearly shot by shot, and although Tuʻungaita is replaced by young men, the scene offers similar close-ups of food preparation, a fire being lit from scratch, and intertitles (such as "Spinach a la Polynesia") that strive to familiarize and domesticate the nonwestern scene. As the sequence turns to dancing, there is an oblique gesture towards O'Brien's Marquesan boy Friday in the name of the featured dancer, Keklafaufaupaopao, translated as "man with legs like exploding eggs." Fayaway follows suit, dancing seductively in front of Lloyd, the white god, who returns her longing glances. At this point we discover that Fayaway is *tapu*, not to be gazed upon amorously by any man.

Advertisements for the film trumpeted the theme of forbidden romance, claiming that here was "the book nobody dared to film—two years of primitive danger to bring it to you!" and ending with the tagline, "It's different!" The accompanying image was of a heroic Monte Blue sweeping a very pale Torres off her feet.[70] Indeed, the film's story does metaphorically and literally embrace difference: Lloyd ultimately goes native and is transformed from a "derelict of the Seven Seas" into the "white god," Matta Loa. Lloyd becomes a beachcomber cast in the mold of figures such as Robarts or Wilson in all but the tattoos, yet with few of the actual hardships or challenges of beachcomber life. This sanitized image of the beachcomber reinforces the spectator's desire to expunge the sins of the west and become reborn into a savage innocence: "The world-worn soul of Matthew Lloyd grew *new* again!" the intertitles exclaim. At this point the film's erotic imagery becomes increasingly embedded in romantic tropes, as an overtly stylized shot of Lloyd and Fayaway embarking on a canoe journey draws our attention. The camera / voyeur stalks the canoe from the shore. Brushing aside foliage as it travels, the camera soon enters into unknown regions marked by increasingly otherworldly visual and aural effects. In a reenactment of Bougainville's appearance of Venus, who "shewed herself to the Phrygian shepherd," Fayaway stands in front of Lloyd and unwraps her clothes. As she stands nude before the "white god," the camera relieves us of our shameful glances by hiding behind leaves, but in a curious move, both camera and canoe then shift direction and begin to lead us away from the site of indiscretion. In a parallel sequence, Rena Bush's character makes innocent love to a young man, as both suggestively pluck morsels from an open fruit. The parallel cutting between Lloyd / Fayaway and the "native" couple exchanging "the flower of love" works to naturalize, and neutralize, the budding relationship between the former couple, momentarily quelling any racial or cultural doubts it might raise.

Soon after, Lloyd is invited to join the tribe after saving the chief's son (Fayaway's brother) from drowning. Primitive nature has helped the doctor to recover his healing powers, and Lloyd is given the gift of the *tapu* Fayaway, according to the Hollywood logic of Polynesian exchange and the patriarchal logic of woman as exchange commodity. But much like that of *Tabu*'s hero, Matahi, who offers the reverse of Lloyd's trajectory by escaping paradise to find sexual freedom among the corrupted mores of the west, Lloyd's personal and cultural newness is built upon a foundation of social transgression and (in Lloyd's case, western) taboo, suggesting that the local *tapu* cannot so easily be lifted. As the boundary between sexual voyeurism and physical participation is crossed, the question of *unnatural* love—miscegenation—becomes increasingly palpable. It is worth recalling that the film appeared only ten years after the legalization of the Asiatic Barred Zone in the US, and only three years after the *United States v. Thind* decision expanded and reinforced popular conceptions of racial difference. The postwar intensification of legislation restricting immigration based on race had no doubt highlighted fears connected to miscegenation—and expanded the conceptual and racial definitions of miscegenation itself.

In advancing a representation of interracial romance, the film has again taken its cue from a wealth of South Seas–themed literature, including Melville's Fayaway, as well as from previous South Seas films such as *The Island of Regeneration* (1915) and *The Fallen Idol* (1919), for sexual taboos are rarely breached in O'Brien's travel account. Though tales of potential miscegenation appear in his later work (such as his screen treatment for *White Shadows* itself), O'Brien's original tends to reinforce the ideological currents that guarantee the failure of Lloyd and Fayaway's relationship. Both O'Brien's book and the film raise the possibility of miscegenation only to quell—or, indeed, kill—the desire: as O'Brien's book argues, "The abyss is impassable" (68). The miscegenation tale in the film does, however—at least initially—appear to venture across this abyss. But the innocent idyll doesn't last: Lloyd is marked by the "unnatural" urges of his race and, in a kind of inversion of the tragic mulatto, whiteness becomes the indelible sign of baseness and psychic disunity, which ultimately resurface in Lloyd's character as a return of the repressed. Lloyd has tried to "pass" as a Marquesan, but when the sight of valuable—and dazzlingly white—pearls sends him into a frenzy of materialistic desire, the film declares, "Across the sun of this paradise crept the first white shadow." The chief's son—like *Moana*'s Pe'a a stock figure of childlike native innocence—curiously watches Lloyd's behavior from a safe distance. It is in these moments that the ironies beneath a notion of whiteness as an immutable and "unmarked" fixture come closest to those in O'Brien's screenplay treatment and to their classic articulation in Melville. White subjectivity is denatured and split, while whiteness itself is, effectively, racialized. The intertitles state, "The instinct of his ruthless race was his: Greed," helping to shift whiteness from an unmarked to a marked category. Though perhaps hardly a radical rupturing of the white / nonwhite opposition, the film at least gestures towards relativizing whiteness in the tradition of South Seas wanderers such as Robarts and Gauguin.

Notably, the central characteristics defining Lloyd's dissolution were assigned, in earlier script treatments, to a "half-caste" character, Mehevi, who serves as the foil to Doctor Lloyd. Lloyd, meanwhile, had originally been conceived as the clean conscience of whiteness: in one of the few lines lifted directly from O'Brien's book, Doyle's screenplay refers to Lloyd as a "brother" to the Polynesians, "who walked in the sunlight."[71] In O'Brien's book, this "brother" is a fictive figure who shows Marquesans "the way" to survive intelligently and thrive in a commercial and technologized world. Doyle's fourth reworking of the script combines the debased desires of the "half-caste" with the generous impulses of the original Doctor Lloyd and conveys a more intriguing view of the dislocations of western subjectivity, torn between conceptions of civilized savages and savage civilizers.[72] Unfortunately, the film's gain in character complexity may have signaled a loss for its utopian narrative. For the irreparably fractured Lloyd, unlike the angelic character of earlier script versions, does not escape the west, marry the native girl, and live to old age on the islands. While the sexual politics of miscegenation could fascinate and titillate, inscribing western and masculine power, they could also encapsulate the horror of breaking social taboos, marking the dangers of racial and cultural contagion.

As Malini Johar Schueller has suggested of *Typee,* MGM's *White Shadows* shows evidence of both reification and resistance. Shades of reification are particularly evident in what Schueller calls "boundary or transgressive situations": moments in the narrative that imply cultural mixing or culture crossing. In *Typee,* these boundary situations are seen in a Calibanesque native figure such as Marnoo, who appropriates the "powers of colonial signifiers," as well as in those colonial figures who desire to go native.[73] It is in these moments of cultural ambivalence, when the integrity and essence of western selfhood is put into question, that the tropes and figures of western cultural difference reassert themselves. These anxieties become evident particularly at the level of bodily inscription, as seen more generally in the obsession in western narratives with the body in all its manifestations, gestures, and encounters: with fantasies of cross-cultural romance, "half-caste" figures of racial mixing, tattooing, and persistent references to "long pig" cannibal feasts. All of these suggest profound western tensions at a bodily level and a preference for looking at, rather than engaging with, what is perceived as other—voyeurism over interaction, spectacle over a becoming that might put the self at risk.

Inevitably, the tensions surrounding Lloyd and Fayaway's transgression mount as the plot rushes to a climax. Lloyd, possessed by white greed, lights a beacon to draw a trading ship to the island, the intertitles proclaiming, "He was only a white man—no god." With Fayaway's help, he manages a change of heart and destroys the fire, but too late: though not seen by the couple, a ship appears on the horizon; a flare streaks across the sky. The following morning, the villagers gather for a chaotic arrival scene that recalls the accounts of early explorers, but this arrival centers on the irony and futility of native joy: they will certainly be destroyed by their own generous impulses. Lloyd, coming to his senses, flails on the shore, desperately trying to stave off the inevitable corruption of his self-contained world of islanders. The return of a tense musical theme heralds the final confrontation between Lloyd and the pearl trader Sebastian, Lloyd attempting to explain that the natives are children of nature—"Like birds...and flowers...they are like man was before he lost the garden of Eden"—but he is ruthlessly shot. There will be no more heroic rescues from actual or psychic death; no efforts can revive him. The islanders flee the beach, and the closing scenes linger over Fayaway's grief as Lloyd lingers into the night, then dies. In a biting coda, the film ends with an island that resembles the wild western debauchery of the opening scenes, the intertitles reminding us of the "white shadows...white shadows." Fayaway mourns while wearing an uncomfortable, missionary-influenced dress; her hair is bound into two tight braids, and shadows fall over the screen.

The Pagan

The fascination with miscegenation narratives and tropical sexuality persisted in films such as *East of Borneo* (1931) and the remake of *Aloha Oe, Aloha* (1931), which returned Raquel Torres to the South Seas genre. A number of Van Dyke's productions included plots or subplots involving interracial romances, including the *White Shadows* sequel, *The Pagan*, and *Never the Twain Shall Meet* (1931). Other films drawn from literary and theatrical sources, such as Erle C. Kenton's *Island of Lost Souls* (1933) and King Vidor's *Bird of Paradise* (1932), presented fantastic variations on the theme, but these relationships were almost always hazardous to the health of one or both parties and failed to offer coherent resistance to dominant prohibitions.[74] Indeed, while many have seen these films as pushing the boundaries of, or at least mildly challenging, the antimiscegenation debate, the films might also—considering their frequently ambiguous takes on interracial romance—be seen to have intervened in the very definitions of miscegenation by visibly rendering uncertain conceptions of what constituted racial difference. Later addenda to the Motion Picture Code of 1930 would, in any event, help to close the screen debate for decades.

Given Van Dyke's personal writings, it is difficult to imagine he would have been comfortable with the miscegenation narrative couched within a fable of a western antihero's redemption. The message of his *Never the Twain Shall Meet,* which strives to confirm that "east is east, west is west, and blood is blood," would seem closer to Van Dyke's position. As earlier suggested, both O'Brien and Flaherty were smitten by so-called Smithed anthropological theories that strove to situate Polynesians within definitions of Aryan origins. Related theories were repeated in various drafts of the MGM screenplay for *White Shadows,* notably in the first treatment, attributed to Eugene Walters, which opens, "There can be little doubt but what the Polynesian people of these days, differing somewhat in the various islands, had all the attributes of the Caucasian race; that they were part of a lost continent."[75] Van Dyke, reading Flaherty's writings in Tahiti, would assert his own racial theories against Flaherty's:

> In one of Flaherty's articles, he asserts that it is very possible that the Polynesians were originally of the Caucasian race. Other writers who have come down here and married native women, like Keable,[76] Stevenson, Lane, Hampton, assert the same thing. I suppose it only natural that when you will sleep with them and marry them that you should want to find some justification for it. . . . If they have an

ounce of Caucasian ancestry in the whole race, then I am a Jersey cow. They smell more like the negroids.[77]

Van Dyke's employment of racial slurs and stereotypes suggests the variety of contesting racial discourses that underlie *White Shadows in the South Seas*. He ascribes fixed and reductive attributes to "white" and "nonwhite" races, while O'Brien's and Flaherty's outputs imagine a more inclusive but perhaps equally hierarchical patterning of Caucasian and non-Caucasian groups.

But the differing positions of Van Dyke and Flaherty also demonstrate the opposing poles and possibilities of racial signification on the screen and the degrees to which the cinema could serve as an operative element in popular conceptions of race. As I have argued, the racializing of Polynesia long depended on the power of the visible—on skin as a visual signifier—and the manipulation of panchromatic "whiteness" and orthochromatic "blackness" towards specific racial types reveals the ways Hollywood could potentially mediate how race signified. This is just one way in which film can impact upon popular ideology, in this case precisely during the period when legislation (as in the *United States v. Thind*) was helping to shift US conceptions of race from "scientific" beliefs towards those held by "common knowledge" and the "common man."

Van Dyke's *The Pagan,* conceived from John Russell's novel as a sequel to *White Shadows,* again engages questions of miscegenation and race mixing, but does so in a far lighter and more comic manner. The opening directly mimics *White Shadows,* depicting images of the wide-open spaces of Pacific islands and sea that shortly lead to a lengthy, left to right traveling shot along the streets of a fallen, hybridized colonial town (Papeete). One key difference in *The Pagan,* however, is in the transitional shots from island paradise to degenerate colonial wilderness, which here focus on the trader, Slater (Donald Crisp), disembarking from his ship anchored at harbor. On deck as he leaves, shot from behind, is a young islander (Tito, played by Dorothy Janis), and this image cuts to a point-of-view shot from her position, watching as the trader's boat is rowed ashore. The feminine point of view established here is important, and will return with some force at the entrance of the film's heartthrob idol, Ramon Novarro, playing the half-caste hero, Henry Shoesmith, Jr. First, however, we are introduced to the film's other central figure, the (white) prostitute Madge (Renée Adorée), whom we glimpse walking the street, after which she propositions Slater while making a transaction at the bank, run by a Chinese banker. The colonial outpost is therefore established as a place marked by flux, racial diversity, freely available sexuality, and (white) feminine mobility, where money rules and anything can be bought for a price. Seeking copra, Slater is sent to find the plantation owner, Henry Shoesmith, who, we are told, is "too much like his native mother," establishing a theme of native torpor (as opposed to the native industry of *White Shadows*) that serves as a comedic—and perhaps Van Dykeian—element throughout the film.

Slater arrives at the Shoesmith store and sends the "native" assistant (first glimpsed asleep behind the desk) to find the owner, after which a tracking shot follows the assistant walking through the exotic foliage in what seems a drug-induced stupor. Novarro is encountered reclining at the base of a palm tree, scantily dressed in a pareu, nibbling fruit, while Madge plays the ukulele at his side; he tells his assistant he is "too busy for business." Though initially depicted as lazy, Henry is unlike the conventional half-caste figure, often portrayed as monstrous or psychologically damaged (as in early script versions of *White Shadows*). Henry is born of a native mother and takes the name of his white father, and as the film progresses he suggests a transitional figure, a mediator between a multiethnic US audience and the native other. Audience identification with "natives" and social outsiders is

FIGURE 7. Madge (Renée Adorée) looks . . . (courtesy of the Academy of Motion Picture Arts and Sciences).

clearly established at this point in the film, but Henry is also an object of desire. This sense is reinforced by the dominant feminine perspective established early on; indeed, unusually in this film women are rarely looked *at* but instead do much of the looking. We see Madge gazing longingly at Novarro's body, after which the camera crawls across it in a point-of-view shot, moving from feet to head while lingering over Novarro's long legs, as in several other shots. The intertitles indicate Madge's unrequited desire for Shoesmith and her regrets at having "fallen" before she met her ideal partner.

Novarro begins singing the film's popular theme, "Pagan Love Song," which is echoed by Tito, who sings while perched on the cabin roof of Slater's boat, offshore. As the two attractive leads meet and enter into their inevitable, mutual infatuation, a synchronized singing sequence shifts into full swing, but Slater suddenly arrives to stop the proceedings. Here the film echoes *The Jazz Singer*'s (1927) strategic staging of synch sound in the famous "Blue Skies" sequence, where Jackie's (Al Jolson) reactionary Jewish father enters the room to stop the song—and the audience's enjoyment of the new (if limited) technology of synch sound—dead.

FIGURE 8. . . . at Henry (Ramon Novarro) (courtesy of the Academy of Motion Picture Arts and Sciences).

Like the "Blue Skies" sequence, "Pagan Love Song" is cut off abruptly, suggesting the uneasy meeting of old and new, the "primitive" and modernity. The film and audience must reenter the world of miming, intertitles, and staid conventionality as the face-off between Shoesmith and Slater begins to take place. We discover that Tito is, like Shoesmith, "half white" and the ward and "Christian duty" of Slater. Moreover, Slater is training her to be "*all* white" (and, as his salacious glances at his ward suggest, *all* his), thus setting in motion the nature versus nurture debate that underlies the film. Slater orders Henry off the ship, establishing his gleaming white vessel as a space of white control and ownership in which the "native" has no place. As Tito does her lessons, reading a moralistic and religious text while Slater surreptitiously strokes her hair, Henry continues to sing "Pagan Love Song" onshore, defiantly facing the camera, now dominating the frame both through the use of medium close-up and the return of synchronized sound, which imbues Novarro's hybrid presence (racially mixed, both "primitive" and modern man) with a sudden immediacy and authority not encountered in the (mainly nonsynch) film up to this point.

A key component of Tito's whitening is an adherence to moral codes and values, as signified in Slater's pious, churchgoing ways, but Tito's eye is constantly drawn to nature and to the voice of her "half-native" beloved. After Slater dupes Shoesmith into giving away his coconut trees for the production of copra, scenes of the previously pristine groves show the island transformed into an industrial buzz of activity. Intertitles offer information about the production of copra and its international value, completing the impression that the copra industry has momentarily hijacked the film. While clearly overrunning the plantation, Slater and his industrial methods are not seen as exceptionally insidious. Unlike *White Shadows'* pearl divers, the copra workers here are portrayed as healthy and businesslike, while Shoesmith is shown shrugging off the invaders of his plantation as if only a temporary distraction. This sequence shows just how radically the tone of *The Pagan* differs from that of *White Shadows:* whereas drama and conflict take place on the level of individuals in the former, the larger social framework and explicit imperial critique of the latter almost entirely fall way, to be replaced by a rosier image of capitalism as the arrival of modernity—of pleasurable goods and synch sound. As Tito and Henry enter into their love affair, Slater aggressively confronts his rival, pushing him to the ground with the words "You half-caste! You sun-baked pagan!" This prejudice is clearly seen as brute ignorance. Slater's ship sails away with Tito weeping on board. Henry is left gazing after her from the shore, with Slater's words, "Borrow money, stock your store, make something of yourself," echoing in his head.

The ensuing scenes chart Henry's awkward efforts to whiten himself by reestablishing the business that carries his white father's name. His comical efforts reinforce the sense that he is a fish out of water, while Madge reminds him that he is going deeper and deeper into debt. Indeed, Henry's efforts at white respectability are visually marked as a masquerade: as he struggles with bolts of fabric for three female customers, he finds himself draped in the cloth, offering an image that suggests an indigenous—and in this case, feminizing—sarong. As far back as Wallis, dressed in tapa in the house of Purea, dressing up has indicated cultural masquerade and identity shifts in the Polynesian context. Joseph Banks, finding his jacket stolen after sleeping alongside Purea, is also encouraged by her to change costume, thus giving an appearance of cultural hybridity: "Oborea [Purea] took care to provide me with cloth to supply the place of my lost Jacket so that I made a motley apearance, my dress being half English and half Indian" (29 May 1769). When Slater's sloop finally reappears, Henry arrives triumphantly as the now fully masculinized replica of Slater, dressed immaculately in white clothes and hat and riding in a rowboat manned by his (one assumes, "full-blooded") native assistant. But the fact that Henry must take a boat at all—which he ridiculously bails as they cross the harbor—when just before he had effortlessly swum out to meet his beloved, suggests the absurdity of his efforts to assimilate.

Indeed, Henry's simplicity and naiveté is underscored when Slater reveals that Henry's bank debts were underwritten by Slater himself, who will now take possession of all Henry's land and goods. Slater, for a second time, orders Henry off of his ship, asserting his white ownership and exhibiting by degrees a slave-owner mentality. He perceives an "unholy light" in Tito's eyes and determines he should "sacrifice himself" for her soul by marrying her, thus saving her from savagery. The scene returns to the site of Madge and Henry's unrequited relationship, and once again the viewer is privileged to a full-body shot of Novarro from Madge's point of view: here Novarro reclines in an elegant, somewhat feminine, position, gazing at his outstretched legs and then settling down, cross-legged. A glamour shot of Novarro's face suggests that Madge—and the viewer—is still smitten with the pretty male figure that can only be voyeuristically gazed upon and never attained. Of course, the extrafilmic "open secret" of Novarro's homosexuality comes into play most strongly in these images, and perhaps De Vinna is to some extent working an in-joke to this effect.[78] But the emphasis on Novarro's seminude, frequently feminized figure in *The Pagan* also speaks to the power of the female box office and to the popularity of safe, feminized yet athletic leading men in the 1920s. Novarro's presence carries with it, however, a blatantly erotic charge not always associated with Hollywood's imaging of the male body that finds perhaps its closest parallel in *Moana* and other tales of exotic masculinity, such as the *Tarzan* series. Here the male body signifies on many levels, sometimes providing a site for projections of power (conventionally linked to masculinity), at other times appearing as a passive, sensuous object of the camera's look (the constructed realm of the feminine).

Slater succeeds in marrying Tito, but Henry abducts her from the chapel and they escape to an idyllic mountain retreat. After a "morning after" scene where the couple recline, shot lovingly in close-up, a long shot shows Tito at the window of their hut, watching as Henry retreats slowly into the distant foliage, an echo of the earlier shot that showed Tito's perspective from the boat as Slater similarly retreated from view across the harbor. Tito turns now to see Slater behind her, dressed uncharacteristically in black: a figure of fate, or death. In another scene displaying synch sound, Henry sings the theme song while coming to the slow realization that Tito has been abducted. The climactic scene on Slater's ship shifts the comic tone of the film to one of tension and tragedy: Slater is shown savagely whipping Tito—she is his "property," after all—with a belt, while in parallel sequencing Henry is shown rushing to her rescue. The parallel montage converges into a slow, agonizing dissolve: Tito is savagely beaten while Henry desperately swims towards her. The final confrontation between Henry and Slater turns to hand-to-hand combat, and here Novarro is transformed from sensuous sloth to the masculine (white) hero par excellence: Madge has already stated that "Henry is half white, and white men *fight* for their women." Slater, on the other hand, is reduced to flailing and hair-pulling, finally begging for his life. As the couple swim away from the ship, Slater equips himself with a suitably phallic compensation for his recent defeat—a large saber. He follows the swimming couple in his boat and attempts to stab Henry, as sharks begin to circle round. Henry tips Slater into the water, where he is quickly devoured by the sharks, leaving the couple to their blissful mountain retreat—though this is now an isolated and perhaps endangered space, like the primitive realm itself.

⌒

THE COMPLEXITY of films such as *White Shadows* and *The Pagan* lies in the interplay between texts and their broader local and global contexts. I am less interested, for example, in condemning Van Dyke on the basis of his writings than in marking the ways his films can work to give rise to anticolonial readings such as Hervé Dumont's, noted at the start of this chapter. As already suggested, *White Shadows* works at other levels, too: the "unmarked" category of whiteness is made palpable, placed within a relativizing framework, even if the racial and cultural otherness depicted on screen is largely fantastic. *The Pagan,* on the other hand, for all its stereotypes, suggests that hybrid "racial" identities might be made up of equally valid components forming part of a single integrated personality, rather than being stunted figures of sterility and latent monstrosity. More problematically, the primitive past in the film engages with a technological, capitalist future, only to find it is cast out into retreat and isolation.

The discovery of Van Dyke's interlocking racist and ethnocentric beliefs behind the scenes, while damaging to a figure such as Malinowski (whose reputation was tarnished when his apparently racist *Diary in the Strict Sense of the Term* was released in 1967), is in many ways hardly a revelation in the case of a self-described populist such as Van Dyke. Van Dyke was a pioneer of the large-scale Hollywood location shoot, and he built his career on exotic adventures such as *White Shadows, The Pagan, Tarzan, the Ape Man,* and *Trader Horn;* but his professional reputation never rested on open declarations of cultural relativism or antiracism. *Trader Horn,* for example, reveals how transparently US xenophobia and racial stereotyping entered into cross-cultural narratives of travel and exploration: a mythical status quo was shored up by these spectacles of difference.

As Ella Shohat and Robert Stam have argued, film is on one level mimesis, but on another it is also "utterance, an act of contextualized interlocution between socially situated producers and receivers."[79] *White Shadows in the South Seas* and *The Pagan* remain interesting and relevant not because of their manifest anticolonialism, but because they exemplify the contours of the modernist South Pacific romance, which allegorizes the rupture of the unified western subject, drawn to the fantasy of lost Edenic unity on distant islands, only to be seduced into an ultimate and problematic erasure of the self. The image of paradise is indelibly marked by a return of the repressed not only abroad, but also at home: miscegenation in *White Shadows* is linked to a loss of self, ending with death, while in *The Pagan,* Henry and Tito must return to their "native" ways. The parallels between imperial narratives and what Hazel V. Carby has called "internal colonization" are thrown into vivid relief when we consider that dime novels such as *Molesca, or the Indian Wife of the White Hunter* were similarly narrating the dangers of crossing into forbidden zones of race mixing.[80] In these films, Hollywood encoded the Janus face of paradise presented to US audiences: a reflection of both the ongoing fascination and distrust that marked the US relationship to Polynesia.

5 The Homoerotic Exotic

From C. W. Stoddard to *Tabu*

Think of the screen for a moment, then, as a mirror—a large mirror, a curiously constructed mirror, with the possibility to reflect all that the screen now reflects, but with an added peculiarity by which your face and figure may be faded into those of the hero and heroine, as the sex may determine.... Who is it that feels so keenly the irresistible lure of the South Seas? Is it the outer self of us? Not by a blue lagoon. We, all of us, on the outside haven't the courage any more than to read about it. We are afraid to lose our jobs, afraid to leave our homes, our families. We are bound up in the sacred shackles that rivet us to the making of profane shekels. We dream of breaking the chains one day.... [But] we aren't men and women enough to really indulge our desires to venture out beyond our conventional depths. It is the inner ego that urges us on to live the fuller measure of adventure; ... to follow the seductive song of Romance, that sings to us of the South Sea Islands on the lapis lazuli beaches, on which we may cavort with Clara Bow and Gilda Gray who think they are Clara and Gilda, but who, you know, are only synthetic shadowgraphs of you and all the other sirens who sit out there in the dark. But only Clara Bow and Gilda Gray are fooled. You recognize your inner self and, at the moment, realize that you have, in the picture, come at last to the Eden where you have always belonged, but which you have been cheated by your outer self.

— George Mitchell, "Movie Audiences Feel Themselves on Screen" (1927)

By the end of the 1920s, the revitalization that film had for some time injected into the well-worn themes of the Polynesian fantasy seemed to be on the wane. O'Brien's popularity—and that of the group of writers that followed him such as Nordhoff and Hall and Robert Dean Frisbie—had dovetailed with an array of films such as *A Virgin Paradise* (1921), with Pearl White; *The Fire Bride* (1922), filmed on location in the Pacific; *Never the Twain Shall Meet* (1925), also partially filmed in Tahiti; *Aloma of the South Seas* (1926), with so-called "shimmy queen" Gilda Gray as a dancer living on "Paradise Island"; *Hula* (1927), a Hawaiian romance featuring Clara Bow; and many others. New forays into the genre, then, were always in danger of simply reproducing clichés or, at worst, becoming self-parodies. *Variety*'s tongue-in-cheek review of the travelogue *Ramu* (1929) hints at just how standardized these conventions had become: "Most of the film shows crew tasting fruit, natives cooking, dancing, and swimming. Hip swinging of heavy breasted native women could have provided the sex bet, which cameraman muffed through apparent fear of close-ups."[1] Clearly, one of the clichés that Hollywood was still interested in perpetuating and further commercializing was the notion of the southern Pacific as heterosexual male fantasy, feeding the desires of its US—and ever-increasing international—audiences.[2] Yet George Mitchell's suggestive take on the role of spectatorship and identification, above, implies that the South Seas spectacle of the 1920s could also work with other genres to intervene in conventional assumptions about gender and sexual desire, allowing viewers to transcend the restraints of artificially constructed "outer selves" and instead "feel themselves"—their "inner selves"—on screen. Mitchell's reading of gender identification is more flexible than fixed, suggesting that audiences might envision themselves cavorting on the beach either alongside, or inhabiting, the synthetic shadowgraph personas of the likes of Gray or Bow.

In the previous chapter I proposed that an analysis of a film such as *The Pagan* might reveal interconnected—and potentially disruptive—racial, sexual, and gender discourses that came to inhabit, over time, even the most mainstream and easily consumable images of Polynesia. This development was arguably also true of other overblown film genres such as the Western of the late 1930s and 1940s or the musical of the 1940s and 1950s: there always seems to be a point at which the generic conventions of mass-marketed narrative forms reach cultural saturation and begin to break into new, more complex and self-referential modes of signification. In the case of *The Pagan,* we might perceive a sort of undertow working within the standards of Hollywood practice, reflecting how the conventions of the exotic romance could facilitate complex identifications and affinities in terms of gender and sexuality. What is particularly interesting is the way that, while certain shots conventionally fetishize the female face and figure, Van Dyke's film encourages female and male viewers alike to look at the "native" male body in openly eroticized ways, exploiting the voyeuristic exoticism embedded in Hollywood's Pacific fantasy while at the same time disturbing conventional hierarchies of gendered looking relations.

This kind of display and fetishization of the male body was not unique to the South Seas genre: Hollywood was accustomed to experimenting with point-of-view and reaction shots (involving, to note just two prominent examples, the camera's gaze at stars such as Rudolph Valentino or Douglas Fairbanks) that could provide *Variety*'s "sex bet" via images of male stars. Yet such images were usually accompanied by the trappings of phallic power, while the South Seas male was commonly feminized. As in *The Pagan*, the appearance of the feminized, fetishized male body is very often aligned to a female look, which fixes the ostensible desire in the film as heterosexual. But as I want to suggest in this chapter, even within this heterosexual coding such images might begin to manipulate and unsettle, if not necessarily unseat, dominant hierarchies of masculine and feminine audience identification, as well as hinting at parallel desires that hover in the margins of the manifest text. As Pamela Cheek concisely argues, exotic identifications were often capable of enabling the exploration of "unavailable models of sexual identity," a phenomenon implied but rarely made explicit in the staged world of Hollywood's Polynesian fantasy.[3] Robert Flaherty and F. W. Murnau's *Tabu*, made independently outside of Hollywood, takes a few more risks in this regard, and as such helps us to make further connections between the less visible sexual and imperial dynamics behind modernist Polynesian-themed texts. *Tabu* could have been enabling for certain modes of subaltern identification and recognition in its audiences, even while—or perhaps because—it also covered its tracks, appearing to endorse many of the familiar stereotypes, tropes, and themes that helped the west to envision its others.

The Look and the Gaze

As chapter 1 suggested, voyeurism and sex tourism have long been embedded in western representations of the South Pacific, and they were given explicit visual form in the virtual tours screened to film viewers in the early decades of the twentieth century—although as a film such as *The Pagan* begins to imply, the appeal of this sex tourism was neither necessarily nor exclusively heterosexual, even if the ostensive audience gaze was framed and coded as such. This chapter thus focuses on two cultural manifestations conjoined in the South Seas film: the destabilizing of sexual and gender assumptions that has been endemic to the Pacific encounter (through western travelers' homoerotic inscriptions as well as encounters with—to name just two local phenomena—*mahū* in Tahiti and the practice of *pekio* in the Marquesas) and the innovative gender work visible in Hollywood films of the 1920s and early 1930s.

Previous chapters have suggested that certain kinds of camera looks at nativized, fetishized male bodies at one level suggest Hollywood's desire to appeal to the box-office power of (heterosexual) female viewers in the 1920s: a manifest level reflected in shots of male bodies that overtly encourage identification with female characters' looks. But at another level—at least in the case of tropical fantasies such as *Moana* and *The Pagan,* both products of heterosexual male directors—moments such as Moana's *siva* or Madge's lengthy, possessive look at Henry's half-naked figure in a pareu arguably engage with a homoerotic subtext, especially when considering in the case of the latter the open secret of Novarro's homosexuality. This might be seen as a latent level of the text—one that uses the fetishized male body as a kind of screen for the projection of aligned desires, allowing for the emergence of homoerotic identifications commonly suppressed in mainstream cultural productions. David Lugowski has taken this a step further, contending in his study of queer Hollywood in the early 1930s that the post–World War I era, with its "disillusioned veterans, feminist struggles, racial and ethnic migrations, shifts and tensions, and widespread contempt for Prohibition," was often "enabling for queerness."[4] As a result, what Noël Burch refers to as the dominant "institutional mode of representation" (IMR) appears to have been far from monolithic, instead permitting and even encouraging diverse forms of spectatorship.[5] Yet it should be said that, as much ideological film criticism has suggested, Hollywood is often able to recuperate such disruptions through hierarchical resolutions in the narrative and other forms of thematic closure that restore "order" to potentially subversive plot and character elements.

Thus even if the camera's look at Henry / Novarro in *The Pagan* is coded as female, and even if behind it is the possibility of a latent homoerotic look, these forms of looking do not necessarily escape being bound to an oppressive regime of the gaze. It should be stressed that these kinds of shots do not, in any definitive way, constitute the disruptive gaze back at the camera; this is not the "gaze returned," if one considers the terms of the dominant modes of visual signification characterized by Laura Mulvey in "Visual Pleasure and Narrative Cinema" as Hollywood's male gaze.[6] Instead these shot sequences indicate a complex and, notably, masculine, imaginary construction of female looks within the gaze of the cinematic apparatus. This fact might lead to other questions: even if we admit that the female look in *The Pagan* is a product of a male gaze, can this look at other levels still pose challenges to dominant ways of seeing, since it encourages uninhibited forms of looking at, and indeed ogling, the spectacle of the—feminized—male body, a body that offers itself up to be looked at?[7]

At this point it might be worth turning to Kaja Silverman's clarification of the difference, according to the work of Jacques Lacan, between the "gaze" and the "look." Lacan's notion of the gaze, Silverman suggests, is not limited to a single individual, but is a collective entity that arises from a variety of angles and vantage points: the gaze is not solely the province of a single character or subject position. The look, on the other hand, can originate from an individual subject or multiple subject positions.[8] As Shohini Chaudhuri elaborates, for Lacan, "The subject is always split, self-divided and alienated from its desire, that is, 'castrated.' Lacan reads castration metaphorically, so for him the look (as well as language), rather than the anatomical body, is the site of castration. The look conveys the looker's desire and *lack*."[9] This might help us to understand why Madge's look at Henry is coded both as desire and as lack. After her longing look takes in every inch of Henry's body, Madge's question implies her confusion about her own lack of sexual appeal: "Henry, why don't you like me?" As E. Ann Kaplan suggests, women in Hollywood film can "receive and return the gaze, but cannot act on it."[10] At the same time, Madge's "marginal" look colludes at other levels with the appropriative gaze of the west over its others: though socially marginalized as woman and prostitute, Madge is also white and possesses a degree of urban mobility (as contrasted to the ship-bound, often locked-up figure of the "native" girl Tito). Madge's look at Henry's "native" body seems to be both feminizing and fetishizing: it thus conspires with the imperial gaze while at the same time foregrounding the disconnected, dysfunctional aspects of voyeurism. Like the audience, Madge can look, but can never touch or possess. In the midst of these female/male, white/native looking relations, the hierarchical gaze of imperial power appears to come undone, replaced by blatant and almost desperate fetishization of the native. I want to pursue some of these ideas in my reading of *Tabu*, a text that envisions a similar admixture of liberating and potentially oppressive looks at native bodies.

Indeed, it could be said that the whole paradoxical nature of 1920s Hollywood attitudes towards sex and cultural difference are encapsulated in some of the shots discussed above, which, often in spite of their best efforts to collude with the regimes of the male and imperial gazes, retain qualities that invite identifications and desires that exceed their framing and that point to some of the problems within monolithic theories of spectatorship. While unpacking the assumptions of received critical positions, critics like Judith Mayne have suggested that there is often a problem in assigning the activity of making meaning to an overly reductive or seemingly unitary source such as the cinematic apparatus or the socially contextualized viewer.[11] It is useful to look instead at the ways that different kinds of filmmakers and viewers—across the spectrum of gender, sexual preference, race, age, class—have produced diverse meanings and confronted, reappropriated, or simply ignored dominant ways of seeing over varying eras. Films such as *Moana, White Shadows in the South Seas, The Pagan,* and *Tabu* all offer specific instances of this diversity, providing windows onto reading and consuming the film text in a variety of ways and revealing that the cinematic gaze on the exotic was paradoxical, problematic, always potentially interesting.

The Homoerotic Exotic

Western representations of Polynesia have, the record suggests, always been crossed and recrossed by inner inconsistencies with respect to gender and sexuality that tend to problematize the (hetero)sexual assumptions that many critics have cited as underlying features of imperial narratives. For example, while Bougainville's description of the nude display of a young Tahitian woman who, like Venus, "shewed herself to the Phrygian shepherd" on the deck of the *Boudeuse* was extensively cited and helped establish notions of the Pacific as a sexual spectacle, an incident that immediately follows in his narrative curiously mirrors the scene, yet with the male gaze at the nude body of the female other—and the western gaze at the Tahitian—abruptly inverted. Bougainville's ship's cook, who had earlier ventured onto shore in order to "content [his] desires," is surrounded and immediately undressed "from head to feet" by the Tahitians, who "tumultuously examin[e] every part of his body" (*Voyage*, 219). Bougainville's published account further suggests the occasional, possibly homoerotic glance. After a few days in Tahiti he makes a special point of noting that he had never seen "men better made, and whose limbs were more proportionate: in order to paint a Hercules or a Mars, one could no where find such beautiful models" (249).

It is worth recalling as well an incident cited in chapter 1, when Joseph Banks received some Tahitian visitors, one of whom displayed "her naked beauties" in an encounter Banks describes as a "ceremony" and seems to interpret as sexual invitation (12 May 1769). The same scene was witnessed by Banks's illustrator, Sydney Parkinson. Banks's "ceremony" has been interpreted as an iconic example of the European eroticization of the Pacific, but an equally interesting yet less fully detailed encounter follows shortly after: Parkinson tersely notes that the next day he "saw a person who had the appearance of a hermaphrodite," but makes no further remarks (13 May). Parkinson's "hermaphrodite" suggests a brief meeting with a *mahū*, a Tahitian male transgender role. For Lee Wallace, the *mahū* figure invokes the Pacific as a space where "the known limits of . . . masculinity come undone"; and perhaps Parkinson's alignment of the "hermaphrodite" with Banks's story might hint at some of the sexual transformations and discoveries taking place beyond those inscribed in the various accounts of Cook's first voyage.[12] Documentation of same-sex practices and nonconventional gender roles was nonetheless limited in Enlightenment voyaging accounts, perhaps because it did not easily gel with the ideal of Polynesia as a sexual Arcadia. But we do have moments such as Cook's observations of *aikāne* in Hawai'i (male sexual favorites of the Hawaiian royalty) and, towards the early years of the nineteenth century, accounts such as the missionary James Wilson's critical observations of the behavior of *mahū*s and Willam Mariner's descriptions of same-sex practice in the Tonga Islands, which were joining ethnographic accounts emerging from around the globe.[13] Rudi Bleys suggests that the very formation of modern western sexual identities were influenced by historical ethnographic accounts of same-sex relations and cross-gender roles, significantly including late-eighteenth- and early-nineteenth-century descriptions of *aikāne, mahū,* and Samoan *fa'afafine*.[14]

By the early 1920s, travel texts such as A. Safroni-Middleton's *South Seas Foam: The Romantic Adventures of a Modern Don Quixote in the Southern Seas* continued to offer ambiguous messages about sexuality, gender, and sexual desires discovered and experienced on Polynesian travels. Safroni-Middleton's "romantic adventures" in Tahiti were clearly bound up in gazing at and assessing the erotic charms of men, as well as women: "The water glistened from their lime-dyed locks and ran down their handsome figures. 'Yarana!' was their oft-iterated salutation. It was hard to tell which were the most attractive, the pretty maids with hibiscus blossoms in their curly hair, or the handsome terra-cotta coloured youths."[15] Homoerotic subthemes have extended from the writings of Melville, Stoddard, London, and Gauguin to more recent work such as photographer Gian Paolo Barbieri's *Tahiti Tattoos* and *Exotic Nudes*. Indeed, Wallace's *Sexual Encounters* ultimately contends that the most "sexually resonant figure inscribed within the representational archive of the Pacific" is that of the male body, not the female.[16]

To frame some of the ways that *Tabu* engages with same-sex curiosity in the Pacific, this chapter first takes a detour into the work of nineteenth-century writer Charles Warren Stoddard, who, Robert Aldrich has suggested, could be considered "one of the most blatantly homoerotic writers of the nineteenth century."[17] Stoddard's work, I suggest, constructs a textual point of view similar to elements of *Tabu*'s queer spectacle. At the same time, this chapter draws to a close the story that began with O'Brien's travels in the Marquesas and that ends with Flaherty's final sojourn in the Pacific. Flaherty and Murnau's coproduction is a film that, like *Moana,* invites nostalgia for the passing of a race while providing a critique of western cultural and capitalist hegemony in the Pacific. Yet simultaneously, *Tabu* stages a largely male and unabashedly homoerotic spectacle that exceeds the sexual undercurrents of *Moana, White Shadows,* and *The Pagan. Tabu's* erotic spectacle makes explicit, but also complicates, assumptions about the kinds of sexual politics encoded in the exotic spectacle, posing alternatives to strictly heteronormative ways of seeing.

In theorizing some of the complexities and pitfalls of what I am calling the homoerotic exotic, it would be useful to recall the cautions outlined in Joseph Boone's essay "Vacation Cruises; or, the Homoerotics of Orientalism," a study that helped to bring to the forefront questions of queer investment in the proliferation of colonial spectacle.[18] After examining Malek Alloula's and Edward Said's readings of the Orient as a field for male westerners to discover and practice sexualities deemed illicit at home, Boone argues that analyses of colonialist erotics need to break out of their "conspicuously heterosexual interpretive frameworks."[19] Specifically, critics who have tended to focus questions of colonial signification and hierarchical oppositions on the juxtaposition of the masculine and feminine often view the connections between colonialism, travel, and erotic projections in terms of heterosexual, masculine travelers gazing at, desiring, and appropriating feminine others. Yet while this feminine trope clearly is thematized throughout a diverse range of colonialist literature, thus binding the force of empire through the collusion of phallocratic and colonial interests (and in the Pacific context this might be seen in accounts such as Paul Theroux's *Happy Isles of Oceania* and Julian Evans's *Transit of Venus*), this feminized other did not, in fact, always correspond to the "female."

Such a debunking of the heteronormative modes of postcolonial criticism, however, has not necessarily been good news for queer studies. As Boone points out, the fact remains that the possibility of homosexual contact in the Orient "underwrites and at times even explains the historic appeal of orientalism as an occidental mode of male perception, appropriation, and control."[20] Mystifications of distance and appropriations of otherness have, paradoxically, opened avenues for validating different contested and subaltern voices in the west, even while reproducing and reinforcing fictions of western cultural and racial superiority over others. Boone's ideas suggest that the work of queer travelers such as Stoddard and Murnau might begin to generate ambiguous and contradictory images of imperial identity. Without, I hope, homogenizing the diverse yet intertwined issues involved in reading the desires of female, lesbian, gay, or—to use a more general term—queer viewers, I want to examine some of the implications of envisioning the "native" male body in the context of Polynesian fantasies that complicate notions of the western gaze as predictable, consistent, or unified.

Queer Looks

Charles Warren Stoddard was born in Rochester, New York, and as a child moved with his family to San Francisco, where he would later establish himself as a member of the West Coast branch of the Bohemians, the New York social group that modeled itself on the experimental artistic life associated with Paris's Left Bank.[21] In San Francisco, Stoddard inhabited a world of "Chopin at twilight, Oriental bric-a-brac, incense, lounging robes, and fragrant cigarettes"—accoutrements that today might suggest some of the obvious clichés of a gay lifestyle.[22] Members of the San Francisco Bohemians included Joaquin Miller and Bret Harte, as well as Stoddard's intimate friends Ina Coolbrith (a poet known to prefer the company of other women) and Samuel Clemens (Mark Twain). Critics have speculated that Stoddard may even have had a short-term sexual relationship with Clemens, Stoddard writing in 1874 that "no one suited him [Clemens] but me, and sometimes I didn't exactly suit. But we were together night and day, and we went deep into each other's lives."[23]

Though Stoddard's literary reputation faded considerably over the course of the twentieth century, a revival of scholarly interest lately coincides with efforts to remap the historical convergences of western sexual identities and the discourses of imperialist expansion.[24] Justin D. Edwards, glossing Leslie Fiedler, sees Stoddard's work as intersecting with a tradition in the US literary imagination of the "cross-cultural male couple traveling through the American wilderness (Huck and Jim) or on the high seas (Ishmael and Queequeg)...a recurring trope that works to disavow the restrictions of a repressed and conservative culture that has alienated itself from the so-called natural primitivism of man."[25] Stoddard, keen to explore the depths of his sexual "nature" amidst exotic Pacific islands, has become an exemplary case study of a queer male traveler writing during a period of extensive US continental and Pacific expansion, and he was in many ways caught up in the potent imaginary power of this westward-looking ideology. Finding only scant success as a poet in San Francisco (his *Poems* was published in 1867), he converted to Catholicism and set out on several trips to the Pacific: Maui, Oahu, and Molokai for six months in 1868, Tahiti for three months in 1870, and—after aborting plans to travel to Samoa—Hawai'i again for several months in 1872. The Pacific region would, a decade later, be included in Sir Richard Burton's infamous delineation of the "Sotadic Zone," the area where "vice is popular and endemic, held at worse to be a mere peccadillo."[26] Stoddard seems to have shared a similar belief that geography could be a primary factor governing social morality. Writing from

Hawai'i to Walt Whitman, he claimed that he was finally able to act as his "nature" prompted him: he had discovered a world of erotic possibility beyond even California, "where men are tolerably bold."[27]

In 1873, Stoddard published a semifictionalized account of his travels as the collection *South Sea Idyls*.[28] The book gained a modest following and is thought to have been a key influence on Stevenson's decision to undertake his long-term sojourn in the Pacific. Stevenson became a faithful admirer of *Idyls,* ranking Stoddard and Herman Melville as the only two writers to have "touched the South Seas with any genius."[29] On receiving a personal copy from Stoddard in 1892, Rudyard Kipling wrote from a wintry Vermont that *South Sea Idyls* had given him "as bad an attack of 'go-fever' as I've had for a long time past." Ironically adopting the persona of a conservative New Englander, Kipling noted that the book was "highly improper, and I doubt not immoral. What has the *hula hula*...to do with New England?...It is sinful beyond telling that a man should wear no clothes. *Therefore* you will see that the South Seas never existed."[30] But the "sinful" undercurrents of *South Sea Idyls* went even further. Emboldened by the passionate male friendships portrayed in works such as Dana's *Two Years before the Mast,* the palpable homoeroticism of Whitman's "Calamus" poems (1860), and Bayard Taylor's *Joseph and His Friend* (1870), Stoddard in his stories makes the sexual undercurrents in works such as Melville's *Redburn* and *Billy Budd* seem relatively staid by comparison. In "Taboo," for instance, Stoddard's first-person narrator is drawn to the sight of "naked and superbly shaped" Polynesian men "stripped to the skin and bareheaded," their "brawny bodies glistening in the sun as though they had been oiled."[31] In "Chumming with a Savage," Stoddard describes a horseback encounter with his sixteen-year-old beloved, Kána-aná: "So Kána-aná brought up his horse, got me on to it in some way or other, and mounted behind me to pilot the animal and sustain me in my first bare-back act" (24). Here are shades of sex tourism and a distinctly American and queer version of Loti's vision of romance in paradise, *Le Mariage de Loti—Rarahu* (1880).

I want to briefly focus on some of *South Sea Idyls*'s more openly homoerotic tales in order to mark the ways that what we might now call Stoddard's queer looks at Pacific Island men inflect his participation in colonial discourses about the Pacific and to note how these looks seem to anticipate the queer cinematic gaze of a film such as *Tabu*. Stoddard's homoerotic descriptions are often organized around acts of scopophilia, foregrounding the power of seeing, and are enabled via the sheer visibility of the native body. Thus a reading that brings concepts of the look and the gaze into focus with issues of sexual and imperial power relations—or what

Jane Gaines refers to in the context of cinema as the "looking relations" governing race, gender, and class—might shed further light on cross-cultural, male-male looking relations in Stoddard's work.[32] E. Ann Kaplan suggests that "like everything in culture, looking relations are determined by history, tradition, power hierarchies, politics, economics. . . . The possibilities for looking are carefully controlled. . . . Looking is power."[33] But I would add to this list the more liminal realms of desire: urges to look that are linked to and monitored by institutional power relations but that also attempt to elude or undermine these dominant structures through the mechanisms of risk, pleasure, and play. Stoddard's textualized queer looks are immersed in other contexts as well, staging encounters that frequently venture beyond a unidirectional western gaze at subordinate others. This may be the mark of the queer traveler coming to grips with an island epistemology: the sense that island encounters can be characterized by the complex and paradoxical nature of islands themselves, which have in many ways confounded, destabilized, and resisted the imperial and taxonomical moves of western powers.

Not unlike the passages from Bougainville and Safroni-Middleton cited above, Stoddard's erotic descriptions tend to foreground the power of seeing, indulging in the pleasures of the (native) male body's visibility. Stoddard's stories frequently involve a first-person narrator describing native masculinity in breathless detail: the central figure is a traveler on the colonial periphery, at a distance from the centers of power and propriety, desiring spaces of erotic possibility away from the conventional codes and prohibitions of the west. There is a seeming paradox here: Stoddard's queer looks were produced from the margins, yet were at the same time absorbed into hegemonic, mainstream literary practices. This chapter thus poses a question that is difficult to fully answer, asking to what extent work such as Stoddard's or Murnau's might have enabled patterns of identification and recognition to emerge from subaltern, queer audiences, even while (or perhaps because) it endorsed the stereotypes of imperial hierarchy—the gaze *at* the subaltern native—and was framed by dominant modes of "us" envisioning "them."

Take, for example, a scene in "A Tropical Sequence" that describes a wordless meeting with a young Tahitian man:

> Suddenly the doorway was darkened by a stalwart brave, whose noiseless step had given no warning of his approach. . . . He paused at the threshold until his friendly greeting had been returned; then he entered with some diffidence, deposited his fruits in the corner, squatted upon the mat near me, and breathed audibly, for his burden was heavy, and the trail no primrose path. Except for the *pareu* that girded his loins, my visitor was quite naked.

The encounter begins with a common alignment from the late-eighteenth and nineteenth centuries between Pacific Islanders and American Indians: the "stalwart brave" is similarly linked to the cliché of an elusive, somewhat mysterious racial other. But quickly the passage shifts—from the narrator observing the other with something akin to an ethnographic detachment to his engaging in an exchange of looks:

> Long we gazed at each other with an earnest, honest gaze that ended in a smile of recognition; we had never met before, but the uncivilized and the overcivilized are brothers. He placed his hand on my shoulder and stroked me fondly. From the back of his ear he drew his tobacco pouch, and rolled a cigarette, of which we took alternate puffs in token of perpetual peace. . . . And then—we had been silent until now—he said, in hesitating English with a childish accent, "I know you; you like me; you come my house." (*Idyls,* 165–166)

The looks and "smile of recognition," followed by fond stroking, hold the promise of an erotic connection. The shared cigarette suggests postcoital bliss or might serve as a (phallic) signifier of sublimated desire: a trope as meaningful and significant, perhaps, as Bette Davis's and Paul Henreid's shared cigarettes in *Now, Voyager* (1942). But what interests me in the passage is the interrelation of looks and gazes in the queer/imperial context. On the one hand it could be argued that Stoddard's imagery and rhetorical style participate in the conventions of a racialized imperial gaze: the Tahitian man is exoticized, infantilized (complete with "childish accent"), and subtly sexualized at the same time. On the other hand, a homoerotic subtext and exchange of looks between the two men has the effect of queering the passage, rendering it unstable, open to multiple and potentially subversive meanings that go against the grain of moral and imperial order.

A similarly problematic exchange takes place in the tale that forms the centerpiece of *South Sea Idyls,* the three-part "Chumming with a Savage," a story based on a relationship Stoddard had with a Hawaiian while traveling through the Halawa valley in Molokai. Here the American narrator's first encounter with his young companion recalls a western tradition of sexualizing, feminizing, and orientalizing Polynesian boys and men, but goes further to suggest a liminal sexual exchange:

> There was no sex to that garment; it was the spontaneous offspring of a scant material and a large necessity. I'd seen plenty of that sort of thing, but never upon a model like this, so entirely tropical—almost Oriental. As this singular phenomenon made directly for me, and, having come within reach, there stopped and

stayed, I asked its name, using one of my seven stock phrases for the purpose; I found it was called Kána-aná. . . . This sage inquirer was, perhaps, sixteen years of age. His eye was so earnest and so honest, I could return his look. I saw a round, full, rather girlish face; lips ripe and expressive, not quite so sensual as those of most of his race; not a bad nose, by any means; eyes perfectly glorious—regular almonds—with the mythical lashes "that sweep," etc., etc. The smile which presently transfigured his face was of the nature that flatters you into submission against your will. (20–21)

While the passage manifestly objectifies and exoticizes the narrator's companion —the "sexless" figure is referred to as "it"—at the same time we might note a queer emphasis on ambiguous gender appearance over sexual essence. Stoddard might be dehumanizing his character in classically imperial fashion, he might be gesturing towards the figure of an *aikāne,* or he might be simply implying sexual ambiguity; in any case, by the end of the passage the telltale pronoun "his" takes over, completing the narrator's and reader's voyage from ambiguity on the level of the visible into the realms of male homoerotic desire.

The status of the look—or more specifically, the look hesitantly returned by Stoddard's narrative persona—is also curious: "His eye was so earnest and so honest, I could return his look." Though Stoddard's look is at first manifestly voyeuristic, he carefully incorporates the look of the other, implying a reciprocation that collapses voyeurism as an act of seeing without being seen, substituting a process of looking and being looked at. This is also a look that comes closer to Freud's original thesis on scopophilia, which contains three stages: first the subject looking towards "an extraneous object"; second, shifting of the scopophilic instinct away from the object towards part of the subject's own body, which prepares the subject to be passively "looked at"; and finally, the introduction of a new subject "to whom one displays oneself in order to be looked at by him."[34] In Stoddard's stories, looking at men implies also being looked at. And common enough as haole were and are in Hawai'i, he carries his own status as something of an outsider, foreign body—a fetish object to be investigated.

Stoddard's queer form of looking further recalls Brian Pronger's discussion of a distinctive "gay gaze": "Most gay men develop a canny ability to instantly discern from the returned look of another man whether or not he is gay. The gay gaze is not only lingering, but also a visual probing, a sometimes satisfying search for recognition."[35] What we are left with is a much more entangled series of looks, probing and threatening to disturb the customary boundaries of culture and sexuality. Following the initial exchange, Kána-aná, according to Stoddard, "weighs [the narrator] in his balance" and, using his "instincts," proceeds to make a direct proposal to the American. Stoddard continues: "You may be sure his instincts didn't cheat him; they don't do that sort of thing—he placed his hands on my two knees, and declared, 'I was his best friend, and he was mine; I must come at once to his house, and there live always with him" (*Idyls,* 21). Stoddard's persona then describes how he was "taken in, fed, and petted in every possible way, and finally put to bed." It is hardly surprising when he adds, "I didn't sleep much, after all. I think I must have been excited" (24). He and his "companion-in-arms" sleep nude together (26), while Kána-aná "would mesmerize me into a most refreshing sleep with a prolonged and pleasing manipulation. It was a reminiscence of the baths of Stamboul not to be withstood" (32). With Kána-aná's relatives sleeping nearby—the couple's own bed hidden behind "numerous shawls"—the narrator exclaims, "How queer the whole atmosphere of the place was!" (25).

Stoddard appears to share in a reciprocated form of queer looking with the likes of Kána-aná and "the bronzed one" of "A Tropical Sequence," but it should be remembered that this look operates on the level of fantasy as the product of a haole, a western figure seeking potential sexual gratification and recognition in the tropics. As Kaplan notes, "Looking relations are never innocent."[36] In fact, there are at least three kinds of looks constructed in the passages: the look of the narrator/Stoddard, the look of the native, and the collaborative looks of (western) readers. To all appearances, the narrator (as did Stoddard, as indicated in his letters)[37] believes he has experienced reciprocated "eye contact," a desiring look at the other mirrored by an equally desiring look returned. But the narrator may be ethnocentrically (or even homo-ethnocentrically) misreading signs of cross-cultural affection as subtextually sexual. Multiple innuendos and double entendres at the same time encourage readers to pleasurably collaborate in this sexual subtext—to exercise, in effect, their own queer looks—as when Stoddard's narrative persona weakly protests that "again and again he [Kána-aná] would come with a delicious banana to the bed where I was lying, and insist upon my gorging myself, when I had but barely recovered from a late orgie of fruit, flesh, or fowl" (32). There may be little that unambiguously confirms a sexual dimension to Stoddard's "real" encounters in the Pacific, yet his stories' prolific imagery of phallic fruit and nude petting directs the attentive reader to conclude that there is a sexual component, at least within the diegesis of the story, without explicitly stating it. Further complicating matters is the fact that "homosexuality" was barely established as a recognized term for a human condition when Stoddard's tales appeared. In 1869 Carl

Maria Benkert proposed the word *Homosexuelle* which, along with *Urning,* would come to be adopted by men engaging in same-sex relations, as well as by medical theorists concerned with this "condition."[38] The exchanged queer looks posited in Stoddard's stories thus can be seen to instill reassurance and recognition in the Stoddard narrator, which in turn constructs a "safe" space for readers who wish to pleasurably engage with, and participate in, the text's homoerotics. This suggests the emergence of a fictional space that indicates, recognizes, and permits same-sex desire, laying the groundwork for imagined spaces of queer identity.

Understandably, Roger Austen was surprised, as late as the 1980s, to find that "during the last one hundred years nearly everyone who has written for publication about [Stoddard] has been unable, or unwilling, to recognize the pervasive undercurrent of sexuality for what it is."[39] Austen argued that homosexuality was "airbrushed" out of historical accounts of Stoddard's fiction, just as it was largely withheld from wider accounts of literature. The scholarly project of drawing out the wider cultural implications of homoerotic codes, begun in earnest in Leslie Fiedler's work, is linked to examining what Jacob Stockinger has called the implicit "homotextuality" of texts. As Bleys suggests, glossing Stockinger, "A document becomes 'of homosexual interest' by its use of carefully chosen adjectives, by the adoption of particular 'signifying' images, names or terms, or by its connection to an Orientalist or Primitivist trope."[40] Stoddard's thinly veiled prose might enact what has been called, in contexts as diverse as political rhetoric and cinematic censorship, a "principle of deniability" that permits the language's sexual content to remain invisible by those who would rather remain unseeing.[41] At the same time, these multilayered rhetorical guises still permitted audiences attuned to the text's homotextuality to engage with, and establish recognition of, shared desires at other levels. Yet it is important to avoid too strictly inscribing Stoddard's work into a linear or progressive reading of queer history and identity. As Ian Barnard cautions,

> Literary and historical projects that attempt to locate and claim a lesbian or gay past, or lesbian and gay "foremothers" and "forefathers" in order to inscribe them into a linear and unified gay tradition, necessarily impose a specifically western and modern teleology of identity, sexuality, and liberation onto historically and culturally diverse (and often alien) subjects, and thus reinforce the imperialist relations that are already inherent in such a project's almost inevitable origin in the white western academy.[42]

Indeed, lest Stoddard's stories appear simply as utopian fictional spaces that invoke a "universal" queer imaginary that subverts the tropes of empire, we should recall that Stoddard's condescension and orientalist fetishizing is at least as overt as his homoeroticism. Moreover, Stoddard's Catholicism may have played a prevailing role in his ambivalent attitude towards Polynesians: he all at once appears to desire, fetishize, and stereotype the other's foreignness.[43] His story "The Chapel of the Palms" describes the noble virtues of missionaries forming a symbiotic relationship with "their" islanders while toiling in poverty and offers a divine future vision of ongoing Christian deliverance after the present missionaries have passed away. It closes by invoking a prayer: "Fever and famine do not stay them.... If there is work to do, it shall be done, and the hands shall be folded, for the young apostles will have followed in the silent footsteps of their flock" (*Idyls*, 238). In a similarly religious vein, part 2 of "Chumming with a Savage" moves away from the homoerotic paradise of Molokai towards the theme "How I Converted My Cannibal," with the Stoddard persona stating that he should "like to show him some American hospitality, and perhaps convert him before I sent him back again" (36). The conversion experiment turns horribly wrong, however, and Kána-aná, now compared to an exotic plant, slowly dies after being plucked from "the luxurious clime of its nativity" (44). Echoing the problematic discourse of the fatal impact, Stoddard's persona is left in self-divided agony. He accuses himself for attempting to "remodel an immortal soul," yet manages to find small comfort in recognizing the errors of tampering with the absolute order of "the Creator" who has placed each creature in its suitable environment. He notes, "I might have known that one reared in the nursery of Nature, as free to speak and act as the very winds of heaven to blow whither they list, could ill support the manacles of our modern proprieties" (61). Kána-aná's death has placed the narrator's own faith in doubt, and he briefly invokes a culturally relative stance, admitting that "each one has his idols" (65). But he returns to the solace of a divine creator who relegates each being in the chain of humanity to their specific "place" and "culture." On learning that Kána-aná had not fully been "corrupted" by his conversion efforts but had died a "devoted and unshaken adherent to the faith of his [Hawaiian] fathers," the narrator feels redeemed, concluding that he "could not but feel that the blood was off my hands" (65).

Boone's conclusions about Joe Orton's and André Gide's homosexual encounters during their North African travels might help us to read the contradictions at the heart of Stoddard's work. Boone notes that "in narratives where the occidental traveler by virtue of his homosexuality is already the other, the presumed *equivalence* of Eastern homosexuality and occidental personal liberation may disguise the specter of colonial privilege and exploitation encoded in the hierarchy of white man/brown boy."[44] Boone's suggestion that there could, in these cases, be an interdependent relationship between queer and imperial discourses is highly germane to texts that have used the Pacific as a stage for visualizing forbidden queer desires. Many of Stoddard's stories seem irreducibly double: providing support for western narratives of queer liberation while also reinforcing the imagined autonomy of whiteness through the racializing and exoticizing tropes of imperial spectacle.

It was an interesting move, then, when the cover of the 1987 edition of Stoddard's stories by San Francisco's Gay Sunshine Press attempted to redress literary history's ignoring of Stoddard's homoeroticism by going to the opposite extreme, rendering the implicit explicit by featuring a photo of a nude Polynesian man leaning against a tree branch. The shot resembles "arty" black-and-white beefcake images that market a variety of gay-themed literature and related merchandise. Unlike most beefcake photos, however—and unlike the reciprocal queer looks imagined by Stoddard in many of his stories—the young Polynesian man on the cover of *Cruising the South Seas: Stories by Charles Warren Stoddard* discretely looks away from, rather than faces, the camera: the figure does not challenge or meet the camera's gaze, but invites the viewer's voyeurism. The portrait not only recalls the tradition of western voyeurism in the Pacific, but also invites the construction of an empowered male gaze and inherently femininized other, a "not looking" relation described by Richard Dyer in the context of the pinup: "In the case of not looking ... the female model typically averts her eyes, expressing modesty, patience and a lack of interest in anything else [while] the male model looks either off or up."[45] Gay Sunshine's edition thus raises the question that Austen and others managed to discreetly elide: if Stoddard's sexuality was underplayed in traditional critical accounts of his work, why was his role in racial and imperial power dynamics often underplayed in queer accounts?

In a number of ways, then, the intersecting problems of queer and imperial ways of seeing to which Stoddard's writings (and their more recent marketing) give rise are intimately related to Flaherty and Murnau's *Tabu*—and not only to the text itself but also to its production and reception. *Tabu* has already been criticized in some detail for its links to the imperial gaze, but it might be read more fully as a text that, like Stoddard's work, inhabits the interstices of queer and imperial spectacles.

Paradise

Reproduced in Lotte Eisner's classic biography of F. W. Murnau is a photograph taken during the making of *Tabu*. She has called it, simply, "Paradise," coyly reflecting the title of the film's part 1. Yet this is a picture of a rather more specific kind of utopia: the figure of Murnau is clad all in white, his hat self-consciously and a bit rakishly angled to one side, and he is nearly lost amidst rows of nearly naked young Polynesian men. This vision of paradise reinscribes some of the classic images of heroic colonialists: vivid white skin and white clothing outlined against anonymous brown bodies, the white figure signifying control at the center of the frame while remaining still comfortably at home among "his" people. Yet the impact of the picture simultaneously runs counter to the conventional, heteronormative discourses of the white colonist. Murnau's vision of paradise is unabashedly homoerotic: the gay filmmaker appears to display with a certain pride a socially censured homosexual desire.

Similarly, and no less problematically, some viewers of *Tabu* might mark Murnau's encoding of his own homoerotic longing as the film's most obvious feature, although the film's homoeroticism has often been underplayed even by recent critics. Fatimah Tobing Rony has suggested that Murnau's participation helped *Tabu* to be "more sexually charged" than Flaherty's other films, but she does not elaborate on how or why this sexual difference is important and ultimately focuses on the ways that the central plot of forbidden heterosexual desire between the two

FIGURE 9. Flaherty (left) and Murnau (right) filming *Tabu* (courtesy of the Academy of Motion Picture Arts and Sciences).

doomed lovers encapsulates the drama of the clash between the modern world and the realm of the ethnographic. Rony's chief concern, of course, is not with the ways that the film inscribes sexual desire but in how it romanticizes and reduces the lives it imagines into museum exhibits for western consumption. Ethnography and history cannot be allowed to overlap without engendering freaks, monsters, the whole realm of teratology: "Monstrosity is present where the Ethnographic meets the Historical," she notes.[46] Assenka Oksiloff similarly offers a cogent analysis of *Tabu* as the embodiment of an "ethnotopia," focusing on the film's overtly nostalgic desire to retrieve an imagined past lost to the west while highlighting the film's obsessive, fetishizing focus on the native body. But whereas Oksiloff acknowledges that the film focuses "above all [on the figures of] the men who are displayed in bold reliefs that accentuate their masculinity," she subsumes this masculine focus to a more general modern regime where "a mythical origin is represented . . . in which sexuality exists in a purportedly 'natural' state."[47] This shift away from engaging with the film's "unnatural" homoeroticism mirrors a general trend in film criticism: Oksiloff contends that the striking shots of male bodies are finally desexualized and that they stress the innocence of their subjects, who appear as beings existing "prior to Western history." While accounts such as Rony's and Oksiloff's are clearly aware of *Tabu*'s filmic and extrafilmic sexual subtexts, it is curious that homoerotics and cross-cultural homosexual contact in the Pacific tend to be subsumed beneath larger concerns about imperial power imbalances and modernist ethnography's obsessions with native bodies in a state of nature.

The point I would make here is that both filmic homoerotics and extrafilmic sexual dynamics are central issues when it comes to *Tabu* and that engaging with these issues might subsequently enrich analyses of the film's imperialist dynamics. The Pacific served as a subcultural space where western writers, artists, and filmmakers could imagine, articulate, and enact desires suppressed at home. Indeed, like Novarro's, Murnau's homosexuality was an open secret in Hollywood; he was known to have surrounded himself with a "virtual repertory" of gay men who would work on his projects on both sides of the camera, including the famous character actor Emil Jannings, who starred in *The Last Laugh* (*Der Letzte Mann*, 1924).[48] But I also would argue that the roots of *Tabu*'s homoerotic spectacle do not lie merely in Murnau's sexuality. Flaherty's participation was of equal importance, as were the complexities of Flaherty's own sexual experiences and attitudes. Taken together, the filmic and extrafilmic tales that *Tabu* tells suggest the fluidity and complexity of sexuality in the imperial context—sexuality as an activity, as social performance, and in representation.

When Murnau and Flaherty met, they were both disaffected exiles from the

Hollywood system. After the critical success of *Sunrise* (1927), Murnau had suffered from the financial failures of *The Four Devils* (1928) and then *Our Daily Bread* (1930), which the studio had taken away from him, adding talking sequences and comic gags, finally releasing it under the title *City Girl.* The commercial disappointment of *Moana,* coupled with his inauspicious withdrawal from *White Shadows in the South Seas,* greatly distanced Flaherty from the Hollywood mainstream and also depleted his financial resources, leaving him feeling alienated even from the United States itself. He wrote to Frances in 1927, "I feel that America and Americans are hopeless—we'll never thrive there."[49] Through Flaherty's brother David, Murnau engineered a rendezvous with Robert in Tucson, Arizona, near where he was collaborating with Frances on a film about the Acoma Indians (which would never be completed after the negative, in a replay of *Nanook*'s origins, burned). Murnau pitched a plan for a collaboration between the two directors on a South Pacific film. Though the Flaherty-Murnau alliance quickly created "quite a stir"—Hollywood gossip "trailed them step by step," notes Eisner[50]—it is difficult now to imagine how Flaherty (though hardly a sexual conservative) and the evidently homosexual Murnau could have managed together. Flaherty's agenda, in any case, was specific and highly personal: he finally had the opportunity to return to paradise, and hoped to redeem past failures: "We'll make the kind of picture they wouldn't let me make of *White Shadows,*" Flaherty stated, a film about the "impact of colonial exploitation on Pacific cultures."[51] The facts surrounding the Flaherty-Murnau partnership are key to reading *Tabu,* since the two men's relationship mirrors many of the cultural and personal undercurrents, sexual and otherwise, that would eventually find their way into the film.

While Flaherty sailed directly to Tahiti to begin setting up the film laboratory, Murnau traveled a more circuitous route on his yacht, the *Bali,* accompanied by David Flaherty, in what was to become a search for physically perfect "types" for the film. He took with him the works of Conrad, Stevenson, Loti, Melville, O'Brien, and Nordhoff and Hall to "strengthen his nostalgia for the islands," and his first stop was the Marquesas, where he found people who appeared like "pictures by Gauguin come to life."[52] At Hanavave, on Fatuiva—where fifteen years earlier O'Brien had observed local swimmers capturing sharks by their tails and contemplated the passing of arts such as tattooing and the making of tapa—Murnau encountered his great "find," Mehao. He wrote, "His smile is like a ray of bright sunshine; you only had to clap your hands for his whole body to sway in a dance of delight."[53] As has already been suggested of the dance sequences in *Moana* and as Murnau's finished film would testify, native dance becomes a thinly veiled, displaced performance of western desire. Furthermore, Murnau's fantasy of sexual control is complemented by the other's supposed willingness to be controlled: an undulating body is produced instantly, by a clap of the hands. Interestingly, Eisner's description of the meeting of filmmaker and the young Polynesian is itself rendered in the style of a sultry South Seas romance and forms a mimicry of Murnau's own embellished prose:

> Under the breadfruit trees, they danced the "tapraita." "It was a dance for the arms and body more than for the feet [wrote Murnau]. The hips are rolled sideways and forwards, faster and faster, more and more voluptuously, perfectly freely. Mehao had more grace, a finer figure, greater passion than any of the rest." Would he not be perfect for the film? Murnau took a photograph of him. Underneath he wrote: "He was an orphan from early childhood and grew up freely and independently, like an animal in the jungle. A pure-bred Polynesian, of extraordinary physical beauty, slim and strong, with simple, natural movements. The marvelous harmony of his figure makes him look like a Greek god, a model for the Olympic games, a delight of nature." [54]

Male-to-male sexual attraction could hardly be considered a subtext here; indeed, his biographer, textually at least, participates in the exciting possibilities of sensual expression away from the "thought of cities and all those people" that had become "repulsive" to Murnau.[55] Dancing with this "animal in the jungle" not only liberates Murnau's own cosmopolitan body, pale and degenerating due to Hollywood's vulgarities and the persistent striving after capital, but also resurrects the social taboo of homosexual desire. He discovers a sexual Arcadia, validated by hearkening back to the Greeks and purified by nature's blessing.

Flaherty's own writings minutely detail his period with Murnau, but conjure up a rather different scenario.[56] In Flaherty's letters to Frances, the opportunity to work with Murnau is presented first as a dream come true. In Hollywood in early 1929, he wrote, "The deal is all set—Murnau is much excited and so am I." Shortly after his arrival in Tahiti he notes in a diary addressed to Frances, "As you say, this collaboration with Murnau will be wonderful."[57] One of the film's chief distinctions from other Pacific romances that had been flooding the market was that it was to be shot in Technicolor—in fact, it was to be the first on-location Pacific film in color. This deal had come about when Murnau proposed a Pacific-themed film to the same Boston-based financial consortium, Colorart, that had offered him a job directing a color version of *Don Quixote*. Flaherty continued with his optimistic account of the new working relationship: "We hope this is the beginning of a series of films under our names."

The differences that ultimately arose between the two directors, which resulted in Flaherty's departure from the set in October of 1930, have commonly been attributed to financial disagreements. After their finance company went bankrupt and left them stranded early on in the production, Murnau decided to sell his assets and finance the film himself. Ultimately, as Rotha has contested, Flaherty was left frustrated because Murnau "held the purse strings."[58] These subtle allusions to a henpecked husband and a marriage gone bad, however, seem to offer little help towards recovering the complexity of the two men's differences. Both Eisner and Richard Griffith have implied certain less apparent aesthetic and personal differences: Flaherty's desire to film a documentary after the style of *Moana,* and his disagreement with Murnau's visualization of Polynesian culture as "white blood under their brown skins," which not only romanticized but "Europeanized" Polynesian psychology and motives.[59] While such disagreements seem serious enough to break off the directors' relationship, certain pieces of the puzzle still fail to fit. First, as previously shown, Flaherty had already manifested his own tendency to visualize "white blood" flowing under brown skin in his own work. Even if he only partially acknowledged this practice, he seems to have had little problem applying western narratives to representations of native life, as long as they expressed the "universals" of human experience. Furthermore, as early screenplays for *Tabu* attest, Flaherty's initial proposal for the film—called *Turia* and begun before the two directors left for Tahiti—was fictional, and ultimately would form the second part of *Tabu.* Thus, even before *Tabu* was very far advanced, Flaherty was approaching the film as a fictional construct.[60] Flaherty wrote at length to Frances about how positive he felt about the film's script. Even though he states that he "loathes" all of this "contriving, this story business" with Murnau and wishes to return to the shooting conditions of *Moana,* he also boasts of having been a prime influence behind the fictional script of *White Shadows in the South Seas.*[61] Thus neither the well-worn euphemism "artistic differences" nor the scenario that pits the faithful ethnographic filmmaker against the Hollywood-influenced showman seems to offer a complete accounting for the Murnau-Flaherty breakup.[62]

That said, Flaherty's writings do in many respects concur with the central elements of the standard version of the story. Even after the collapse of Colorart, he continues to write to Frances of being enraptured with his working relationship with Murnau: "Murnau really is great—you'd love him. My respect for him grows and grows. We collaborate perfectly—he worships the country and the people. How you'd love to work with him. . . . He stands for everything we do."[63] Assuming that Murnau shared his affection for time-consuming ethnographic methods, a small crew, and native actors, Flaherty embarked on gathering material with his

Akeley camera, writing excitedly that "it will almost be like *Moana* again." After the two men had spent over six months in the Pacific, mainly in Tahiti, the unit moved to Bora Bora to find a more pristine filming location. But around this time, Flaherty begins to make mention of the "terrible German will" in his letters to Frances, who was herself living in Germany with their children at the time. Flaherty writes, "Every peculiarity you mention [about the Germans], this fear of contamination . . . this strain the Germans put on everything, this fanaticism is all here in one man—and he is Murnau."[64] By April of 1930, after almost a year away from the US, and from Frances and his children, Flaherty is showing evidence of his exasperation, arguing that Murnau is "in no way creative. . . . Unless he is supplied with story structure and continuity he is completely clueless."[65] By the following month he writes, "In this terrible year the blood in me has almost dried"; he is "disgusted sick and tired of everything."[66] By 22 October 1930, after nearly a year and a half in the Pacific with Murnau, Flaherty was on board the *Maunganui* heading east to the US, having sold his interest in the film back to Murnau for $25,000.

Few have cited Murnau's homosexuality as a possible cause for disagreement between the men. Flaherty himself wrote in no uncertain terms to Frances that "there isn't a particle of truth in the gossip of Hollywood concerning [Murnau's] 'queerness'—that is all rot."[67] Still, this was relatively early in the shoot—and it implies that Flaherty preferred Murnau without the queerness. According to Rotha, immediately after his departure from the *Tabu* set in 1930, Flaherty went to Berlin to reunite with his family, where he was assaulted by the "shop window displays of sexual and particularly sadistic literature and photographs; the lesbian and homosexual bars and night spots horrified the man who had only recently come from the innocence of Tahiti."[68]

But Flaherty was far from innocent, though the myth established by works such as Arthur Calder-Marshall's *The Innocent Eye: The Life of Robert J. Flaherty* (1963, based on material by Paul Rotha and Basil Wright) might suggest a rather different view. As W. S. Van Dyke wrote from the set of *White Shadows in the South Seas,* "You will not see the funny part of this [joke about Flaherty] unless you know that Flaherty sleeps with everything and anything there is in town. . . . [Monte] Blue, or was it Clyde [de Vinna], called the shots the other day when he said that Flaherty acts like a little boy that has done something in his pants . . . trying to stave off discovery till the last moment."[69] Even during his "golden age" experience making *Moana* in relative isolation in Samoa, Flaherty and his family lived amidst a far-from-innocent environment. There were rumors on Savai'i that their German host, the retired officer and trader Felix David, was homosexual, and formal

accusations were later made against him. Finally, a homosexual colonial administrator involved with Felix David, who had allegedly "committed offenses against
Samoan boys," committed suicide while in custody.[70] Felix David was himself a
rather odd and colorful character, known for getting drunk and singing opera arias
at the top of his lungs, often well into the night, from his house in Safune, and he
became the inspiration behind Flaherty's bizarre, unfilmed, semifictional screenplay about a German ex-officer with an opera fetish, called *A Singer of the South
Seas*. Shortly after the Flahertys left Safune, Felix David was himself arrested, ban-
ished from Savai'i and, in Rotha's words, "withered away and died"—something
like the Wicked Witch of the West—a few years later.[71] Like a subhuman figure,
"he slinks about in dark corners where no one can see him," David Flaherty wrote
of the demise of the now-unspeakable Felix David, relating the story in his *Asia*
article called "Serpents in Eden." Here the evil serpents in paradise—the Flahertys'
"enemies"—are the two homosexual German men. Felix David is said to give
David Flaherty "the queerest feeling," while the resident commissioner is finally
revealed at the article's end as a "degenerate, guilty of unmentionable debauchery
of the natives."[72] Several years after this incident, Flaherty was in Tahiti filming
with the reasonably private and self-protective but rumored-to-be homosexual
Murnau; it is thus difficult to imagine a "horrified" Flaherty in Berlin having just
returned from South Pacific innocence or to dismiss the role that Murnau's sexuality, or even the (homo)erotic elements of his shot choices, might have played in
Flaherty's decision to leave the production.

Moreover, Flaherty, having been away from his wife and children for more
than a year, had complications within his own marriage. While he was off filming
Tabu Frances experienced serious financial difficulties. She was traveling and taking care of the children on her own, and via letters she finally demanded an "economic separation" from her husband. "My reason for doing this," she wrote, "is
to make up to the children in the only way I can some measure of what they have
already lost through your failure to live up to your part of the partnership arrangement."[73] Around the same time, Frances was writing to her husband of having met
a woman called "Alice" who had become "a husband in everything but sex." "Alice
is offering everything I need for myself and the children," she continues; "I wish
you could love her. I love her."[74]

But precisely what all of this meant to Flaherty as he spent weeks, months,
and finally over a year in Tahiti and Bora Bora—drinking through the night with
his close friend James Norman Hall, conversing about film with Henri Matisse
during his visit to the set, arguing and making up with the increasingly imperious and perfectionist Murnau—is impossible to state with absolute certainty. On

some level extrafilmic "gossip" always works itself into film interpretation, though its value is not always obvious. We know that Flaherty left the production, nervous but optimistic about making a silent film in the age of talkies, hoping that *Tabu* might still turn a profit and still suggesting that he might work with Murnau in the future. Murnau was left to finish the production on his own, which he managed to do in a few months' time.

Tabu

Unfolding in two symmetrical chapters, *Tabu* continues the tradition of layering western narratives over South Pacific peoples and places. It also returns us to the central concerns that marked the explorers' accounts discussed at this book's start and that underlie the western image of the South Pacific: the ways that the pleasures of voyeurism are bound up with fears and disgust via the self's corruption and spoliation of the other. The film's first chapter, "Paradise," presents Bora Bora as a landscape "untouched by the hand of civilization," an Eden that consists of strikingly shot male and female bodies choreographed to a westernized beat. The film's establishing shots present the island as an all-male paradise featuring Murnau's star, Matahi,[75] heroically perched on a rock while several young men wait nearby with fishing spears. Shot from a slightly low angle, Matahi's statuesque pose conjoins the Hellenistic physicality ascribed to South Sea islanders with celebrations of the Greek male nude found in late-nineteenth- and early-twentieth-century Uranian cults such as Edward Carpenter's. In the carefully composed group shot that follows, the torsos of the two men in the foreground dominate the frame, emphasizing their status as physical objects to be looked at. Like the statuesque nude and seminude males found in photography ranging from Wilhelm von Gloeden's turn-of-the-century fantasies to Bruce Weber's or Herb Ritts's arty black-and-white poses, these shots, which now market the commercial video and DVD versions of the film, suggest an aesthetic of the male body that recalls (in spite of the homogenizing overtones of the term) a gay male iconography.

These early scenes might also be compared to the fetishism found in the German cult of physical culture, which would soon link up with the ideals of national socialism in the early 1930s; Leni Riefenstahl's *Olympische Spiele 1936* was filmed only six years later. But this is a problematic and perhaps forced association: Murnau lived under the "ominous shadow," Eisner writes, of paragraph 175 of the pre-1918 German Penal Code, which outlawed homosexuality; likewise Murnau's idealized bodies are not, at least overtly, Aryan. Still, a skeptical Murnau had taken

Flaherty's advice to shoot the film on panchromatic stock, which can be linked to a regime of bleaching Polynesian skin tones to achieve "superior" aesthetic effects. The voyeurism of *Tabu*'s early scenes thus suggests an obsession with healthy and racially pure bodies—an obsession that here intersects with the pleasures of homo-erotic voyeurism. Writing to publisher Kurt Korff with hopes of some prerelease publicity in *Illustrierte Zeitung* or *Dame* in Berlin, Murnau suggests how he chose these idealized physical types: "I am sending you herewith some photographs of our main characters, who, we think, while they have all the qualities of the pure native appearance, still will appeal to a white audience. Personally I think these people, with their childlike charm and grace, would be a sensation if they entered European or American studios."[76]

Murnau's assessment of the aesthetic and erotic demands of white audiences echoes Frances Flaherty's stated concerns over casting *Moana,* since, she thought, Polynesian skin tones might get a lukewarm reception at home. Murnau's lingering preoccupation with white responses to visible racial difference thus coincides with concerns over "pure native appearance" that go beyond the mere desire to authenticate his work by demonstrating that he used "real" native actors. The wider racial implications of Murnau's interests are clearly on show in *Tabu*'s opening titles, which declare that "only native-born South Seas islanders appear in this picture with a few half-castes and Chinese." Concerns about racial corruption and degeneration in the distant colonies here work to delineate and reinforce racial paranoia at home.

Murnau did not live long enough to demonstrate the extent to which his fetishization of the body and apparent preoccupation with racial purity might have drawn him into the ascendant fascist ideologies of the 1930s. One can only assume that, like Fritz Lang, Max Ophüls, or Murnau's screenwriter, Carl Mayer, he would have remained an expatriate. In any case, he would not have lasted long in Germany: if homosexuality was at first quietly tolerated and even to an extent institutionalized during the rise of national socialism, it was just as swiftly rendered a social evil—medicalized, vilified, sentenced to death. And in spite of Flaherty's insistence that Murnau personified the "terrible German will," Murnau in fact was seen by many as "despairingly alien" to German culture.[77] As it stands, Murnau's sexuality would end up providing titillating rumors for a gossiping public even beyond the grave. His death in a car accident near Santa Barbara became linked to stories that he was in an act of fellatio with his fourteen-year-old Filipino driver while the car was moving.[78]

As *Tabu* moves from an ethnopornotopia of male bodies to a female-centered world, we see a close-up of a flower garland flowing down a forest stream towards the men bathing together below, an object that forms a link between two distinctly gendered worlds. Matahi briefly wears the garland as he climbs towards the women, perhaps momentarily and humorously evoking a *mahū* figure, while the musical score shifts from a jaunty pace to a tinkling, magical air. The next scene of the young women bathing in a forest pool is highly reminiscent of the "first contact" episode in *White Shadows in the South Seas,* complete with the escape—here more playful than terrified—of the women when they perceive they are being looked at, signaled by a point-of-view camera shot from the perspective of the men. The film's female lead, Reri (Anna Chevalier), is represented as an exotic bird perched among leaves, and her calls to Matahi are synchronized on the soundtrack to the birdlike peeping of flutes. Arguably, however, the voyeuristic focus of the film continues to revolve around Matahi even while the dominant mise-en-scène occupies the realm of the women: Chevalier is photographed discreetly, and her sacklike costume conceals most of her body. Eisner, skillful at projecting Murnau's desires, problematically lingers on Chevalier's appearance; she "is not especially goodlooking, and as, like all island girls, she has rather short legs, she doesn't compare very well with the magnificent young men. But she is charming, especially when she smiles."[79] Eisner's generalization, based on glimpsing Chevalier through Murnau's lens, could be seen to duplicate Murnau's voyeuristic appreciation of the male stars and the visual elision of the female.[80]

After a slapstick-style scuffle between Reri and another of the bathing women, Matahi tosses the offending rival down a waterfall and settles down to comfort his beloved. The audience is privileged to an intimate clutch between the two, though native sensuality is closely linked to innocence. Furthermore, these shots recall a Flahertyesque ethnographic mode: the couple is watched from afar, reminiscent of the *siva* scene in *Moana.* As they decorate each other with garlands, neither individual is privileged to a point-of-view shot that might endow them with subjectivity, and the extreme close-ups of their hands reaching for garlands are offered as purely informational ethnographic images, not as psychologically motivated as, for example, a shot-reverse-shot structure might have suggested.

The couple's moment of seclusion is abruptly halted by the arrival of a ship, and in a series of stunning action shots (including crowd-pleasing images of a child steering a miniature outrigger canoe), the village is shown stirring to life and finally arriving en masse at the boat—the *Moana* of Papeete—anchored just beyond the coral reef. Here the film introduces the character of Hitu, stooped and white haired: he appears not only as a judge and a figure of the absolute Law, but of death amidst the untrammeled youthfulness of the opening scenes. Hitu, however, turns out to be merely a messenger for a conspicuously absent authority (one never shown in the film), reading out a document that proclaims Reri has been named as the sacred Virgin, therefore she is *tabu*,[81] and "man must not touch her or cast upon her the eye of desire."

With this intrusion—not only into the paradise of Bora Bora, but into the idyllic lives of the two lovers—the film introduces a number of predominant themes in quick succession. Most important, perhaps, is Hitu's text, which implies the invasion of the written word into the setting, linking the realm of writing to the image of the *tabu*. Written text functions symbolically on several levels: within the film's diegesis it suggests the opposition made later by Claude Lévi-Strauss between "primitive" speech and writing, the latter of which Lévi-Strauss sees as embodying and acting as the harbinger of all the competitive and exploitative structuring principles of civilization.[82] As Lévi-Strauss bluntly suggests, the role of writing is to implement hierarchies where none previously existed; writing invokes the integration of individuals into political and legal systems, and its primary function historically has been to "facilitate slavery."[83] Better, it would seem, to return to an innocent time before the introduction of writing and the brutal hierarchies of civilization. A similar opposition is established in *Tabu:* before the introduction of Hitu's written text, the loving couple existed in a timeless, purely sensual universe. Writing heralds the separation of the couple by classifying Reri as a publicly and divinely possessed object, identifying her "virtue" and "royal blood" while at the same time classifying her as *tabu*, thus relegating her to a life of chastity and isolation. Furthermore, it is only after Hitu arrives that the key writing figures of white men appear: first the ship's captain, who is keeping a log that briefly provides the audience with missing exposition, then the white trader of the film's second chapter, who keeps a written diary of the couple's activities. Writing appears to inscribe and even determine their lives: it authors and delineates their fates. Similarly, the appearance of the written sign "Tabu" in the film's second part is a visual reminder of a death, psychic or physical or both, already inscribed, lurking always beyond the boundaries of the frame. Finally, Reri's succumbing to her *tabu* status at the end of the film is marked by the fanciful narrative gesture of having her write (as *Variety* complained, in "Oxford English")[84] a farewell note to Matahi, who, as the plot has suggested rather explicitly up to this point, can barely read or write himself.

Hitu's text perhaps implies one more, in this case extrafilmic, dimension: the "perfect form" of the silent film, Murnau wrote, would be one without a single intertitle, where the meanings could be projected entirely through the wordless signals of light, gesture, and music.[85] The written text thus also ruptures the cinematic perfection of this exotic paradise. Hitu's message suggests yet another issue in the realm of the visual: man must not "cast upon her the eye of desire," a phrase that links seeing to sexuality and perhaps strikes a warning note about the western voyeuristic gaze at the female "native" body. Ironically and perhaps self-referentially, the male heterosexual gaze at the film's female star is thus coded as forbidden, while heteroerotic female and homoerotic male looks are facilitated by frequent and lingering shots of Matahi and other young men—heroically ferrying boats, hanging languorously from the ship's rigging—who dominate the frame throughout most of these early scenes.

Whatever power the word and the invisible authority represented by Hitu may hold, Matahi has every intention of going against tradition: Reri's discarded flower garland, signifying her desire, lies on the deck in the bright sunlight, but Matahi's shadow—perhaps already a harbinger of his death—steals slowly across it, and his hand reaches out to snatch it while the shadow recedes. As the scene shifts back to the island, excited preparations for the celebration of the Virgin are contrasted with shots of Reri weeping in her house and Matahi adopting a forlorn yet classical pose against a wall outside. Crosscutting here emphasizes the arbitrary separation of the couple and suggests a more general critique of social restrictions and constraints on sexual freedom. Briefly, Reri's gaze meets Hitu's and they exchange looks—but he is clearly in authority, shown in a position above her, looking down. After the ceremony, Reri is led away beneath the overarching palm-leaf roof of the ceremonial canoe that will convey her to the *Moana*. Framed through the churchlike, sloping roof, the scene invokes both a wedding and a funeral. The music is mournful, with Reri now completely covered in cloth, like an anonymous corpse, connoting the veiling of her sexuality but also recalling, perhaps, the missionary prohibitions on indigenous dress much reviled by the likes of Flaherty and Murnau.

If the film's first chapter resembles the timeless exotic worlds that Flaherty was famous for conjuring up, the second chapter, "Paradise Lost," seems closer to Murnau in its themes of the protagonists' unavoidable fate, its existential unease, and its carefully composed Expressionist visuals. Matahi has stolen away with Reri in the night, and the couple is washed up on "some island of the pearl trade, where the white man rules and the gods are forgotten." They quickly recover, according to the written account of the local pearl trader, though they are never far from the ever-present shadow of the *tabu* that hangs over their illicit affair. It is logical to read *Tabu*'s second part, as have a number of critics, as the movement from purity to spoliation or, as Rony suggests, from the realm of the racially pure to the teratological realms of miscegenation and cultural mixing. The second chapter's early scenes—which emphasize the space of the island as chaotic, diverse, and messily inhabited by Chinese traders and "half-caste" laborers—suggest "Adam and Eve trapped in a network of language, writing, and money, and the end result can only be annihilation or perversion."[86] Matahi, a "born diver" who has brought numerous pearls to the surface, is lofted above the crowd, and a makeshift and raucous dance ensues, led by an accordion player and the Chinese café owner's liberal distribution of champagne (at Matahi's expense, we soon learn). A close-up of the dancers' feet shows a mixture of barefooted women dancing with shoed men, and shoed women dancing with barefooted men, signifying the tumult of cultural and racial—and perhaps also sexual, since the feet at times appear genderless—mixing and implying the degeneration of civilized manners alongside the sullying of native life. Champagne is drunk out of both glasses and coconut shells, while the accordion player does a camp imitation of Polynesian dancing, wiggling his hips and striking extreme and grotesque poses.

While the scene is marked by an overarching sense of corruption, hysteria, and western decadence, Matahi and Reri remain in a slightly elevated position for most of the time, overlooking the proceedings; then, as they lead the dance, they become psychically removed and rapturously absorbed in each other's motions.

Figure 10. Reri (Anna Chevalier) and Matahi amidst the drunken crowd (courtesy of the Academy of Motion Picture Arts and Sciences).

Notably, they are at all times detached from the crowd, and though plied with alcohol, neither ever appears drunk. We are left to presume that (unlike Stoddard's Kána-aná, who withers away in a foreign environment) they are relatively resilient in the face of western hybridization. Or perhaps the portrait of modernity here is also somewhat more ambivalent—or compromising—than it is in *Moana* or *White Shadows*. The couple's dance is on one level a hollow reenactment of the (forbidden) dance they performed in Bora Bora, yet at the same time on this island their passion is fully legal, even encouraged. The constraints of "primitive" tradition do not bind in a land where money, enterprise, and youth rule. This is a fleeting glimpse of a US populist dream: two individuals free from external laws and determined to forge on their own a new physical and moral universe. As a frantic form of jazz bellows on the soundtrack, for a moment *Tabu* seems that it might be embracing the mobilities and transnational spaces endemic to modernity—echoing something like the problematic but intriguing racial shape-shifting and youthful stumbling towards the new allegorized in *The Jazz Singer* a few years earlier. But the couple's worries quickly return: a ship arrives, its prow slicing into the left of the frame. For the second time, the ship interrupts the couple's state of blissful transport, just as Hitu had also interrupted their forbidden dance at the ceremony of the Virgin. The ship quickly returns the figure of Law and tradition to the scene as the couple, now terrified, read the word *Moana* on its stern. Matahi locks them inside their hut, but it is made of thin palm fronds: its fragility belies their inability to seal themselves away from the world.

Writing once again signals the invasion of Matahi's and Reri's ideal state, as the trader who has been previously inscribing their fate appears at the door with a notice, in French, that a five-hundred-franc reward has been offered for their arrest. Matahi, quick to learn the underhanded power of capital, successfully offers a pearl to bribe the trader in return for his silence. At this point the film establishes both a dominant dramatic space—the interior of the couple's hut, their last refuge—and a dominant point of view: Reri's. Reri peeks out from behind Matahi's shoulder, and we watch her scrutinize the trader, who is laughing at Matahi's bribe. Reri's look begins to motivate several shots of the doorway to the sea beyond, which beckons with the promise of freedom, signifying either the possibility of flight or its foreclosure as the foreboding figure Hitu rises up to block the view. Hitu's first appearance in the doorway is noticed only by Reri, and the image explicitly recalls the nightmarish appearance of the vampire Orlock at Hutter's door in Murnau's *Nosferatu* (1922): both figures visualize a return of the repressed, the dangers of sexuality, and the inability to escape one's fate. Shortly after Hitu's appearance, the trader erects the "*tabu*" sign over the shark-infested diving area, the word now an ever-present reminder of the proscribed fate that awaits what the intertitles call the "guilty couple."

As the couple sleeps, palm branches throw sharply defined shadows across their faces.[87] Another shadow steals across the sand, and again a written missive enters the frame to mark their fate. As Reri reads the note from Hitu, Matahi continues to sleep, but his face now gives the appearance of a death mask. Reri looks up at the space left by the now-retreating figure of Hitu, then looks at the sleeping Matahi, then gazes at the camera with an expression of dread and accusation, subtly drawing the audience into the web of deceit and denial. Now Reri knows what we know, and what Matahi—now arguably well established as the fetishized object of the gaze—does not know.

As the scene shifts to daylight, the nightmare is dispelled by Matahi's laughing face, shot again from Reri's point of view, a visual oxymoron given what she, and we, now know. As Matahi leaves for his dive, she remains in the hut, sullen and alone. Reri has taken over as conveyor and protagonist of the tale, and there is a brief moment of respite and hope as she discovers that a steamer is leaving for Papeete in two days. With the promise of escape, the horizons open up again, and in another point-of-view shot Reri gazes through the door of the hut, now open with an unobstructed view to the sea. A fantasy-like close-up of Reri's face, cradled safely in Matahi's lap, completes the episode.

The film begins to move towards a climax, and here Matahi's dilemma becomes central. He is prepared to buy the tickets for their passage, but the Chinese café owner, Kong Ah, appears with thousands of francs' worth of bills. Inside the hut, Reri cheerfully plays her guitar, her cares lifted: now it is she who is blissfully unaware of the danger, taking the position that Matahi had occupied in the previous sequence. That night, shadows again cut across the couple's sleeping bodies. Jumbled, dreamlike images flash on the screen: Matahi, half awake, imagines Kong Ah with handfuls of bills, sees the seabed covered in oysters and giant pearls and so is fully drawn into the vicious cycle of capital and desire for material wealth. Hitu again appears to Reri, and she throws herself at his feet. When Hitu leaves, Matahi steals away towards the *tabu* area of the lagoon, leaving Reri alone, feigning sleep, now herself appearing frightfully close to death.

When Reri rises to write her letter, her act begins to sum up and clarify a number of interpretive issues raised by the film up to this point. It is worth turning once more, albeit briefly, to Lacan. If the couple once occupied a state of visual perfection and wordless sounds (Reri's birdlike "peeping") in their paradise—resembling, in effect, infants—in the Lacanian view, the entry into language would also suggest the entry into the world of social communication. In Lacan's view this world, the realm of the symbolic order, is governed by the Law.[88] Yet this Law is also, importantly, overseen by the Name of the Father—the realm of phallic power, of heteronormative patriarchal law. It is this emphasis on the controlling phallus and patriarchal law that begins to shift the analysis of *Tabu* away from a view that positions language and writing in the film as always marking a fall from grace and a break from paradise. Indeed, as Reri writes her letter, she appears for the first time to be fully acknowledging this realm of written communication, which is also the realm of the unseen "primitive" Law of which Hitu is the messenger. Matahi and Reri's relationship, then, which has desperately tried to forge an alternative to this patriarchal, restrictive world, is not only *tabu;* it might also be seen as "queer"—that is, queer in the sense of desire rendered perverse because it is exercised outside the bounds of circumscribed patriarchal laws and norms. Paradoxically, Reri's acceptance of the Name of the Father leaves her utterly isolated, contra Lacan: she is disallowed from entering into the (patriarchal) community of others and becomes merely a silent object of tribal exchange.

I would therefore argue against readings of the film that posit a clear opposition between the worlds of "Paradise" and "Paradise Lost." Oksiloff very effectively links the first chapter to the realm of the visual and the second to the realm of "fallen" language, suggesting that behind this lies Murnau's (and of course Flaherty's) own elevation of silent cinema aesthetics over the coming of "corrupt" talkies. Indeed, during his final months on the shoot with Murnau, Flaherty was writing to Frances of his hopes that new silent projects by major figures such as Chaplin and Fairbanks would kill the talkies, declaring that "talking pictures had failed" and would now become Hollywood's "Frankenstein."[89] But perhaps the film's two symmetrical parts should not be read as quite so oppositional, but as worlds in collusion: paradise is, in effect, always the projection of the couple's desires—it exists in a waterfall and a bathing pool, but even in these locations lurk conflict, rivalry, and violence. Both worlds are ruled by an absent patriarchal authority, and both enslave and commodify their subjects (Reri's female body in paradise, Matahi's laboring body on the pearl island). As the French government's document demanding the couple's arrest states, "The government desires to avoid conflict," that is, authority exercised in the "primitive" world and authority overseeing the pearl trader's island are in collusion rather than opposition. Both are marked by seemingly arbitrary demands and *tabu*s, both announce their demands through written declarations.

On a final note, it is worth measuring the metaphorical impact of the film's theme—sexual *tabu*—more carefully against Murnau's homosexuality, in that this tale of "forbidden love" might be seen as a more generalized allegory of desires both unspeakable and unrepresentable. It is true that the idea of sexual desire, knowledge, and transgression as causes for the Fall returns us again to narratives so regularly imposed upon the South Pacific scene. But in *Tabu,* the transgression of an arbitrarily determined social and sexual prohibition, handed down by absent figures of authority, is further shown not only to be the cause of social exclusion and exile, but also to instill spiritual homelessness, ejecting the lovers from their sexual Arcadia. Murnau, himself displaced from both Germany and Hollywood, wandering the Pacific in search of aesthetic and physical stimulation, was hoping to abolish the "guilt feelings," Eisner writes, "inherent in European morality," and in the process he arguably produced an allegory of socially proscribed queer desire.[90] Indeed, the insertion of the idea of *tabu* love into the story likely came from Murnau.[91] At the end of the film, Matahi, failing to orchestrate yet another escape for the lovers, succumbs to the physical (and social) death signified in transgressing the sexual *tabu.* Hitu's knife (perhaps another phallic, patriarchal symbol) cuts the rope, and the man Murnau had personally selected as his magnificent star is left swimming frantically after his desire, but never attaining it, finally sinking beneath the waves.

⮑

BUT HOW do we incorporate these homoerotic subthemes within the broader problems of the film, particularly—to use Rony's phrase—the eroticization of genocide?[92] What were then still seen as rapidly diminishing Polynesian cultures are eroticized in *Tabu* to an even greater extent than previous texts we've seen here that engaged in fatal impact discourse. The erotic spectacle of Polynesian actors is intermixed with themes of transgression, colonial spoliation, and imminent death. I think that briefly returning to Rony's concept of the "third eye" might be instructive here. Using W. E. B. Du Bois's concept of "double consciousness," where a young person of color learns to recognize the practice of "always looking at one's self through the eyes of others," Rony elaborates: "Perhaps we Savages, plunged in darkness, do understand each other.... The racially charged glance can also induce one to see the very process which creates the internal splitting, to witness the conditions which give rise to the double consciousness described by Dubois."[93] In *Tabu* we perhaps begin to witness the opening up of yet another point of view: the gaze split between the unifying voyeurisms of imperial power and the painful silencing of queer sexual desire. It is a marginal, homoerotic gaze at others that at the same time seeks power and reassurance in collective, and oppressive, imperial identities. It is this tricky convergence of the imperialist and modernist gazes, and the incipient heterogeneity of each, that begins to suggest a multiple discursive field not adequately explained simply by positing a colonial, masculine viewer as governing acts of looking at others.

Tabu debuted in March 1931, to mixed reviews. *Variety* compared it unfavorably to *White Shadows* and *Moana,* noting that "in the first runs ... it is going to need strong support and well-handled exploitation, [yet] it is still not going to set anything on fire."[94] By the end of 1931, however, the *New York Times* had named it one of the ten best films of the year. Floyd Crosby, the cinematographer chiefly responsible for *Tabu*'s exotic visual pleasures, would end up the film's biggest winner, taking home the Oscar in 1932.[95] Just a week before the film's release, Murnau had died of a fractured skull in a car accident near Santa Barbara. A few months later, Frederick O'Brien saw *Tabu* in a local San Francisco cinema and had only the highest praise, calling it "the finest South Sea picture ever made."[96] Yet O'Brien would also not live much longer: severely ill with heart disease and the cumulative effects of lifelong alcoholism, he died three months later at his home in Sausalito, his companion Margaret Wickham Watson at his side. Flaherty would never return to the South Pacific, and *Tabu* in many ways marks the end of this chapter in the US romance with Polynesia and in the nation's ever shifting but ongoing obsessions with physically and psychically appropriating the vast oceanic spaces to its west.

Afterword

For K. R. Howe, the renewed preoccupation in the early twentieth century with the Pacific island paradise can be attributed to increasing tourism, which helped to demystify and reshape some of the largely hostile images of Oceania produced throughout the nineteenth century.[1] As I've suggested, however, a duality and ambivalence persisted in this collective obsession: post–World War I Polynesiana arrived in the US when an increasingly urbanized population was still flush with the relative newness of fast travel, fast communication, and the cinema—all hallmarks of modernity—yet on many fronts weaving nostalgic fictions of the country's own disappearing pastoral roots. Aspects of westward expansionist optimism and the nostalgia of the 1920s began to wane as the 1930s brought the grim fact of the Great Depression into everyday lives, crystallized in remarkable cinematic set-pieces such as Busby Berkeley's "Remember My Forgotten Man" number in *Gold Diggers of 1933* and in literature such as John Steinbeck's biting, ironic reinscription of the manifest destiny myth in *The Grapes of Wrath,* where westward mobility comes to embody a nation marked by diaspora, vagrancy, corruption, and widespread disaffection. Meanwhile, talk was established on movie screens, rupturing and displacing the purist aesthetic regime of the visual found in silent film. In the era of the Depression and the talkie, the screen image of the South Pacific, it seemed, was to be pushed even further into escapism, excess, and hyperbole.

For quite some time, sound film failed to bring the anticipated narrative, aesthetic, and technical progress that many thought would rapidly occur; in fact, at least in terms of Polynesian-themed films, it arguably heralded visual and narrative regression to some of the west's earliest and most simplistic primitivist fantasies. Larry Langman notes that "a wave of visual and thematic sophistication swept across the island film during the 1920s. During the Depression era of the 1930s, Hollywood switched chiefly to light romance, musicals, and comedies."[2] While it would hardly be useful to wax nostalgic for the ethnographic valorization and eroticized colonialism in the 1920s Polynesian romance, clearly the downturn in the US economy coupled with the coming of synch sound was causing major generic shifts in Hollywood that tended to reduce the complexities found in certain key 1920s genres while giving rise to others, such as the all-talking comedy. In the South Seas genre, women now seemed to be leaping into volcanoes with increasing frequency, as in the Raquel Torres vehicle *Aloha* (1931) and the RKO adaptation of the play *Bird of Paradise* (1932), with Dolores Del Rio taking the plunge. In 1933, Erle C. Kenton's *Island of Lost Souls* (an adaptation of H. G. Wells's *The Island of Dr. Moreau* [1896]) made more explicit the psychic and western cultural associations of island savagery, animality, and monstrosity. Perhaps the most significant change, however, was the stricter enforcement of the Production Code after 1934; such enforcement radically altered the style and content of the South Seas genre— which was after all largely predicated on displays of sensuality and nudity—and of Hollywood filmmaking as a whole. Before 1934, films such as *Balinese Love* (1931), *Isle of Paradise* (1932), and *Virgins of Bali* (1932) continued to offer the expected "sex bet" to audiences by openly screening female nudity, along with Henry de la Falaise's semidocumentary *Legong: Dance of the Virgins* (1933)—billed as "true— actually filmed in Bali"—a film that realized Flaherty and Murnau's ambitions of a Pacific production in two-color Technicolor.[3]

By 1935, when *Tabu* was resubmitted to the Production Code Administration (PCA) of the MPPDA for a Code Certificate of Approval, the climate had radically changed, even for films with ostensibly documentary-ethnographic credentials. *Tabu*'s distributors were told to remove several "minor" items, including all shots of "dancing girls with breasts exposed," a "shot of a nude child," "shots where girl and partner dance in a sensuous manner," and the scenes of Matahi and Reri lying on a sleeping mat in their hut.[4] Clearly, these "minor" changes would render the film effectively unintelligible, as the film's distributors indeed argued at the time. In 1939, responding to another request for a code certificate for rerelease, Joseph Breen called Murnau's picture "unacceptable under the provisions of the Production Code."[5] As a later MPPDA memo noted, "It was considered that this particular film did not come within the requirements of the Code on 'natives in their native habitat,' because it is an entertainment film with nothing of the 'travelogue flavor' to it." It was further noted that the film's director had "not shot it indiscriminately, but had very carefully selected the young girls for his cast with obviously handsome breasts."[6] By 1950, the film's owners had given up hope altogether of exhibiting the film with a PCA seal of approval and sought permission for independent release on the emerging "art house" circuit.

MGM's 1935 version of Nordhoff and Hall's hugely popular *Mutiny on the Bounty* found itself potentially in a similar dilemma with the new enforcement of the code, here because the story is grounded in the interracial romantic relations of Fletcher Christian, Roger Byam, and other members of the crew. As Michael Sturma suggests, MGM managed to deflect criticism and the wary eyes of the PCA by highlighting the bonding of Christian and Byam and underplaying relations with their Tahitian love interests. As *Variety* noted in its review at the time, "The boys must have worn out plenty of kid gloves in slipping in this part of the story with diplomacy. Polynesians are considered members of the white race by many experts, but whether they are so held by the majority of laymen is questionable. . . . But it is all done so neatly kicks won't be numerous."[7] Shortly afterwards, John Ford's screen version of Nordhoff and Hall's *The Hurricane* (1937) was helping to usher in a generation of artfully draped, Americanized figures of South Seas masculinity (now noticeably more hypermasculine than before, in the Tarzan mode) in the form of the lead, Jon Hall, and femininity, in the iconic figure of Dorothy Lamour.

Perhaps, as Howe implies, the Hollywood dream factory's remythification of the South Seas was linked to the actual Pacific's demystification and increasingly easy access. Certainly as the 1930s progressed, the geopolitical struggles for Pacific control, anticipated by the likes of Melville and Twain and observed (if not always documented) by the travelers discussed in this book, was being rapidly stepped up, taking on even more powerful ideological force. If US political concerns appeared to be chiefly cast towards Europe in the later years of the 1930s, Pacific islands were becoming the staging grounds for the imperial powers' second Great War, finally leading to Oceania's "total militarization" as Japan and the US battled for mastery of the Pacific basin.[8] As Rob Wilson notes, the *idea* of the "American Pacific" began to take root as early as imperialist struggles for Samoa and Hawai'i in the late-nineteenth century, but the actualization of the American Pacific was realized only after these World War II battles, "when the United States had defeated Japan and took control, via 'strategic trust,' over Micronesia and territories of strategic interest."[9] This process of US intervention and mass military occupation was anatomized in microcosm in James Norman Hall's *Lost Island* (1944), where the loss of paradise to bulldozers and runways clearly parallels Hall's own nostalgia for the lost Eden of his agrarian, Midwestern roots in Iowa. Interestingly, the book's jacket blurb intimately links the US mainland and Polynesia as spaces that both signify "home" to Americans, noting, "In this novel whose prose is memorable for its purity and poignancy, James Norman Hall has shown us the human impact of war as it strikes home, even in Polynesia."[10]

A rather different but by this time dominant portrait of the US military transformation of Pacific island sites was presented in Margaret Mead's anthropological study of Manus off the northern coast of New Guinea, an island that would become a fueling and training station for millions of US troops during the war, leaving an indelible physical and cultural impact. Mead assesses this impact as positive change and progress in her monumental hymn to the growth of the American Pacific, *New Lives for Old: Cultural Transformation—Manus, 1928–1953*. In 1953, Mead revisited the island where she had performed a detailed study of child rearing in 1928–1929, only to discover the miracle of "a people who have moved in fifty years from darkest savagery to the twentieth century, men who have skipped over thousands of years of history in just the last twenty-five years," a people who could thus offer "food for the imagination of Americans, whom the people of Manus so deeply admire."[11] US civilization was exciting and "new" for Mead, and its hegemony in the Pacific was crucial to the present and future to the people of Manus and Oceania at large. Such were the benefits of free-market capitalism and the unidirectional flow—from "us" to "them"—of information and goods: "American civilization is new because it has come to rest on a philosophy of production and plenty instead of saving and scarcity, and new because the men who built it have themselves incorporated the ability to change and change swiftly as need arises."[12]

By the post–World War II period, the psychic hegemony of the American Pacific was so complete that James Michener's *Tales of the South Pacific* could present what Michener called the "trivial islands" of the Pacific region essentially as the nostalgic playgrounds of American soldiers and their orientalized love interests.[13] Shortly afterwards, the phenomenal success of the "cold war master narrative" *South Pacific*—both as stage musical (1949) and film (1958)—based on Michener's *Tales,* demonstrated that wartime nostalgia for exotic islands where conflict, desire, and victory had all come together for Americans now could be actualized in "real spaces" via fast travel and tourism back to Polynesia's paradise.[14] In the film *South Pacific,* half-dressed sailors perform the number "There Ain't Nothing Like a Dame" while the grinning, beetle-nut-chewing figure of Bloody Mary—effectively sexless but the only "dame" in the vicinity—is visually linked to a skull that serves as a prop in the dance; thus she appears as a kind of death's-head that both seduces and threatens annihilation. *South Pacific* thus strangely both revisits and mocks the ghosts of recent war and present nuclear annihilation—and perhaps suggests a palimpsest of the fatal impact—amidst the intense pleasures of tropical islands, implicitly revisiting the "Et in Arcadia ego" theme established with some of the South Pacific's earliest European illustrators such as William Hodges. In "Bali Hai" Bloody Mary sings, "Come to me, I am your own special island": the mystical, uncanny lure of the Pacific island is established, recalling Enlightenment voyages of desire while sounding the call for innumerable Polynesian tourist ads to come.

Bali Hai itself is envisioned as a space of excess marked by the extremes of the fictionalized and cinematic exotic; it appears in turns African or intensely Oriental, luring the masculine gaze with its feminine intrigue: "We are a very pretty people, no?" asks Bloody Mary of the film's lust-struck military protagonist.

In this book my aim has been to chart some of the major images and conceptions of Polynesia during a period of transition and upheaval in the US, shortly before the post–World War II American Pacific typified by Mead's free-market liberalist attitudes would come to dominate popular global consciousness, before saleable commodities such as "Pacific Rim" cuisine and the transnational markets of the "Asia-Pacific" region came to dominate and absorb western conceptions of the Pacific and its islands. Many have contested this image: Subramani, for example, argues that even a seemingly monolithic term such as "American Pacific" is actually only part of a wider Pacific in a process of ongoing decolonization, and only part of a multicentered region that speaks to and has long confronted a range of imperial centers.[15] Recent work such as Mel Kernahan's *White Savages in the South Seas* (1995), on one level playing on O'Brien's legacy, offers a self-aware portrait of the ironies of Pacific tourism and the ways that Pacific islands are not just isolated monads or cultural artifacts awash in a distant ocean but are integrally connected to and part of global movement and exchange.[16] Vanessa Warheit and Amy Robinson's film *The Insular Empire: America's Pacific Frontier* addresses related issues of the paradoxes of presumed isolation versus actual transnational and transcultural interactions in the Mariana Islands and the complex and simultaneous processes of colonization and decolonization, charting everyday life as it goes on in regions that form part of the US's ambiguous, frequently "unincorporated" or largely ignored spaces of empire. On the other end of the spectrum, Steve James's *Reel Paradise* (2005), which opens with film producer John Pierson screening the Three Stooges' *Some More of Samoa* (1941) to an enraptured crowd (of mostly children) in Fiji, suggests in the perpetually exasperated and condescending figure of Pierson the tiredness and embeddedness of western cultural hierarchies of us and them, US sophistication versus Pacific island cultural simplicity and "backwardness."

In the texts of the 1920s and the early 1930s examined here, we see the byproducts of the growing regime of the American Pacific and the ambivalences and determination of the US superpower and so-called mainland towards its Oceanic neighbors. We also glimpse a nation's desires, its subconscious fears, its seemingly endless hunger for alliances, appropriation, and annihilation. Yet these were the texts that also helped to bring an uneven and contested image of other cultural practices, the "out there," back to US audiences. The figures examined in this book often failed in attempting to represent the cultures with which they engaged, yet they also reveal ideological cracks in the seamless veneer of imperial discursive practices. They show personal and social norms stretched to the breaking point in the face of difference, a reflection of the failures not only of fully knowing the other, but, when pressed into self-reflection, of fully knowing the self. And as the producers of these texts struggle to identify, to name themselves in the midst of otherness, they also illuminate and exemplify a transitional moment in the US's own process of historical, cultural, and imperial naming.

Notes

Introduction

1. Dudley A. Siddal, "Artists Flock to Tahiti," *Publisher's Weekly* 99 (22 January 1921): 199. Also qtd. in Charles Robert Roulston, "Eden and the Lotus Eaters: A Critical Study of the South Sea Island Writings of Frederick O'Brien, James Norman Hall, and Robert Dean Frisbie," Ph.D. dissertation (University of Maryland, 1965).

2. Amy Kaplan, *The Anarchy of Empire in the Making of U.S. Culture* (Cambridge: Harvard University Press, 2002), 18.

3. See, for example, Donald Denoon et al., eds., *The Cambridge History of the Pacific Islanders* (Cambridge: Cambridge University Press, 1997), 8; Ernest S. Dodge, *Islands and Empires: Western Impact on the Pacific and East Asia* (Minneapolis: University of Minnesota Press, 1976), 114–115. "Oceania," according to Martin W. Lewis and Karen Wigen in *The Myth of Continents: A Critique of Metageography* (Berkeley: University of California Press, 1997)—the invention of which cartographically isolated Southeast Asia, the Pacific, and Australia from the Asian continent—was the invention of French geographers as part of the political mapping that went on during nineteenth-century colonization (219).

4. Epeli Hauʻofa, "Our Sea of Islands," in *A New Oceania: Rediscovering Our Sea of Islands,* ed. Eric Waddell, Vijay Naidu, and Epeli Hauʻofa (Suva: University of the South Pacific Press, 1993), 8.

5. Jocelyn Linnekin, "Contending Approaches," in *The Cambridge History of the Pacific Islanders,* ed. Donald Denoon et al. (Cambridge: Cambridge University Press, 1997), 8.

6. Alfred Gell, *Wrapping in Images: Tattooing in Polynesia* (Oxford: Clarendon Press, 1993), 4.

7. Herman Melville, "The South Seas" (*Baltimore American and Commercial Daily Advertiser* [9 February 1859]), in *The Portable Melville,* ed. Jay Leyda (New York: Viking, 1952), 576.

8. John R. Eperjesi, *The Imperialist Imaginary: Visions of Asia and the Pacific in American Culture* (Hanover, NH: Dartmouth College Press, 2005), 15.

9. Qtd. in Rob Wilson, *Reimagining the American Pacific: From South Pacific to Bamboo Ridge and Beyond* (Durham, NC: Duke University Press, 2000), 111.

10. Wilson, 23–24. See also Christopher L. Connery's "Pacific Rim Discourse: The US Global Imaginary in the Late Cold War Years," in *Asia / Pacific as Space of Cultural Production,* ed. Arif Dirlik and Rob Wilson (Durham, NC: Duke University Press, 1995), 47–56. For a reading of "Asia / Pacific" as a space of emerging cultural formations, see David Palumbo-Liu in *Asian /American: Historical Crossings of a Racial Frontier* (Palo Alto: Stanford University Press, 1999). See also Bruce Cumings, "Rimspeak: or, The Discourse of the 'Pacific Rim,'" in *What Is in a Rim? Critical Perspectives on the Pacific Region Idea,* ed. Arif Dirlik (Boulder, CO: Westview, 1993), 53–72.

11. See Malini Johar Schueller, *U.S. Orientalisms: Race, Nation, and Gender in Literature, 1790–1890* (Ann Arbor: University of Michigan Press, 1998); Mary A. Renda, *Taking Haiti: Military Occupation and the Culture of U.S. Imperialism, 1915–1940* (Chapel Hill: University of North Carolina Press, 2001).

12. Eperjesi, 4–13.

13. See "Colonial Discourse and Post-Colonial Theory: An Introduction," in *Colonial Discourse and Post-Colonial Theory: A Reader,* ed. Patrick Williams and Laura Chrisman (New York: Columbia University Press, 1994), 1–4.

14. Eperjesi, 5; Martin Jacques, "Strength in Numbers," *The Guardian,* 23 October 2004, sec.1: 23.

15. Albert Wendt, ed., *Nuanua: Pacific Writing Since 1980* (Honolulu: University of Hawaiʻi Press, 1990), 2; Wendt, "Towards a New Oceania," *Writers in East-West Encounter: New Cultural Bearings,* ed. Guy Amirthanayagam (London: Macmillan, 1982), 213.

16. Neil Rennie, *Far-Fetched Facts: The Literature of Travel and the Idea of the South Seas* (Oxford: Clarendon Press, 1995), 30–82.

17. Describing the loss of the mythic in German culture, Nietzsche further notes,

> Man today, stripped of myth, stands famished among all his pasts and must dig frantically for roots, be it among the most remote antiquities. What does our great historical hunger signify, our clutching about us of countless other cultures, our consuming desire for knowledge, if it is not the loss of myth, of a mythic home, the mythic womb? We should consider whether our feverish and frightening agitation is anything but the greedy grasping for food of a hungry man.

"The Birth of Tragedy" *and* "The Genealogy of Morals," trans. Francis Golffing (New York: Doubleday, 1956), 137.

18. Gayatri Chakravorty Spivak, "The Rani of Sirmur," in *Europe and Its Others,* vol. 1, ed. Francis Barker, Peter Hulme, Margaret Iversen, and Diana Loxley (Colchester: University of Essex Press, 1985), 128.

19. Robert Young, *White Mythologies: Writing History and the West* (New York: Routledge, 1990), 7.

20. Rod Edmond, *Representing the South Pacific: Colonial Discourse from Cook to Gauguin* (Cambridge: Cambridge University Press, 1997), 12–13.

21. Ibid., 11.

22. Rod Edmond and Vanessa Smith, "Editor's Introduction," in *Islands in History and Representation,* ed. Edmond and Smith (London: Routledge, 2003), 6.

23. Nicholas Thomas, *Entangled Objects: Exchange, Material Culture, and Colonialism in the Pacific* (Cambridge: Harvard University Press, 1991), 35–36.

24. Nicholas Thomas, *In Oceania: Visions, Artifacts, Histories* (Durham, NC: Duke University Press, 1997), 16.

25. J. G. A. Pocock, "Nature and History, Self and Other: European Perceptions of World History in the Age of the Encounter," in *Voyages and Beaches: Pacific Encounters, 1769–1840,* ed. Alex Calder, Jonathan Lamb, and Bridget Orr (Honolulu: University of Hawai'i Press, 1999), 32–33.

26. 'Okusitino Māhina, "Myth and History," in *Voyages and Beaches: Pacific Encounters, 1769–1840,* ed. Alex Calder, Jonathan Lamb, and Bridget Orr (Honolulu: University of Hawai'i Press, 1999), 62.

27. 'I. F. Helu, "South Pacific Mythology," in Calder et al., 49. See also Malama Meleisea, "The Postmodern Legacy of a Premodern Warrior Goddess in Samoa," in Calder et al., 55–60.

28. I am not intervening here in what Edmond calls the "gladiatorial" Sahlins-Obeyesekere debate (*Representing,* 62), but simply citing it as an example of textual instability, where myth and history, Oceania and the west, have become entangled (another might be the equally prominent Margaret Mead–Derek Freeman debates, though the latter could also be described, to paraphrase Trinh-T. Minh-ha, as a case of "us talking to us about them"). See Gananath Obeyesekere, *The Apotheosis of Captain Cook: European Mythmaking in the Pacific* (Princeton, NJ: Princeton University Press, 1992), and Marshall Sahlins's response in *How "Natives" Think: About Captain Cook, for Example* (Chicago: University of Chicago Press, 1995), 1–15; also Calder et al., "Introduction: Postcoloniality and the Pacific," in Calder et al., 8–11. Edmond notes that Cook's death could have come as the result of an increasingly frequent and dangerous habit of taking native hostages as collateral for stolen goods or to procure demands (*Representing,* 51).

29. Ali Behdad, *Belated Travelers: Orientalism in the Age of Colonial Dissolution* (Durham, NC: Duke University Press, 1994), 1.

30. I have in mind Foucault's interviews in *Power/Knowledge:* "In reality, power in its exercise goes much further, passes through much finer channels, and is much more ambiguous, since each individual has at his disposal a certain power, and for that very reason can also act as the vehicle for transmitting a wider power." Michel Foucault, *Power/Knowledge: Selected Interviews and Other Writings, 1972–1977,* ed. Colin Gordon (New York: Pantheon, 1980), 72.

31. Ibid., 119.

32. Lisa Lowe, *Critical Terrains: French and British Orientalisms* (Ithaca, NY: Cornell University Press, 1991), ix; Behdad, 13.

33. Qtd. in Schueller, *U.S. Orientalisms,* 8.

34. Dennis Porter, *Haunted Journeys: Desire and Transgression in European Travel Writing* (Princeton, NJ: Princeton University Press, 1991), 4.

35. A good overview of the period can be found in Michael Sturma, *South Sea Maidens: Western Fantasy and Sexual Politics in the South Pacific* (Westport, CT: Greenwood Press, 2002), 123–145.

36. See Chris Friday, "Where to Draw the Line? The Pacific, Place, and the US West," in *A Companion to the American West,* ed. William Deverell (Oxford: Blackwell, 2004), 276.

37. I am indebted to Wilson, who usefully summarizes this concept (175–176). See Antonio Gramsci, *Selections from Cultural Writings,* ed. David Forgacs and Geoffrey Nowell-Smith, trans. William Boelhower (Cambridge: Harvard University Press, 1985), 356.

38. "Summer Smiles This Winter in Hawaii" (advertisement for the Hawai'i Tourist Bureau), *Asia* 25 (October 1925): 899.

39. Qtd. in Rennie, 221.

40. Mark Twain, *Following the Equator: A Journey around the World* [1897] (New York: Dover, 1989), 61.

41. William Maxwell Wood, *Wandering Sketches of People and Things in South America, Polynesia, California, and Other Places Visited, during a Cruise on Board of the US Ships* Levant, Portsmouth, *and* Savannah (Philadelphia: Carey and Hart, 1849), 189–190.

42. As Wilson notes, "The semiotics of 'South Pacific' scenery and the eros of bodily bliss still serve as tourist flow allure," leading locals in Hawai'i to insist on calling what many refer to as the "Hollywood of the Pacific" the "*Haole*-wood" of the Pacific (ix).

43. Edmond, *Representing,* 20–21.

44. Jean-Louis Comolli and Jean Narboni, "Cinema/Ideology/Criticism (1)," *Screen Reader 1: Cinema, Ideology, Politics,* trans. Susan Bennett (London: Society for Education in Film and Television, 1977), 3.

45. Rennie, 1.

46. Porter, 12.

Chapter 1: The Garden and the Wilderness

1. Louis-Antoine de Bougainville, *The Pacific Journal of Louis-Antoine de Bougainville, 1767–1768,* ed. and trans. John Dunmore (London: Hakluyt Society, 2002), 63; subsequent page references in text. Bougainville, *Voyage autour du monde (A Voyage round the World),* trans. John [Johann] Reinhold Forster (London: J. Nourse and T. Davies, 1777), 228–229, 244; subsequent page references in text.

2. Qtd. in Roy Porter, "The Exotic as Erotic: Captain Cook at Tahiti," in *Exoticism in the Enlightenment,* ed. G. S. Rousseau and Roy Porter (Manchester: Manchester University Press, 1990): 119.

3. Joseph Banks, *The* Endeavour *Journal of Joseph Banks, 1768–1771* (entry 13 April 1769), in "South Seas Voyaging and Cross Cultural Encounters in the Pacific (1760–1800)," http://southseas.nla.gov.au/journals/banks/17690426.html (accessed 1 August 2004). Subsequent date-of-entry references in text.

4. Jonathan Lamb, ed., "Introduction," special issue, *Eighteenth Century Life* 18.3 (November 1994): 7.

5. Pamela Cheek, *Sexual Antipodes: Enlightenment Globalization and the Placing of Sex* (Stanford, CA: Stanford University Press, 2003), 2.

6. I am indebted in this and the previous paragraph to Alex Calder, Jonathan Lamb, and Bridget Orr's fine reading of Greg Dening in their "Introduction: Postcoloniality and the Pacific," 13–19.

7. I use "deployment" rather than "experimentation" because aboveground explosions destroyed vast areas and displaced thousands of people. Between 1966 and 1996, France deployed 44 nuclear tests in the atmosphere and 115 underground, causing widespread radiation contamination. One test, which took place amidst high winds on 11 September 1966 on the Moruroa atoll and was witnessed by Charles De Gaulle, resulted in radiation contamination as far west as Samoa, Tonga, Fiji, and Tuvalu. The region's location vis-à-vis the Asian continent made it key for strategic displays of US military power. According to Glenn Alcalay's discussion of nuclear activity in Micronesia, "One navy commander was reported to have suggested killing off the populace as the simplest course to take" ("The United States Anthropologist in Micronesia: Toward a Counter-Hegemonic Study of Sapiens," in *Confronting the Margaret Mead Legacy,* ed. Lenora Foerstel and Angela Gilliam [Philadelphia: Temple University Press, 1992], 182). The relocation of thousands of people to facilitate atomic and hydrogen bomb testing was common US policy, particularly in the Marshall Islands from 1946 to 1958. This included the "largest and dirtiest bomb experiment," called Bravo, on 1 March 1954, which resulted in immediate and long-term contamination of the local populace (Alcalay, 184–185). Paul Breco's film *Marshall Islands: A Matter of Trust* (1988) documents the rapid physical, cultural, and economic devastation in the Marshalls. In 2003, islanders called for an official public apology.

8. Many sources document the events, including Wallis's logbook, the journal of George Robertson (the master of the *Dolphin*), and the first volume of John Hawkesworth's novelistic account of the British voyages. See Wallis, "The Discovery of Tahiti," in *Exploration and Exchange: A South Seas Anthology, 1680–1900,* ed. Jonathan Lamb, Vanessa Smith, and Nicholas Thomas (Chicago: University of Chicago Press, 2000), 57–72; Robertson, *The Discovery of Tahiti, a Journal of the Second Voyage of the H.M.S. Dolphin round the World, 1766–1768,* ed. Hugh Carrington (London: Hakluyt Society, 1948); Hawkesworth, *An Account of the Voyages Undertaken by the Order of his*

Present Majesty for Making Discoveries in the Southern Hemisphere, vols. 1–3 (London: W. Strahan and T. Cadell, 1773); subsequent page references for all three sources in text. Except for some fictional embellishments, Hawkesworth's account roughly conforms to Robertson's journal and to sections of Wallis's logbook (Hawkesworth had access to dozens of logbooks but probably drew on only twelve or so). Rennie calls Robertson's journal the "fullest account from the British point of view" (84), while Jonathan Lamb in Lamb, Smith, and Thomas, *Exploration and Exchange*, notes that Robertson's account is "more racy and vivid" than Wallis's (57). Wallis's logbook in three volumes is in the State Library of New South Wales, Sydney.

9. Lee Wallace, *Sexual Encounters: Pacific Texts, Modern Sexualities* (Ithaca, NY: Cornell University Press, 2003), 1. For an overview of British Pacific voyages as sexual spectacle, see Margaret Jolly, "From Point Venus to Bali Ha'i: Eroticism and Exoticism in Representations of the Pacific," in *Sites of Desire, Economies of Pleasure: Sexualities in Asia and the Pacific*, ed. Lenore Manderson and Margaret Jolly (Chicago: University of Chicago Press, 1997), 99–122.

10. See, for example, Sturma, 27.

11. John Dunmore, "Introduction" to Bougainville, *Pacific Journal*, lvii. Denis Diderot notes with irony in his *Supplément au voyage de Bougainville*, ed. Paul-Edouard Levayer (Paris: Librairie Générale Française, 1995) that "the tone of [Bougainville's *Voyage*] is simplicity and clearness, especially when one is familiar with the language of sailors" (27).

12. Philibert Commerson was, however, an admirer of Rousseau's controversial idealization of the savage in *Discours sur l'origine et les fondements de l'inégalité parmi les hommes* (1754). Commerson believed that they had come upon "the state of natural man, born essentially good, free from all preconceptions," with instincts that had "not yet degenerated into reason" (qtd. in Dunmore, lvi).

13. Bougainville, *Voyage*, 265n. Cheek notes that Aotourou had acquired the reputation of being rude and "coarsely sexual" (19).

14. Arranged by the Royal Society to provide observations of the transit of Venus, this was the first of Cook's three Pacific expeditions, the last of which would end in his violent death during the Makahiki festival in Hawai'i in 1779. J. C. Beaglehole's *Exploration of the Pacific* (London: A. & C. Black, 1934) and *The Life of Captain James Cook* (Stanford, CA: Stanford University Press, 1974) largely established the parameters of modern Cook scholarship. Two recent books further revise the legend: Peter Aughton's *Resolution: Captain Cook's Second Voyage of Discovery* (London: Weidenfeld and Nicolson, 2004) and Nicholas Thomas's *Discoveries: The Voyages of Captain Cook* (London: Allen Lane, 2004).

15. Qtd. in Bernard Smith, *Imagining the Pacific: In the Wake of the Cook Voyages* (New Haven, CT: Yale University Press, 1992), 207.

16. In spite of this edict, Obeyesekere suggests, "secret instructions" from the Admiralty demanded the accumulation of territories for the English. See Obeyesekere, 13.

17. Sydney Parkinson, *Parkinson's Journal* (entry 15 April 1769), in "South Seas Voyaging and Cross Cultural Encounters in the Pacific (1760–1800)," http://southseas.nla.gov.au/journals/parkinson/046.html (accessed 15 August 2004). Subsequent date-of-entry references in text.

18. R. Porter, 132.

19. See Thomas, *Discoveries*, 68–69. In a footnote to Cook, Beaglehole cites the diary of Maximo Rodriguez, which relates a similar encounter in 1775 and calls it a festival of *taurua*. Beaglehole concludes that "there was no impropriety about the ceremony." Captain James Cook, *The Journals of Captain James Cook on His Voyages of Discovery*, vol. 1: *The Voyage of the* Endeavour, *1768–1771*, ed. J. C. Beaglehole (Cambridge: Hakluyt Society, 1955), 93n. Page references in text.

20. Rennie outlines some of Hawkesworth's changes (99). The scene is also discussed by, for example, Cheek (149–150) and Wallace (65–66).

21. In his response to George Forster's *A Voyage round the World*, William Wales offers a different theory, that the scene was a "contrivance" of Purea and that the participants were "two actors" who were indeed "terrified" in performing the act. William Wales, *Remarks on Mr. Forster's Account of Captain Cook's last Voyage round the World*, in George Forster, *A Voyage round the World* [1777], vols. 1–2, ed. Nicholas Thomas and Oliver Berghof (Honolulu: University of Hawai'i Press, 2000), 724. This would suggest Cook's use of "want" in the sense of desire rather than need. Nicholas Thomas confirms this idea, suggesting that Purea was publicly parodying the outlandish sexual behavior of Cook's sailors (G. Forster, 2:831n).

22. Cheek suggests a similar "othering" of Purea—though earlier described as "white" with "uncommon intelligence and sensibility in her eyes"—based on this scene. Focusing on the ways that sentimental recognition of somatic clues helped identify British cultural belonging in the eighteenth century, Cheek notes, "Hawkesworth never invited 'Oberea' into the British culture of sensibility via her recognizable display of appropriate sentiment" (152).

23. Cheek, 142.

24. Rennie, 101; and Jonathan Lamb, "Circumstances Surrounding the Death of John Hawkesworth," special issue, *Eighteenth Century Life* 18.3 (November 1994): 97–113.

25. Sturma, 19.

26. Critics such as Rennie (100–102) and Roy Porter (124) have commented on the passage's sexual display.

27. Bridget Orr, "'Southern passions mix with northern art': Miscegenation and the *Endeavour* Voyage," special issue, *Eighteenth Century Life* 18.3 (November 1994): 213.

28. Diderot, 35.

29. Orr argues in her reading of the "Oberea cycle" of satirical poems (1774) that what is highlighted is not "indecent" Polynesian practices (as focused on in newspapers

and private correspondence), but Banks's reported activities, where the specter of miscegenation appears with force: "O shame! Were we, great George, thy gallant crew,/ And had we—damn it—nothing else to do,/ But turn thy great design to filthy farce,/ And search for wonders on an Indian's a——?" (qtd. in Orr, 220).

30. Cheek, 191.

31. Vanessa Agnew cogently argues that the Pacific "occupies an ambiguous position within the emergent discourse of biological race" during the last decades of the eighteenth century. See Agnew, "Pacific Island Encounters and the German Invention of Race," in Edmond and Smith, 92.

32. Edmond, *Representing*, 7.

33. Cheek, 143–144.

34. Lamb, Introduction, special issue, *Eighteenth Century Life* 18.3 (November 1994): 5. In *Preserving the Self in the South Seas, 1680–1840* (Chicago: University of Chicago Press, 2001), Lamb stresses the complexity of the Forsters' experiences and the need to avoid reducing their aims merely to the "production of truth for imperial purposes" (7).

35. George Stocking, *Race, Culture, and Evolution: Essays in the History of Anthropology* (Chicago: University of Chicago Press, 1982), 44–45. Subsequent page references in text.

36. Nicholas Thomas, "'On the Varieties of Human Species': Forster's Comparative Ethnology," in Johann Reinhold Forster, *Observations Made during a Voyage round the World,* ed. Nicholas Thomas, Harriet Guest, and Michael Dettelbach (Honolulu: University of Hawai'i Press, 1996), xxvi. Thomas's useful summary informs my reading here.

37. Kay Flavell, "Mapping Faces: National Physiognomies as Cultural Prediction," special issue, *Eighteenth Century Life* 18.3 (November 1994): 9; J. Forster, *Observations,* 153. Subsequent page references in text.

38. For George Forster, following his father's theories, there was a stark contrast between the "beautifully formed" Society Islanders and the "deformed savages" of Tierra del Fuego, who were reduced by climatic conditions to a state "next to brutes" (2:684).

39. Smith, *Imagining,* 54.

40. John Bonehill, "Hodges and Cook's Second Voyage," in *William Hodges, 1744–1797: The Art of Exploration,* ed. Geoff Quilley and John Bonehill (New Haven, CT: Yale University Press, 2004), 75.

41. Flavell, 8–9.

42. Nicholas Thomas, "Hodges as Anthropologist and Historian," in Quilley and Bonehill, 33.

43. Wales, 699. See also Thomas, "Introduction" to G. Forster, *Voyage,* 1:xxii. Forster was later livid when denied the expected privilege of writing up the official account of the voyage. For details see Thomas, "Johann Reinhold Forster and his *Observations,*" in J. Forster, *Observations,* xviii–xix.

44. Qtd. in Bonehill, "Hodges and Cook's Second Voyage," 74.

45. Ibid., 97.

46. Thomas, "Hodges as Anthropologist," 31.

47. Smith, *Imagining*, 132. Hodges would later implicitly combine his indebtedness to the neoclassical painter Richard Wilson, his mentor, and his views of the South Pacific in *Landscape, Ruins, and Figures* (1790), which exactly duplicates the ample female figure in the foreground of *View Taken in the Bay* and *Tahiti Revisited* while removing the tattoos, placing the figure against a landscape of classical ruins. Sturma offers an overview of these typical "classical bodies" of the South Seas (80–83).

48. Bonehill, "Hodges's Post-voyage Work," in *William Hodges, 1744–1797: The Art of Exploration*, ed. Geoff Quilley and John Bonehill (New Haven, CT: Yale University Press, 2004), 123.

49. Alan Bewell, "Constructed Places, Constructed Peoples: Charting the Improvement of the Female Body in the Pacific," special issue, *Eighteenth Century Life* 18.3 (November 1994): 52; see also Sturma, 23–24.

50. See, for example, James Cook, *The Journals of Captain James Cook on His Voyages of Discovery*, vol. 2: *The Voyage of the* Resolution *and* Adventure, *1772–1775*, ed. J. C. Beaglehole (Cambridge: Hakluyt Society, 1961), 175.

51. G. Forster, *Voyage*, 1:121–122. William Wales, the astronomer on Cook's second voyage, argued that this text was largely the work of the elder Forster. Thomas notes that the work was "based on his father's journals" (*Voyage*, 1:xxviii).

52. Smith, *Imagining*, 208–209.

53. David N. Leff, *Uncle Sam's Pacific Islets* (Stanford, CA: Stanford University Press, 1940), 3.

54. The "American Pacific," as defined by Wilson, is "the US vision of the Pacific as this had been won through commerce, missionary work, and war" (62). Citing Subramani, he sees the contemporary American Pacific as one of just several postcolonial regions "oriented towards the power that colonized it." As constructed after the post–World War II seizing of territories from defeated Japan, it includes the Republic of the Marshall Islands, the Republic of Belau, the Federated States of Micronesia, the Commonwealth of the Northern Marianas, Guam, and American Samoa (68).

55. Renda, 7.

56. For a list of ships visiting The Marquesas between 1774 and 1842 see Greg Dening, *Islands and Beaches: Discourse on a Silent Land, Marquesas 1774–1880* (Honolulu: University of Hawai'i Press, 1980), 196–301.

57. Qtd. in John Carlos Rowe, *Literary Culture and U.S. Imperialism: From the Revolution to World War II* (Oxford: Oxford University Press, 2000), 83.

58. Captain David Porter, *Journal of a Cruise Made to the Pacific Ocean in the United States Frigate* Essex *in the Years 1812, 1813, and 1814*, vol. 2 (New York: Wiley and Halstead, 1822), 105. Subsequent page references in text. Melville claims in *Typee* that he did not read Porter, only knowing the account from Charles S. Stewart's *A Visit to the South Seas* (1831). Critics such as T. Walter Herbert cite "incontestable" evidence

to the contrary. See Herbert, *Marquesan Encounters: Melville and the Meaning of Civilization* (Cambridge: Harvard University Press, 1980), 159. Porter's influence on Melville is outlined in Rowe, *Literary Culture,* 77–88. I am indebted to Nicholas Thomas's discussion in *Marquesan Societies: Inequality and Political Transformation in Eastern Polynesia* (Oxford: Clarendon, 1990), 133–142.

59. Herbert, 79.

60. Renda, 21.

61. Dening, in *Islands and Beaches,* attributes this insult to the Hapa'a and renders the phrase as "the Americans were the posteriors to the Teii privates" (27). This (homo)sexual implication does not appear in Porter's 1822 edition.

62. Thomas, *Marquesan Societies,* 135. On the attentiveness to ethnographic detail in early accounts see, for example, Calder et al., "Introduction," 5–7.

63. W. Patrick Strauss, *Americans in Polynesia, 1783–1842* (East Lansing: Michigan State University Press, 1963), 153; on Porter versus Calvinistic missionary presumptions see Herbert, 84–88. Sturma cites accounts of missionaries themselves participating in sexual liaisons with Pacific Islanders (4), while Schueller notes the mutual connections between imperial (military) and missionary discourses after US independence (*U.S. Orientalisms,* 39–40).

64. The categories of "soft primitivism" and "hard primitivism" can be traced to George Boas and Arthur O. Lovejoy's *Primitivism and Related Ideas in Antiquity* (1935). Bernard Smith links these two categories to imagery produced on Cook's voyages. The former depicted the Society Islands as "the lands of free love and easy living, where life could be lived without toil or labour" (as in Hodge's *Tahiti Revisited* [1776]), while the latter depicted the same site as occupied by godless, aggressive savages practicing unspeakable rites (as in John Webber's *Human Sacrifice at Otaheite* [1777]) (*Imagining,* 188).

65. John S. Jenkins, *Voyage of the U.S. Exploring Squadron Commanded by Captain Charles Wilkes of the United States Navy in 1838, 1839, 1840, 1841, and 1842* (Auburn, NY: James M. Alden, 1850), 206–207.

66. Qtd. in John Curtis Perry, *Facing West: Americans and the Opening of the Pacific* (Westport, CT: Praeger, 1994), 52–53. See also Strauss, 136; Dodge, *Islands and Empires,* 117; and Charles Erskine, *Twenty Years Before the Mast: With the More Thrilling Scenes and Incidents While Circumnavigating the Globe Under the Command of the Late Admiral Charles Wilkes, 1838–1842* (Boston: Charles Erskine, 1890; rept. Washington, DC: Smithsonian Institution Press, 1985). Wilkes's squadron was "rediscovered" with the popularity of Nathaniel Philbrick's *Sea of Glory: America's Voyage of Discovery, the US Exploring Expedition, 1838–1842* (New York: Viking, 2003).

67. See Donald D. Johnson and Gary Dean Best in *The United States in the Pacific: Private Interests and Public Policies, 1784–1899* (Westport, CT: Greenwood Press, 1995), xvi–xvii.

68. Arthur P. Dudden, *The American Pacific: From the Old China Trade to the Present* (New York: Oxford University Press, 1994), xix.

69. Edward Soja, *Postmodern Geographies: The Reassertion of Space in Critical Social Theory* (London: Verso, 1989), 190.

70. On whaling, see Ernest S. Dodge, *New England and the South Seas* (Cambridge: Harvard University Press, 1965), 55–56.

71. On his death in 1891, Melville's obituary in the *New York Press* announced the "Death of a Once Popular Author" and suggested that "of late Mr. Melville . . . has fallen into a literary decline, as the result of which his books are now little known." Qtd. in Jay Leyda, *The Melville Log: A Documentary Life of Herman Melville, 1819–1891* (New York: Harcourt, 1951), 836.

72. Herbert, 149.

73. Herman Melville, *Typee: A Peep at Polynesian Life* [1846], ed. John Bryant (New York: Penguin, 1996), 27 (chap. 4). Subsequent page references in text.

74. John Bryant, "Introduction," in Melville, *Typee,* xxiii.

75. Schueller, "Indians, Polynesians, and Empire Making: The Case of Herman Melville," in *Genealogy and Literature,* ed. Lee Quinby (Minneapolis: University of Minnesota Press, 1995), 52. Subsequent page references in text. In *U.S. Orientalisms,* Schueller presents Melville's *Clarel* as more unambiguously "subversive," suggesting that it questions the presumed opposition of the New World and Near East through the "circulation of homoerotic desire" (15, 126–140).

76. John Carlos Rowe, "Melville's *Typee:* US Imperialism at Home and Abroad," in *National Identities and Post-Americanist Narratives,* ed. Donald E. Pease (Durham, NC: Duke University Press, 1994), 258. Subsequent page references in text. A revised version of the article appears in Rowe, *Literary Culture,* 77–96.

77. Schueller, *U.S. Orientalisms,* 8.

78. Herman Melville, *Moby-Dick* [1851] (London: Penguin, 1994), 456 (chap. 111). Wilson cites this passage, noting that *Moby-Dick* is Melville's ominous vision of the Pacific as an "oceanic American plantation" (36).

79. Wood, 151–152.

80. Dening, *Islands and Beaches,* 149.

81. Leff, 7–8.

82. Johnson and Best, 127.

83. Ernest N. Paolino, *The Foundations of the American Empire: William Henry Seward and US Foreign Policy* (Ithaca, NY: Cornell University Press, 1973), 4, 32. See also Walter LaFeber on Seward in *The New Empire: An Interpretation of American Expansion, 1860–1898* (Ithaca, NY: Cornell University Press, 1998), 24–32.

84. Johnson and Best, 123.

85. LaFeber, 55, 61.

86. J. W. Davidson, *Samoa mo Samoa: The Emergence of the Independent State of Western Samoa* (Melbourne: Oxford University Press, 1967), 60. Meleisea stresses that this period encapsulates a long-standing European preoccupation with the centralization of localized Samoan polities and districts. See Malama Meleisea, *Change and*

Adaptations in Western Samoa (Christchurch: Macmillan Brown Centre, University of Canterbury, 1992), 9–10.

87. Dodge, *New England,* 47.

88. In the case of Hawai'i, Queen Liliuokalani had been overthrown in 1893 by American forces as a direct result of increasing commercial exploitation of the sugar industry in the islands, but the act was not a fait accompli. Grover Cleveland was known to have opposed Hawaiian annexation because of the great resistance of the islanders, though local colonialists refused to allow Liliuokalani's return to power, setting up an interim colonial administration, with Sanford B. Dole as president. William McKinley, however, favored annexation. See Ronald Takaki, *Pau Hana: Plantation Life and Labor in Hawai'i, 1835–1920* (Honolulu: University of Hawai'i Press, 1983); Noel J. Kent, *Hawai'i: Islands under the Influence* (Honolulu: University of Hawai'i Press, 1993); Tom Coffman, *Nation Within: The Story of America's Annexation of the Nation of Hawai'i* (Kāne'ohe, HI: EpiCenter, 1998).

89. John Robert Procter, "Isolation or Imperialism" [*Forum* 26 (September 1898)]; qtd. in Richard E. Welch, *Imperialists vs. Anti-imperialists: The Debate over Expansionism in the 1890s* (Itsaca, IL: F. E. Peacock, 1972), 21.

90. Dudden, xviii.

91. See, for example, William Ellis, *Polynesian Researches* [1831] (Rutland, VT: Charles Tuttle, 1969), 122.

92. Qtd. in Welch, 26.

93. Qtd. in Dudden, 84.

94. Vincent L. Rafael, *White Love and Other Events in Filipino History* (Durham, NC: Duke University Press, 2000), 21–22.

95. Advertisement for the American Asiatic Association, *Asia* 25 (August 1925): 709.

96. Qtd. in LaFeber, 410. See also Eperjesi's study of the association, 86–104.

97. William James, letter to Senator G. F. Hoar, 11 May 1900; qtd. in Welch, 108–109.

98. See, for example, Rebecca Solnit, *River of Shadows: Eadweard Muybridge and the Technological Wild West* (New York: Viking, 2003), 5.

99. Qtd. ibid., 9.

100. David M. Wrobel, *The End of American Exceptionalism: Frontier Anxiety from the Old West to the New Deal* (Lawrence: University of Kansas Press, 1993), 29–41.

101. Hubert Howe Bancroft, *The New Pacific,* rev. ed. (New York: Bancroft Company, 1912), 13–14.

102. Wilson makes this interesting connection specifically between Soja's notion of peripheralization and Hawaiian annexation (94).

103. Emily S. Rosenberg, *Spreading the American Dream: American Economic and Cultural Expansion, 1890–1945* (New York: Hill and Wang, 1982), 7–9.

104. Overviews of the exposition and its ideological implications can be found in Robert W. Rydell, *All the World's a Fair: Visions of Empire at American International*

Expositions, 1876–1916 (Chicago: University of Chicago Press, 1984); Rosenberg, 3–13; and Julie K. Brown, *Contesting Images: Photography and the World's Columbian Exposition* (Tucson: University of Arizona Press, 1994).

105. Robert Aldrich, *The French Presence in the South Pacific, 1840–1940* (Honolulu: University of Hawai'i Press, 1990), 273, 252–253.

106. As early as 1880, with the announcement of French intentions to span the Panamanian isthmus (then controlled by Colombia), President Rutherford B. Hayes addressed a message to Congress that clearly outlined the value of an American canal. But as late as 1901—when McKinley was assassinated in office by the (possibly) anarchist Leon Czolgosz—plans for the canal were still only partially in place. With the passage of the Spooner Bill in 1902, signed by Teddy Roosevelt, the preferred site for an American canal moved from Nicaragua to Panama, where France had already failed in its canal-building attempts. Roosevelt later claimed that Panama had agreed to sell the designated six-mile-wide strip of the isthmus to the US but that Colombia refused to relinquish control. With rumors of a Panamanian revolution imminent, the battleship *Nashville* moved in, sent by Roosevelt to "protect American lives in Panama." Panama declared its independence from Colombia, and the new Panamanian government was immediately recognized by the US in early 1904. The canal was soon in business, opening in 1914. See Johnson and Best, 120; Tyler Jones, "The Panama Canal: A Brief History," http://www.june29.com/Tyler/nonfiction/pan2.com (accessed 5 April 2002); see also Ira Bennett, *History of the Panama Canal* (Washington, DC: Historical Publishing Co., 1915).

107. Qtd. in Aldrich, *French Presence,* 260.

108. Ibid., 261.

109. Rosenberg, 28.

110. Joseph Hiery, *The Neglected War: The German South Pacific and the Influence of World War I* (Honolulu: University of Hawai'i Press, 1995), 23–27; see also Michael J. Field, *Mau: Samoa's Struggle against New Zealand Oppression* (Wellington: Reed Publishers, 1984), 14–15.

111. Aldrich, *French Presence,* 273.

112. Beatrice Grimshaw, *In the Strange South Seas* (Philadelphia: J. B. Lippincott, 1908), 307.

113. J. H. M. Abbott, *Peeps at Many Lands: The South Seas* (London: Adam and Charles Black, 1908), 29–30.

114. A. J. A. Douglas and P. H. Johnson, *The South Seas of To-day* (London: Cassell, 1926), 90.

115. Linnekin, 8.

116. Douglas Rannie, *My Adventures Among South Sea Cannibals; an account of the experiences and adventures of a government official among the natives of Oceania* (London: Seeley, Service, 1912).

117. Anne Maxwell, *Colonial Photography and Exhibitions: Representations of the 'Native' People and the Making of European Identities* (London: Cassell, 1999), 12–13.

118. Qtd. in Richard Drinnon, *Facing West: The Metaphysics of Indian-Hating and Empire-Building* (New York: Meridian, 1980), 248.

119. R. Porter, 138.

120. These constructions of Polynesian "whiteness" differ from, though are not unrelated to, the kind of "whitening" of Polynesian culture explored in the poetry of Talosaga Tolovae. In "Polynesian Old Man" Tolovae marks the effects of whitening on the gestures of the body itself: "I wonder why/old man/I guess you feared meeting a pale shade/of your brown Polynesian son/with a white-man's stride." "Polynesian Old Man," in Wendt, *Nuanua*, 289.

121. Pedro Fernández de Quirós, *The Voyages of Pedro Fernández de Quirós, 1595 to 1606*, vol. 1, ed. and trans. Sir Clements Markham (London: Hakluyt Society, 1904), 16.

122. Qtd. in Cheek, 139.

123. J. Forster, *Observations*, 154–164.

124. Cheek, 166. Sturma notes an opposite yet related image of the nineteenth century: interbreeding having a positive impact on island "races," creating, as George Angas noted of intermarriages between Europeans and daughters of New Zealand chiefs, "perhaps the finest half-castes in the world" (qtd. in Sturma, 60).

125. Sturma makes the point that female bodies were frequently noted as having less distinctively "racial" characteristics than male, linking gender politics and masculine heterosexual erotic projections to racial perceptions; the long tradition of homoerotic idealization of male Polynesian bodies is not mentioned in this section of his account (60).

126. Homi Bhabha, "Of Mimicry and Man: The Ambivalence of Colonial Discourse," in *The Location of Culture* (New York: Routledge, 1994), 85–92.

127. Herman Melville, *White Jacket, or, The World in a Man-of-War* (New York: Holt, Rinehart, 1967), 394. See James Baird, *Ishmael* (Baltimore: Johns Hopkins Press, 1956), 256–277.

128. Melville, *Moby-Dick*, 193 (chap. 42).

129. Peter Bellwood, *The Polynesians: Prehistory of an Island People* (London: Thames and Hudson, 1987), 17.

130. Roland Burrage Dixon, "A New History of Polynesian Origins," *Proceedings: American Philosophical Association* 59 (1920): 261–267.

131. Louis R. Sullivan, *Marquesan Somatology with Comparative Notes on Samoa and Tonga, Based on the Field Studies of E. S. Craighill Handy and Willowdean C. Handy* (New York: Kraus Reprints, 1974). This influence seems to inhere in current racial theories: in the introductory textbook *Anthropology*, for example, Conrad P. Kottack suggests that links between physical appearance and racial categories persist in current thinking. See Kottack, *Anthropology*, 5th ed. (New York: McGraw Hill, 1991), 25.

132. James Belich, *Paradise Reforged: A History of New Zealanders from the 1880s to the Year 2000* (Auckland: Allen Lane, 2001), 206–210. Belich shows the resilience of these theories well into the 1970s (208).

133. Henry Adams, *Tahiti: Memoirs of Arii Taimai e Marama of Eimeo, Teriirere of Tooarai, Terrinui of Tahiti, Tauraatua i Amo (Memoirs of Marau Taaroa, Last Queen of Tahiti)* [1901], ed. Robert E. Spiller (New York: Scholars' Facsimiles and Reprints, 1947), 7. This discussion easily becomes bound up in white racist discourse, as even a cursory investigation on the Internet reveals, and much widely disseminated information continues to be speculative and unreliable. "Aryan" is considered a racial term used by the Arii as a tribal name in Persia; some sources link Arii to the name "Bavaria."

134. "White Shadows: A Play," Turner/MGM Script Collection, Margaret Herrick Library, Academy of Motion Picture Arts and Sciences, Beverly Hills, folder 1.

135. See Roger Daniels, *The Politics of Prejudice: The Anti-Japanese Movement in California and the Struggle of Japanese Exclusion* [1962] (Berkeley: University of California Press, 1991); also Jeanette Roan, "Exotic Explorations: Travels to Asia and the Pacific in Early Cinema," in *Collecting Early Asian America: Essays in Cultural History,* ed. Josephine Lee, Imogene L. Lim, and Yuko Matsukawa (Philadelphia: Temple University Press, 2002), 187–199.

136. Supreme Court of the United States, *United States v. Bhagat Singh Thind,* no. 202, 261 U.S. 204, 43 S.Ct. 338, 67 L.Ed. 616. Argued 11, 12 January 1923. Decided 19 February 1923.

137. Qtd. in Marian L. Smith, "Race, Nationality, and Reality: INS Administration of Racial Provisions in US Immigration and Nationality Law since 1898," *Immigration Daily,* 16 June 2003, http://www.ilw.com/lawyers/articles/2003,0616–smith.shtm (accessed 5 October 2004).

138. Abraham Fornander, *An account of the Polynesian race; its origins and migrations, and the ancient history of the Hawaiian people to the times of Kamehameha I,* 3 vols. (London: Trübner & Co., 1878, 1880, 1885), 1:2. Fornander traces the origin of his theories to Fanz Bopp, "Über die Verwandtschaft der Malaysich-Polynesischen Sprachen mit den Indisch-Europäischen" (1841), cited in 3:2.

139. Josiah Nott, a southern slavery advocate who had contributed an appendix to Count de Gobineau's notorious "On the Intellectual and Moral Diversity of Races," was one such scientific figure in the miscegenation debate. As glossed in J. L. Cabell's mid-century defense of monogenism, *The Unity of Mankind* (1859), Nott concluded that miscegenation directly resulted in the racial degeneration of both blacks and whites. See J. L. Cabell, *The Testimony of Modern Science to the Unity of Mankind* (New York: Robert Carter and Brothers, 1859), 127–128. Cheek, however, highlights a history of eugenics where the principle of selective interbreeding was seen to give rise to the reinvigoration and perfection of the race (126). See also Schueller on Nott in *U.S. Orientalisms,* 37–38.

140. Peter Bellwood, *Man's Conquest of the Pacific: The Prehistory of Southeast Asia*

and Oceania (New York: Oxford University Press, 1979), 305. Macmillan Brown also put forward a now-familiar sunken continent migration theory.

141. Albert Churchward, *Origin and Evolution of the Human Race* (London: George Allen and Unwin, 1921), 69; see also Stocking, *Race,* 61.

142. Stocking, *Race,* 64.

143. Ibid., 65.

144. Ibid., 68.

145. Bancroft, x.

146. Ross Chambers, "The Unexamined," in *Whiteness: A Critical Reader,* ed. Mike Hill (New York: New York University Press, 1999), 189.

147. Interestingly, Amy Kaplan in *The Anarchy of Empire* seizes on precisely the ways that ambiguity—racial, national, territorial—was crucial to the process of US empire building. Puerto Rico's status as an "unincorporated territory" exemplifies the manner in which overseas expansion relied on the creation of ambiguous and often "stateless" spaces occupying liminal realms between clear-cut definitions of "foreign" and "domestic" territories (15).

148. Stocking, *Race,* 88.

149. *"Tubora Tumaida"* and *"Tootahau"* appear in Parkinson's journal (20 April and 4 May 1769).

150. Talal Asad, "The Concept of Cultural Translation in British Social Anthropology," in *Writing Culture: The Poetics and Politics of Ethnography,* ed. James Clifford and George E. Marcus (Berkeley: University of California Press, 1986), 149; emphasis in original.

151. Vanessa Smith, "Pitcairn's 'Guilty Stock': The Island as Breeding Ground," in Edmond and Smith, 123.

152. Edward Robarts, *The Marquesan Journal of Edward Robarts, 1797–1824,* ed. Greg Dening (Honolulu: University of Hawai'i Press, 1974), 268.

153. Paul Gauguin, *Noa Noa* [1919], ed. and trans. O. F. Theis (New York: Noonday, 1957), 30.

154. Advertisement for *Noa Noa, Publisher's Weekly,* 17 January 1920: 151. In 1923, Dodd, Mead and Co. published an edition of Gauguin's letters featuring an Introduction by Frederick O'Brien.

155. Alfred St. Johnston, *Camping among Cannibals* (London: Macmillan Colonial Library, 1889), 171. Subsequent page references in text.

156. Qtd. in Asad, 141.

157. Stocking, *Race,* 69.

158. Ibid., 169.

159. Ibid., 180.

160. Franz Boas, "Foreword," in Margaret Mead, *Coming of Age in Samoa* [1928] (New York: William Morrow, 1961), ii–iii.

161. Robert W. Rydell, *World of Fairs: The Century of Progress Expositions* (Chicago: University of Chicago Press, 1993), 38.

162. See Margaret Mead, *An Anthropologist at Work: Writings of Ruth Benedict* (Boston: Houghton Mifflin, 1959); Jane Howard, *Margaret Mead: A Life* (New York: Simon and Schuster, 1984), 67–75.

163. Edward Sapir, "Culture, Genuine and Spurious," in *Culture, Language, and Personality: Selected Essays* [1949], ed. David G. Mandelbaum (Berkeley: University of California Press, 1966), 95–96. Subsequent page references in text.

164. Margaret Mead, *From the South Seas: Studies of Adolescence and Sex in Primitive Societies* (New York: William Morrow, 1939), xxvii.

Chapter 2: Idylls and Ruins

1. The basis for this account is Robert Flaherty's "Synopsis" to *Singer of the South Seas,* box 42, Robert J. Flaherty Papers, Butler Library, Columbia University (hereafter Flaherty Papers); also Robert Flaherty, "Film: The Language of the Eye," *Theatre Arts* 36.5 (May 1951): 34. Similar versions appear in Richard Griffith, *The World of Robert Flaherty* [1953] (Westport, CT: Greenwood, 1970), 50; Frances Flaherty, "Setting Up House and Shop in Samoa," *Asia* 25 (August 1925): 639–640; and Paul Rotha, *Robert J. Flaherty: A Biography,* ed. Jay Ruby (Philadelphia: University of Pennsylvania Press, 1983), 52–53.

2. Rotha, 52.

3. Letter to Charmian London, 29 June 1921. Jack London Collection 15987-16038, Henry E. Huntington Library and Art Gallery, Pasadena (hereafter JLC). Their affair started after an exchange of letters relating to *White Shadows in the South Seas* beginning in June 1920.

4. The friend was Dr. Malcolm Douglas.

5. Frances Flaherty, "Setting Up," 639.

6. Eric Howard, "Famous Californians: Frederick O'Brien," *San Francisco Call and Post,* 3 September 1923: 1.

7. "The Literary Spotlight XXVIII: Frederick O'Brien," *Bookman* 59.1 (March 1924): 57.

8. Letter to Charmian London, 29 June 1921 (Apia, Samoa), JLC.

9. "Literary Couriers to Distant Places," *Travel* (New York), 37 (October 1921): 14.

10. James D. Hart, ed., *Oxford Companion to American Literature* (New York: Oxford University Press, 1995), 482. Jean Simon's *La Polynésia dans l'art et la littérature de l'occident* (Paris: Gallimard, 1939) also credits O'Brien with reviving interest in Polynesia after the war but devotes only a page to his work (232–233). Per-

haps the most in-depth examination of O'Brien to date is found in Roulston. See also Paul Lyons, *American Pacificism: Oceania in the U.S. Imagination* (London: Routledge 2006), 133–135.

11. Frederick O'Brien, "The Author of *White Shadows*," *Bookman* 52 (December 1920): 297–298.

12. Diary of Margaret Wickham Watson, 2 September 1925; MS 2272, California Historical Society, San Francisco (hereafter MWW diary).

13. Dening, *Islands*, 130. For further work on beachcomber life and writings see I. C. Campbell, "*Gone Native*" *in Polynesia: Captivity Narratives and Experiences from the South Pacific* (Westport, CT: Greenwood, 1998); Vanessa Smith, *Literary Culture and the Pacific: Nineteenth-Century Textual Encounters* (Cambridge: Cambridge University Press, 1998).

14. See Newton Arvin's analysis of Melville's episodic form in *Herman Melville: A Critical Biography* (New York: William Sloane, 1950), 80–81.

15. O'Brien, "Author," 299.

16. Frederick O'Brien, *White Shadows in the South Seas* (New York: Century, 1919), 376. Subsequent page references in text.

17. Edmond Terence Casey, "Frederick O'Brien Day by Day" [Obituary], *Sausalito News* (15 January 1932). There are conflicting accounts of O'Brien's date of birth. I am using 1869, widely cited in his obituaries, though Leon Stanley, his close friend and physician who attended him at his death, stated the date was 1868. See "Doctor Leo Stanley" in *Ross Valley Reporter,* 24 November 1971: 4–5. Further details about O'Brien's life have been drawn from the O'Brien clippings file in the Sausalito Historical Society, Sausalito: Charles Willcox, "The Lost Autobiographical Works of Once Famous Sausalito Author Frederick O'Brien," *Sausalito Historical Society Quarterly,* Winter 1994: 1–2; Eric Howard, "Famous Californians: Frederick O'Brien," *San Francisco Call and Post,* 3 September 1923; "O'Brien's Ashes to be Cast in Golden Gate," *San Francisco News,* 11 January 1932; "Loving Life, O'Brien Did Not Fear Death" [Obituary], *San Francisco Examiner,* 10 January 1932; "O'Brien Loved His Sausalito," *Sausalito News,* 15 January 1932; "Death Claims O'Brien, Noted World Writer" [Obituary], *San Francisco Chronicle,* 10 January 1932.

18. "Loving Life, O'Brien Did Not Fear Death"; Willcox, 1–2.

19. Letter to Charles Peirson, 10 May 1924, JLC.

20. Letter to Sara Bard (Field) Wood, 6 February 1920, WD box 177, JLC.

21. Letter to Sarah Bard Field and Charles Erskine Scott Wood, no date (1927), WD box 177, JLC.

22. In 1899–1901, US troops battled and finally suppressed the independence movement led by Emilio Aguinaldo, a former American ally against the Spanish. Twain was also part of the Anti-Imperialist League working in support of Aguinaldo, though he was hardly averse to the Americanization of the Pacific in the form of Hawaiian annexation.

23. Letter to Sara Bard (Field) Wood, 5 January 1921, WD box 177, JLC.

24. 13 June 1925, MWW diary.

25. O'Brien, "Author," 299. The house, at 1 Edwards Avenue, was razed in the 1930s to make way for the Golden Gate Bridge and Highway 101.

26. George Biddle, *Tahitian Journal* (Minneapolis: University of Minnesota Press, 1968), 70.

27. Casey, 1.

28. O'Brien, "Author," 298.

29. Figures for 1920 are from *Publisher's Weekly* 99.5 (29 January 1921): 281; for 1921 are from *Publisher's Weekly* 101.4 (28 January 1922): 198.

30. "The Weekly Record of New Publications," *Publisher's Weekly* 96 (27 September 1919): 910.

31. Cartoon, *Current Opinion* 70 (June 1921): 735.

32. Letter to Charmian London, dated "Sunday noon" (August 1920?), JLC.

33. "Travel Books to the Fore Again," *Publisher's Weekly* (6 December 1919): 1540.

34. Wrobel, *End,* 98.

35. Ibid., 29–41.

36. Frederick Jackson Turner, *The Frontier in American History* (New York: Henry Holt, 1920), 1, 15.

37. Wrobel, 98.

38. Ibid., 92.

39. Advertisement for *The Man of the Forest, Publisher's Weekly* (3 January 1920): 6–7.

40. Bancroft, ix.

41. Controversy later surrounded the extent to which Lane contributed to the manuscript. In the mid-1920s she sued him for failing to credit her.

42. Vaitahu is spelled "Vait-hua" throughout *White Shadows,* probably an editorial error. O'Brien claimed that the book was prepared for publication and released while he was in Hong Kong ("Author," 299). The error is corrected in *Atolls of the Sun* (New York: Century, 1922).

43. *"White Shadows in the South Seas," Outlook* (29 October 1919): 123.

44. St. Johnston, 1.

45. See Joseph Bristow, *Empire Boys* (London: Harper Collins, 1991).

46. Charles S. Stewart, *A Visit to the South Seas in the U.S. Ship* Vincennes, *During the Years 1829 and 1830* (New York: John P. Haven, 1831), 317.

47. See Johannes Fabian, *Time and the Other: How Anthropology Makes Its Object* (New York: Columbia University Press, 1983).

48. O'Brien, *Atolls,* 30–33. O'Brien wrongly cites Darwin: while not categorically dismissing submerged continent theories, Darwin betrayed a skepticism towards figures such as Edward Forbes, who posited a lost continent in the Atlantic to explain the

dispersion of species around the planet. Confining his theories to the dispersion of flora, Darwin put forward instead a theory of "accidental" or "occasional" distribution, that is, accidents of nature that allowed for seeds crossing oceans on floating timber, carried by birds, and so on. See Charles Darwin, *On the Origin of Species* [1859] (New York: Atheneum, 1972), 357–358.

49. D. H. Lawrence, "Psychoanalysis and the Unconscious" *and* "Fantasia of the Unconscious" [1922] (Cambridge: Cambridge University Press, 2004), 7. See also John Macmillan Brown's *The Riddle of the Pacific* (Boston: Small, Maynard, 1924); also Bellwood, 305–306. Marianna Torgovnick, in *Gone Primitive: Savage Intellects, Modern Lives* (Chicago: University of Chicago Press, 1990), glosses the Lawrence passage in her reading of *The Plumed Serpent:* "After the flood, these 'life' orientations survived in isolated South Sea islands and among what he calls the 'savages' of Africa; they survived as well in certain individuals who were misfits in Western civilization, and also in the myths of Western culture" (160). Unlike O'Brien, however, Lawrence made little effort to ground his ideas in scientific or historical sources, stating clearly at the outset that these ideas help to form a spiritual universe, and he is not interested in whether others share his ideas or not (276).

50. Qtd. on "James Churchward" Web site, http://www.churchward.com/cw/james .html (accessed 26 November 2004).

51. James Churchward, *The Lost Continent of Mu, the Motherland of Man* (New York: William Edwin Rudge, 1926), 1.

52. R. M. Watson, *History of Samoa* (Wellington: Whitcombe and Tombs, 1918), 33.

53. See, for example, Mgr. René Ildefonse Dordillon, *Grammaire et dictionnaire de la langue des Iles Marquises* [1904] (Papeete: Societé des Études Océaniennes, 1999).

54. De Quirós, 18–19.

55. Ibid., 24–25.

56. Percy S. Allen, *Stewart's Handbook of the Pacific Islands: A Reliable Guide to All the Inhabited Islands of the Pacific Ocean for Traders, Tourists, and Settlers* (Sydney: McCarron, Stewart, 1922), xvii, 231. O'Brien provides similar figures: "A hundred years ago there were a hundred and sixty thousand Marquesans on these islands. Twenty years ago there were four thousand. To-day I am convinced that there remain not twenty-one hundred" (*White Shadows*, 162). In 1921, E. S. Craighill Handy estimated there were eighteen hundred people; see Handy, *The Native Culture in the Marquesas* (Honolulu: Bernice P. Bishop Museum Bulletin 9, 1923), 5. Aldrich establishes that the population of the Marquesas was at least halved within fifty years of European contact (*French Presence,* 176–178). Recent census reports cite the population as seventy-five hundred.

57. Thomas, *Entangled Objects,* 121–122.

58. Dening, *Islands,* 239.

59. Edmond, *Representing,* 14.

60. This proverb, with references going back to the missionaries William Ellis and John Davies, was widely cited and transmuted; it served as the epigraph to London's short story "The Chinago" and was cited by Loti, Stevenson, Melville, and others.

61. Dening, *Islands,* 278.

62. Henry David Thoreau, *Walden,* in *"Walden," and Civil Disobedience,* ed. Owen Thomas (New York: W. W. Norton, 1966), 23; qtd. in Schueller, "Indians," 52.

63. Robert Louis Stevenson, *In the South Seas* [1900] (Honolulu: University Press of Hawai'i, 1971), 25. Subsequent page references in text. Stevenson cruised for seven months on the yacht *Casco* (1888), and later for six months on the schooner *Equator* (1889), a trip he intended to benefit his failing health. O'Brien expresses little reverence for Stevenson, in spite of his influence. In *Atolls of the Sun,* O'Brien criticizes Stevenson for his lack of respect for the art of Marquesan tattooing, noting that Stevenson expressed "a real sympathy for the iconoclastic ignorance that was destroying tattooing here" (338).

64. Dening, *Islands,* 277.

65. Edmond, *Representing,* 167.

66. Douglas and Johnson, 95.

67. In keeping with such claims, in the 1830s William Ellis argued that areas of Polynesia were recovering and populations "rapidly increasing" as a result of the "renovating and genial principles of true religion and the morality with which this is inseparably connected." Ellis, 108.

68. Wendt, *Nuanua,* 3.

69. Dening, *Islands,* 238.

70. Margaret Mead, *Blackberry Winter: My Earlier Years* (New York: Simon and Schuster, 1972), 127.

71. Critics such as Edmond have linked this aestheticization to the "narcissistic appropriation" and feminizing of Pacific islands in writers such as Loti and Melville, respectively. See Edmond, *Representing,* 245.

72. Edward Said, "Representing the Colonized: Anthropology's Interlocutors," *Critical Inquiry* 15.2 (Winter 1989): 222–223.

73. The end of *A Passage to India* becomes a moment in which, Said suggests, "Forster notes, and confirms the history behind, a political conflict between Dr. Aziz and Fielding—Britain's subjugation of India—and yet [Forster] can neither recommend decolonization, nor continued colonization. 'No, not yet, not here,' is all Forster can muster by way of resolution" ("Representing," 223). But the passage actually reads, "'No, not yet,' and the sky said, 'no, not *there*'" (E. M. Forster, *A Passage to India* [New York: Harcourt Brace, 1952], 320). Beyond Forster's—perhaps meaningful—inscription of the distance between the "here" and the "there" of novelistic description, it could be argued that the passage implies that it is precisely imperial subjugation that prevents "friendship" and reconciliation between the two men.

74. Dening, *Islands,* 53.

75. Ibid., 88. Thomas, in *Marquesan Societies,* stresses the role muskets played in the transformation of the indigenous political system in the Marquesas (139–141).

76. Handy, 4–5.

77. Dening, *Islands,* 283.

78. Behdad, 78.

79. Raymond Williams, *Keywords: A Vocabulary of Culture and Society* [1976] (Oxford: Oxford University Press), 49.

80. Walter Benjamin, *Origin of the German Tragic Drama* [1928], trans. John Osborne (New York: Verso, 1977), 178.

81. Ann Laura Stoler discusses these discourses in Foucauldian terms in *Race and the Education of Desire* (Durham, NC: Duke University Press, 1996).

82. Baufré's character reappears in *Atolls of the Sun,* this time called Peyral.

83. See Alfred Gell, *Wrapping in Images: Tattooing in Polynesia* (Oxford: Clarendon Press, 1993), 194–195.

84. Behdad, 76.

85. Benjamin, *Origin,* 95.

86. Robarts, 256.

87. Gell, 175–176.

88. Lyons, *American Pacificism,* 135.

89. Wilson, 24.

90. Advertisement for *White Shadows in the South Seas,* in *Publisher's Weekly,* 6 March 1920: 668.

91. Wrobel, 90.

92. Robarts, 270.

93. "The Literary Spotlight XXVIII," 54.

94. *American Library Association* 16 (December 1919): 86; *New York Call,* 26 October 1919: 11; *Outlook* 123 (29 October 1919): 243; *Review* 2 (10 January 1920): 37.

95. *New York Times,* 17 April 1921: 7.

96. Letter to Charmian London, 19 June, 1921, JLC; emphasis in original.

97. Letter to Charmian London, 29 October, 1921, JLC.

98. Letter to Charmian London, 20 November 1921, JLC.

99. Walter E. Taprock [a.k.a. George S. Chappell], *The Cruise of the* Kawa: *Wanderings in the South Seas* (New York: G. P. Putnam's Sons, 1921), ix.

100. Ben Macomber, "Fred O'Brien Brings Up Gorgeous South Sea Haul" (review of *Atolls of the Sun*), *San Francisco Chronicle,* 22 October 1922. O'Brien clippings file, Sausalito Historical Society.

101. 2 April 1924, MWW diary.

102. 14 June 1925, MWW diary.

103. Lane's contributions should not be underestimated, and she was likely responsible at the very least for the highly readable and fluid style of the text. Though

there is not space here to fully consider Lane's contribution, see Betty Ren Wright, *The Ghost in the House: A Life of Rose Wilder Lane* (Columbia: University of Missouri Press, 1995). Though she helped to prepare and refine the manuscript, and coauthored article publications that fed into *White Shadows,* the idea of coauthorship, or ghost writing, as several Web sites suggest (see, for example, the Rose Wilder Lane Web site at http://webpages.marshall.edu/irby1/laura/rose/html), seems to overstate the case.

104. Letter to Charmian London, 4 February 1922, JLC.

105. 21 October 1932, MWW diary.

Chapter 3: Searching for Moana

1. "The Screen," *New York Times,* 12 June 1922: 16.

2. "Pictures of 1922," *New York Times,* 2 July 1922, sec. 4:3. For *Nanook*'s costs and earnings see William T. Murphy, *Robert Flaherty: A Guide to References and Resources* (Boston: G. K. Hall, 1978), 10.

3. Rotha, 51.

4. Letter to David Flaherty, 19 February 1923; box 2, Flaherty Papers.

5. For a contemporary example of this notion of Polynesian origins, see William R. Castle, Jr., *Hawaii: Past and Present* (New York: Dodd, Mead, 1926), 13. On Nafanua see Meleisea, "Postmodern Legacy."

6. Tensions between Samoan leaders and the policies of the New Zealand administrator, Brigadier General George Spafford Richardson, escalated through the 1920s and initiated the rise of the anticolonial movement the Mau, with violent skirmishes between New Zealand police and Mau protestors in the late 1920s. See Meleisea, *Change and Adaptations,* 42–46. J. W. Davidson notes that ultimately Richardson "wished to subject the Samoans to his will in order that he could impose on them a comprehensive policy of social and economic development. The actions of the government and its Samoan officials thus impinged upon the ordinary lives of the people far more extensively than ever before" (112–113).

7. André Bazin, *What Is Cinema?,* vol. 1, ed. and trans. Hugh Gray (Berkeley: University of California Press, 1967), 155.

8. Orson Welles, "Portrait of Robert Flaherty," BBC Broadcast, 2 September 1952; qtd. in Rotha, 321.

9. Fred Zinnemann, "About Robert Flaherty," article draft, 24 March 1976, Fred Zinnemann Collection, Margaret Herrick Library, Academy of Motion Picture Arts and Sciences, Beverly Hills.

10. Jay Ruby, "A Reexamination of the Early Career of Robert J. Flaherty," *Quarterly Review of Film Studies* (Fall 1980): 431.

11. Ruby calls Flaherty the "American father figure of documentary film" ("The Ethics of Image-Making," in *New Challenges for Documentary,* ed. Alan Rosenthal [Berke-

ley: University of California Press, 1988], 312) and has anatomized the ways that the figure of the maverick filmmaker and independent artist was constructed first through the self-image Flaherty created in his own writings and interviews and then through the efforts of biographers such as Richard Griffith and Arthur Calder-Marshall (Ruby, "The Aggie Will Come First: The Demystification of Robert Flaherty," in *Robert J. Flaherty Photographer/Filmmaker: The Inuit, 1910–1922*, ed. Jo-Anne Birnie Danzker [Vancouver: Vancouver Art Gallery, 1980], 67–74, 94–96). For a discussion of Flaherty related to the arguments in this section, see my "*Nanook of the North:* Fiction, Truth, and the Documentary Contract," in *Film Analysis: A Norton Reader,* ed. Jeffrey Geiger and R. L. Rutsky (New York: W. W. Norton, 2005), 118–137.

12. Qtd. in Murphy, 57.

13. Ibid., 71.

14. Fatimah Tobing Rony, *The Third Eye: Race, Cinema, and Ethnographic Spectacle* (Durham, NC: Duke University Press, 1996), 102.

15. Ibid., 99.

16. Ruby, "Ethics," 313.

17. Bill Nichols, *Representing Reality: Issues and Concepts in Documentary* (Bloomington: Indiana University Press, 1991), 231; emphasis in original.

18. See Linda Williams, "Mirrors without Memories: Truth, History, and the New Documentary," *Film Quarterly* 46.3 (Spring 1993): 9–21.

19. G. Forster, *Voyage,* 1:232. Forster's attack on the engraving might also be related to the report that his father, Johann Forster, was angry to be denied not only the opportunity to write the official account of Cook's voyages, but also access to engravings that were known to greatly enhance sales of travel accounts (*Voyage,* 1:xxvii–xxviii).

20. See B. Smith, *Imagining,* 72.

21. Wales, *Remarks,* 712.

22. B. Smith, *Imagining,* 72.

23. Flaherty was a great admirer of Vertov, as he was of Eisenstein, urging Frances to read Vertov's work in the journal *The Realist* (1929). See Letter to Frances Flaherty, 3 February 1930; box 1, Flaherty Papers.

24. "The Screen," *New York Times,* 12 June 1922: 16.

25. L. D. Froelick, "Moana of the South Seas," *Asia* 25 (May 1925): 389.

26. L. D. Froelick, "Along the Trail with the Editor" *Asia* 25 (May 1925): 375.

27. "Flaherty and Film" (Robert Gardner interview with Frances Flaherty, 1960), *Nanook of the North,* Criterion Collection DVD (1999).

28. Frances Flaherty, "Behind the Scenes with Our Samoan Stars," *Asia* 25 (September 1925): 748. Subsequent page references in text. The *Asia* series was edited and reprinted in Griffith, *The World of Robert Flaherty,* 52–71.

29. I was unable to find any mention of Finauga's real name in the Flaherty papers at Columbia University.

30. For further details about Flaherty's background as explorer and prospector see

Rotha, 7–42; Rony, 109–111; and Richard M. Barsam, *The Vision of Robert Flaherty: The Artist as Myth and Filmmaker* (Bloomington: Indiana University Press, 1988), 11–25.

31. Qtd. in Rotha, 12.

32. See Rony, 113; also Danzker; and Ruby, "Reexamination." All offer overviews of the contexts of *Nanook of the North*'s creation.

33. Qtd. in Murphy, 57.

34. Qtd. in Richard Corliss, "Robert Flaherty: The Man in the Iron Myth," in *Nonfiction Film Theory and Criticism*, ed. Richard Meran Barsam (New York: E. P. Dutton, 1976), 230.

35. Ibid.

36. George Stocking, "The Ethnographic Sensibility of the 1920s and the Dualism of the Anthropological Tradition," in *Romantic Motives: Essays on Anthropological Sensibility*, ed. George Stocking (Madison: University of Wisconsin Press, 1989), 212.

37. Susan Hegeman, *Patterns for America: Modernism and the Concept of Culture* (Princeton, NJ: Princeton University Press, 1999), 6.

38. Sapir, "Culture, Genuine and Spurious," 93.

39. Robert S. Lynd and Helen Merrell Lynd, *Middletown: A Study in Modern American Culture* (New York: Harcourt, Brace and World, 1929), 16, 21.

40. Stocking, "Ethnographic Sensibility," 220.

41. Qtd. in Jay Ruby, *Picturing Culture: Explorations of Film and Anthropology* (Chicago: University of Chicago Press, 2000), 71. The quotation is from an early draft of an article that was to become "How I Filmed *Nanook of the North*" (1922).

42. Qtd. in Ruby, *Picturing Culture*, 84.

43. Ibid.

44. Mead, *Coming of Age*, 7.

45. Mead, *Blackberry Winter*, 154. This must refer to one of Frances's articles for *Asia*.

46. "I had seen Nanook before I went to Samoa, and an article by Flaherty in Asia Magazine provided me with pictures that I used in making a Samoan picture interpretation test. . . . My Samoan diorama in the Peoples of the Pacific Hall [in the American Museum of Natural History], finished in 1972, is based upon a scene from *Moana*" (Letter to Jay Ruby, 20 September 1976; qtd. in Ruby, *Picturing Culture*, 85).

47. Trinh T. Minh-ha, "Outside In Inside Out," *Questions of Third Cinema*, ed. Jim Pines and Paul Willemen (London: British Film Institute, 1989), 134.

48. Ernst Bloch, "Ungleichzeitigkeit and Pflicht zu ihrer Dialektik" [1932], in *Erbschaft dieser Zeit* (Frankfurt: Suhrkamp, 1962), 326.

49. In *Patterns of Culture* Ruth Benedict offers a caution regarding Spengler's reduction of western society to classifications that amount to "a couple of catchwords" (even if she was less cautious about offering up portraits of "simpler peoples" in a similar manner). Ruth Benedict, *Patterns of Culture* (New York: Houghton Mifflin, 1934), 54–55.

50. Qtd. in Fabian, 45.

51. Sapir, "Culture: Genuine and Spurious," 93.

52. Donna Haraway, *Simians, Cyborgs, and Women: The Reinvention of Nature* (New York: Routledge, 1991), 191.

53. Margaret Mead, *Growing Up in New Guinea* [1930] (New York: Dell, 1968), 21–22.

54. See Rotha, 31.

55. Frances Flaherty, "Setting Up House and Shop," 648–649. Subsequent page references in text.

56. See Rotha, 70.

57. Trinh, "Outside In," 134.

58. James Clifford, *The Predicament of Culture: Twentieth-Century Ethnography, Literature, and Art* (Cambridge: Harvard University Press, 1988), 230.

59. Stevenson, *In the South Seas,* 31.

60. Mead, *Blackberry Winter,* 183.

61. Ibid., 127.

62. Bronislaw Malinowski, *Argonauts of the Western Pacific* [1922] (New York: Dutton, 1961), xv.

63. George E. Marcus, "Contemporary Problems of Ethnography in the Modern World System," in *Writing Culture: The Poetics and Politics of Ethnography,* ed. James Clifford and George E. Marcus (Berkeley: University of California Press, 1986), 165.

64. Mead, Introduction to *Anthropologist at Work,* xviii.

65. James Clifford, "Of Other Peoples: Beyond the Salvage Paradigm," in *Discussions in Contemporary Culture,* no. 1, ed. Hal Foster (Seattle, WA: Bay Press, 1987), 122.

66. Mead, *Growing Up in New Guinea,* 16.

67. The notion of documenting "whole cultures" was central to Mead's work. See, for example, *Blackberry Winter,* 202; *Growing Up in New Guinea,* 18. Interestingly, according to her biographer Jane Howard, Mead was not very interested in the salvage of concrete artifacts, though in her capacity as curator of the American Museum of Natural History, this was one of her main responsibilities, including the establishment of her famous Hall of the Peoples of the Pacific. Quoting Mead's colleagues Junius Bird and Phillip Gifford, Howard concludes, "collecting was never really Mead's forte" (132).

68. Clifford, "Of Other Peoples," 123.

69. Robert Flaherty, letter to Gifford Pinchot, 15 October 1929; box 23, Flaherty Papers.

70. James Norman Hall, letter to Gifford Pinchot, 15 October 1929; box 23, Flaherty Papers.

71. For a study of photography in Samoa preceding and including part of the period discussed in this chapter, see Alison Devine-Nordstrom, ed., *Picturing Paradise: Colonial Photography of Samoa, 1875–1925* (Oxford: Pitt-Rivers Museum, 1995).

72. Gilberto Perez, *The Material Ghost: Films and Their Medium* (Baltimore, MD: Johns Hopkins University Press, 1998), 34.

73. See Maxwell, *Colonial Photography,* 165–179.

74. *"Moana"* (review) *New York Times,* 31 October 1926; box 25 (clippings), Flaherty Papers.

75. André Gide, *The Journals of André Gide,* vol. 2, ed. and trans. Justin O'Brien (New York: Knopf, 1948), 382.

76. Rony, 28. Assenka Oksiloff, who cites Rony, further notes, "It is as if, precisely when 'modern' bodies lose their legitimacy as cognizable autonomous objects, the primitive body steps in to ensure the persistence of an older visual regime.... Visions of non-Westerners provided a stronghold against the impinging forces of modernist subjective vision." Assenka Oksiloff, *Picturing the Primitive: Visual Culture, Ethnography, and Early German Cinema* (New York: Palgrave, 2001), 10.

77. Nichols, *Representing,* 223–224.

78. Ibid., 183.

79. Griffith, *World,* 50.

80. Ibid., 51.

81. Patricia Zimmerman, "Midwives, Hostesses, and Feminist Film," *Wide Angle* 17 (1995): 200.

82. 22 April 1923, MWW diary.

83. Letter to Frances Flaherty, 12 June 1929; box 2, Flaherty Papers.

84. "New Lighting for Movies," *New York Times,* 12 February 1928.

85. 22 February 1925; box 23, Flaherty Papers.

86. Letter to L. D. Froelick, January–June 1925; box 23, Flaherty Papers.

87. Frances Flaherty, "Fa'a Samoa" *Asia* 25 (December 1925): 1085. Subsequent page references in text.

88. Qtd. in Rotha, 53.

89. Murphy, 66.

90. Barsam, 37. Barsam acknowledges the extent of Frances's contributions to the making of the film (38), but nonetheless suggests that her presence worked to the film's disadvantage.

91. Frances Flaherty, "A Search for Animal and Sea Sequences," *Asia* 25 (November 1925): 1003. Subsequent page references in text.

92. Froelick, "Moana of the South Seas," 390.

93. Meleisea, *Change and Adaptations,* 20.

94. Robert Littell, *"Moana,"* review in *The New Republic* 46 (3 March 1926): 46.

95. John Grierson, "Flaherty's Poetic *Moana,*" in *The Documentary Tradition,* ed. Lewis Jacobs (New York: W. W. Norton, 1979), 25.

96. Mikhail Bakhtin, *The Dialogic Imagination: Four Essays,* ed. Michael Holquist, trans. Caryl Emerson and M. Holquist (Austin: University of Texas Press, 1981), 17.

97. Ibid., 15–16.

98. Ibid., 13.

99. Robert Flaherty, "The Handling of Motion Picture Film under Various Climatic Conditions," *Transactions of the Society of Motion Picture Engineers* 26: 85–93, http://nimbus.ocis.temple.edu/~jruby/wava/Flaherty/ (accessed 30 October 2004).

100. Sturma offers a useful overview of this cliché and the "semiotics of exposed breasts" in *South Sea Maidens,* 83–87.

101. Froelick, "Moana of the South Seas," 390.

102. Barsam, 41.

103. See, for example, David MacDougall, "The Subjective Voice in Ethnographic Film," in *Fields of Vision: Essays in Film Studies, Visual Anthropology, and Photography,* ed. Leslie Devereaux and Roger Hillman (Berkeley: University of California Press, 1995), 217–255.

104. Rotha, 72.

105. *"Moana"* (review), *Variety,* 10 February 1926.

106. Qtd. in Drinnon, 245–246.

107. Barsam, 41.

108. Rony, 178. Rony glosses Michelle Wallace, *Invisibility Blues: From Pop to Theory* (London: Verso: 1990).

109. Frances's caption to her photo accompanying Froelick's "Moana of the South Seas," 390.

110. Steve Neale, "Masculinity as Spectacle: Reflections on Men and Mainstream Cinema," in *Feminism and Film,* ed. E. Ann Kaplan (New York: Oxford University Press, 2000), 262–263.

111. On the feminization of the Polynesian male, particularly as it relates to homoeroticism, see, for example, Wallace; Rod Edmond, "The Pacific/Tahiti: Queen of the South Sea Isles," in *The Cambridge Companion to Travel Writing,* ed. Peter Hulme and Tim Youngs (Cambridge: Cambridge University Press, 2002), 144–149. More will be said on this subject in chapter 5. Of the female cinemagoer of the 1920s, Gaylyn Studlar notes, "Although box office records of the time are untrustworthy and studies of the gender differentiation of the audience nonexistent, the female portion of the American film audience was estimated by exhibitors' trade journals, fan magazines, and numerous casual observers as being between 75 and 83 percent. For example, in 1925 *Exhibitors Trade Herald* warned its readers: DON'T FORGET HER!" See Gaylyn Studlar, "Barrymore, the Body, and Bliss: Issues of Male Representation and Female Spectatorship in the 1920s," in *Fields of Vision: Essays in Film Studies, Visual Anthropology, and Photography,* ed. Leslie Devereaux and Roger Hillman (Berkeley: University of California Press, 1995), 160.

112. David Flaherty, "Samoa Journal"; box 24, Flaherty Papers.

113. Ibid.

114. See Murphy, 15.

115. Barsam, 36.

116. Meleisea, *Change and Adaptations,* 22–23; Rotha, 68–69.

117. Gell, 38; Albert Wendt, *"Tatau*ing the Post-Colonial Body: Reading the

Samoan *Tatau* as Literature," paper presented to the MELUS conference, Honolulu, Hawai'i (April 1997). Published as "*Tatau*ing the Post-Colonial Body," in *Inside Out: Literature, Cultural Politics, and Identity in the New Pacific,* ed. Vilsoni Hereniko and Rob Wilson (Lanham, MD: Rowman and Littlefield, 1999), 399–412. The pain endured in the process, in Wendt's view, may be seen as broadly analogous to the difficult and painful emergence of postcolonial literatures in the Pacific: they are both indigenous aesthetic and spiritual practices, "clearing space alongside other bodies and literatures," practices partly modified and innovated upon through past colonial restrictions and traditions. Wendt has produced films documenting the revival of Samoan *tatau*ing in New Zealand.

118. Gell, 34.

119. Ibid., 97–98.

120. Wallace, 85–86.

121. Studlar, 172.

122. Ibid., 174.

123. Qtd. in Murphy, 16. Flaherty's original cut was twelve reels (approximately 120 minutes); see Rotha, 71.

124. Rotha, 72.

125. Letter from Chas. Shire, Lincoln Theater, to Paramount, 6 November 1925; box 23, Flaherty Papers.

126. Letter from Ernest Morrison, Imperial Theater, to Paramount, 29 October 1925; box 23, Flaherty Papers.

127. Letter from Irwin Wheeler, Auditorium Theater, to Jesse Lasky, 21 August 1925; box 23, Flaherty Papers.

128. Robert Sherwood, "Film of the Month," *McCall's* (June 1926): 25; John S. Cohen, Jr., "The Ten Best Films," *New York Sun,* 18 December 1926: 6; box 25 (clippings), Flaherty Papers.

129. Letter from the Catholic Mission, Apia, to David Flaherty, 10 July 1926; box 23, Flaherty Papers.

130. Letter from Ta'avale to Robert and Frances Flaherty, 23 March 1925; box 23, Flaherty Papers.

131. Letter from Tu'ungaita to Robert and Frances Flaherty, 2 April 1925; box 23, Flaherty Papers.

132. Letter from Nancy Phelan to Richard Griffith, 17 August 1954; box 23, Flaherty Papers.

Chapter 4: The Front and Back of Paradise

1. Qtd. in Hervé Dumont, "Woody S. Van Dyke et l'age d'or de Hollywood," *Travelling* 37 (Summer 1973): 18 (my translation).

2. Ibid., 16.

3. Bazin, 155; see also Rony, 144–145.

4. The journal, written as a long letter to Van Dyke's then-girlfriend in Los Angeles, Josephine Chippo, was discovered in Chippo's attic in her Los Angeles home after she died. Rudy Behlmer edited and annotated the letter, focusing primarily on production details. See Behlmer, *W. S. Van Dyke's Journal: "White Shadows in the South Seas"* (Lanham, MD: Scarecrow Press, 1996). Many of Behlmer's omissions needed to be recovered for the purposes of my argument here.

5. Comolli and Narboni, 7.

6. Letter to Charmian London, 20 February 1922, JLC.

7. Letter to Charmian London, undated (1922), JLC.

8. O'Brien, *Atolls*, 337. Missionary laws forbidding tattooing were still in force during O'Brien's time.

9. Ibid., 349, 355. In the screen scenario Titihuti is half white, reprising a subplot from O'Brien's earlier theatrical version of *White Shadows*.

10. Will Durant, "The Modern Woman (Philosophers Grow Dizzy as She Passes By)," *Century* 113.4 (February 1927): 418, 422.

11. O'Brien, *Atolls*, 356.

12. "Outline sketch of scenario by Frederick O'Brien," April 18, 1927. Turner/MGM Script Collection, Margaret Herrick Library, Academy of Motion Picture Arts and Sciences, Beverly Hills (hereafter Turner/MGM Script Collection).

13. O'Brien, *Atolls*, 363.

14. Gell, 39.

15. See Larry Langman's comprehensive catalogue of films set in the South Pacific, which surveys the cinematic evolution of the genre's primary themes, including escapism, regeneration, and interracial romance. Langman, *Return to Paradise: A Guide to South Sea Island Films* (Lanham, MD: Scarecrow Press, 1997).

16. Sigmund Freud, *Civilization and Its Discontents* [1930], trans. James Strachey (New York: W. W. Norton, 1961), 79–80.

17. O'Brien, *Atolls*, 363.

18. For a discussion of the South Seas film as a genre, looking at the themes of the noble savage, western spoliation, and interracial romance, see Glenn K. S. Man, "Hollywood Images of the Pacific," *East-West Film Journal* 5.2 (July 1991): 16–29.

19. See the Grauman's Chinese Theater program, folder 10, Josephine Chippo Collection, Margaret Herrick Library, Academy of Motion Picture Arts and Sciences, Beverly Hills (hereafter Chippo Collection).

20. According to Rudy Behlmer, "The negative cost recorded in the in-house M-G-M 'Operating Results by Picture' ledger was $365,000 (the original budget was approximately $150,000). The net profit realized (domestic and foreign) was eventually $450,000" (71).

21. Raymond F. Betts, "The Illusionary Island: Hollywood's Pacific Place," *East-West Film Journal* 5.2 (July 1991): 32.

22. "*White Shadows*" (review), *Variety,* 8 August 1928: 12.

23. *Film Daily,* 5 August 1928. "*White Shadows*" clippings file, Chippo Collection.

24. Howard Sharpe, "The Star Creators of Hollywood" (interview with W. S. Van Dyke), *Photoplay,* December 1936: 71–73.

25. Mark Langer notes that Flaherty was initially set to collaborate with director John McCarthy, but after McCarthy's refusal, he was replaced with Van Dyke. Selznick was against the Van Dyke/Flaherty collaboration. He told Kevin Brownlow, "Either man could do it perfectly well, but not the two of them. . . . In any case, I got into a terrible argument with Stromberg, and that was the end of my connection—my abortive connection—with *White Shadows.*" Qtd. in Mark Langer, "Flaherty's Hollywood Period," *Wide Angle* 17 (1995): 53. See also Rotha, 85; Murphy, 49.

26. Robert C. Cannom, *Van Dyke and the Mythical City, Hollywood* (Culver City, CA: Murray and Gee, 1948), 160–161.

27. Folder 19, Chippo Collection. All of Van Dyke's quotations are taken from the original journals in the Chippo Collection unless otherwise noted.

28. Behlmer, 46. Georges Sadoul, Marcel Martin, and others have claimed that the film was largely Flaherty's (see Dumont, 15). William Murphy, Richard Griffith, and others offer the more widely accepted theory that no more than a dozen of Flaherty's original shots made the finished film (Murphy, 49; Griffith, *The World,* 76). Floyd Crosby, assistant cameraman, concurs: "Flaherty had no idea of how to direct a story film . . . Van Dyke did the whole thing" (Langer, 43).

29. See the IMDb, "Filming Locations for *White Shadows in the South Seas,*" http: www.imdb.com/title/tt0019574/locations (accessed 8 February 2004). The case of *White Shadows* is an example of the trivializing of cultural and geographical specificity that has gone on in mainstream cinema. Though *White Shadows* was filmed in Tahiti, MGM publicity claimed it was filmed in the Marquesas. The premiere program for Grauman's Chinese Theater repeats MGM's claim that the film was made with "authentic" Marquesans and filmed in the Marquesas Islands. The myth continues in the American Film Institute Catalog, which states "photographed on location in the Marquesas Islands" (Kenneth Munden, ed., *American Film Institute Catalog of Motion Pictures Produced in the United States: Feature Films 1921–1930* [New York: Bowker, 1971], 895). A recent review of Behlmer's edition repeats the claim. See Diane MacIntyre, "*W. S. Van Dyke's Journal:* White Shadows in the South Seas," *Classicfilms* network, www.mdle. com//classicfilms/featurebook/book14 (accessed 1 March 2003).

30. Letter to Josephine Chippo, 6 February 1928; folder 8, Chippo Collection.

31. Behlmer, 24.

32. Ibid., 41.

33. Griffith, *The World,* 76.

34. Letter to Frances Hubbard Flaherty, autumn 1927; box 1, Flaherty Papers. The letters also show that Flaherty was still in close contact with O'Brien. Several screenplay treatments were considered by MGM in the preliminary stages, including those

by Eugene Walters, Ray Doyle, and O'Brien. Paul Rotha has noted that Robert Flaherty was involved in an earlier version of the script: "Laurence Stallings was called in to collaborate with Flaherty in trying to work out a story line [for *White Shadows*]. They tried instead to sell Thalberg the idea of making [Herman Melville's] *Typee* . . . but the young studio boss stuck to his choice of *White Shadows*" (85). The script, at one stage entitled "Southern Skies," went through numerous major revisions. Supporting Mark Langer's theory that Flaherty's ideas were instrumental, the final shooting script shows the strong influence of *Typee*. See Langer, 53.

35. Letter to Frances Hubbard Flaherty, "Monday," December 1927; box 1, Flaherty Papers.

36. Letter to Frances Hubbard Flaherty, 6 February 1927; box 1, Flaherty Papers.

37. Letter to Frances Hubbard Flaherty, 12 December 1927; box 1, Flaherty Papers.

38. Letter to Frances Hubbard Flaherty, 20 January 1928; box 4, Flaherty Papers.

39. Letter to Frances Hubbard Flaherty, 6 February 1928; box 1, Flaherty Papers.

40. "M.G.M. Backs Van Dyke," *Variety*, 21 March 1928: 1–4.

41. David O. Selznick interviewed by Kevin Brownlow; qtd. in Langer, 53.

42. Behlmer, 24–25.

43. Sander L. Gilman, *Disease and Representation: Images of Illness from Madness to AIDS* (Ithaca, NY: Cornell University Press, 1988), 256.

44. Bram Dijkstra traces related concepts that linked the figure of woman to social degeneration in fin-de-siècle Europe. See Dijkstra, *Idols of Perversity: Fantasies of Feminine Evil in Fin-de-Siècle Culture* (Oxford: Oxford University Press, 1986), 219–222, 274–275.

45. Fifty pages of Van Dyke's journals and numerous telegrams repeat his passionate declarations of love and jealousy, much in an alphabetic code he developed while in Tahiti. Van Dyke intended to have Josephine Chippo accompany him on his assignment in Tahiti in her professional capacity as a script clerk, but MGM assigned this position instead to Mrs. Grant Whytock, the wife of the film's studio-appointed on-location supervisor. See Behlmer, 9. This was a serious point of contention for Van Dyke, who frequently wired the studio while in Tahiti requesting permission to have Chippo sent over. Van Dyke had sworn to celibacy while in Tahiti, claiming to abstain even from masturbation, and makes frequent references to a "promise" made with Chippo that he seems anxious she not break. Van Dyke's thoughts of Chippo are described as "a torture," and a month later he is writing, "No more sister . . . go ahead and carouse to your hearts content (if you think you will get away with it)" (folder 19, Chippo Collection).

46. Behlmer, 27.

47. Folder 19, Chippo Collection. Robert Cannom comments that Van Dyke had a "hypersensitive skin condition" that made him highly paranoid about being touched on the face, though he does not mention the specific name of the condition, nor that Van Dyke would normally refuse to shake hands (167).

48. Folder 19, Chippo Collection.

49. Ibid.

50. Folder 16, Chippo Collection.

51. I am indebted here to Henrietta Moore, who, in the context of anthropological writing, argues that an imaginary pact and a unitary sense of purpose exists between western authors and audiences. See Moore, *A Passion for Difference* (Bloomington: Indiana University Press, 1994), 107–128. See also Betts, 34.

52. The blurb accompanies a publicity still of Torres in the Turner/MGM Stills collection, Margaret Herrick Library, Beverly Hills. Flaherty noted that Torres had "a voice as pleasing as a crumb-plugged mouth organ" (Letter to Frances Flaherty, 6 February 1928; box 4, Flaherty Papers).

53. Behlmer, 33.

54. Betts further discusses the practice of using lead actors who were "hyphenated" in their ethnic origin (36).

55. Jane Gaines, "*The Scar of Shame:* Skin Color and Caste in Black Silent Melodrama," in *Representing Blackness: Issues in Film and Video,* ed. Valerie Smith (New Brunswick, NJ: Rutgers University Press, 1997), 75.

56. Letter to Frances Flaherty, January 1930; box 1, Flaherty Papers.

57. Folder 16, Chippo Collection.

58. Grierson, 25–26.

59. See Rony, 172.

60. See, for example, Joseph A. Boone, "Vacation Cruises; or, the Homoerotics of Orientalism," *PMLA* 110.1 (January 1995): 89–107.

61. See Langman, 27, 31; on the theme of alcoholism, see 55.

62. Betts, 40. See also Man's contention that the critique of western culture often at the heart of the South Seas genre is subverted through "certain pro-Western elements which ultimately dominate" (21).

63. Folder 19, Chippo Collection.

64. Moore, 115.

65. Nichols, *Representing,* 201–228.

66. Ray Doyle, screenplay treatment for *White Shadows in the South Seas,* 10 September 1927; Turner/MGM Script Collection.

67. Nichols, *Representing,* 225.

68. Cook, 1:85. Cook's spelling is erratic; he also uses "Obarea," "Obariea," and "Obaria."

69. Cheek, for example, cites Horace Walpole's contemporary letter attacking Hawkesworth, which concluded by noting, "Dr. Hawkesworth is still more provoking—an old black gentlewoman of forty carries Capt. Wallis cross a river, when he was too weak to walk, and the man represents them as a new edition of Dido and Aeneas." Qtd. in Cheek, 144.

70. See, for example, the "White Shadows" advertisement, *San Francisco Examiner,* 3 October 1928.

71. Ray Doyle, screenplay treatment for *White Shadows in the South Seas,* 10 September 1927; Turner/MGM Script Collection. The line appears in O'Brien, *White Shadows,* 166.

72. Doyle, screenplay treatment for *White Shadows in the South Seas,* 24 October 1927; Turner/MGM Script Collection. A number of South Seas films included themes of dissolution, rehabilitation, and greed, but Lloyd's character suggests a more unusual confluence of these elements. See Langman, 55–56.

73. Schueller, "Indians, Polynesians, and Empire Making," 59.

74. See Man, 27; also Langman, 56–57. Few texts focus exclusively on Pacific Islanders in this context. Gina Marchetti discusses interracial romance involving Asians and Asian Americans in *Romance and the "Yellow Peril": Race, Sex, and Discursive Strategies in Hollywood Fiction* (Berkeley: University of California Press, 1994). See also Matthew Bernstein and Gaylyn Studlar, eds., *Visions of the East: Orientalism in Film* (New Brunswick, NJ: Rutgers University Press, 1997).

75. Turner/MGM Script Collection, file 4.

76. Probably the author Robert Keeble, also an acquaintance of O'Brien.

77. Folder 19, Chippo Collection.

78. For an in-depth discussion of Novarro's life, including an account of his homosexuality, see Andre Soares, *Beyond Paradise: The Life of Ramon Novarro* (New York: St. Martin's, 2002).

79. Ella Shohat and Robert Stam, *Unthinking Eurocentrism: Multiculturalism and the Media* (London: Routledge, 1994), 180.

80. Hazel V. Carby, "'On the Threshold of Woman's Era': Lynching, Empire, and Sexuality in Black Feminist Theory," in *"Race," Writing, and Difference,* ed. Henry Louis Gates, Jr. (Chicago: University of Chicago Press, 1986), 304. See also Anne McClintock, "The Angel of Progress: Pitfalls of the Term Post-colonialism," in Williams and Chrisman, 295; and Torgovnick, 262n.

Chapter 5: The Homoerotic Exotic

1. Waly, "Ra-mu" (review), *Daily Variety,* 13 February 1929: 24.

2. By 1925, US films comprised roughly 95 percent of all films shown in Britain and Canada, 70 percent of those shown in France, and 80 percent in South America. See Rosenberg, 100.

3. Cheek, 3.

4. David M. Lugowski, "Queering the (New) Deal: Lesbian and Gay Representation and the Depression-Era Cultural Politics of Hollywood's Production Code," *Cinema Journal* 38.2 (Winter 1999): 5.

5. See Noël Burch, "A Primitive Mode of Representation?" in *Early Cinema: Space, Frame, Narrative,* ed. Thomas Elsaesser (London: BFI, 1990), 220–227.

6. Laura Mulvey, "Visual Pleasure and Narrative Cinema," *Screen* 16.3 (1975): 6–18.

7. There are limits to this reading: the absence of lesbian looks, for example.

8. Kaja Silverman, "Fassbinder and Lacan: A Reconsideration of Gaze, Look, and Image," *Camera Obscura* 19 (1989): 54–85. I am indebted to Shohini Chaudhuri for directing my attention to this article.

9. Shohini Chaudhuri, "*Ali:* An Anatomy of Racism," in *Film Analysis: A Norton Reader,* ed. Jeffrey Geiger and R. L. Rutsky (New York: Norton, 2005), 650; emphasis in original. Chaudhuri's reading of *Ali* is instructive here.

10. E. Ann Kaplan, "Is the Gaze Male?" in *Feminism and Film,* ed. E. Ann Kaplan (New York: Oxford University Press, 2000), 121.

11. See Judith Mayne, *Cinema and Spectatorship* (London: Routledge, 1993), 94.

12. Wallace, 13. Rudi C. Bleys offers an archeology of the notion of the hermaphrodite in the western ethnographic imagination, arguing that by the late-eighteenth century cultural perceptions of hermaphrodites and sodomites were becoming more interchangeable. That is, a tendency in the discourse to heighten roles like the North American berdache—and, if Parkinson's ambiguity is any indication, the *mahū*—might have helped to detach the concept of the hermaphrodite from being grounded in the appearance of sex organs and moving it towards conceptions of same-sex behavior and cross-gender roles. See Bleys, *The Geography of Perversion: Male-to-Male Sexual Behaviour outside the West and the Ethnographic Imagination, 1750–1918* (London: Cassell, 1996), 70–73.

13. Bleys, 77–78; see also William Mariner, *William Mariner's Account: An Account of the Natives of the Tonga Islands in the South Pacific Ocean, with an Original Grammar and Vocabulary of their Language* (Neiafu, Vavaʻu, Tonga: Vavaʻu Press, 1981).

14. Bleys, 77–78. This point returns us to the debate, as suggested by Bleys and Wallace, of whether modern homosexual identities were forged in the dissemination of encounters with third-sex categories of the "New World" or whether homosexual identity was an ethnocentric imposition of western sexual categories onto nonwestern "others." It seems to me, as Bleys suggests (70–81), that any cause and effect analysis is overly simplistic: homosexual identity in the west emerged in a fluid and uneven manner alongside the western projects of geographical and ethnographic mapping.

15. A. Safroni-Middleton, *South Seas Foam: The Romantic Adventures of a Modern Don Quixote in the Southern Seas* (New York: George H. Doran, 1920), 73.

16. Wallace, 1.

17. Robert Aldrich, *Colonialism and Homosexuality* (London: Routledge, 2003), 130.

18. See also Ross Chambers's analysis of the gay sex tourism of Roland Barthes in *Loiterature* (Lincoln: University of Nebraska Press, 1999), 250–269, as well as Aldrich, *Colonialism and Homosexuality.*

19. Boone, "Vacation Cruises," 90.

20. Ibid.

21. In this section I use "queer" in the critical sense described, for example, by Michele Aaron, in *New Queer Cinema: A Critical Reader* (Edinburgh: Edinburgh University Press, 2004), following the work of Judith Butler, Margery Garber, and others: "Queer represents the resistance to, primarily, the normative codes of gender and sexual expression . . . but also the restrictive potential of gay and lesbian sexuality. In this way, queer, as a critical concept, encompasses the non-fixity of gender expression and the non-fixity of both straight and gay sexuality" (5). Aaron continues, "Queer is not just about gender and sexuality, but the restrictiveness of the rules governing them and their intersection with other aspects of identity" (7).

22. Roger Austen, *Genteel Pagan: The Double Life of Charles Warren Stoddard,* ed. John W. Crowley (Amherst: University of Massachusetts Press, 1991), 54.

23. Qtd. in Andrew J. Hoffman, "Mark Twain and Homosexuality," *American Literature* 67.1 (March 1995): 42. Hoffman stresses that sexual contact between the two men cannot be substantiated, but that their romantic friendship left Stoddard bereft when Twain parted, after two months, from their cohabitation arrangement in England.

24. See, for example, Aldrich's *Colonialism and Homosexuality,* Christopher Mark McBride's *The Colonizer Abroad: American Writers on Foreign Soil, 1846–1912* (London: Routledge, 2004), and Justin D. Edwards's *Exotic Journeys: Exploring the Erotics of US Travel Literature, 1840–1930* (Hanover, NH: University Press of New England [for] University of New Hampshire, 2001).

25. Edwards, 2–3.

26. Richard F. Burton, trans. and ed., *The Book of a Thousand Nights and a Night: Plain and Literal Translation of the Arabian Nights' Entertainments,* vol. 10 (London: Burton Club private edition, 1885–1886), 206.

27. Qtd. in Austen, *Genteel, Pagan,* 42.

28. Reprinted and revised in 1892; reprinted by Routledge in 2005. Chatto and Windus in Great Britain published *South Sea Idyls* under the title *Summer Cruising in the South Seas.*

29. Stevenson, *In the South Seas,* 26.

30. Rudyard Kipling, letter to Charles Warren Stoddard, 30 October 1892 (emphasis in original). Charles Warren Stoddard collection, box 1, C-H 53, Bancroft Library, UC Berkeley.

31. Charles Warren Stoddard, *South Sea Idyls* [1873], 2nd ed. (New York: Charles Scribner's, 1892), 87. Subsequent page references in text.

32. Gaines, 12. Critics such as Joan Copjec (*Read My Desire: Lacan against the Historicists* [Cambridge: MIT Press, 1994], 5–38) and Kaja Silverman (*Male Subjectivity at the Margins* [New York: Routledge, 1992], 130) have pointed out that, though derived from Lacanian theory, theories of the look and gaze commonly associated with film theory (such as those of Laura Mulvey and E. Ann Kaplan, whom I loosely draw upon here) are not precisely equivalent to Lacan's conceptions of the gaze.

33. E. Ann Kaplan, *Looking for the Other: Feminism, Film, and the Imperial Gaze* (London: Routledge, 1997), 4.

34. Qtd. in Vanessa Smith, "Pitcairn's 'Guilty Stock,'" 117. I am indebted to Smith's formulation of scopophilia as an "ambivalent uncovering" in the context of Pacific island encounters.

35. Brian Pronger, *The Arena of Masculinity,* excerpted in *A Queer Reader,* ed. Patrick Higgins (London: Fourth Estate, 1993), 214–215.

36. E. Ann Kaplan, *Looking,* 6.

37. See Austen, *Genteel Pagan,* 42–43.

38. Bleys, 157–158.

39. Roger Austen, "Introduction," in *Cruising the South Seas: Stories by Charles Warren Stoddard,* ed. Winston Leyland (San Francisco: Gay Sunshine Press, 1987), 17. Perhaps demonstrating his own skill with double entendres, however, William Dean Howells did once refer to Stoddard's "A Prodigal in Tahiti" as one of the "few such delicious bits of literature in the language." Howells, "Introductory Letter," in Stoddard, *South Sea Idyls,* i.

40. Bleys, 11.

41. See, for example, Ruth Vasey, *The World according to Hollywood, 1918–1939* (Exeter: Exeter University Press, 1997), 107.

42. Ian Barnard, "The United States in South Africa: (Post)Colonial Queer Theory?" in *Postcolonial and Queer Theories: Intersections and Essays,* ed. John C. Hawley (Westport, CT: Greenwood Press, 2001), 136.

43. Gregory Tomso considers Stoddard's Catholicism, homoeroticism, and interest in leprosy, looking at the "pleasures of suffering and redemption" in Stoddard's short work *The Lepers of Molokai* (1885). See Tomso, "The Queer History of Leprosy and Same-Sex Love," *American Literary History* 14.4 (2002): 758. In his excellent Introduction to Austen's posthumously published *Genteel Pagan,* John W. Crowley addresses some of the ways in which Stoddard's prose was "thoroughly in keeping with the prevailing racialism and imperialism of the American Gilded Age" (xxix).

44. Boone, "Vacation Cruises," 104.

45. Richard Dyer, "Don't Look Now: The Instabilities of the Male Pin-up," in *Only Entertainment* [1992] (London: Routledge, 2002), 123.

46. Rony, 149, 153.

47. Oksiloff, 171.

48. Murphy, 78.

49. Letter to Frances Hubbard Flaherty, 1? December 1927; box 2, Flaherty Papers.

50. Lotte Eisner, *Murnau* [1964] (Berkeley: University of California Press, 1973), 216.

51. Rotha, 91. The best published account of this period in Flaherty's career can be found in Rotha, 88–94; for a detailed narrative of Murnau's relationship with Flaherty, see Eisner, *Murnau,* 202–220.

52. Eisner, *Murnau*, 210–211.

53. Ibid.

54. Ibid., 211–212.

55. Ibid., 213.

56. It should be kept in mind that Flaherty's accounts were written to his wife and children and were likely self-censored.

57. Letter to Frances Flaherty, "Tuesday" 1929; box 2, Flaherty Papers. Diary (to Frances Flaherty), 13–24 June 1929; box 2, Flaherty Papers.

58. Rotha, 91.

59. Richard Griffith, "Flaherty and *Tabu*," *Film Culture* 20 (1959): 12. For negative reviews of the film that resented what was seen as the imposition of a Hollywood plot on Polynesian life, see Malcolm Cowley, "*Tabu*," *New Republic* 66 (1 April 1931): 183; and Harry Alan Potamkin, "Lost Paradise: *Tabu*," *Creative Art* 8 (June 1931): 462–463.

60. Eisner, *Murnau*, 217. With the help of David Flaherty, the screenplay for *Turia* was reprinted in a special issue of *Film Culture* 20 (1959).

61. Letter to Frances Flaherty, 12 June 1929; box 2, Flaherty Papers.

62. Richard Griffith also focuses on artistic differences between the two men, arguing that "there was a more fundamental cleavage between the Murnau and the Flaherty approach than is indicated by the story alone" (Griffith, *The World of Robert Flaherty*, 79).

63. Letter to Frances Flaherty, 20 August 1929; box 2, Flaherty Papers.

64. Letter to Frances Flaherty, January 1930; box 2, Flaherty Papers.

65. Letter to Frances Flaherty, 29 April 1930; box 2, Flaherty Papers.

66. Letter to Frances Flaherty, 26 May 1930; box 2, Flaherty Papers.

67. Letter to Frances Flaherty, 20 August 1929; box 2, Flaherty Papers.

68. Rotha, 95.

69. Folder 17, Josephine Chippo Collection.

70. Rotha, 70.

71. Ibid., 71.

72. David Flaherty, "Serpents in Eden," *Asia* 25 (October 1925): 898. The "serpents" are given the pseudonyms of Bauer (for Felix David) and Philip Rice-Ewing (for the resident commissioner). Bauer is lengthily described as Prussian, nervous, loquacious, a "gross sensualist," lonely, histrionic, theatrical, and frequently drunk, while Rice-Ewing is presented as "quite insane," with "the weakest mouth I have ever seen . . . chinless as a shark," and a "peculiar lack of ruggedness in his make-up. . . . There was about his whole frame, his whole person, a sort of inadequacy—I do not know how to describe it" (861).

73. Letter to Robert Flaherty, 1929; box 11, Flaherty Papers.

74. Letter to Robert Flaherty, 1929; box 11, Flaherty Papers.

75. Matahi replaced Murnau's initial Marquesan star, Mehao.

76. Qtd. in Eisner, *Murnau*, 208.

77. Lotte H. Eisner, *The Haunted Screen: Expressionism in the German Cinema* [1952] (Berkeley: University of California Press, 1977), 98.

78. Eisner disputes these rumors, offering instead two eyewitness but nonetheless conflicting versions of the accident (*Murnau*, 221–226).

79. Ibid., 203.

80. Chevalier took the name of her character, Reri, later becoming a dancer, according to Eisner, "somewhere on Broadway" (*Murnau*, 203). Almost without exception, Polynesian actors in these Pacific films rarely found work in film again.

81. As the film consistently uses *tabu*, the Tongan variant of *tapu*, I use this spelling throughout the chapter.

82. Claude Lévi-Strauss, *Tristes Tropiques*, trans. John and Doreen Weightman (New York: Atheneum, 1974), 337–338. Oksiloff goes into great detail on the role of writing versus speech in the film; see 169–171.

83. Lévi-Strauss, *Tristes Tropiques*, 338.

84. *"Tabu"* (review), *Variety* (weekly), 25 March 1931: 17.

85. F. W. Murnau, "The Ideal Picture Needs No Titles," *Theatre Magazine* (New York), 47 (January 1928).

86. Rony, 151.

87. For Eisner, Murnau's faces become forms of "landscape," which "the inquisitive eye of the lens explores indefatigably down to its most hidden recesses." In *Sunrise, Nosferatu, The Last Laugh,* and *Tabu,* Murnau's play of light and shadow on faces and bodies tends to indicate psychological depth, while also acting as a form of narrative exposition, implying histories and fates of which certain characters are not themselves conscious (Eisner, *The Haunted Screen*, 269).

88. Jacques Lacan, *Freud's Papers on Technique, 1953–1954* (seminar of Jacques Lacan), trans. John Forrester, ed. Jacques Miller (New York: W. W. Norton, 1991), 230.

89. Letter to Frances Flaherty, 22 October 1930; box 2, Flaherty Papers.

90. Eisner, *The Haunted Screen*, 98.

91. The insertion of the *tabu* idea into Flaherty's script seems to have come some time after the two directors had arrived in Tahiti, and there is no written evidence (that is, in extant scripts) to back up David Flaherty's claim that the *tabu* concept was based on his brother Robert's experiences in Samoa (see Eisner, *Murnau*, 218). Most critics, in any case, have argued that Murnau's "invention" of the *tabu* theme was yet another expropriation—taking an indigenous theme and sloppily translating it for western consumption—while legend has it that Murnau's own obsession with, and fears about, local *tabu*s and their coinciding specters pursued him to his early death.

92. Rony, 113.

93. Rony, 4.

94. *"Tabu,"* 17.

95. Eisner discusses the extensive footage cut out of the final print, much of it likely Flaherty's (*Murnau*, 206).

96. 3 October 1931, MWW diary.

Afterword

1. K. R. Howe, *Nature, Culture, and History: The "Knowing" of Oceania* (Honolulu: University of Hawai'i Press, 2000), 21–22.

2. Langman, x.

3. *Legong: Dance of the Virgins* (1933), dir. Henry de la Falaise (Milestone DVD, 2004).

4. Letter from Vincent G. Hart to H. Innes (Paramount), 2 August 1935; *Tabu* MPAA file, Margaret Herrick Library, Academy of Motion Picture Arts and Sciences, Beverly Hills (hereafter *Tabu* MPAA file).

5. Letter from Joseph I. Breen to Herman J. Kleinheinz, 4 May 1939; *Tabu* MPAA file.

6. Memo dated 7 June 1950; *Tabu* MPAA file.

7. Qtd. in Sturma, 46.

8. Wilson, 83. Wilson offers a detailed reading of this idea, noting that Melville was "uncanny in his attempt to survey, enlist, and map powerful Asian interests in this new, interlinked Pacific" of the international whaling industry (82). See further Akira Iriye, *Pacific Estrangement: Japanese and American Expansion, 1897–1911* (Cambridge: Harvard University Press, 1972).

9. Wilson, 106.

10. James Norman Hall, *Lost Island* (Boston: Little, Brown, 1944), front inside jacket cover.

11. Margaret Mead, *New Lives for Old: Cultural Transformation—Manus, 1928–1953* [1956] (New York: Dell, 1971), 33.

12. Ibid., 31.

13. Qtd. in Lyons, *American Pacificism,* 28. See also Wilson, 83–84.

14. Wilson, 165–166.

15. See Subramani, *South Pacific Literature: From Myth to Fabulation* (Suva, Fiji: University of the South Pacific Press, 1985).

16. See Edmond's reading in "The Pacific/Tahiti," 152–153.

Bibliography

Aaron, Michele, ed. *New Queer Cinema: A Critical Reader.* Edinburgh: Edinburgh University Press, 2004.

Abbott, J. H. M. *Peeps at Many Lands: The South Seas.* London: Adam and Charles Black, 1908.

Adams, Henry Brook. *The Education of Henry Adams: An Autobiography* [1907, 1918]. Boston: Houghton Mifflin, 1961.

———. *Tahiti: Memoirs of Arii Taimai e Marama of Eimeo, Teriirere of Tooarai, Terrinui of Tahiti, Tauraatua i Amo (Memoirs of Marau Taaroa, Last Queen of Tahiti)* [1901]. Ed. Robert E. Spiller. New York: Scholars' Facsimiles and Reprints, 1947.

Agnew, Vanessa. "Pacific Island Encounters and the German Invention of Race." In *Islands in History and Representation,* ed. Rod Edmond and Vanessa Smith, 81–94. London: Routledge, 2003.

Alcalay, Glenn. "The United States Anthropologist in Micronesia: Toward a Counter-Hegemonic Study of Sapiens." In *Confronting the Margaret Mead Legacy,* ed. Lenora Foerstel and Angela Gilliam, 173–204. Philadelphia: Temple University Press, 1992.

Aldrich, Robert. *Colonialism and Homosexuality.* London: Routledge, 2003.

———. *The French Presence in the South Pacific, 1840–1940.* Honolulu: University of Hawai'i Press, 1990.

Allen, Percy S. *Stewart's Handbook of the Pacific Islands: A Reliable Guide to All the Inhabited Islands of the Pacific Ocean for Traders, Tourists, and Settlers.* Sydney: McCarron, Stewart, 1922.

Anderson, Benedict. *Imagined Communities: Reflections on the Origin and Spread of Nationalism.* London: Verso, 1983.

Arens, William. *The Man-Eating Myth: Anthropology and Anthropophagy.* New York: Oxford University Press, 1979.

Arvin, Newton. *Herman Melville: A Critical Biography.* New York: William Sloane, 1950.

Asad, Talal. "The Concept of Cultural Translation in British Social Anthropology." In *Writing Culture: The Poetics and Politics of Ethnography,* ed. James Clifford and George E. Marcus, 141–164. Berkeley: University of California Press, 1986.

Aughton, Peter. *Resolution: Captain Cook's Second Voyage of Discovery.* London: Weidenfeld and Nicolson, 2004.

Austen, Roger. *Genteel Pagan: The Double Life of Charles Warren Stoddard.* Ed. John W. Crowley. Amherst: University of Massachusetts Press, 1991.

———. "Introduction" to Charles Warren Stoddard, *Cruising the South Seas: Stories by Charles Warren Stoddard.* Ed. Winston Leyland. San Francisco: Gay Sunshine Press, 1987.

Babcock, Barbara A. "'Not in the Absolute Singular': Rereading Ruth Benedict." In *Women Writing Culture,* ed. Ruth Behar and Deborah Gordon, 104–130. Los Angeles: University of California Press, 1995.

Baird, James. *Ishmael: A Study of the Symbolic Mode in Primitivism.* Baltimore: Johns Hopkins Press, 1956.

Bakhtin, Mikhail. *The Dialogic Imagination: Four Essays.* Ed. Michael Holquist, trans. Caryl Emerson and M. Holquist. Austin: University of Texas Press, 1981.

Ballantyne, R. M. *The Coral Island* [1858]. Bristol: Purnell Books, 1985.

Bancroft, Hubert Howe. *The New Pacific* [1900]. Rev. ed. New York: The Bancroft Company, 1912.

Banks, Joseph. *The* Endeavour *Journal of Joseph Banks, 1768–1771.* "South Seas Voyaging and Cross-Cultural Encounters in the Pacific (1760–1800)." http://southseas .nla.gov.au/journals/banks/17690426. html (accessed 1 August 2004).

Barker, Francis; Peter Hulme; and Margaret Iversen, eds. *Cannibalism and the Colonial World.* Cambridge: Cambridge University Press, 1998.

Barnard, Ian. "The United States in South Africa: (Post)Colonial Queer Theory?" In *Postcolonial and Queer Theories: Intersections and Essays,* ed. John C. Hawley, 129–138. Westport, CT: Greenwood Press, 2001.

Barsam, Richard M. *The Vision of Robert Flaherty: The Artist as Myth and Filmmaker.* Bloomington: Indiana University Press, 1988.

Barthes, Roland. *Camera Lucida.* Trans. Richard Howard. New York: Noonday Press, 1981.

———. *Image-Music-Text.* Ed. and trans. Stephen Heath. New York: Noonday Press, 1977.

Bazin, André. *What Is Cinema?* Vols. 1–2. Ed. and trans. Hugh Gray. Berkeley: University of California Press, 1967.

Beaglehole, J. C. *The Exploration of the Pacific.* London: A. and C. Black, 1934.

———. *The Life of Captain James Cook.* Stanford, CA: Stanford University Press, 1974.

Beck, Ulrich. *What Is Globalization?* Trans. Patrick Camiller. Cambridge: Polity, 2000.

Behdad, Ali. *Belated Travelers: Orientalism in the Age of Colonial Dissolution.* Durham, NC: Duke University Press, 1994.

Behlmer, Rudy, ed. *W. S. Van Dyke's Journal:* "White Shadows in the South Seas." Lanham, MD: Scarecrow Press, 1996.

Belich, James. *Paradise Reforged: A History of the New Zealanders from the 1880s to the Year 2000.* London: Allen Lane, 2001.

Bellwood, Peter. *Man's Conquest of the Pacific: The Prehistory of Southeast Asia and Oceania.* New York: Oxford University Press, 1979.

———. *The Polynesians: Prehistory of an Island People.* London: Thames and Hudson, 1987.

Benedict, Ruth. "Anthropology and the Abnormal." In *An Anthropologist at Work: Writings of Ruth Benedict,* ed. Margaret Mead, 262–283. Boston: Houghton Mifflin, 1959.

———. *Patterns of Culture.* Boston, New York: Houghton Mifflin, 1934.

Benjamin, Walter. *Origin of the German Tragic Drama* [1928]. Trans. John Osborne. New York: Verso, 1977.

Bennett, Ira. *History of the Panama Canal.* Washington, DC: Historical Publishing Co., 1915.

Bernstein, Matthew, and Gaylyn Studlar, eds. *Visions of the East: Orientalism in Film.* New Brunswick, NJ: Rutgers University Press, 1997.

Betts, Raymond F. "The Illusionary Island: Hollywood's Pacific Place." *East-West Film Journal* 5.2 (July 1991): 30–45.

Bewell, Alan. "Constructed Places, Constructed Peoples: Charting the Improvement of the Female Body in the Pacific." Special issue, *Eighteenth Century Life* 18.3 (November 1994): 37–54.

Bhabha, Homi K. *The Location of Culture.* London: Routledge, 1994.

Biddle, George. *Tahitian Journal.* Minneapolis: University of Minnesota Press, 1968.

Bleys, Rudi C. *The Geography of Perversion: Male-to-Male Sexual Behavior outside the West and the Ethnographic Imagination, 1750–1918.* London: Cassell, 1996.

Bloch, Ernst. "Ungleichzeitigkeit and Pflicht zu ihrer Dialektik" [1932]. *Erbschaft dieser Zeit.* Frankfurt: Suhrkamp, 1962.

Boas, Franz. *Anthropology and Modern Life* [1928]. New York: W. W. Norton, 1962.

———. "The Mind of Primitive Man." *Journal of American Folklore* 14 (1901): 1–11.

———. *Primitive Art* [1927]. New York: Dover, 1955.

Bonehill, John. "Hodges and Cook's Second Voyage." In *William Hodges, 1744–1797: The Art of Exploration,* ed. Geoff Quilley and John Bonehill, 74–108. New Haven, CT: Yale University Press, 2004.

———. "Hodges's Post-voyage Work." In *William Hodges, 1744–1797: The Art of Exploration,* ed. Geoff Quilley and John Bonehill, 109–136. New Haven, CT: Yale University Press, 2004.

Boon, James A. *Other Tribes, Other Scribes: Symbolic Anthropology in the Comparative Study of Cultures, Histories, Religions, and Texts.* Cambridge: Cambridge University Press, 1982.

Boone, Joseph Allen. *Libidinal Currents: Sexuality and the Shaping of Modernism.* Chicago: University of Chicago Press, 1998.

———. "Vacation Cruises; or, The Homoerotics of Orientalism." *PMLA* 110.1 (January 1995): 89–107.

Bougainville, Louis-Antoine de. *The Pacific Journal of Louis-Antoine de Bougainville, 1767–1768.* Ed. and trans. John Dunmore. London: Hakluyt Society, 2002.

————. *Voyage autour du monde (A Voyage round the World).* Trans. John [Johann] Reinhold Forster. London: J. Nourse and T. Davies, 1777.

Briand, Paul L. *In Search of Paradise: The Nordhoff-Hall Story.* New York: Duell, Sloan, and Pearce, 1966.

Bristow, Joseph. *Empire Boys: Adventures in a Man's World.* London: Harper Collins, 1991.

Brown, John Macmillan. *The Riddle of the Pacific.* Boston: Small, Maynard, 1924.

Brown, Julie K. *Contesting Images: Photography and the World's Columbian Exposition.* Tucson: University of Arizona Press, 1994.

Burch, Noël. "A Primitive Mode of Representation?" In *Early Cinema: Space, Frame, Narrative,* ed. Thomas Elsaesser, 220–227. London: BFI, 1990.

————. *To the Distant Observer: Form and Meaning in Japanese Cinema.* Berkeley: University of California Press, 1979.

Burton, Richard F., trans. and ed. *The Book of a Thousand Nights and a Night: Plain and Literal Translation of the Arabian Nights' Entertainments.* Vol. 10. London: Burton Club private edition, 1885–1886.

Butler, Judith. *Bodies That Matter: On the Discursive Limits of 'Sex'.* New York: Routledge, 1993.

Cabell, J. L. *The Testimony of Modern Science to the Unity of Mankind.* New York: Robert Carter and Bros., 1859.

Calder, Alex; Jonathan Lamb; and Bridget Orr, eds. *Voyages and Beaches: Pacific Encounters, 1769–1840.* Honolulu: University of Hawai'i Press, 1999.

Campbell, I. C. *"Gone Native" in Polynesia: Captivity Narratives and Experiences from the South Pacific.* Westport, CT: Greenwood, 1998.

Cannom, Robert C. *Van Dyke and the Mythical City, Hollywood.* Culver City, CA: Murray and Gee, 1948.

Carby, Hazel V. "'On the Threshold of Woman's Era': Lynching, Empire, and Sexuality in Black Feminist Theory." In *"Race," Writing, and Difference,* ed. Henry Louis Gates, Jr., 301–316. Chicago: University of Chicago Press, 1986.

Casey, Edmond Terence. "Frederick O'Brien Day by Day" (obituary). *Sausalito News,* 15 January 1932: 1.

Castle, William R., Jr. *Hawaii: Past and Present.* New York: Dodd, Mead, 1926.

Chambers, Ross. *Loiterature.* Lincoln: University of Nebraska Press, 1999.

————. "The Unexamined." In *Whiteness: A Critical Reader,* ed. Mike Hill, 187–203. New York: New York University Press, 1999.

Chaudhuri, Shohini. "*Ali:* An Anatomy of Racism." *Film Analysis: A Norton Reader,* ed. Jeffrey Geiger and R. L. Rutsky, 640–657. New York: Norton, 2005.

Cheek, Pamela. *Sexual Antipodes: Enlightenment, Globalization, and the Placing of Sex.* Stanford, CA: Stanford University Press, 2003.

Chrisman, Laura, and Patrick Williams. "Colonial Discourse and Post-Colonial Theory: An Introduction." In *Colonial Discourse and Post-Colonial Theory: A Reader,* ed. Patrick Williams and Laura Chrisman, 1–20. New York: Columbia University Press, 1994.

Churchward, Albert. *Origin and Evolution of the Human Race.* London: George Allen and Unwin, 1921.

Churchward, James. *The Lost Continent of Mu, the Motherland of Man.* New York: William Edwin Rudge, 1926.

Clifford, James. "Of Other Peoples: Beyond the Salvage Paradigm." In *Discussions in Contemporary Culture,* no. 1, ed. Hal Foster, 121–130. Seattle: Bay Press, 1987.

———. *The Predicament of Culture: Twentieth-Century Ethnography, Literature, and Art.* Cambridge: Harvard University Press, 1988.

Clifford, James, and George Marcus, eds. *Writing Culture: The Poetics and Politics of Ethnography.* Berkeley: University of California Press, 1986.

Coffman, Tom. *Nation Within: The Story of America's Annexation of the Nation of Hawaiʻi.* Kāneʻohe, HI: EpiCenter, 1998.

Cohen, John S., Jr. "The Ten Best Films." *New York Sun* 18 December 1926: 6.

Comolli, Jean-Louis, and Jean Narboni. "Cinema/Ideology/Criticism (1)." In *Screen Reader 1: Cinema, Ideology, Politics,* 2–11. Trans. Susan Bennett. London: Society for Education in Film and Television, 1977.

Connery, Christopher L. "The Oceanic Feeling and the Regional Imaginary." In *Global/ Local: Cultural Production and the Transnational Imaginary,* ed. Rob Wilson and Wimal Dissanayake, 284–311. Durham, NC: Duke University Press, 1996.

———. "Pacific Rim Discourse: The US Global Imaginary in the Late Cold War Years." In *Asia/Pacific as Space of Cultural Production,* ed. Arif Dirlik and Rob Wilson, 47–56. Durham, NC: Duke University Press, 1995.

Cook, Captain James. *The Journals of Captain James Cook on His Voyages of Discovery.* Vol. 1: *The Voyage of the* Endeavour, *1768–1771.* Ed. J. C. Beaglehole. Cambridge: Hakluyt Society, 1955.

———. *The Journals of Captain James Cook on His Voyages of Discovery.* Vol. 2: *The Voyage of the* Resolution *and* Adventure, *1772–1775.* Ed. J. C. Beaglehole Cambridge: Hakluyt Society, 1961.

Corliss, Richard. "Robert Flaherty: The Man in the Iron Myth." In *Nonfiction Film Theory and Criticism,* ed. Richard Meran Barsam, 230–238. New York: E. P. Dutton, 1976.

Cowley, Malcolm. *"Tabu"* (review). *New Republic* 66 (1 April 1931): 183.

Cumings, Bruce. "Rimspeak: or, The Discourse of the 'Pacific Rim.'" In *What Is in a Rim? Critical Perspectives on the Pacific Region Idea,* ed. Arif Dirlik, 53–72. Boulder, CO: Westview, 1993.

Dampier, William. *A New Voyage around the World* [1697]. Ed. Sir Albert Gray. New York: Dover, 1968.

Dana, Richard Henry, Jr. *Two Years before the Mast: A Personal Narrative* [1840]. New York: Signet, 2000.

Daniels, Roger. *The Politics of Prejudice: The Anti-Japanese Movement in California and the Struggle of Japanese Exclusion* [1962]. Berkeley: University of California Press, 1991.

Danzker, Jo-Anne Birnie, ed. *Robert J. Flaherty, Photographer/Filmmaker: The Inuit, 1910–1922.* Vancouver: Vancouver Art Gallery, 1980.

Darnell, Regna. *Invisible Genealogies: A History of Americanist Anthropology.* Lincoln: University of Nebraska Press, 2001.

Darwin, Charles. *On the Origin of Species* [1859]. New York: Atheneum, 1972.

———. *The Voyage of the* Beagle [1860]. New York: American Museum of Natural History and Anchor Books, 1962.

Davidson, J. W. *Samoa Mo Samoa: The Emergence of the Independent State of Western Samoa.* Melbourne: Oxford University Press, 1967.

Daws, Gavin. *A Dream of Islands: Voyages of Self-Discovery in the South Seas.* Honolulu, HI: Mutual Publishing, 1980.

Debord, Guy. *Society of the Spectacle* [1967]. Detroit, MI: Black and Red, 1983.

De Certeau, Michel. *Heterologies: Discourse on the Other.* Trans. Brian Massumi. Minneapolis: University of Minnesota Press, 1986.

Defoe, Daniel. *New Voyage round the World, by a Course Never Sailed Before.* London: A. Bettesworth and W. Mears, 1725.

———. *Robinson Crusoe* [1719]. Oxford: Oxford University Press, 1972.

Deleuze, Giles. *Cinema 1: The Movement Image.* Trans. Hugh Tomlinson. Minneapolis: University of Minnesota Press, 1986.

Dening, Greg. *Islands and Beaches: Discourse on a Silent Land, Marquesas, 1774–1880.* Honolulu: University of Hawai'i Press, 1980.

———, ed. *The Marquesan Journal of Edward Robarts, 1797–1824.* Honolulu: University of Hawai'i Press, 1974.

———. *Mr. Bligh's Bad Language: Passion, Power, and Theatre on the* Bounty. Cambridge: Cambridge University Press, 1993.

Denoon, Donald, et al., eds. *The Cambridge History of the Pacific Islanders.* Cambridge: Cambridge University Press, 1997.

Devine-Nordstrom, Alison, ed. *Picturing Paradise: Colonial Photography of Samoa, 1875–1925.* Oxford: Pitt-Rivers Museum, 1995.

Diderot, Denis. *Supplément au voyage de Bougainville.* Ed. Paul-Edouard Levayer. Paris: Librairie Générale Française, 1995.

Dijkstra, Bram. *Idols of Perversity: Fantasies of Feminine Evil in Fin-de-Siècle Culture.* Oxford: Oxford University Press, 1986.

Dirlik, Arik, ed. *What Is in a Rim? Critical Perspectives on the Pacific Region Idea.* Boulder, CO: Westview, 1993.

Dirlik, Arif, and Rob Wilson, eds. *Asia/Pacific as Space of Cultural Production.* Durham, NC: Duke University Press, 1995.

Dixon, Roland Burrage. "A New History of Polynesian Origins." *Proceedings: American Philosophical Association* 59 (1920): 261–267.

Dodge, Ernest S. *Islands and Empires: Western Impact on the Pacific and East Asia.* Minneapolis: University of Minnesota Press, 1976.

———. *New England and the South Seas.* Cambridge: Harvard University Press, 1965.

Dominguez, Virginia R. "Exporting US Concepts of Race: Are There Limits to the US Model?" *Social Research* 65.2 (Summer 1998): 369–400.

———. "Of Other Peoples: Beyond the Salvage Paradigm." In *Discussions in Contemporary Culture,* no. 1, ed. Hal Foster, 131–137. Seattle, WA: Bay Press, 1987.

Dordillon, René Ildefonse. *Grammaire et dictionnaire de la langue des Iles Marquises* [1904; Le Père Siméon Delmas]. Papeete: Societé des Études Océaniennes, 1999.

Douglas, A. J. A., and P. H. Johnson, *The South Seas of To-day.* London: Cassell, 1926.

Drinnon, Richard. *Facing West: The Metaphysics of Indian-Hating and Empire-Building.* New York: Meridian, 1980.

Dudden, Arthur P. *The American Pacific: From Old China Trade to the Present.* New York: Oxford University Press, 1994.

Dumont, Hervé. "Woody S. Van Dyke et l'age d'or de Hollywood." *Travelling* (Paris), 37 (Summer 1973): 13–35.

Dunmore, John. "Introduction." In *The Pacific Journal of Louis-Antoine de Bougainville, 1767–1768.* Ed. and trans. John Dunmore. London: Hakluyt Society, 2002.

Durant, Will. "The Modern Woman (Philosophers Grow Dizzy as She Passes By)." *Century* 113.4 (February 1927): 418–429.

Dyer, Richard. *Only Entertainment* [1992]. London: Routledge, 2002.

———. *White.* New York: Routledge, 1997.

Edmond, Rod. "Missionaries on Tahiti, 1797–1840." In *Voyages and Beaches: Pacific Encounters, 1769–1840,* ed. Alex Calder, Jonathan Lamb, and Bridget Orr, 226–240. Honolulu: University of Hawai'i Press, 1999.

———. "The Pacific/Tahiti: Queen of the South Sea Isles." In *The Cambridge Companion to Travel Writing,* ed. Peter Hulme and Tim Youngs, 139–155. Cambridge: Cambridge University Press, 2002.

———. *Representing the South Pacific: Colonial Discourse from Cook to Gauguin.* Cambridge: Cambridge University Press, 1997.

Edmond, Rod, and Vanessa Smith, eds. *Islands in History and Representation.* London: Routledge, 2003.

Edwards, Elizabeth. *Anthropology and Photography, 1860–1920.* New Haven, CT: Yale University Press, 1992.

Edwards, Justin D. *Exotic Journeys: Exploring the Erotics of US Travel Literature, 1840–1930.* Hanover, NH: University Press of New England [for] University of New Hampshire Press, 2001.

Eisner, Lotte H. *The Haunted Screen* [1952]. Berkeley: University of California Press, 1977.

———. *Murnau*. [1964]. Berkeley: University of California Press, 1973.

Ellis, Jack C. *The Documentary Idea: A Critical History of English Language Documentary Film and Video*. Englewood Cliffs, NJ: Prentice Hall, 1989.

Ellis, William. *Polynesian Researches* [1831]. Rutland, VT: Charles Tuttle, 1969.

Eperjesi, John R. *The Imperialist Imaginary: Visions of Asia and the Pacific in American Culture*. Hanover, NH: Dartmouth College Press, 2005.

Erskine, Charles. *Twenty Years before the Mast: With the More Thrilling Scenes and Incidents while Circumnavigating the Globe under the Command of the Late Admiral Charles Wilkes, 1838–1842*. Boston: Charles Erskine, 1890. Rept. Washington, DC: Smithsonian Institution Press, 1985.

Evans, Julian. *Transit of Venus: Travels in the Pacific*. London: Secker and Warburg, 1992.

Fabian, Johannes. *Time and the Other: How Anthropology Makes Its Object*. New York: Columbia University Press, 1983.

Felski, Rita. *The Gender of Modernity*. Cambridge: Harvard University Press, 1995.

Field, Michael J. *Mau: Samoa's Struggle against New Zealand Oppression*. Wellington: Reed Publishers, 1984.

Fielder, Leslie. *Love and Death in the American Novel*. New York: Stein and Day, 1966.

———. *The Return of the Vanishing American*. London: Jonathan Cape, 1968.

Flaherty, David. "A Few Reminiscences." *Film Culture* 20 (1959): 14–16.

———. "Serpents in Eden." *Asia* 25 (October 1925): 858–869, 895–898.

Flaherty, Frances Hubbard. "Behind the Scenes with Our Samoan Stars (The Trials and Tribulations of Casting a Typical Samoan Family)." *Asia* 25 (September 1925): 747–753, 795–796.

———. "Faʻa Samoa (The Old Primitive Polynesian Life—A Fleeting Ghost—Caught for the American Screen)." *Asia* 25 (December 1925): 1085–1090, 1096–1100.

———. *The Odyssey of a Filmmaker: Robert Flaherty's Story* [1960]. New York: Arno Press, 1972.

———. "Samoan Immortals" (photographs). *Asia* 25 (May 1925): 393–400.

———. "A Search for Animal and Sea Sequences (Wherein 'Natural Drama' Goes Under and 'Faʻa Samoa' Comes Out on Top)." *Asia* 25 (November 1925): 954–962, 1000–1004.

———. "Setting Up House and Shop in Samoa (The Struggle to Find Screen Material in the Lyric Beauty of Polynesian Life)." *Asia* 25 (August 1925): 639–651, 709–711.

Flaherty, Robert J. "Film: The Language of the Eye." *Theatre Arts* 36.5 (May 1951): 30–36.

———. "The Handling of Motion Picture Film under Various Climatic Conditions."

Transactions of the Society of Motion Picture Engineers 26: 85–93. http://nimbus
.ocis.temple.edu/~jruby/wava/Flaherty/ (accessed 1 March 2004).

———. "Picture Making in the South Seas." *Film Yearbook 1924,* 9–13. http://nimbus.
ocis.temple.edu/~jruby/wava/Flaherty/ (accessed 1 March 2004).

Flaherty, Robert J., and F. W. Murnau. "*Turia,* An Original Story." *Film Culture* 20
(1959): 17–26.

Flaherty, Robert J., with Frances Hubbard Flaherty. *My Eskimo Friends.* Garden City,
NY: Doubleday, 1924.

Flavell, Kay. "Mapping Faces: National Physiognomies as Cultural Prediction." Special
issue, *Eighteenth Century Life* 18.3 (November 1994): 8–22.

Fletcher, C. Brunsdon. *The Problem of the Pacific.* London: Heinemann, 1918.

Foerstel, Lenora, and Angela Gilliam, eds. *Confronting the Margaret Mead Legacy.* Philadelphia: Temple University Press, 1992.

Fornander, Abraham. *An account of the Polynesian race; its origins and migrations, and
the ancient history of the Hawaiian people to the times of Kamehameha.* Vols. 1–3.
London: Trübner, 1878, 1880, 1885.

Forster, E. M. *A Passage to India* [1924]. New York: Harcourt Brace, 1952.

Forster, George. *A Voyage round the World* [1777]. Vols. 1–2. Ed. Nicholas Thomas and
Oliver Berghof. Honolulu: University of Hawai'i Press, 2000.

Forster, Johann Reinhold. *Observations Made during a Voyage round the World* [1778].
Ed. Nicholas Thomas, Harriet Guest, and Michael Dettelbach. Honolulu: University of Hawai'i Press, 1996.

Foster, Gwendolyn Audrey. *Captive Bodies: Postcolonial Subjectivity in Cinema.* Albany:
SUNY Press, 1999.

Foucault, Michel. *Discipline and Punish: The Birth of the Prison.* Trans. Alan Sheridan.
New York: Random House, 1977.

———. *The Order of Things: An Archeology of the Human Sciences* [1966]. New York:
Vintage Books, 1973.

———. *Power/Knowledge: Selected Interviews and Other Writings, 1972–1977.* Ed.
Colin Gordon, trans. John Gordon, Leo Marshall. New York: Pantheon, 1980.

Frassetto, Monica Flaherty. "New Birth for *Moana.*" *Wide Angle* 17 (1995): 408–413.

Friday, Chris. "Where to Draw the Line? The Pacific, Place, and the US West." In *A
Companion to the American West,* ed. William Deverell, 271–286. Oxford: Blackwell, 2004.

Frisbie, Robert Dean. *The Book of Puka Puka* [1928]. Honolulu: Mutual Publishing,
1957.

———. *My Tahiti.* Boston: Little, Brown, 1937.

Freud, Sigmund. *Beyond the Pleasure Principle* [1920]. Trans. James Strachey. New York:
W. W. Norton, 1961.

———. *Civilization and Its Discontents* [1930]. Trans. James Strachey. New York:
W. W. Norton, 1961.

Froelick, L. D. "Along the Trail with the Editor." *Asia* 25 (May 1925): 375.

———. "Moana of the South Seas." *Asia* 25 (May 1925): 389–390.

Gaines, Jane. "*The Scar of Shame:* Skin Color and Caste in Black Silent Melodrama." In *Representing Blackness: Issues in Film and Video,* ed. Valerie Smith, 61–82. New Brunswick, NJ: Rutgers University Press, 1997.

Gauguin, Paul. *Noa Noa* [1919]. Ed. and trans. O. F. Theis. New York: Noonday, 1957.

———. *Paul Gauguin's Intimate Journals* [*Avant et Après,* 1918]. Trans. Van Wyck Brooks. Bloomington: Indiana University Press, 1958.

Geertz, Clifford. *The Interpretation of Cultures.* New York: Basic Books, 1973.

———. *Works and Lives: The Anthropologist as Author.* Stanford, CA: Stanford University Press, 1988.

Geiger, Jeffrey. "*Nanook of the North:* Fiction, Truth, and the Documentary Contract." In *Film Analysis: A Norton Reader,* ed. Jeffrey Geiger and R. L. Rutsky, 118–137. New York: W. W. Norton, 2005.

Gell, Alfred. *Wrapping in Images: Tattooing in Polynesia.* Oxford: Clarendon Press, 1993.

Gibson, Arrell Morgan, with John Whitehead. *Yankees in Paradise: The Pacific Basin Frontier.* Albuquerque: University of New Mexico Press, 1993.

Gide, André. *The Journals of André Gide.* Vol. 2. Ed. and trans. Justin O'Brien. New York: Knopf, 1948.

Gilman, Sander L. *Disease and Representation: Images of Illness from Madness to AIDS.* Ithaca, NY: Cornell University Press, 1988.

Gramsci, Antonio. *Selections from Cultural Writings.* Ed. David Forgacs and Geoffrey Nowell-Smith, trans. William Boelhower. Cambridge: Harvard University Press, 1985.

Gray, J. A. C. *Amerika Samoa.* New York: Arno Press, 1980.

Grey, Zane. *The Man of the Forest* [1920]. Lincoln: University of Nebraska Press, 1996.

———. *Tales of Tahitian Waters* [1928]. New York: Derrydale Press, 1990.

Grierson, John. "Flaherty's Poetic *Moana*" [*New York Sun,* 8 February 1926]. In *The Documentary Tradition,* ed. Lewis Jacobs, 25–26. New York: W. W. Norton, 1979.

Griffith, Richard. "Flaherty and *Tabu.*" *Film Culture* 20 (1959): 12–13.

———. *The World of Robert Flaherty* [1953]. Westport, CT: Greenwood, 1970.

Grimshaw, Beatrice. *In the Strange South Seas.* Philadelphia: J. B. Lippincott, 1908.

Guest, Harriet. "Cook in Tonga: Terms of Trade." In *Island in History and Representation,* ed. Rod Edmond and Vanessa Smith, 95–115. London: Routledge, 2003.

Hall, James Norman. *Lost Island.* Boston: Little, Brown, 1944.

———. *My Island Home: An Autobiography.* Boston: Little, Brown, 1952.

Handy, Edward Smith Craighill. *The Native Culture in the Marquesas.* Honolulu, HI: Bernice P. Bishop Museum, 1923.

Haraway, Donna. *Simians, Cyborgs, and Women: The Reinvention of Nature.* New York: Routledge, 1991.

————. "Teddy Bear Patriarchy: Taxidermy in the Garden of Eden, New York City, 1908–1936." *Social Text* 11 (Winter 1984–1985): 20–64.

Harvey, Bruce. *American Geographics: U.S. National Narratives and the Representation of the Non-European World, 1830–1865.* Stanford, CA: Stanford University Press, 2001.

Hau'ofa, Epeli. "The Ocean in Us." *Contemporary Pacific: A Journal of Island Affairs* 10.2 (Fall 1998): 392–409.

————. "Our Sea of Islands." In *A New Oceania: Rediscovering Our Sea of Islands,* ed. Eric Waddell, Vijay Naidu, and Epeli Hau'ofa, 2–16. Suva: University of the South Pacific Press, 1993.

Hawkesworth, John. *An Account of the Voyages Undertaken by the Order of his Present Majesty for Making Discoveries in the Southern Hemisphere.* Vols. 1–3. London: W. Strahan and T. Cadell, 1773.

Hegeman, Susan. *Patterns for America: Modernism and the Concept of Culture.* Princeton, NJ: Princeton University Press, 1999.

Helu, 'I. Futa. "South Pacific Mythology." In *Voyages and Beaches: Pacific Encounters, 1769–1840,* ed. Alex Calder, Jonathan Lamb, and Bridget Orr, 45–54. Honolulu: University of Hawai'i Press, 1999.

Hempenstall, Peter. *Pacific Islanders under German Rule: A Study in the Meaning of Colonial Resistance.* Canberra: Australian National University Press, 1978.

Herbert, T. Walter. *Marquesan Encounters: Melville and the Meaning of Civilization.* Cambridge: Harvard University Press, 1980.

Hereniko, Vilsoni. "Clowning as Political Commentary: Polynesia, Then and Now." *Contemporary Pacific* 6.1 (1994): 1–28.

————. "Representations of Cultural Identities." In *Inside Out: Literature, Cultural Politics, and Identity in the New Pacific,* ed. Vilsoni Hereniko and Rob Wilson, 406–434. Lanham, MD: Rowman and Littlefield, 1999.

Hiery, Joseph. *The Neglected War: The German South Pacific and the Influence of World War I.* Honolulu: University of Hawai'i Press, 1995.

Hill, Mike, ed. *Whiteness: A Critical Reader.* New York: New York University Press, 2000.

Hoffman, Andrew J. "Mark Twain and Homosexuality." *American Literature* 67.1 (March 1995): 23–49.

Howard, Eric. "Famous Californians: Frederick O'Brien." *San Francisco Call and Post,* 3 September 1923: 1.

Howard, Jane. *Margaret Mead: A Life.* New York: Simon and Schuster, 1984.

Howe, K. R. *Nature, Culture, and History: The "Knowing" of Oceania.* Honolulu: University of Hawai'i Press, 2000.

————. *Where the Waves Fall: A New South Seas History from First Settlement to Colonial Rule.* Honolulu: University of Hawai'i Press, 1984.

Howells, William Dean. "Introductory Letter." In Charles Warren Stoddard, *South Sea Idyls* [1873]. 2nd ed. New York: Charles Scribner's, 1892.

Hulme, Peter, and Tim Youngs, eds. *The Cambridge Companion to Travel Writing.* Cambridge: Cambridge University Press, 2002.

Iriye, Akira. *Pacific Estrangement: Japanese and American Expansion, 1897–1911.* Cambridge: Harvard University Press, 1972.

Jacques, Martin. "Strength in Numbers." *The Guardian* (Manchester/London), 23 October 2004, sec. 1: 23.

Jenkins, John S. *Voyage of the U.S. Exploring Squadron Commanded by Captain Charles Wilkes of the United States Navy in 1838, 1839, 1840, 1841, and 1842.* Auburn, NY: James M. Alden, 1850.

Johnson, Donald D., and Gary Dean Best. *The United States in the Pacific: Private Interests and Public Policies, 1784–1899.* Westport, CT: Greenwood Press, 1995.

Johnson, Martin. *Through the South Seas with Jack London* [1913]. Cedar Springs, MI: Wolf House Books, 1972.

Jolly, Margaret. "From Point Venus to Bali Ha'i: Eroticism and Exoticism in Representations of the Pacific." In *Sites of Desire, Economies of Pleasure: Sexualities in Asia and the Pacific,* ed. Lenore Manderson and Margaret Jolly, 99–122. Chicago: University of Chicago Press, 1997.

Jones, Tyler. "The Panama Canal: A Brief History." http://www. june29.com/Tyler/nonfiction/pan2.com (accessed 1 March 2003).

Kaplan, Amy. *The Anarchy of Empire in the Making of U.S. Culture.* Cambridge: Harvard University Press, 2002.

Kaplan, Amy, and Donald E. Pease, eds. *Cultures of United States Imperialism.* Durham, NC: Duke University Press, 1993.

Kaplan, E. Ann. "Is the Gaze Male?" In *Feminism and Film,* ed. E. Ann Kaplan, 120–131. New York: Oxford University Press, 2000.

———. *Looking for the Other: Feminism, Film, and the Imperial Gaze.* London: Routledge, 1997.

Kapur, Geeta. "Globalization and Culture: Navigating the Void." In *The Cultures of Globalization,* ed. Fredric Jameson and Masao Miyoshi, 191–217. Durham, NC: Duke University Press, 1998.

Kemp, Philip. "F. W. Murnau." *World Film Directors,* ed. John Wakeman. New York: H. W. Wilson, 1987.

Kent, Noel J. *Hawai'i: Islands under the Influence.* Honolulu: University of Hawai'i Press, 1993.

Kirby, Lynne. *Parallel Tracks: The Railroad and Silent Cinema.* Durham, NC: Duke University Press, 1997.

Klein, Kerwin Lee. *Frontiers of the Historical Imagination: Narrating the European Conquest of Native America, 1890–1990.* Berkeley: University of California Press, 1997.

Kottack, Conrad P. *Anthropology*. 5th ed. New York: McGraw Hill, 1991.

Krusenstern, A. J. V. *Voyage round the World in the Years 1803, 1804, 1805, and 1806 by Order of His Majesty Alexander the First*. London: John Murrray, 1813.

Lacan, Jacques. *Freud's Papers on Technique, 1953–1954*. Seminar of Jacques Lacan. Trans. John Forrester, ed. Jacques Miller. New York: W. W. Norton, 1991.

La Farge, John. *Reminiscences of the South Seas*. New York: Doubleday Page, 1912.

LaFeber, Walter. *The New Empire: An Interpretation of American Expansion, 1860–1898* [1963]. Ithaca, NY: Cornell University Press, 1998.

Lamb, Jonathan. "Circumstances Surrounding the Death of John Hawkesworth." Special issue, *Eighteenth Century Life* 18.3 (November 1994): 97–113.

———, ed. Special issue, *Eighteenth Century Life* 18.3 (November 1994).

———. *Preserving the Self in the South Seas, 1680–1840*. Chicago: University of Chicago Press, 2001.

Lamb, Jonathan; Vanessa Smith; and Nicholas Thomas, eds. *Exploration and Exchange: A South Seas Anthology, 1680–1900*. Chicago: University of Chicago Press, 2000.

Langer, Mark. "Flaherty's Hollywood Period." *Wide Angle* 17 (1995): 39–57.

Langman, Larry. *Return to Paradise: A Guide to South Sea Island Films*. Lanham, MD: Scarecrow Press, 1997.

Langsdorff, Georg H. von. *Voyages and Travels in Various Parts of the World* [1813–1814]. Vols. 1–2. New York: Da Capo, 1968.

Lawrence, D. H. "Psychoanalysis and the Unconscious" *and* "Fantasia of the Unconscious" [1922]. Cambridge: Cambridge University Press, 2004.

Leff, David N. *Uncle Sam's Pacific Islets*. Stanford, CA: Stanford University Press, 1940.

Leprohon, Pierre. *L'Exotisme et le cinema*. Paris: Les Éditions J. Susse, 1945.

Lévi-Strauss, Claude. *Tristes Tropiques* [1955]. Trans. John and Doreen Weightman. New York: Pocket Books, 1977.

Lewis, Martin W., and Karen Wigen. *The Myth of Continents: A Critique of Metageography*. Berkeley: University of California Press, 1997.

Leyda, Jay. *The Melville Log: A Documentary Life of Herman Melville, 1819–1891*. New York: Harcourt, 1951.

Linnekin, Jocelyn. "Contending Approaches." In *The Cambridge History of The Pacific Islanders,* ed. Donald Denoon et al., 3–31. Cambridge: Cambridge University Press, 1997.

"Literary Couriers to Distant Places." *Travel* (New York), 37 (October 1921): 14.

"The Literary Spotlight XXVIII: Frederick O'Brien" (with a caricature by William Gropper). *Bookman* 59.1 (March 1924): 54–58.

Littell, Robert. *"Moana"* (review). *New Republic* 46 (3 March 1926): 46–47.

London, Charmian [Kittredge]. *The Log of the* Snark. New York: Macmillan, 1915.

London, Jack. *The Cruise of the* Snark. New York: Macmillan, 1911.

———. *Tales of the Pacific*. Ed. Andrew Sinclair. London: Penguin, 1989.

Lowe, Lisa. *Critical Terrains: French and British Orientalisms.* Ithaca, NY: Cornell University Press, 1991.

Lugowski, David M. "Queering the (New) Deal: Lesbian and Gay Representation and the Depression-Era Cultural Politics of Hollywood's Production Code." *Cinema Journal* 38.2 (Winter 1999): 3–35.

Lynd, Robert S., and Helen Merrell Lynd. *Middletown: A Study in Modern American Culture.* New York: Harcourt, Brace and World, 1929.

Lyons, Paul. *American Pacificism: Oceania in the U.S. Imagination.* London: Routledge, 2006.

———. "From Man-Eaters to Spam-Eaters: Literary Tourism and the Discourse of Cannibalism from Herman Melville to Paul Theroux." In *Multiculturalism and Representation: Selected Essays,* ed. John Rieder and Larry Smith, 67–86. Honolulu: University of Hawai'i Press, 1996.

MacDougall, David. "The Subjective Voice in Ethnographic Film." In *Fields of Vision: Essays in Film Studies, Visual Anthropology, and Photography,* ed. Leslie Devereaux and Roger Hillman, 217–255. Berkeley: University of California Press, 1995.

Mackay, David. "Myth, Science, and Experience in the British Construction of the Pacific." In *Voyages and Beaches: Pacific Encounters, 1769–1840,* ed. Alex Calder, Jonathan Lamb, and Bridget Orr, 100–113. Honolulu: University of Hawai'i Press, 1999.

Macomber, Ben. "Fred O'Brien Brings Up Gorgeous South Sea Haul." Review of *Atolls of the Sun. San Francisco Chronicle,* 22 October 1922.

Māhina, 'Okusitino. "Myth and History." In *Voyages and Beaches: Pacific Encounters, 1769–1840,* ed. Alex Calder, Jonathan Lamb, and Bridget Orr, 61–88. Honolulu: University of Hawai'i Press, 1999.

Malinowski, Bronislaw. *Argonauts of the Western Pacific* [1922]. New York: Dutton, 1961.

———. *A Diary in the Strict Sense of the Term.* New York: Harcourt, Brace and World, 1967.

Man, Glenn K. S. "Hollywood Images of the Pacific." *East-West Film Journal* 5.2 (July 1991): 16–29.

Marchetti, Gina. *Romance and the "Yellow Peril": Race, Sex, and Discursive Strategies in Hollywood Fiction.* Berkeley: University of California Press, 1994.

Marcus, George E. "Contemporary Problems of Ethnography in the Modern World System." In *Writing Culture: The Poetics and Politics of Ethnography,* ed. James Clifford and George E. Marcus, 165–193. Berkeley: University of California Press, 1986.

Marcus, George E., and Michael M. J. Fischer. *Anthropology as Cultural Critique: An Experimental Moment in the Human Sciences.* Chicago: University of Chicago Press, 1986.

Martin, Robert K. *Hero, Captain, and Stranger: Male Friendship, Social Critique, and*

Literary Form in the Sea Novels of Herman Melville. Chapel Hill: University of North Carolina Press, 1986.

Maxwell, Anne. *Colonial Photography and Exhibitions: Representations of the 'Native' People and the Making of European Identities.* London: Cassell, 1999.

Mayne, Judith. *Cinema and Spectatorship.* London: Routledge, 1993.

McBride, Christopher Mark. *The Colonizer Abroad: American Writers on Foreign Soil, 1846–1912.* New York: Routledge, 2004.

McClintock, Anne. "The Angel of Progress: Pitfalls of the Term Post-colonialism." In *Colonial Discourse and Post-Colonial Theory: A Reader,* ed. Patrick Williams and Laura Chrisman, 291–304. New York: Columbia University Press, 1994.

Mead, Margaret, ed. *An Anthropologist at Work: Writings of Ruth Benedict.* Boston: Houghton Mifflin, 1959.

———. *Blackberry Winter: My Earlier Years.* New York: Simon and Schuster, 1972.

———. *Coming of Age in Samoa* [1928]. New York: William Morrow, 1961.

———. *From the South Seas: Studies of Adolescence and Sex in Primitive Societies.* New York: William Morrow, 1939.

———. *Growing Up in New Guinea* [1930]. New York: Dell, 1968.

———. *Letters from the Field, 1925–1975.* New York: Harper and Row, 1977.

———. *New Lives for Old: Cultural Transformation—Manus, 1928–1953* [1956]. New York: Dell, 1971.

Meleisea, Malama. *Change and Adaptations in Western Samoa.* Christchurch: Macmillan Brown Centre, University of Canterbury, 1992.

———. "The Postmodern Legacy of a Premodern Warrior Goddess in Modern Samoa." In *Voyages and Beaches: Pacific Encounters, 1769–1840,* ed. Alex Calder, Jonathan Lamb, and Bridget Orr, 55–60. Honolulu: University of Hawai'i Press, 1999.

Melville, Herman. *Moby-Dick* [1851]. London: Penguin, 1994.

———. *Omoo* [1847]. New York: Library of America, 1982.

———. "The South Seas" [*Baltimore American and Commercial Daily Advertiser,* 9 February 1859]. *The Portable Melville,* ed. Jay Leyda, 575–583. New York: Viking Press, 1952.

———. *Typee: A Peep at Polynesian Life* [1846]. Ed. John Bryant. New York: Penguin, 1996.

———. *White Jacket, or, The World in a Man-of-War.* Ed. Hennig Cohen. New York: Holt, Rinehart, 1967.

Memmi, Albert. *The Colonizer and the Colonized.* Boston: Beacon Press, 1967.

"M.G.M. Backs Van Dyke." *Variety,* 21 March 1928: 1–4.

Mitchell, George. "Movie Audiences Feel Themselves on Screen." *New York Times,* 15 October 1927.

"*Moana.*" Review. *New York Times,* 31 October 1926.

"*Moana.*" Review. *Variety,* 10 February 1926: 40.

Montag, Warren. "The Universalization of Whiteness: Racism and the Enlightenment."

In *Whiteness: A Critical Reader*, ed. Mike Hill, 281–293. New York: New York University Press, 1999.

Montaigne, Michel de. "On Cannibals." In *Essays*. Trans. J. M. Cohen. New York: Penguin Books, 1958.

Moore, Henrietta. *A Passion for Difference*. Bloomington: Indiana University Press, 1994.

Moorhead, Alan. *The Fatal Impact: An Account of the Invasion of the South Pacific, 1767–1840*. New York: Harper and Row, 1966.

Mudimbe, V. Y. *The Invention of Africa: Gnosis, Philosophy, and the Order of Knowledge*. Bloomington: Indiana University Press, 1988.

Mulvey, Laura. "Visual Pleasure and Narrative Cinema." *Screen* 16.3 (1975): 6–18.

Munden, Kenneth W., ed. *American Film Institute Catalogue of Motion Pictures Produced in the United States: Feature Films, 1921–1930*. New York: R. R. Bowker, 1971.

Murnau, F. W. "The Ideal Picture Needs No Titles." *Theatre Magazine* (New York), 47 (January 1928).

Murphy, William T. *Robert Flaherty: A Guide to References and Resources*. Boston: G. K. Hall, 1978.

Neale, Steve. "Masculinity as Spectacle: Reflections on Men and Mainstream Cinema." In *Feminism and Film*, ed. E. Ann Kaplan, 253–264. New York: Oxford University Press, 2000.

"New Lighting for Movies." *New York Times*, 12 February 1928.

Nichols, Bill. *Ideology and the Image: Social Representation in the Cinema and Other Media*. Bloomington: University of Indiana Press, 1981.

———. *Representing Reality: Issues and Concepts in Documentary*. Bloomington: Indiana University Press, 1991.

Nichols, Bill; Christian Hansen; and Catherine Needham. "Pornography, Ethnography, and the Discourses of Power." In *Representing Reality: Issues and Concepts in Documentary*, Bill Nichols, 201–228. Bloomington: Indiana University Press, 1991.

Nietzsche, Friedrich. "The Birth of Tragedy" *and* "The Genealogy of Morals." Trans. Francis Golffing. New York: Doubleday, 1956.

Nordhoff, Charles, and James Norman Hall. *Faery Lands of the South Seas*. Garden City, NY: Garden City Publishing, 1921.

———. *The Hurricane*. New York: Triangle Books, 1935.

Obeyesekere, Gananath. *The Apotheosis of Captain Cook: European Mythmaking in the Pacific*. Princeton, NJ: Princeton University Press, 1992.

O'Brien, Frederick. *Atolls of the Sun*. New York: Century, 1922.

———. "The Author of *White Shadows*." *Bookman* 52 (December 1920): 295–299.

———. "Flowing Kava Bowl." *Asia* 9 (July 1919): 638–644.

———. "The Lure of the South Seas." *Mentor* 10.1 (1922): 7–31.

———. *Mystic Isles of the South Seas*. New York: Century, 1921.

———. *White Shadows in the South Seas*. New York: Century, 1919.

O'Brien, Frederick, and Rose Wilder Lane. "Atuona Goes to Church." *Asia* 19 (September 1919): 830–835.

———. "O Lalala, the Gambler." *Century* 98 (August 1919): 446–454.

Odencrantz, Louise Christine. *Italian Women in Industry.* New York: Russell Sage Foundation, 1919.

Oksiloff, Assenka. *Picturing the Primitive: Visual Culture, Ethnography, and Early German Cinema.* New York: Palgrave, 2001.

Orr, Bridget. "'Southern passions mix with northern art': Miscegenation and the *Endeavour* Voyage." Special issue, *Eighteenth Century Life* 18.3 (November 1994): 212–231.

Palumbo-Liu, David. *Asian/American: Historical Crossings of a Racial Frontier.* Stanford, CA: Stanford University Press, 1999.

Paolino, Ernest N. *The Foundations of the American Empire: William Henry Seward and US Foreign Policy.* Ithaca, NY: Cornell University Press, 1973.

Parkinson, Sydney. *Parkinson's Journal.* "South Seas Voyaging and Cross Cultural Encounters in the Pacific (1760–1800)." http://southseas.nla.gov.au/journals/parkinson/046.html (accessed 1 August 2004).

Pearson, Bill. *Rifled Sanctuaries: Some Views of the Pacific Islands in Western Literature.* Auckland: Auckland University Press, 1984.

Perez, Gilberto. *The Material Ghost: Films and Their Medium.* Baltimore, MD: Johns Hopkins University Press, 1998.

Perloff, Nancy. "Gauguin's French Baggage: Decadence and Colonialism in Tahiti." In *Prehistories of the Future: The Primitivist Project and the Culture of Modernism,* ed. Elazar Barkan and Ronald Bush, 226–269. Stanford, CA: Stanford University Press, 1995.

Perry, John Curtis. *Facing West: Americans and the Opening of the Pacific.* Westport, CT: Praeger, 1994.

Philbrick, Nathaniel. *Sea of Glory: America's Voyage of Discovery, the US Exploring Expedition, 1838–1842.* New York: Viking, 2003.

"Pictures of 1922." *New York Times,* 2 July 1922, sec. 4: 3.

Pocock, J. G. A. "Nature and History, Self and Other: European Perceptions of World History in the Age of the Encounter." In *Voyages and Beaches: Pacific Encounters, 1769–1840,* ed. Alex Calder, Jonathan Lamb, and Bridget Orr, 25–44. Honolulu: University of Hawai'i Press, 1999.

Porter, David. *Journal of a Cruise Made to the Pacific Ocean in the United States Frigate Essex in the Years 1812, 1813, and 1814.* Vols. 1–2. New York: Wiley and Halstead, 1822.

Porter, Dennis. *Haunted Journeys: Desire and Transgression in European Travel Writing.* Princeton, NJ: Princeton University Press, 1991.

Porter, Roy. "The Exotic as Erotic: Captain Cook at Tahiti." In *Exoticism in the Enlight-*

enment, ed. G. S. Rousseau and Roy Porter, 117–143. Manchester: Manchester University Press, 1990.

Potamkin, Harry Alan. "Lost Paradise: *Tabu.*" *Creative Art* 8 (June 1931): 462–463.

Pratt, Mary Louise. *Imperial Eyes: Travel Writing and Transculturation.* New York: Routledge, 1992.

Procter, John Robert. "Isolation or Imperialism." *Forum* 26 (September 1898). In *Imperialists vs. Anti-imperialists: The Debate over Expansionism in the 1890s,* ed. Richard E. Welch. Itsaca, IL: F. E. Peacock, 1972.

Pronger, Brian. *The Arena of Masculinity.* Excerpted in *A Queer Reader,* ed. Patrick Higgins, 214–215. London: Fourth Estate, 1993.

Quilley, Geoff, and John Bonehill, eds. *William Hodges, 1744–1797: The Art of Exploration.* New Haven, CT: Yale University Press, 2004.

Quirós, Pedro Fernández de. *The Voyages of Pedro Fernández de Quirós, 1595 to 1606.* Vol. 1. Ed. and trans. Sir Clements Markham. London: Hakluyt Society, 1904.

Rafael, Vincent L. *White Love and Other Events in Filipino History.* Durham, NC: Duke University Press, 2000.

Rannie, Douglas. *My Adventures Among South Sea Cannibals; an account of the experiences and adventures of a government official among the natives of Oceania.* London: Seeley, Service, 1912.

Renda, Mary A. *Taking Haiti: Military Occupation and the Culture of US Imperialism, 1915–1940.* Chapel Hill: University of North Carolina Press, 2001.

Rennie, Neil. *Far-Fetched Facts: The Literature of Travel and the Idea of the South Seas.* Oxford: Clarendon Press, 1995.

Reyes, Luis I. *Made in Paradise: Hollywood's Films of Hawai'i and the South Seas.* Honolulu, HI: Mutual Publishing, 1995.

Roan, Jeanette. "Exotic Explorations: Travels to Asia and the Pacific in Early Cinema." In *Collecting Early Asian America: Essays in Cultural History,* ed. Josephine Lee, Imogene L. Lim, and Yuko Matsukawa, 187–199. Philadelphia: Temple University Press, 2002.

Robarts, Edward. *The Marquesan Journal of Edward Robarts, 1797–1824.* Ed. Greg Dening. Honolulu: University of Hawai'i Press, 1974.

Robertson, George. *The Discovery of Tahiti, a Journal of the Second Voyage of the H.M.S. Dolphin round the World, 1766–1768.* Ed. Hugh Carrington. London: Hakluyt Society, 1948.

Rony, Fatimah Tobing. *The Third Eye: Race, Cinema, and Ethnographic Spectacle.* Durham, NC: Duke University Press, 1996.

Rosenberg, Emily S. *Spreading the American Dream: American Economic and Cultural Expansion, 1890–1945.* New York: Hill and Wang, 1982.

Rosenthal, Alan, ed. *New Challenges for Documentary.* Berkeley: University of California Press, 1988.

Rotha, Paul. *Robert J. Flaherty: A Biography.* Ed. Jay Ruby. Philadelphia: University of Pennsylvania Press, 1983.

Roulston, Charles Robert. "Eden and the Lotus Eaters: A Critical Study of the South Sea Island Writings of Frederick O'Brien, James Norman Hall, and Robert Dean Frisbie." Ph.D. Dissertation. University of Maryland, 1965.

———. *James Norman Hall.* Boston: Twayne, 1978.

Rowe, John Carlos. *Literary Culture and U.S. Imperialism: From the Revolution to World War II.* Oxford: Oxford University Press, 2000.

———. "Melville's *Typee:* US Imperialism at Home and Abroad." In *National Identities and Post-Americanist Narratives,* ed. Donald E. Pease, 255–278. Durham, NC: Duke University Press, 1994.

Ruby, Jay. "The Aggie Will Come First: The Demystification of Robert Flaherty." In *Robert J. Flaherty, Photographer/Filmmaker: The Inuit, 1910–1922,* ed. Jo-Anne Birnie Danzker, 67–74, 94–96. Vancouver: Vancouver Art Gallery, 1980.

———. "The Ethics of Image-Making." In *New Challenges for Documentary,* ed. Alan Rosenthal, 308–318. Berkeley: University of California Press, 1988.

———. *Picturing Culture: Explorations of Film and Anthropology.* Chicago: University of Chicago Press, 2000.

———. "A Re-examination of the Early Career of Robert J. Flaherty." *Quarterly Review of Film Studies,* Fall 1980: 431–456.

Rydell, Robert W. *All the World's a Fair: Visions of Empire at American International Expositions, 1876–1916.* Chicago: University of Chicago Press, 1984.

———. *World of Fairs: The Century of Progress Expositions.* Chicago: University of Chicago Press, 1993.

Safroni-Middleton, A. *South Seas Foam: The Romantic Adventures of a Modern Don Quixote in the Southern Seas.* New York: George H. Doran, 1920.

Sahlins, Marshall. *How "Natives" Think: About Captain Cook, for Example.* Chicago: University of Chicago Press, 1995.

Said, Edward. *Culture and Imperialism.* New York: Alfred A. Knopf, 1993.

———. *Orientalism.* New York: Vintage, 1979.

——— "Representing the Colonized: Anthropology's Interlocutors." *Critical Inquiry* 15.2 (Winter 1989): 205–225.

———. *The World, the Text, and the Critic.* Cambridge: Harvard University Press, 1983.

Sapir, Edward. *Culture, Language, and Personality: Selected Essays* [1949]. Ed. David G. Mandelbaum. Berkeley: University of California Press, 1966.

Schmidt, Johanna. "Redefining Fa'afafine: Western Discourses and the Construction of Transgenderism in Samoa." *Intersections* 6 (August 2001). http://www.sshe.murdoch.edu.au/intersections/issue6/schmidt.html (accessed 1 August 2004).

Schueller, Malini Johar. "Indians, Polynesians, and Empire Making: The Case of Herman Melville." In *Genealogy and Literature,* ed. Lee Quinby, 48–67. Minneapolis: University of Minnesota Press, 1995.

———. *U.S. Orientalisms: Race, Nation, and Gender in Literature, 1790–1890.* Ann Arbor: University of Michigan Press, 1998.

"The Screen." *New York Times,* 12 June 1922: 16.

Sharpe, Howard. "The Star Creators of Hollywood." Interview with W. S. Van Dyke. *Photoplay,* December 1936: 71–73.

Sherwood, Robert. "Film of the Month." *McCall's,* June 1926: 25.

Shohat, Ella, and Robert Stam. *Unthinking Eurocentrism: Multiculturalism and the Media.* London: Routledge, 1994.

Siddal, Dudley A. "Artists Flock to Tahiti." *Publisher's Weekly* 99 (22 January 1921): 199.

Silverman, Kaja. "Fassbinder and Lacan: A Reconsideration of Gaze, Look, and Image." *Camera Obscura* 19 (1989): 54–85.

Simon, Jean. *La Polynésia dans l'art et la littérature de l'occident.* Paris: Gallimard, 1939.

Smith, Bernard. *European Vision and the South Pacific.* New Haven, CT: Yale University Press, 1985.

———. *Imagining the Pacific: In the Wake of the Cook Voyages.* New Haven, CT: Yale University Press, 1992.

Smith, Marian L. "Race, Nationality, and Reality: INS Administration of Racial Provisions in US Immigration and Nationality Law Since 1898." *Immigration Daily.* http://www.ilw.com/lawyers/articles/2003,0616–smith.shtm (accessed 1 August 2004).

Smith, Vanessa. *Literary Culture and the Pacific: Nineteenth-Century Textual Encounters.* Cambridge: Cambridge University Press, 1998.

———. "Pitcairn's 'Guilty Stock': The Island as Breeding Ground." In *Islands in History and Representation,* ed. Rod Edmond and Vanessa Smith, 116–132. London: Routledge, 2003.

Soares, Andre. *Beyond Paradise: The Life of Ramon Novarro.* New York: St. Martin's, 2002.

Soja, Edward. *Postmodern Geographies: The Reassertion of Space in Critical Social Theory.* London: Verso, 1989.

Solnit, Rebecca. *River of Shadows: Eadweard Muybridge and the Technological Wild West.* New York: Viking, 2003.

Spivak, Gayatri Chakravorty. "Can the Subaltern Speak?" In *Colonial Discourse and Postcolonial Theory,* ed. Patrick Williams and Laura Chrisman, 66–111. New York: Columbia University Press, 1994.

———. *The Post-Colonial Critic: Interviews, Strategies, Dialogues.* Ed. Sarah Harasym. London: Routledge, 1990.

———. "The Rani of Sirmur." In *Europe and Its Others,* ed. Francis Barker, Peter

Hulme, Margaret Iversen, and Diana Loxley, 1:128–151. Colchester: University of Essex Press, 1985.

Spurr, David. *The Rhetoric of Empire: Colonial Discourse in Journalism, Travel Writing, and Imperial Administration.* Durham, NC: Duke University Press, 1993.

Stevenson, Robert Louis. *In the South Seas: Being an account of experiences and observations in the Marquesas, Paumotus and Gilbert Islands in the course of two cruises, on the yacht* "Casco" *(1888) and the schooner* "Equator" *(1889)* [1900]. Honolulu: University Press of Hawai'i, 1971.

———. *Island Nights' Entertainments* [1893]. London: Chatto and Windus, 1987.

———. *The Letters of Robert Louis Stevenson.* Vols. 7–8. Ed. Bradford A. Booth and Ernest Mehew. New Haven, CT: Yale University Press, 1995.

Stewart, Charles S. *A Visit to the South Seas in the U.S. Ship* Vincennes, *during the Years 1829 and 1830.* New York: John P. Haven, 1831.

St. Johnston, Alfred. *Camping among Cannibals.* London: Macmillan Colonial Library, 1889.

Stocking, George. "The Ethnographic Sensibility of the 1920s and the Dualism of the Anthropological Tradition." In *Romantic Motives: Essays on Anthropological Sensibility,* ed. George Stocking, 208–276. Madison: University of Wisconsin Press, 1989.

———. *Race, Culture, and Evolution: Essays in the History of Anthropology* [1968]. Chicago: University of Chicago Press, 1982.

———. *The Shaping of American Anthropology, 1883–1911: A Franz Boas Reader.* New York: Basic Books, 1974.

Stoddard, Charles Warren. *Cruising the South Seas: Stories by Charles Warren Stoddard.* Ed. Winston Leyland. San Francisco: Gay Sunshine Press, 1987.

———. *Exits and Entrances: A Book of Essays and Sketches.* Boston: Lothrop, 1903.

———. *South Sea Idyls* [1873]. 2nd ed. New York: Charles Scribner's, 1892.

Stoler, Ann Laura. *Race and the Education of Desire: Foucault's History of Sexuality and the Colonial Order of Things.* Durham, NC: Duke University Press, 1996.

Strauss, W. Patrick. *Americans in Polynesia, 1783–1842.* East Lansing: Michigan State University Press, 1963.

Studlar, Gaylyn. "Barrymore, the Body, and Bliss: Issues of Male Representation and Female Spectatorship in the 1920s." In *Fields of Vision: Essays in Film Studies, Visual Anthropology, and Photography,* ed. Leslie Devereaux and Roger Hillman, 160–180. Berkeley: University of California Press, 1995.

Sturma, Michael. *South Sea Maidens: Western Fantasy and Sexual Politics in the South Pacific.* Westport, CT: Greenwood Press, 2002.

Subramani. "Emerging Epistemologies." Paper Presented to the conference "South Pacific Literatures," Noumea, New Caledonia, 20–24 October 2003. www.usp.ac.fj/fileadmin/files/others/vakavuku/subramani.doc (accessed 1 September 2004).

———. "The Oceanic Imaginary." *Contemporary Pacific* 13.1 (2001): 149–162.

————. *South Pacific Literature: From Myth to Fabulation.* Suva: University of the South Pacific, 1985.

Sullivan, Louis R. *Marquesan Somatology with Comparative Notes on Samoa and Tonga, Based on the Field Studies of E. S. Craighill Handy and Willowdean C. Handy.* New York: Kraus Reprints, 1974.

"*Tabu.*" Review. *Variety,* 25 March 1931: 17.

Takaki, Ronald. *Pau Hana: Plantation Life and Labor in Hawai'i, 1835–1920.* Honolulu: University of Hawai'i Press, 1983.

Taprock, Walter E. [George S. Chappell]. *The Cruise of the* Kawa: *Wanderings in the South Seas.* New York: G. P. Putnam's Sons, 1921.

Theroux, Paul. *The Happy Isles of Oceania: Paddling the Pacific.* New York: Putnam, 1992.

Thomas, Nicholas. *Discoveries: The Voyages of Captain Cook.* London: Allen Lane, 2004.

————. *Entangled Objects: Exchange, Material Culture, and Colonialism in the Pacific.* Cambridge: Harvard University Press, 1991.

————. "Hodges as Anthropologist and Historian." In *William Hodges, 1744–1797: The Art of Exploration,* ed. Geoff Quilley and John Bonehill, 27–34. New Haven, CT: Yale University Press, 2004.

————. *In Oceania: Visions, Artifacts, Histories.* Durham, NC: Duke University Press, 1997.

————. "Introduction" to George Forster, *A Voyage round the World* [1777]. Vols. 1–2. Ed. Nicholas Thomas and Oliver Berghof. Honolulu: University of Hawai'i Press, 2000.

————. "Johann Reinhold Forster and his Observations." In Johann Reinhold Forster, *Observations Made during a Voyage round the World* [1778]. Ed. Nicholas Thomas, Harriet Guest, and Michael Dettelbach. Honolulu: University of Hawai'i Press, 1996.

————. *Marquesan Societies: Inequality and Political Transformation in Eastern Polynesia.* Oxford: Clarendon, 1990.

————. "'On the Varieties of Human Species': Forster's Comparative Ethnology." In Johann Reinhold Forster, *Observations Made during a Voyage round the World* [1778]. Ed. Nicholas Thomas, Harriet Guest, and Michael Dettelbach. Honolulu: University of Hawai'i Press, 1996.

Thoreau, Henry David. *Walden.* In *"Walden," and Civil Disobedience.* Ed. Owen Thomas. New York: W. W. Norton, 1966.

Tomso, Gregory. "The Queer History of Leprosy and Same-Sex Love." *American Literary History* 14.4 (2002): 747–775.

Torgovnick, Marianna. *Gone Primitive: Savage Intellects, Modern Lives.* Chicago: University of Chicago Press, 1990.

"Travel Books to the Fore Again." *Publisher's Weekly,* 6 December 1919: 1540.

Trinh T. Minh-ha. "Outside In Inside Out." In *Questions of Third Cinema,* ed. Jim Pines and Paul Willemen, 133–149. London: British Film Institute, 1989.

Turner, Frederick Jackson. *The Frontier in American History.* New York: Henry Holt, 1920.

Turner, Victor. *The Anthropology of Performance.* New York: PAJ Publications, 1988.

Twain, Mark. *Following the Equator: A Journey around the World* [1897]. New York: Dover, 1989.

———. *Mark Twain's Letters from Hawaii.* Ed. A. Grove Day. Honolulu: University Press of Hawai'i, 1966.

———. *Roughing It.* Hartford, CT: American Publishing, 1872.

Vasey, Ruth. *The World According to Hollywood, 1918–1939.* Exeter: Exeter University Press, 1997.

Wales, William. *Remarks on Mr. Forster's Account of Captain Cook's Last Voyage round the World.* In George Forster, *A Voyage round the World* [1777]. Vol. 2. Ed. Nicholas Thomas and Oliver Berghof. Honolulu: University of Hawai'i Press, 2000.

Wallace, Lee. *Sexual Encounters: Pacific Texts, Modern Sexualities.* Ithaca, NY: Cornell University Press, 2003.

Wallis, Captain Samuel. "The Discovery of Tahiti." Journal excerpt. In *Exploration and Exchange: A South Seas Anthology, 1680–1900,* ed. Jonathan Lamb, Vanessa Smith, and Nicholas Thomas, 57–72. Chicago: University of Chicago Press, 2000.

Waly. "*Ra-mu.*" Review. *Daily Variety,* 13 February 1929: 24.

Watson, R. M. *History of Samoa.* Wellington: Whitcombe and Tombs, 1918.

Welch, Richard E., ed. *Imperialists vs. Anti-imperialists: The Debate over Expansionism in the 1890s.* Itasca, IL: F. E. Peacock, 1972.

Wendt, Albert, ed. *Nuanua: Pacific Writing since 1980.* Honolulu: University of Hawai'i Press, 1990.

———. "*Tatau*ing the Post-Colonial Body: Reading the Samoan *Tatau* as Literature." Paper presented to the MELUS conference, Honolulu (April 1997). *SPAN* 42/43 (1996): 15–29.

———. "Towards a New Oceania." In *Writers in East-West Encounter: New Cultural Bearings,* ed. Guy Amirthanayagam, 202–215. London: Macmillan, 1982.

"*White Shadows (in the South Seas) (sound).*" Film review. *Variety,* 8 August 1928: 12.

Willcox, Charles. "The Lost Autobiographical Works of Once Famous Sausalito Author Frederick O'Brien." *Sausalito Historical Society Quarterly,* Winter 1994: 1–2.

Williams, Linda. "Mirrors without Memories: Truth, History, and the New Documentary." *Film Quarterly* 46.3 (Spring 1993): 9–21.

Williams, Patrick, and Laura Chrisman, eds. *Colonial Discourse and Post-Colonial Theory: A Reader.* New York: Columbia University Press, 1994.

Williams, Raymond. *Culture and Society, 1780–1950* [1958]. New York: Columbia University Press, 1983.

————. *Keywords: A Vocabulary of Culture and Society* [1976]. Rev. ed. Oxford: Oxford University Press, 1985.

Wilson, Rob. *Reimagining the American Pacific: From South Pacific to Bamboo Ridge and Beyond.* Durham, NC: Duke University Press, 2000.

Wilson, Rob, and Arif Dirlik, eds. *Asia/Pacific as Space of Cultural Production.* Durham, NC: Duke University Press, 1995.

Wood, William Maxwell, M.D. *Wandering Sketches of People and Things in South America, Polynesia, California, and Other Places Visited During a Cruise on Board of the U.S. Ships* Levant, Portsmouth, *and* Savannah. Philadelphia: Carey and Hart, 1849.

Wright, Betty Ren. *The Ghost in the House: A Life of Rose Wilder Lane.* Columbia, MO: University of Missouri Press, 1995.

Wrobel, David M. *The End of American Exceptionalism: Frontier Anxiety from the Old West to the New Deal.* Lawrence: University of Kansas Press, 1993.

Young, Robert. *White Mythologies: Writing History and the West.* New York: Routledge, 1990.

Zimmerman, Patricia. "Midwives, Hostesses, and Feminist Film." *Wide Angle* 17 (1995): 197–216.

Index

Adams, Henry, 54, 56, 152, 247n133; *Tahiti*, 61
Adler, William F., *Shipwrecked Among Cannibals* (film), 55
Adorée, Renée, 185–186
aikāne, 198, 204
Akeley, Carl, 121
Aldrich, Robert, 54, 198
Allakariallak ("Nanook"), 100, 121–122
American exceptionalism, 2, 101; refuted by O'Brien, 105–106
American Indians, 45–46, 49, 65, 97, 114, 128, 134, 203
American Pacific: and decolonization, 231; defined, 241n54; growth of, 38–39, 41–45, 47–52, 229; and Second World War, 229–230
Andrew, Thomas, 136
annexations: of 1898–1899, 48–51, 76; of Pacific territories, 2, 14, 47
anthropology, 128–136, 229–230; amateur, 52, 128–130; cultural, 71, 128–131; physical, 55–56, 60–61, 64, 70; and relativism, 60, 66, 71–73, 115; as salvage, 99–100, 133–136. *See also* ethnography; relativism
anthropometry, 55–56, 60–61, 64
anticolonialism, 14, 84, 160, 211. *See also* colonialism; imperialism
anti-imperialism, 44–46, 50–54, 79–80, 100–102, 105–106, 114–115. *See also* colonialism; imperialism
Aotourou, 23
Asad, Talal, 67
Asiatic Barred Zone, 62–63, 181
Austen, Roger, 206

Baker, Josephine, 86
Bakhtin, Mikhail, 78, 147–148
Balboa, Vasco Nuñez de, 4
Ballantyne, R. M., *The Coral Island*, 88
Bancroft, Hubert Howe, 2, 51, 65, 83, 92
Banks, Joseph, 18, 22, 23–25, 30, 54, 189, 197–198, 240n29; and relativism, 66; and sexual fantasy, 25–26, 197; and sunken continent theory, 91
Barnard, Ian, 206
Barsam, Richard, 143, 150, 154
Barthes, Roland, 87
Bateson, Gregory, 99
Bayard, Thomas, 48
Bazin, André, 120, 160
beachcombers, 54, 77–78, 104, 162, 180; and cultural crossings, 46, 67–69, 110–111, 154
Becke, Louis, 54, 87
Behdad, Ali, 11–12, 103, 107–108
Belich, James, 61

Bellwood, Peter, 60, 64
Benedict, Ruth, 71, 257n49
Benjamin, Walter, 106, 108
Benkert, Carl Maria, 206
Best, Gary Dean, 47–48
Betts, Raymond F., 165, 175, 262n21
Bhabha, Homi, 44–45, 59
Biddle, George, 74, 80
biological determinism, 56–57, 69–70
Bird of Paradise (stage play and film), 15, 184, 228
blackbirding, 48, 54
Bleys, Rudi C., 198, 206, 267nn12, 14
Bloch, Ernst, 130
Blue, Monte, 172, 174
Blumenbach, Johann Friedrich, 31, 35, 55, 57
Boas, Franz, 69–72, 129; and Jesup North Pacific Expedition, 60; and salvage anthropology, 133
Bonehill, John, 36
Boone, Joseph Allen, 199, 207–208
Bopp, Franz, 63
Bora Bora, 14, 168, 215–216, 222
Bougainville, Louis-Antoine de, 18, 22–23, 57, 66, 73, 89, 99, 236n1; and appearance of "Venus," 22, 181, 197
"boy's own" stories, 88
Brown, J. Macmillan, 60, 64
Buchan, Alexander, 32–35
Buffon, George-Louis Leclerc de, *Histoire naturelle*, 34
Burch, Noël, 195
Burton, Sir Richard, 200
Byron, Captain John, 20

Cabri, Jean, 77
Calder-Marshall, Arthur, 214
Calvinism, 23, 42, 154
Camper, Petrus, 56
cannibalism, 44, 55, 86, 88, 99
Carby, Hazel V., 191
Carpenter, Edward, 216
Chambers, Ross, 65
Chaudhuri, Shohini, 196
Cheek, Pamela, 19, 27, 29, 58, 194, 239n22, 365n69
Chevalier, Anna ("Reri"), 218, 271n80
China trade, 6, 14, 38–39, 42–43, 50, 53, 83
Chinese Exclusion Act, 62. *See also* Asiatic Barred Zone
Chippo, Josephine, 166–167, 169, 262n4; and W. S. Van Dyke, 170–171, 264n45
Chrisman, Laura, 6
chronophotography, 33–34

Churchward, Albert, 64
Churchward, James, *The Lost Continent of Mu*, 91
classicism, 66; and images of Pacific Islanders, 36–37, 57, 124, 153, 241n47. *See also* "South Seas maiden"
Clifford, James, 133–135
colonialism, 8–9; compared to imperialism, 6, 105–106; discourses of, 10–12, 44–45, 85, 107–108; dissemination of idea of, 54; and Enlightenment, 37–38; as ruin, 103–107. *See also* anticolonialism; imperialism
Commerson, Philibert, 18, 57, 238n12
Comolli, Jean-Louis, 16, 161
Connery, Christopher, 5
Cook, Captain James, 23–27, 30, 32, 34, 36–38, 59, 88–89, 99; death of, 10–11; and relativism, 66; and "rites of Venus," 26–27; scholarship about, 10–11, 238n14
Coolbrith, Ina, 200
Conrad, Joseph, 88, 211
Corliss, Richard, 121
craniology, 55–56
Crisp, Donald, 185
Crosby, Floyd, 165, 168, 226
Cruise of the Kawa, The (Walter E. Taprock), 115–116
Cunningham, Jack, 164
Curtis, Edward S., 128
Cuvier, Georges, 56

Dana, Richard Henry, *Two Years before the Mast*, 43, 201
Dance in Otaheite, A (John Keyes Sherwin), 37
Darwin, Charles, 63, 90, 251n48. *See also* evolutionary theory
Davenport, Charles B., 70
David, Felix, 119, 214–215, 270n72
Davidson, J. W., 48
degeneration, 106–107, 169–170, 217; and civilization, 37–38, 81, 105, 175, 183; and culture contact, 97, 99, 220–221. *See also* miscegenation
Delmas, Père Siméon, 91, 104
Dening, Greg, 20, 46, 67, 77, 102, 110, 114; on depopulation, 96–97, 99–100
depopulation, 95–99, 101–102, 134; as self-inflicted, 99, 133. *See also* fatal impact
depression (economic), 51; of 1870s, 47; of 1890s, 79; the Great Depression, 13, 117, 227–228
De Vinna, Clyde, 165, 167, 171, 176, 179, 189, 214
Diderot, Denis, 9, 66, 68
Dixon, Roland Burrage, 60, 64
documentary: and authenticity, 120–127, 136, 138; drawing, 32–33, 36–37, 123–124; film, 33, 120–123, 124–127, 143, 147, 231; observational, 151
Doyle, Ray, 164, 168, 176, 182
Du Bois, W. E. B., 73, 225
Dudden, Arthur P., 42–43, 49
Dumont, Hervé, 160–161, 190

Dumont D'Urville, J. S. C., 3–4
Durant, Will, "The Modern Woman," 162
Dyer, Richard, 208

Eden. *See* prelapsarian return
Edmond, Rod, 8–9, 16, 30, 96–97, 98, 235n28, 260n111
Edwards, Justin D., 200
Eisner, Lotte, 208–209, 211–213, 218, 225
Ellis, William, 65, 253n67
encounters: textualization of, 21, 27, 89–90; and violence, 20–28, 37–41, 42, 46, 92–93, 105
Engstfeld, Axel, *Second Glance* (film), 159
Enlightenment, 7, 18–19, 30, 38; and nonconventional gender roles, 198, 267nn12, 14; and race, 30–32, 56, 57; and ruins, 106; as self-contradictory, 24, 37–38, 40, 42; and the US, 20, 38–41
Eperjesi, John, 5–6
eroticism: in *Moana*, 145, 153–154; in O'Brien's writings, 108–110; of Polynesian encounters, 21–23, 25–28, 36–37; in *White Shadows* (film), 176–181. *See also* fetishism; homoeroticism
Erskine, Charles, 42
ethnography: amateur, 102; and authority, 130–131, 144; early visual, 33–38; and pornography, 137–138, 176, 178–180; and race, 28–38; romantic, 121–122; as a "safe" framing device, 86, 138, 153–154, 155, 180; as salvage, 99–100, 133–136; shared, 131–132, 145; as spectacle, 52, 126, 173; in voyaging accounts, 41
eugenics, 69–71, 247n139
Euhemerus of Messene, *Sacred Scripture*, 7–8
evolutionary theory, 56, 63, 90, 92. *See also* Darwin
expansionism, 38, 47–54, 84, 92, 114. *See also* frontier; manifest destiny

fa'afafine, 198
Fa'angase *(Moana)*, 146, 148–149, 151–153, 159
Fabian, Johannes, 90, 130, 147
fatal impact, 23, 46, 95–103, 134, 207, 230; as aesthetic contemplation, 96, 99–100, 104, 133; and socioeconomic critique, 101–102. *See also* depopulation
feminization: of the "native" male, 153, 189, 195–196, 203–204, 260n111; of the tropics, 162
fetishism, 216; of females, 21–22, 25–26, 86, 108–109, 181, 246n125; of males, 151–156, 189–197, 207–210, 216–217; of "native" bodies, 86, 137, 210. *See also* classicism; eroticism; homoeroticism; "South Seas maiden"
Fiedler, Leslie, 200, 206
Field, Sarah Bard, 79
film stock: and racial representation, 141–143, 172, 185, 216–217
Finauga ("Pe'a"), 126, 148, 150–151, 155, 159
First World War. *See* wars
Flaherty, David, 118–119, 153–154, 157, 167, 211; "Serpents in Eden," 215
Flaherty, Frances Hubbard, 13–14, 74–75, 119,

129, 132–133, 217, 263n34; and *Acoma,* 140, 167, 211; *Asia* articles, 125–126, 140–145; and the female gaze, 139–145; and professional identity, 132–133, 140; racial attitudes of, 141–142, 217; relationship with Robert Flaherty, 139–140, 215. See also *Moana*

Flaherty, Robert J., 13–14, 60, 74–75, 117–159, 184; and box-office returns, 75, 118, 157; and criticism of "talkies," 224; and ethnography, 129–130, 213–214, 218; and imperialism, 126–128; legacy of, 120–128, 255n11; *Louisiana Story,* 120, 138, 139; *Man of Aran,* 121, 139; *My Eskimo Friends,* 127; *Nanook of the North,* 74, 100, 118–120, 121–122, 125–127, 129, 136, 139; as outsider, 120, 210–211; relationship with F. W. Murnau, 140, 210–216; relationship with W. S. Van Dyke, 165–168, 214, 263n25; *A Singer of the South Seas,* 215. See also *Moana; Tabu; White Shadows in the South Seas* (MGM)

Flavell, Kay, 31, 34

Fornander, Abraham, 63–64, 91, 247n138

Forster, E. M., *A Passage to India,* 100, 253n73

Forster, George, 30, 37–38, 98, 240n38; and dispute with William Hodges, 123–124; and sunken continent theory, 91

Forster, Johann Reinhold, 30–32, 35, 57–58, 141–142; critique of Aotourou, 23

Foucault, Michel, 11–12, 45, 235n30

Freud, Sigmund, 17, 162–163

Frisbie, Robert Dean, 115, 192

Froelick, L. D., 125, 145–147

frontier: and 1920s crisis, 81–84; official closure of, 51; and US expansion, 3, 14–15, 50–52. *See also* manifest destiny

Gaines, Jane, 172, 202

Gauguin, Paul, 68, 85, 109, 182, 198, 211; burial place of, 105

gaze: and Enlightenment voyages, 21–22, 197; female, 140–145, 156, 187; and imperialism, 196, 202–203, 208, 225; queer, 195–202, 204–205; returned, 173, 195; and tourism, 52, 199. *See also* scopophilia; voyeurism

Gell, Alfred, 4, 111, 154–155, 163

Gide, André, 137, 207

Gilman, Sander, 169

globalization, 43; and Enlightenment, 19; and modernity, 111–113

Gloeden, Wilhelm von, 216

Gobineau, Count de, 65

"going native," 107, 110–111, 168, 170, 176, 179–181. *See also* beachcombers

Golem, The (film), 132

Gramsci, Antonio, 13

Grant, Madison, 70–71; *The Passing of the Great Race,* 65

Grant, Ulysses S., 51

Grass (film), 141

Gray, Gilda, 192, 193

Grey, Zane, 82–83, 118

Grierson, John, 121, 147, 156, 173

Griffith, D. W., 165; *The Birth of a Nation* (film), 71

Griffith, Richard, 139, 213

Grimshaw, Beatrice, 119; *In the Strange South Seas,* 54, 55

haka'iki, 102, 104

"half caste": in film, 182, 186, 188–189, 191

Hall, James Norman, 77, 115, 135–136, 168, 192, 211, 215, 218, 228; *Lost Island,* 229

Halley, Edouard, 104

Handy, Edward Smith Craighill and Willowdean, 60–61, 102

Hapa'a, 39–40

Haraway, Donna, 121, 130

Hau'ofa, Epeli, 4, 7

havai'i, 100

Hawai'i, 14–15, 39, 52, 200; in Stoddard's writings, 203–205; US annexation of, 48–49, 229, 244n88

Hawkesworth, John, 21–22, 25–28, 29, 62, 123–124, 178–179

Hay, John, 152; "Open Door Notes," 83

Hays, Will, 129

Heads of divers natives (Sydney Parkinson), 35

Hegeman, Susan, 128

hegemony, 13, 98; in the Pacific, 5, 229–230; and resistance, 13, 45, 108

Helu, I. F., 10

Herbert, T. Walter, 39, 242nn58, 63

history: and myth, 3–4, 7–8, 9–10, 82–83, 89–92; and relativism, 130, 257n49; and ruins, 106

Hodges, William, 35–36, 57, 123–124, 230

homoeroticism, 14; and Bougainville, 197; and exoticism, 197–199, 207–212, 216–217, 225–226; and male friendship, 200; and *Moana,* 153–154, 155–156; and *The Pagan,* 189–190, 193–195; and Stoddard's writings, 198–208; and *Tabu,* 208–209, 212, 217–220, 224–225; and *White Shadows* (O'Brien), 109. *See also* eroticism; homosexuality

homosexuality: and Enlightenment observations, 198; and "homotextuality," 206–207; and *Moana,* 215; as modern identity, 198, 206–207, 267n14; origins of term, 205–206; prohibitions against, 216–217, 224–225; and *White Shadows* (film), 174. *See also* homoeroticism

Hough, Emerson, *The Passing of the Frontier,* 84

Howe, K. R., 227, 229

Hurricane, The (film), 172, 177, 229

hybridity, 29, 91, 188, 191; cultural, 15, 99, 112, 185, 189, 222; of genres, 123

immigration, 3, 62–63, 70, 181; and Americanization, 81–82; Immigration Act of 1917, 62. *See also* naturalization; Supreme Court

imperialism, 8–9, 10–12, 47–54, 126–128; and colonialism, 6, 38–39, 105–106; defined, 6; discourses of, 10–13, 16, 44–45; foundations of US, 38–39; gaze of, 196, 202–203, 208, 225; and modernism, 100, 225; "preventive," 48. *See also* anti-imperialism; colonialism

Ingraham, Joseph, 39
Insular Empire, The (film), 231
interracial romance. *See* miscegenation
Inuits, 122, 131
Iotete, 104
Island of Lost Souls (film), 184
islands: from continental perspectives, 9, 14; and
  paradoxes of representation, 12, 202

James, William, 50
Janis, Dorothy, 185
Jannings, Emil, 210
Jazz Singer, The (film), 187–188, 222
Johnson, Donald, 47–48
Johnson, Major A. P. A., 54, 99
Johnson, Martin, 87
Jolly, Margaret, 238n9

Kames, Lord H. H., *Sketches of the History of
  Man,* 31
Kant, Immanuel, 30
Kaplan, Amy, 3, 248n147
Kaplan, E. Ann, 196, 202, 205, 268n32
Keatonui ("Gattenewa"), 39
Kernahan, Mel, *White Savages in the South Seas,*
  85–86, 231
King Kong (film), 153
Kipling, Rudyard, 75, 201
Kroeber, Alfred, 71, 134
Krusenstern, Adam J. von, 41
Kyrou, Ado, 160

Lacan, Jacques, 195–196, 223–224, 268n32
Ladebat, Laffon de, 104
LaFeber, Walter, 48
Lamb, Jonathan, 18, 31
Lamour, Dorothy, 172, 176–177, 229
Lane, Rose Wilder, 84, 116–117, 254n103
Langman, Larry, 227, 262n15, 265n61, 266n72
Langsdorff, George H. von, 41, 44
Lasky, Jesse L., 118
Lavater, Johann Caspar, 34
Lawrence, D. H., 90–91, 252n49
Leff, David N., 38
Le Moine, Charles Alfred, 85, 108, 110
Lévi-Strauss, Claude, 118, 219
Linné, Carl von, 30–31. *See also* taxonomy
Linnekin, Jocelyn, 4, 55
Littell, Robert, 147
lome lome, 109, 178–180
London, Charmian Kittredge, 75, 81, 113–114,
  116, 161; affair with O'Brien, 74; *Log of the
  Snark,* 113
London, Jack, 18, 87, 110, 114
Loti, Pierre, 54, 109, 110, 201, 211
Lowie, Robert H., 69–71
Lugowski, David, 195
Lynd, Robert A. and Helen Merrell, *Middletown,*
  128
Lyons, Paul, 111

Mackenzie, Sir William, 127
Magellan, Ferdinand, 20

Māhina, 'Okusitino, 10
mahū, 194, 197–198, 218
Malinowski, Bronislaw, 99, 129, 134–135; *Diary
  in the Strict Sense of the Term,* 191
manifest destiny, 3, 49–52, 114. *See also* expan-
  sionism; frontier
Marcus, George, 134
Marey, Etienne-Jules, 34
Mariana Islands, 231
Mariner, William, 198
Marquesas Islands: beachcombers in, 77–78;
  claimed as film location, 263n29; and
  encounter with Mendaña, 92–93; ethnog-
  raphies of, 102–103; and "fatal impact," 46,
  95–103; and French possession, 39, 40, 94;
  population of, 95, 252n56; US claims on,
  39–41. *See also* Murnau, F. W.; O'Brien,
  Frederick
Marshall, Edison, 82
Marshall Islands, 237n7, 241n54
Matahi, 181, 216–225
Maxwell, Anne, 56
Mayne, Judith, 196
McKinley, President William, 49–50
Mead, Margaret, 69, 70–72, 114, 130–131,
  229–230, 255n11; *Coming of Age in Samoa,*
  70, 129–130; *Growing Up in New Guinea,* 131,
  134; *New Lives for Old,* 230; and Peoples of
  the Pacific Hall, 257n46, 258n67; and salvage
  anthropology, 99, 133
Melanesia, 3–4; and First World War, 54; western
  conceptions of, 55, 86, 141–142
Meleisea, Malama, 10, 119, 243n86
Melville, Herman, 5, 19, 20, 39, 75, 85, 98, 115,
  229; *Billy Budd,* 201; decline of popularity,
  243n71; *Moby-Dick,* 45, 59–60; *Omoo,* 43, 77;
  Redburn, 201; and theme of whiteness, 58–60,
  65–66; *Typee,* 18, 43–46, 58–59, 77, 88–89,
  94, 150, 160, 177–178, 181, 241n58; *White
  Jacket,* 59
Mendaña, Alvaro de, 20, 24, 59, 92–93
MGM, 117, 160–162, 164–166, 168, 172, 184,
  263n29
Michener, James, *Tales of the South Pacific,* 230
Micronesia, 3–4, 55, 229, 241n54; and nuclear
  deployment, 237n7
miscegenation, 57; and degeneration theories,
  64, 106, 170–171, 220, 247n139; eighteenth
  century conceptions of, 28–29, 57, 240n29;
  and Hollywood films, 180–186, 191, 228–229,
  266n74; in Melville's writings, 58–59; in
  O'Brien's writings, 106, 109–110, 182; and
  regeneration, 29, 58, 180, 246n124
missionaries, 41–42, 50, 52, 53, 69, 91, 99, 220,
  242n63, 253n67; review of *Moana,* 157–158;
  in Stoddard's writings, 207; and tattooing
  prohibitions, 154–155, 162
Mitchell, George, 192–193
Moana (film), 14, 118–159, 213–214; casting
  of, 125–127; close reading of, 145–156; and
  domesticity, 143, 149–150; influence on
  White Shadows (film), 180; New York premiere, 151; as primeval fantasy, 92, 145–148;

reviews of, 151; Samoan premiere, 157; test screenings of, 156–157; and "whitening," 141–142, 213
modernism, 13, 16, 54, 77, 100, 225; and primitivism, 86; and relativism, 72
modernity, 112, 222, 227
monogenism, 31, 247n139. *See also* polygenism
Monroe Doctrine, 53, 76
Montagu, Ivor, 121
Montaigne, Michel de, 66
Moore, Henrietta, 176
Moore, Michael, *Fahrenheit 9/11* (film), 122–123
Morea, 14
Morton, Samuel George, *Crania Americana,* 34–35, 56
Motion Picture Producers and Distributors of America (MPPDA), 129, 228
mulattos: and "tragic mulatto," 182; and voyager observations, 28, 57. *See also* miscegenation
Mulvey, Laura, 195, 268n32
Murnau, F. W., 13–14, 135, 208–226; death of, 217, 226; *Four Devils,* 211; and homosexuality, 208–212, 214, 216–217, 224–225; and the Marquesas, 211–212; *Nosferatu,* 222; as outsider, 211, 217, 225; relationship with Robert Flaherty, 140, 210–216; *Sunrise,* 211. *See also Tabu*
Mutiny on the Bounty (film), 172, 228–229
Muybridge, Eadweard, 33
myth: and history, 10; of Polynesia, 7–8, 16, 18–19, 230–231

Nafanua (warrior goddess), 119, 155
name-exchange, 111–112
Narboni, Jean, 16, 161
naturalization, 62–63, 181. *See also* immigration; Supreme Court
Neal, Steve, 153
Nichols, Bill, 122, 137–138, 176, 178
Nietzsche, Friedrich, 7, 234n17
Nordhoff, Charles, 77, 115, 135, 168, 192, 211, 228–229
Nott, Josiah, 35, 247n139
Novarro, Ramon, 185–190; and homosexuality, 189, 266n78

Oberea. *See* Purea.
Obeyesekere, Gananath, 66, 235n28, 238n16
O'Brien, Frederick, 13–14, 39, 60, 74–117, 119, 137, 161–164, 180, 184, 211; *Atolls of the Sun,* 74–75, 84–85, 89–91, 101–102, 116, 160, 162; and culture crossing, 110–112; death of, 117, 226; life of, 78–80, 116–117, 250n17; *Mystic Isles of the South Seas,* 80–81, 84, 89; popularity of, 75–76, 80–81, 115–116; relationship with Robert Flaherty, 74–75, 119, 140; *White Shadows* (stage play), 61, 117, 161. See also *White Shadows in the South Seas*
Oceania: definitions of term, 4; militarization of, 229–230; and scholarship, 10
Oksiloff, Assenka, 210, 224, 259n76
Omai (Mai), 23, 29, 62
Orientalism, 11, 62, 107, 206

Orr, Bridget, 29, 240n29
orthochromatic. *See* film stock

Pacific Rim, 231; definitions, 5
Paetini ("Piteenee"), 39
Pagan, The (film), 14, 161; close reading of, 184–190; compared to *White Shadows* (film), 188, 190; female gaze in, 187, 189; theme of "whitening" in, 189; use of synch sound in, 187–188, 190
Panama Canal, 53, 245n106
panchromatic. *See* film stock
papalagi: defined, 147; and images of Polynesia, 16, 147, 155
Paramount Pictures, 126, 151, 156–157; and Robert Flaherty's contract, 75, 118–119, 158
Parkinson, Sydney, 24–26, 32–36, 38, 98; observes "hermaphrodite," 197–198
Patagonia, 32–33
paternalism, 40, 41, 119–120
Pe'a *(Moana). See* Finauga.
pe'a *(tatau),* 155
pekio, 110, 114, 194
Pelleray, Eugène (Comité de l'Océanie française), 53
Perez, Gilberto, 136
peripheralization, 43, 51–52, 244n102
Phelan, Nancy, 158–159
Philippines, 6, 49–50, 80, 250n22. *See also* wars
physiognomy: and difference, 28–29; as pseudoscience, 34; and somatology, 246n131. *See also* taxonomy; typologies
Pigafetta, Antonio, 20
Plessy v. Ferguson (1896), 62
Pocock, J. G. A., 9
Poedua, 37
polygenism, 35, 64. *See also* monogenism
Polynesia: ambiguity of classification, 29–30, 240n31; instability of representations of, 7–8, 27, 66; invention of term, 3–4; as myth and fantasy, 1–2, 7–9, 18–19, 27–28, 36–37, 73, 171, 176, 227–228; popular vogue for, 13–14, 80–84, 116; and racial origin narratives, 57, 61, 63–64, 90–92, 141, 184–185, 247n133; and western conceptions of innocence, 23, 38, 137, 144, 174, 183; and "whiteness," 19, 57–66, 141–142. *See also* prelapsarian return
pornography: in the eighteenth century, 21–22, 27; and ethnography, 137–138, 176, 178–180. *See also* fetishism; voyeurism
Porter, Captain David, 19, 39–41, 42, 43–46, 111; influence on Melville, 39, 46, 241n58; and O'Brien's writings, 105–106; on skin color, 58–59
Porter, Dennis, 12, 17
Porter, Roy, 25, 56
postcolonial studies, 6; and ethnography, 137. *See also* anti-imperialism; colonialism; imperialism
prelapsarian return: as cinematic theme, 73, 145, 148, 173, 175–176, 191; and fatal impact, 96, 99, 134; and the "new America," 51, 82; Polynesia as, 17–19, 32, 60, 73, 76, 90–92, 111

primitivism, 66, 86, 137, 163, 176, 190, 227–228; and Flaherty's films, 121, 127–128; "hard" and "soft," 41–42, 55–56, 93, 242n64
Procter, John R., 48–49, 92
Production Code, 184, 228–229
Pronger, Brian, 204
prostitution, 28, 185
Purea ("Oberea"), 26–27, 109, 178–179, 189, 239n22

queer: definition of, 268n21; looking relations, 199, 201–206
Quirós, Pedro Fernández de, 20, 24, 57, 92–93

race mixing: See miscegenation
Rafael, Vincent, 50
Reel Paradise (film), 231
regeneration, 1–2, 68–69, 212. See also miscegenation
Regnault, Félix-Louis, 34
relativism: cultural, 60, 66–73, 115, 128–131; historical, 130, 257n49
Renda, Mary, 5, 38, 40
Rennie, Neil, 7, 16
Richardson, General George Spafford, 119, 255n6
Riefenstahl, Leni, 216
Ripley, William Z., 64, 125
Robarts, Edward, 67–68, 77, 110, 114, 162, 180, 182
Robertson, George, 28, 57
Rony, Fatimah Tobing, 121, 126, 137, 153, 209–210, 225, 259n76
Roosevelt, Teddy, 76, 82
Rosenberg, Emily, 52
Rotha, Paul, 118, 154, 213–214
Roulston, Robert, 250n10
Rousseau, Jean-Jacques, 23, 42, 66
Rowe, John Carlos, 45
Royal Society, 24, 238n14
Ruby, Jay, 122, 129, 255n11

Safroni-Middleton, A., 119, 198
Said, Edward, 11, 100, 199, 253n73
Samoa: as cultural "sanctuary," 135; and fa'a Samoa, 119, 143, 145; German influence in, 119; and US interests, 48. See also Moana; Savai'i
Sapir, Edward, 69, 71–72, 128
Savai'i: Falealupo, 155, 214–215; Safune, 74–75, 119, 147, 155
Schueller, Malini Johar, 5, 12, 44–45, 183, 243n75
scopophilia, 136–138, 143, 176–177; and homoeroticism, 201–202, 204. See also gaze; voyeurism
Second World War. See wars
Selznick, David O., 166, 168, 263n25
Seward, William Henry, 47, 49, 51
Sherwin, John Keyes, 37, 124
Shohat, Ella, 191
Silverman, Kaja, 195–196
siva, 151–154, 195
slavery, 219; in the Pacific, 48, 54; in the US, 3, 45–46, 49, 50, 247n139

Smith, Bernard, 32, 34, 38, 123–124
Smith, Stephenson Percy, 61, 63, 91, 184
Smith, Vanessa, 67
Soja, Edward, 52
Solander, Carl, 30
South Pacific (stage musical and film), 230–231
South Seas: as 1920s literary fad, 2, 14, 80–84, 115–116; definitions, 4–5; as exhibit, 52, 257n46, 258n67; as myth and fantasy, 7, 17–19, 38, 136–137, 212. See also Polynesia
"South Seas maiden," 86, 108–109, 149, 161; and degeneration, 170. See also fetishism; voyeurism
Spanish-American War. See wars
Spengler, Oswald, Decline of the West, 130, 257n49
Spivak, Gayatri, 8–9
Spöring, Herman, 33
St. Johnston, Alfred, Camping Among Cannibals, 69, 88
Stallings, Laurence, 168
Stam, Robert, 191
Stefansson, Vilhjalmur, 121
Steinbeck, John, The Grapes of Wrath, 227
Steinberger, Albert B., 48
Stevenson, Robert Louis, 54, 77, 87, 97–100, 119, 184, 201, 211; and cultural crossing, 110; O'Brien's criticism of, 253n63
Stewart, Charles S., 59, 90, 242n58
Stewart's Handbook of the Pacific Islands (1922 ed.), 95, 252n56
Stocking, George, 31, 34, 64, 66, 70, 128–129
Stockinger, Jacob, 206
Stoddard, Charles Warren, 54, 87, 222; and Catholicism, 200, 207, 269n43; "Chumming with a Savage," 201, 203–206; and homoeroticism, 198–208; and sex tourism, 109, 198–201, 203, 205; "Taboo," 201; "A Tropical Sequence," 202, 205
Stoler, Ann Laura, 106
Stromberg, Hunt, 166, 263n25
Studlar, Gaylyn, 155–156
Sturma, Michael, 241n47, 246nn124, 125
Subramani, 99, 231
Sullivan, Louis R., The Essentials of Anthropometry, 60–61, 64
Supreme Court (of the United States): race-based cases, 62–63, 181, 185

Ta'avale ("Moana"), 148, 151–156, 158–159
taboo (tabu, tapu), 102, 109, 111, 181, 219–220, 222–225, 271nn81, 91
Tabu (film), 14, 135, 194, 198; censorship of, 228; close reading of, 216–225; and Flaherty's contributions, 120, 209, 213, 218, 271n91; and homoeroticism, 208–209, 212, 217–220, 224–225; preproduction for, 211–212; reviews of, 226; and theme of escape, 181, 222–223; and theme of writing, 219–220, 223–224. See also Flaherty, Robert; Murnau, F. W.
Taft, President William Howard, 53
Tahiti, 200; Arioi performers, 27; and Cook's artists, 34–37; and Enlightenment encounters, 18–28; and First World War, 54; and rumor